SHARJAH

1965 International Co-operation Year

80

HARRISON AND SONS LTD LONDON

4d

ČESKOSLOVENSKO

1·40 kčs

Charlie Chaplin
ČESKOSLOVENSKÁ KOMISE UNESCO

Dr. CHRISTIAN BARNARD "Adelantos de Medicina
TRANSPLANTE DE CORAZON 1965"

$ 0.25

CORREO DEL PARAGUAY

A SZOCIALISTA ORSZÁGOK POSTAÜGYI MINISZTEREINEK VI. ÉRTEKEZLETE·1965

60

MAGYAR POSTA

RÉPUBLIQUE ISLAMIQUE DE MAURITANIE

POSTE AÉRIENNE

50F

MAHATMA GANDHI · 1869-1948
DELRIEU

POLSKA

J. A. GAGARIN

1961-IV-12 ·RUSZ

CZŁOWIEKA W KOSMOS

P.W.P.W

NEW ZEALAND   ROYAL VISIT

4d

H. M. QUEEN ELIZABETH II   THE DUKE OF EDINBURGH

ČESKOSLOVENSKO

ČESKOSLOVENSKÁ KOMISE UNESCO

D1465884

25/-
(in U.K.only)

NAME-DROPPER

PROFILES OF THE TOP NAMES OF OUR TIMES

By Peter Hildreth

McWHIRTER PUBLISHING COMPANY LIMITED
24 Upper Brook Street, London W1

Printed offset lithography by
Redwood Press Limited,
Trowbridge & London

Made and Printed in Great Britain

CONTENTS

Notes on the Author

Name-Dropper has all the attraction of the ear at the eaves and the eye at the keyholes of the headliners of this century – without any of the risk of your being caught in a ridiculous posture.

The author, Peter Hildreth, was educated at Ratcliffe and Downing College, Cambridge. His father represented India as a sprinter in the 1924 Olympic Games at Paris, and Hildreth himself became an Olympian in 1952 when he represented Great Britain at Helsinki as a high hurdler, reaching the semi-finals.

Hildreth stayed in athletics well into his thirties achieving many distinctions including a place in Britain's 1956 (Melbourne) and 1960 (Rome) Olympic teams, many European and British hurdling records, and more representative appearances for Britain than any other athlete.

Peter Hildreth works in the editorial department of a London publisher and since 1961 has covered athletics for the *Sunday Telegraph* and has written two very successful coaching books.

Hildreth's first love since retiring from a remarkable career in sport has been patient and unblinking research into really great news makers of recent times – their intimate details, what they have said about their contempories, what has been said about them, what they look like, how they write, and how much they earn and exactly what they have achieved.

Author's Preface

'As you know', wrote Shakespeare nearly 400 years ago, 'what great ones do the less will prattle of.' His words still have a pungent relevance in an age when the presentation of the news in any medium is linked with the names of famous people. Such at any rate is the pretext for my book on famous people of today and recent times.

Various criteria were used to select the subjects but, in essence, their achievements made each a natural choice. Their names, moreover, fall easily within the scope of popular identification. No apology is made for including certain twentieth-century 'villains'; their record provides the inevitable minus against which the constructive lives of others may be weighed.

Space has prohibited the inclusion of some deserving subjects. They will have priority for treatment in future editions in the preparation of which the author welcome suggestions from readers.

London, March 1970

HRH Prince Philip in the full dress uniform of an Admiral of the Fleet with the Sash and Star of the Order of the Garter, and the Star of the Order of the Thistle. From the collar hangs the badge of the Grand Master of the Order of the British Empire.

HRH THE PRINCE PHILIP

Though not at the time attired in wig and gown, Lord Justice Birkett[1] once gave a summing-up which will forever put the work of Prince Philip's biographers into perspective: 'He can talk with crowds and walk with kings and yet remain the exemplar of all that is worthiest and noblest in our national life. This country is exceedingly fortunate in having a leader of such versatility and of such devotion to public service.' A similar reference was made by Dr Kurt Hahn, former headmaster of Gordonstoun, Prince Philip's old school, who reported: 'He has the greatest sense of service of all the boys in the school . . . Prince Philip will make his mark in any profession where he will have to prove himself in a full trial of strength.'

The chosen profession of the man who was to marry the future Queen of England was the Royal Navy. He made his mark at the Battle of Cape Matapan[2] when he was in charge of searchlight control aboard the battleship HMS *Valiant*. His commanding

The Royal Family together at Frogmore, Windsor Great Park, in April 1968 with one of the Queen's four Corgi dogs.

officer reported that 'Thanks to his alertness and appreciation of the situation we were able to sink in five minutes two eight-inch-gun cruisers.' Lt. Mountbatten, RN, was mentioned in despatches by Admiral Sir Andrew Cunningham, Commander-in-Chief, Mediterranean.

Whether in uniform or plain clothes, Prince Philip was always in a hurry to go places and get things done. On the eve of his wedding he was stopped for speeding in London but disarmed a policeman, pencil poised for details, by apologizing: 'Sorry officer, but I've got an appointment with the Archbishop of Canterbury.' Though pressure of engagements impelled him to exceed the official limits of safe motoring on other occasions, the urge for speed was not inconsistent with his competitive philosophy, outlined in a speech at the British Olympic Association's dinner on 21 Nov. 1955: '. . . the urge to pit one's skill or ability against others is present in everyone from childhood', he pointed out,

'and has been with man as a whole since he ran races up and down the trees, or threw a stone axe.'

In sports Prince Philip has won a wide measure of popularity. He threw the javelin 129 feet $8\frac{1}{2}$ inches, played goalkeeper at Association Football, and is recognized as a fearless (handicap 5) polo player. His cricket was the subject of warm approval from Sir Donald Bradman: 'I have watched films of the Duke's bowling', commented Sir Don, 'and he shows the perfect action for the right-arm off-spinner.' Afloat, he rates in the estimation of Uffa Fox: 'the best man sailing across the tide I have ever sailed with. . . . If he could get in more sailing, he would be the finest helmsman in the country.'

---

[1] William Norman Birkett, 1st Baron Birkett (1883–1962), Lord Justice of Appeal (1950–57).

[2] The battle between the British and Italian navies took place from 18–19 March 1941 at a point about 100 miles from Cape Matapan on the southern tip of the Peloponese and roughly 300 miles from Prince Philip's birthplace at Corfu.

As president or patron of hundreds of associations and professional bodies, the Prince has a tight daily schedule often necessitating several changes of clothes for successive engagements. A specially-designed wardrobe at Buckingham Palace, fitted with push-button sliding panels and robot arms, enables him to select the appropriate uniform or suit in rapid order, effecting a full change in the impressive time of one minute flat.

Much of his time is spent making speeches, none of them ghosted for him. 'Some people have what I can only describe as a positive genius for saying absolutely nothing in the most charming language', he has remarked. 'Neither my English nor my imagination are good enough for that, so I try to say something which I think might be interesting or at least constructive.' In his public utterances he is barred from, but has not always avoided, making political comment,[1] but this does not prevent him exerting influence indirectly. 'I can't get up in public and say: "I think you're making a nonsense." But I can talk to somebody in private about any political situation.'

Some of his best talks have arisen from personal experience and observation as 'Royal Ambassador Extraordinary'. In 1956, following a four-month 40,000-mile tour with the Queen in the Royal Yacht *Britannia* to Antarctica, the Indian Ocean, Australia, and New Zealand, he gave a 52-minute talk on BBC television, des-cribed as the longest *ad-lib* broadcast ever made on the Corporation's channels. Early in 1957 the National Geographical Society presented him with a medal inscribed with a reference to his 'questing spirit' which had 'taken him to the far corners of the globe and brought to millions a better under-standing of our planet and its peoples.'

By 1962 Prince Philip had visited 66 nations on official duties, many of which have since been re-visited and new ones added to the tally. His travels, coupled with his duties at home, make him one of the hardest-worked men in the British Commonwealth. At all times he must be conscious of his public image, can never appear to be bored or fatigued, should always be informed about and interested in the people he meets and their work. He must, furthermore, endure the complaints of those who feel that his Civil List income of £40,000 (now $96,000) is excessive. In fact his presence often gives a bigger boost to exports or fund-raising than the slickest salesman. On his visit to the United States and Canada in 1966 he helped to raise $1,100,000 (£392,857) for children's causes. As a result of this the Variety Club of Great Britain contributed £100,000 ($280,000) to the Duke of Edinburgh Award Scheme. The Variety Club, of which he is a Gold Card Life Member, raised £500,000 ($1,400,000) for children's charities in 1966. After his appearance at a miniature motor show at Los Angeles that year, more than £70,000 ($196,000) worth of orders were taken for British make cars.

One of the more delicate tasks of royalty, constantly in the full glare of publicity, is handling the press. Prince Philip has demonstrated that it is possible to knock the fourth estate and get away with it. Remarks such as 'The *Daily Express* is a bloody awful newspaper', and the rhetorical broadside at Gibraltar: 'Which are the photographers and which are the apes?' have not arched too many backs. In general, his adroitness and good humour in parrying even the crassest irrelevance at interview assure him of a

---

[1] It is a condition of constitutional monarchy that Royalty shall not give public expression to contentious political opinions.

[2] Voted on the accession of Queen Elizabeth II in 1953. Prince Philip previously earned £12 ($34) a week as a lieutenant in the Royal Navy. On his marriage to Princess Elizabeth in 1947 he was voted £10,000 (then $40,000) a year out of which he had to pay the salaries of his personal staff.

12

good press. Asked in America if he wore polka-dot underwear, he sidestepped: 'I'll wear almost anything providing it fits.'

Prince Philip scored one of his most memorable hits at the Royal Gala Performance at the London Palladium on 29 Nov. 1966, when two of the stars of the popular TV series, *Coronation Street*, presented to him in the line-up of celebrities, gave spontaneous voice to their impressions. Said Elsie Tanner (Pat Phoenix): ''E's gorgeous – and so brown'. Replied Ena Sharples (Violet Carson): 'He ought to be – he is always abroad. I'd tame 'im if 'e were mine.'

A descendant of Queen Victoria, and of Astrid, sister of King Canute (995–1035), the Duke of Edinburgh, Earl of Merioneth, and Baron Greenwich probably cherishes no title more than the one bestowed on him in New Guinea: 'Number-One-Fellah-Belong-Missus-Queen'.

The Queen and Prince Philip at luncheon with Princess Anne and Prince Charles at Windsor Castle.

Prince Philip was asked whether a businessman visiting South America should wear a bowler hat or a sombrero: 'It doesn't really matter. But it would be better to send a bowler-hatted man speaking Spanish, than a man wearing a sombrero who could only speak English.' (1962)

'The trouble with senior management to an outsider is that there are too many one-ulcer men holding down two-ulcer jobs.' (1963)

'All money nowadays seems to be produced with a natural homing instinct for the Treasury.' (1964)

'It's no good shutting your eyes and saying "Britain is best" three times a day after meals and expecting it to be so.' (1966)

'People say this is a permissive society. But we live in the most regimented society ever in this country. You have practically to have a licence to breathe – you cannot move without people asking what you are doing.' (1968)

PRINCE PHILIP'S TOURS ABROAD

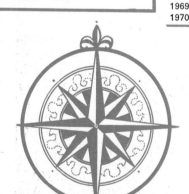

Year	Countries visited
1952	Kenya, Norway, Sweden, Finland, France, Malta.
1953	Germany, Newfoundland, Bermuda, Jamaica, Panama, Fiji, New Zealand.
1954	New Zealand (cont.), Australia, Tasmania, Australia, Cocos Islands, Ceylon, Aden, Uganda, Libya, Malta, Gibraltar, France, Germany, Canada.
1955	Germany, Malta, France, Gibraltar, Norway, Germany, Denmark.
1956	Nigeria, Gibraltar, Corsica, Sardinia, Germany, Sweden, Gibraltar, Seychelles, Ceylon, Malaya, New Guinea, Australia, New Zealand, Chatham Island, Deception Island.
1957	Falkland Islands, South Georgia, Gough Island, Tristan da Cunha, St Helena, Gambia, Gibraltar, Portugal, France, Denmark, Germany, Canada, USA.
1958	Germany, Belgium, Netherlands, Germany, Canada, Germany, Holland.
1959	Tripoli, Aden, India, Pakistan, Burma, Singapore, Sarawak, Brunei, North Borneo, Hong Kong, Solomon Islands, Gilbert & Ellice Islands, Panama, Bahamas, Bermuda, USA, Canada, Ghana.
1960	Malta, Switzerland, Germany, Canada, USA, Denmark, Holland, Germany, Italy.
1961	Cyprus, India, Pakistan, India, Nepal, India, Iran, Turkey, Sardinia, Vulcano Island, Italy, Vatican City, Italy, Germany, Ghana, Liberia, Sierra Leone, Gambia, Tanganyika, Greece.
1962	British Guiana, Venezuela, Colombia, Ecuador, Peru, Bolivia, Chile, Paraguay, Uruguay, Brazil, Argentine, Grand Cayman, British Honduras, Germany, Netherlands, Canada, USA, Canada, USA, Australia, Germany.
1963	Canada, Honolulu, Fiji, New Zealand, Australia, Fiji, Canada, Germany, USA, Germany, Sudan, Zanzibar, Kenya, Sudan.
1964	Greece, Iceland, Sudan, Malawi, Uganda, Germany, Greece, Malta, Canada, Nassau, Mexico, Galapagos Islands, Panama, Trinidad, Tobago, Grenada, St Vincent, Barbados, St Lucia, Dominica, Anguilla, Montserrat, Antigua, Germany, France, Belgium, Italy, Morocco, France, Liechtenstein.
1965	Ethiopia, Sudan, Saudi Arabia, Pakistan, India, Malaysia, Singapore, Australia, Singapore, Malaysia, Thailand, India, Nepal, India, Pakistan, Bahrein, Greece, Italy, Germany, France, Germany, Italy, France, Switzerland, Belgium, Liechtenstein.
1966	Liechtenstein (cont.), Newfoundland, West Indies (22 islands), British Guiana, USA, Canada, Labrador, Greenland, Iceland, Netherlands, Norway, Belgium, Germany, Jamaica, Argentine, Germany, Monaco, Italy, France.
1967	Italy, Greece, Jordan, Iran, Pakistan, Singapore, Australia, Singapore, Thailand, Pakistan, Quatar, Lebanon, France, Netherlands, Italy, Canada, Malta, Germany, Belgium.
1968	Libya, Trucial Oman, India, Malaysia, Indonesia, Australia, New Zealand, Australia, Singapore, India, Pakistan, Saudi Arabia, Malta, Mexico, Belgium, Germany.
1969	Libya, Ethiopia, Kenya, Sudan, Egypt, Libya, Paris, Aachen, Canada, USA.
1970	Australia, New Zealand, Figi, Tonga, Canada.

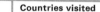

Neil Armstrong

Neil Alden Armstrong, the first man to set foot on the surface of the Moon.

As a schoolboy Neil Armstrong looked at the Moon and predicted : 'Someday I'm going to be up there. I'm going to be on that Moon.' No Man ever lived up to a loftier prediction.

Full name Neil Alden Armstrong.

Born Tues. 5 Aug. 1930, Wapakoneta, Ohio, USA.

Characteristics About 5' 11″; about 165*lb.* (11*st.* 11*lb.*) having slimmed by about 15*lb.* for the Moon mission; sandy hair; blue eyes; pulse rate when landing on the Moon 156 per minute; described as 'tight-lipped and phlegmatic'; blushes easily; slight tendency to stammer; smokes and drinks occasionally.

Married 1956 Janet Shearon 2*s.*

HERE MEN FROM THE PLANET EARTH
FIRST SET FOOT UPON THE MOON
JULY 1969, A. D.
WE CAME IN PEACE FOR ALL MANKIND

NEIL A. ARMSTRONG
ASTRONAUT

MICHAEL COLLINS
ASTRONAUT

EDWIN E. ALDRIN
ASTRONAU

RICHARD NIXON
PRESIDENT, UNITED STATES OF AMERICA

'I am going to step off the module now. That is one small step for man, one giant leap for mankind' With these words Commander Neil Armstrong lowered his left foot from the ninth rung of the egress ladder on the lunar module *Eagle* and became the first inhabitant of the Earth to set foot upon the Moon. The time was 02 56 hours and 20 seconds GMT on Mon. 21 July in the year AD 1969. An audience of 600 million televiewers over 232,000 miles away witnessed the culmination of the most astounding achievement in the annals of human science and exploration just over one second after it had happened, the time it took for the picture to be transmitted to Earth. Minutes later President Richard M. Nixon spoke to Armstrong on the radio telephone from the White House, Washington: 'For one priceless moment in the whole history of man, all of the people on this Earth are truly one – one in their pride for what you have done, and one in our prayers that you will return safely to Earth.'

The safe return seemed almost routine after the deeds of 21 July: lift-off by *Eagle*, docking with the command module *Columbia*, exit from Lunar gravity, re-entry into the Earth's gravitation at a speed of 24,250 mph (nearly seven miles per second), and splashdown in the Pacific Ocean 940 miles south-west of Honolulu at 16.49 hours GMT on 24 July. Armstrong, Aldrin, and Michael Collins, pilot of *Columbia* orbiting the Moon while the others landed on it, all underwent three weeks' quarantine before emerging in public for an earthbound heroes' welcome.

The son of a civil servant, probably of Scottish ancestry, Neil Armstrong made his first flight at the age of six. At Wapakoneta High School he was a keen Boy Scout and played the baritone horn. He always had a passion for flying and earned his pilot's licence on his 16th birthday, the earliest legal age, before he could drive a car. After reading aeronautical engineering at Purdue University, he was drafted at 19 for service in Korea. He won three Air Medals, surviving 78 combat missions, and flying one aircraft which had 77 patches over enemy bullet holes.

Returning home to graduate from Purdue in 1955, Armstrong joined NASA (National Aeronautics and Space Administration), first at the Lewis Flight Propulsion Laboratory and later at the High Speed Flight Station. As a civilian research pilot, he flew the X-15 rocket plane at 3,989 mph at an altitude of 207,500 feet, both records at that time. He had his share of brushes with eternity. The X-15 dived out of control on one flight, the rocket motor firing just in time for him to pull out. Commanding the Gemini-8 for the first docking with the Agena target vehicle in 1966, he had to make an emergency splashdown when the spacecraft's thrusters developed a short circuit. In 1968 he had to eject from a lunar-landing research vehicle crashing out of control at only 100 feet.

The head of the United States Space-craft Programme is Dr Wernher von Braun, the German-born American-naturalized scientist who figured prominently in the development of the World War II V-2 rocket. He was away from the V-2 rocket base at Peenemünde, East Germany on the night of a massive Allied air raid in 1945 in which several German scientists were killed.

In 1957 von Braun predicted that 'we should be able to send people to the Moon and back within 25 years'. The rate of progress in rocketry and allied sciences during the next decade was such that in a 1967 interview he was able to refer to the Moon voyage as 'a picnic, a trifle, a party trick'. He then foreshadowed that men would go to Mars by 'about 1985 or 1990', a journey of about two years there and back. In 1969 he revised this estimate, predicting that the trip might take place by 1982.

Neil Armstrong

American Space Flights

Dates	Flight	Astronauts	Achievements
5 May 1961	Mercury 3	Alan B. Shepard Jr.	First US manned sub-orbital space-flight.
21 July 1961	Mercury 4	Virgil I. Grissom	Further sub-orbital experience; spacecraft sank.
20 Feb. 1962	Mercury 6	John H. Glenn Jr.	First US manned orbital flight.
24 May 1962	Mercury 7	M. Scott Carpenter	Experiments towards future space flights; landed 250 miles from target.
3 Oct. 1962	Mercury 8	Walter M. Schirra Jr.	Developed techniques relevant to extended space journeys; landed 5 miles from target.
15–16 May 1963	Mercury 9	L. Gordon Cooper Jr.	Spent one day in space; final aim of Mercury programme.
23 March 1965	Gemini 3	Virgil I. Grissom John W. Young	First US two-man space-flight and orbital manoeuvres.
3–7 June 1965	Gemini 4	James McDivitt Edward H. White, II	First US spacewalk, 21 minutes, by White.
21–29 Aug. 1965	Gemini 5	L. Gordon Cooper Jr. Charles Conrad Jr.	Proved human capacity for sustained efficiency in space, duration 8 days.
4–18 Dec. 1965	Gemini 7	Frank Borman James A. Lovell Jr.	World's longest manned orbital flight, duration 330 hours 35 minutes.
15–16 Dec. 1965	Gemini 6A	Walter M. Schirra Jr. Thomas P. Stafford	World's first successful space rendezvous; came within one foot of Gemini 7.
16–17 March 1966	Gemini 8	Neil A. Armstrong David R. Scott	First docking of two vehicles in space; emergency splashdown (*see page* 11).
3–6 June 1966	Gemini 9A	Thomas P. Stafford Eugene A. Cernan	Rendezvous of spacecraft and target vehicle thrice; 127-minute spacewalk by Cernan.
18–21 July 1966	Gemini 10	John W. Young Michael Collins	Target used as source of thrust for first time; new altitude record of 475 miles.
12–15 Sept. 1966	Gemini 11	Charles Conrad Jr. Richard F. Gordon Jr.	Rendezvous and docking in first orbit; first multiple docking; highest manned orbit, about 853 miles.
11–15 Nov. 1966	Gemini 12	James A. Lovell Jr. Edwin E. Aldrin Jr.	Lovell walked and worked outside orbiting spacecraft for over $5\frac{1}{2}$ hours; first space photograph of solar eclipse.
11–22 Oct. 1968	Apollo 7	Walter M. Schirra Jr. Donn F. Eisele R. Walter Cunningham	Perfected two manoeuvres essential for eventual flight to the Moon.
21–27 Dec. 1968	Apollo 8	Frank Borman James A. Lovell Jr. William A. Anders	First men to leave Earth's gravity, orbit the Moon, and observe its hidden side.
3–13 March 1969	Apollo 9	James A. McDivitt David R. Scott Russell L. Schweikart	First successful test of lunar module; first transfer from manned to unmanned spacecraft.
18–26 March 1969	Apollo 10	Thomas P. Stafford John W. Young Eugene A. Cernan	Tested lunar module in lunar environment; descended to within nine miles of Moon's surface.
16–24 July 1969	Apollo 11	Neil A. Armstrong Edwin E. Aldrin Jr. Michael Collins	First man on the Moon; collected lunar samples.
14–24 Nov. 1969	Apollo 12	Charles Conrad Jr. Richard F. Gordon Jr. Alan Bean	Exploration in Ocean of Storms area. Further samples taken.

N.B: On 27 Jan. 1967 Apollo 204 was burned out while being tested on the launching pad at Cape Kennedy. Virgil I. Grissom, Edward H. White II, and Roger B. Chaffee were killed. Their widows each received a sum of $100,000 (£41,666) plus a large pension from the Time-Life Corporation.

Salaries of the Apollo 11 Crew

Armstrong	$30,054	£12,522
Aldrin	$18,622	£7,760
Collins	$17,147	£7,144

In addition the Time-Life Corporation has set up a fund reported to be more than $1,000,000 (£416,666) for distribution among the 60-plus astronauts in active training.

TWIGGY

Full name Lesley Hornby. Justin de Villeneuve chose the name Twiggy (nicknames include: 'Skinny', 'Oxfam', and 'the Matchstick').

Born Mon. 19 Sept. 1949 at 93 St Raphael's Way, London NW 10, England.

Characteristics About 5′ 6½″; about 91*lb.* (6*st.* 7*lb.*); bust 31″; waist 22″; hips 32″; wrist 5½″; ankle 8″; shoes English size 4½; mousy-brown hair; grey eyes; cockney accent: 'If I tried to go la-di-da it wouldn't be me so I speak as I've always done.' Bites her nails.

When a girl is pictured on the cover of a Japanese magazine every week for six months, no prizes are offered for concluding that the girl is popular in Japan. It could even be argued and widely believed that the Japanese loved her. But, joking aside, there is no doubt that Twiggy loved them back: 'I'm crazy about the kimono', she peeped. 'I want to make a Western style out of it.'

Evidence proved the Japs were not the only ones in step. Around the world the raves were heard in equal volume. Scandinavia was truly wowed. Paris she took by storm. Germans simply oozed goodwill. American dollies spent $10,000,000 (now (£4,166,666) on her fashions in 1967. That year she was named the Briton who made the 'greatest impact' on the US scene – greater still, some whispered, than previous winners Richard Burton and Lord Rootes. In Canada she was the rage of Expo 67.

So small a girl, so big a reputation: how did she do it? asked the Press. Justin de Villeneuve told them: 'There's never been anything like Twiggy. She's more than a model: she's the biggest teenage influence *ever*. The biggest in history.' Soviet papers detected other influences, accusing her of being a 'Capitalist pawn' and Western

Justin de Villeneuve took this photograph of Twiggy wearing a spectacular head-dress in Dynel by Leonard. Twiggy is joint owner with Leonard of a hairdressing salon in Chelsea.

leaders of exploiting her to make teenagers think about false eyelashes instead of high ideals. Twiggy took these grumbles cheerfully: 'It's a load of old codswallop', she chirped. 'I get a lot of fan mail from behind the Iron Curtain. Maybe that's what's worrying them.'

Twiggy was 16 when she left Brondesbury and Kilburn Grammar School where her nickname was 'Sticks'. She had earned £1 for working on Saturdays only. Justin helped her make a start in modelling, taking her to a London hairdresser. Off came her long tresses and the short were streaked with a lemon-silver highlight. Photographed by a friend of Justin's she was featured in the *Daily Express* as the 'Face of 1966'. The next year she was earning £100 ($240) an hour modelling in America where Twiggy tights, sweaters, dolls, and eye make-up (produced by Yardley's) went on the market. Her rate for modelling in England was not published but she was quoted as admitting: 'I know that if someone put all my money into my hand I would faint.' Her hairdresser flew to New York exclusively for a single consultation; the bill was £257 14s. ($720).

The frailty that grew famous has been variously described. 'A body to fit the clothes rather than clothes to fit the body' was one attempt. Somebody else came up with 'she's an ectomorph'.[1] Twiggy herself was asked how she would describe her figure and was ready with the baffling answer: 'I dunno'. Bob Hope did know: 'She's the world's sexiest X-ray', he cracked. 'When I met her I didn't know whether to kiss her or smoke her.'

Twiggy's gym-slip silhouette and 22-inch waist[2] are not maintained by dieting. She eats almost anything, drinks orange juice, and smokes a little. She enjoys swimming and dancing but dances only at private parties and seldom stays up after 10.30 at night because she insists on getting nine hours' sleep.

The original 1966–67 Twiggy image set off her pipecleaner legs with mini-skirts 8–10 inches above the knee. Short hair and Twiggy eyelashes (three pairs) were in. A preference for long, hip-hugging trousers, flared at the bottoms, featured in the 1968 look. The eyelashes were discarded and the hair was longer with curls or ringlets and perhaps a bandeau. Minis were still in favour, especially in the summer. Observers in New York detecting slightly more rounded contours, confirmed that she had abandoned her flattening body-stocking and now wore a bra. Twiggy runs up some of her dresses on her own sewing machine but if she is shopping she seldom spends more than £20 ($48) on a dress and prefers Biba and Quorom in London because they can fit her.

In 1969 nine factories around the world were producing Twiggy merchandise and most of the well-known stores in London stocked Twiggy dresses. Twiggy appeared on the cover of *Harper's Bazaar* causing the magazine to reach an all-time circulation peak. Prosperity enabled her to buy her parents a home at Twickenham where she lives with them. Justin, who masterminded much of her success, had discarded his Rolls-Royce and chosen instead an £11,000 ($26,400) Lamborghini.

[1] According to the somatotype system of classifying human physique everybody has elements of three main tendencies: endomorphy (globularity), mesomorphy (muscularity), and ectomorphy (linearity).

[2] Compare this with the measurements of the heaviest woman in British history, Nellie Lambert, who had an 88-inch waist and 26-inch arms.

21

CASSIUS CLAY

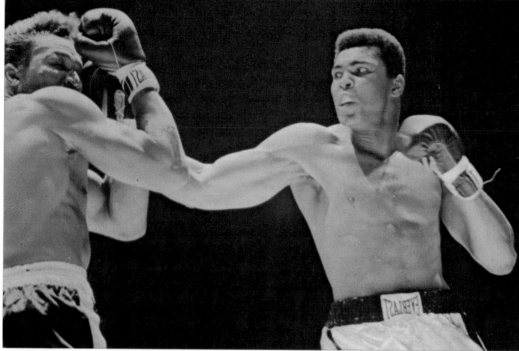

In his fifth title defence of 1966, Clay disposed of the pretensions of Cleveland 'Big Cat' Williams. The referee stopped the fight in the third round.

Full name Cassius Marcellus Clay (Given the title Muhammad Ali by the Black Muslim sect in 1964; stripped of this title in 1969 and banned from the Black Muslims for a year).

Born Sun. 18 Jan. 1942, Louisville, Kentucky, USA.

Characteristics About 6' 2½"; for the Terrell fight in 1967 the following physical details were reported: weight 218*lb.* (15*st.* 8*lb.*); chest normal 42½"; chest expanded 44½"; waist 34"; thigh 25"; calf 17"; fist 13"; biceps 15". Black hair and brown eyes.

Married (1) 1964 Sonji Roy (div. 1966)[1]; (2) 1967 Belinda Boyd. 1*d.*

[1] Clay was made liable to pay alimony of $15,000 (£5,357) a year for 10 years plus $22,500 (£8,000) legal fees.

Though it may not already have occurred to the world at large, the cosmic discovery that he was 'the greatest' first dawned on the consciousness of Cassius Clay after he had won the Olympic light-heavyweight title at Rome in 1960. 'I'm better than Floyd Patterson was at the same age. Right? I bet Sugar Ray Robinson wasn't as good as me when he was 18. Right? Right. So I guess I must be real good.' The sublime logic of his reasoning was supported by the evidence of unusual speed in the ring though this let him down in a race, unofficially staged at Rome, against Wilma Rudolph, Olympic sprint champion: 'I couldn't see any lady beating me', he complained, 'but I was going with wide-open speed and she left me so fast the last couple of blocks it was pitiful.'

Backed by a syndicate of 12 millionaires and giving out his constant theme 'They must fall in the round I call', Clay outlined his professional boxing ambitions in 1961: 'When I've got me a $100,000 house, another quarter-million stuck in the bank, and the world title latched on to my name, then I'll be in heaven.' The lesser heavyweights duly fell in the specified round while reigning champion Sonny Liston was softened up for the kill with such Clay-tailored invective as: 'You so ugly, when you cry, the tears run down the back of your head. You so ugly, you have to sneak up on the mirror so it won't run off the wall.' Coupled with this came a barrage of self-promotion: 'I'm so beautiful I should be chiselled in gold. Look at that build. It's pretty. I mean it's ready to dance. Right now!' And: 'I am the greatest. I am the prettiest. I am so pretty that I can hardly stand to look at myself . . . I am the fastest heavyweight that you ever did see. Next to me, Liston will look like a dump-truck.' Though this latter part of his forecast was fulfilled, Liston retired in the sixth round of their first world heavyweight title bout. Clay had promised an eighth-round fall.

Bank officials were startled when the new champion demanded his winnings in $1,000 (then £357) notes and 40 had to be sent from the Federal Bank on his insistence. He had already delivered a shock to the world with his announcement that he had joined the Black Muslim sect and assumed the name Muhammad Ali. The paradox of this *volte face* was underlined by the Muslim leader, Elijah Muhammad, who stated: 'We Muslims don't believe in beating up our brothers for the entertainment of whites and the making of money. We just don't care nothing about that.' Manager Angelo Dundee opined: 'This boy is incapable of hate. I think he is involved with these Muslims just because people don't want him to be.' Whatever his motivation, Clay appeared utterly sincere about his religion and became a lay preacher. He also passed over substantial commercial offers on the ground that they would infringe his principles: 'The white man want me hugging on a white woman, or endorsing some whisky or skin bleach, lightening the skin when I'm promoting black as the best.' Parenthetically, he went on record with this description of his ideal woman: 'My ideal is tall, 5 feet 8 inches; she hides her limbs under long wrap-around dresses like the Pakistanis wear and she exudes the radiance of soul.'

Clay further emphasized his convictions by refusing to serve in the US army in Vietnam. This cost him a fine of $10,000 (£4,166), and a five-year sentence passed on 24 July 1969.[1] His vacant title was fought for and two versions of the world title were extant in 1969 held by Americans Joe Frazier and Jimmy Ellis[2], the latter a former sparring partner of Clay's. The ex-champion asserted that Ellis was 'slow and flat-footed, just like the old dead pugs used to be', and that he could 'whup' the pair of them in one night. Hopes that he might come back were raised when it was reported he might meet his next opponent in London in 1970.

Clay's opinion of previous world heavyweight champions has been summed up briefly as follows: 'Take Louis, strictly a shuffler, a six-inch jabber. Walcott was a

23

good mover with a good swing, left and right. Patterson was too light and his reach was too short. Johansson had a good left jab, a hard right, but no rhythm. Marciano had no skill but he was strong and had good defence. Charles was a master boxer.'[3]

Several heavyweights have placed on record their opinion of Clay. Henry Cooper: 'Cassius is a damaging puncher. He can cut and hurt you. But he can't knock you out, not with one punch, any-way.' Joe Walcott: 'I think he's one of the best heavyweight champions we ever had. He thinks in the ring and he's well-conditioned. I was in the ring when he knocked out Liston in the second bout and I *know* he can punch.' Rocky Marciano: 'I was the first guy who made the prediction he'd be champion . . . he's not a bad champion, not in the ring.' Joe Louis: 'I don't think anybody will ever know how good he is. There ain't anybody around to test him. . . . He can't punch. He can't hurt you. He move too fast. If he slow down maybe he punch harder.' In another article Louis opined that Clay would have been beaten not only by himself but also by Germany's Max Schmeling, world heavy-weight champion (1930–32), by Joe Walcott, and by Rocky Marciano.

But, whatever the suppositions, the facts of Clay's supremacy do not admit of any argument. He disposed of his nine challengers conclusively, without manifesting any marks of battle. This alone is probably unique in the annals of pugilism. In 29 professional bouts he was unbeaten.

Moreover, he profited from his prowess on a generous scale, amassing total estimated ring earnings from title fights of about $4,648,941 (£1,660,000) up to March 1967. As a rule, his manager took 40 per cent and paid all the expenses.

Praise and prejudice for Clay's fistic attainments are well-aired but his incipient literary talents have yet to be seriously reviewed. Pending further published evidence, the following sample of doggerel may serve as an earnest example of latent poetic aptitude:

> 'I'm not saying this just
> to be funny.
> I'm fighting Terrell 'cause *he*
> needs the money.'

LP Recording

Highlights from 21 Years of BBC's Sports Report (BBC Radio Enterprises REC29M). Includes commentaries of the Rome Olympics and the Clay-Cooper fight in 1963. Clay's voice is heard.

[1] Clay's appeal was still pending in 1970.
[2] Ellis held the World Boxing Association's version of the title; Frazier held the title according to the New York Boxing Commission.
[3] Joe Louis was world heavyweight champion from 1937–1949, Ezzard Charles from 1949–51, Rocky Marciano from 1952–56, Floyd Patterson from 1956–59 and 1960–62, and Ingemar Johansson from 1959–60.

CASSIUS CLAY'S 10 SUCCESSFUL WORLD HEAVYWEIGHT TITLE FIGHTS					
Date	Venue	Opponent	Result	Round	Reported Purses
25 Feb. 1964	Miami	Sonny Liston (USA)	Retired	6	$600,000 (£214,286) less a fine of $2,500 (£900) for yelling and jumping around at the weigh-in.
25 May 1965	Lewiston, Maine	Liston	KO	1	$480,650 (£171,660)
22 Nov. 1965	Las Vegas	Floyd Patterson (USA)	RSF	12	$750,000 (£267,857)
29 March 1966	Toronto	George Chuvalo (Canada)	Points	15	total of about $2,000,000 (£714,280)
21 May 1966	London	Henry Cooper (England)	RSF	6	
6 Aug. 1966	London	Brian London (England)	KO	3	
10 Sept. 1966	Frankfurt	Karl Mildenberger (Germany)	RSF	12	
14 Nov. 1966	Houston, Texas	Cleveland Williams (USA)	RSF	3	
6 Feb. 1967	Houston, Texas	Ernie Terrell (USA)	Points	15	$556,293 (£198,675)
22 March 1967	New York	Zora Folley (USA)	KO	7	$261,998 (£93,570)
		RSF - Referee stopped fight			

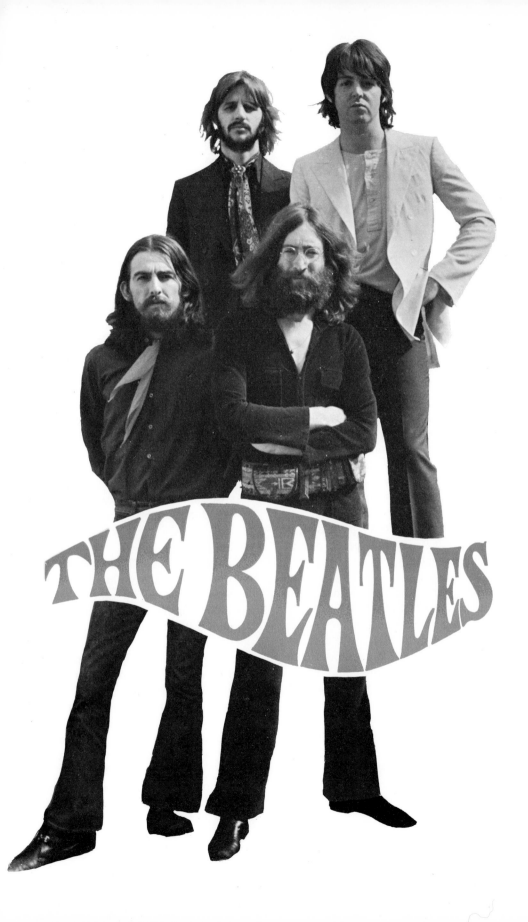

Full name George Harrison, MBE (1966).
Born Thurs. 25 Feb. 1943 at 12 Arnold Grove, Wavertree, Liverpool, England.
Characteristics About 5′ 11″; about 142*lb.* (10*st.* 1*lb.*); brown hair; hazel eyes.
Married 1966 Patty Boyd.

Full name John (Winston) Lennon, MBE (1966). (John returned his MBE insignia on 26th Nov. 1969.)
Born 18.30 hours, Wed. 9 Oct. 1940, Maternity Hospital, Oxford Street, Liverpool, England.
Characteristics About 5′ 11″; about 159*lb.* (11*st.* 5*lb.*); brown hair and eyes.
Married (1) 1962 Cynthia Powell (div. 1968) 1*s.*; (2) 1969 Mrs Yoko Ono Cox (Yoko had her second miscarriage in Oct. 1969).

Full name (James) Paul McCartney, MBE (1966).
Born Thurs. 18 June 1942, Walton Hospital, Allerton, Liverpool, England.
Characteristics About 5′ 11″; about 158*lb.* (11*st.* 4*lb.*); brown hair; hazel eyes; left-handed.
Married 1969 Linda Eastman (1*d.* by previous marriage) 1*d.*

Full name Richard Starkey (Ringo Starr), MBE (1966).
Born just after midnight, Sun. 7 July 1940 at 9 Madryn Street, Dingle, Liverpool, England.
Characteristics About 5′ 8″; about 132*lb.* (9*st.* 8*lb.*); brown hair; blue eyes.
Married 1965 Maureen Cox. 2*s.*

George has said

About fame: 'I asked to be successful. I never asked to be famous.' (1966)

About his public image: 'I have what may be termed a Beatles life and a private life. It isn't always easy to separate the two.' (1966)

On taking up the sitar: 'Before I discovered the sitar, I think my outlook on music was too narrow. The Beatles were regarded as a good pop group with limitations. . . . It was through the sitar that I realized that we are involved in *music* – but not just pop music, but music generally.' (1966)

Fined £500 ($1,200) for possession of drugs in 1969: 'I shall never possess marijuana again.'

John has said

About writing: 'I write what I think of, when I think of it.' (1964)

Has success changed him?: 'Yes, it's made me richer.' (1964)

About composing: 'Sometimes I write the whole thing – words and music. Sometimes Paul does. Most times we work on each number together, one of us contributing some words and some music. We'd never dream of allowing somebody else's composition to go out under our name.' (1964)

Does he think happiness is egg-shaped?: 'It depends how the egg is cooked.' (1966)

About Maharishi Mahesh Yogi[1]: 'What he says about life is the same message that Jesus, Buddha[2], Krishna[3], and all the big boys were putting over.' (1967)

More about the Maharishi: 'If we'd met him before we'd taken LSD[4] we wouldn't have needed to take it.' (1967)

About Yoko Ono: 'Her work is naked, basically simple and childlike and truthful.' (1968)

Fined £150 ($360) for being in possession of the drug cannabis in Nov. 1968, John said: 'The drug scene is now over.'

Paul has said

About the fans: 'I don't despise them. I don't think fans are humiliating themselves. I queued up at the Liverpool Empire for Wee Willie Harris's autograph. I don't think I was being stupid.' (1966)

About composing: 'I can hear a whole song in one chord. In fact, I think you can hear a whole song in one note, if you listen hard enough. But nobody ever listens hard enough.' (1966)

About lyrics: '. . . nearly all our songs start with the first line suggesting itself from books or newspapers.' (1967)

Whom does he admire?: 'When we started off our idols were Elvis [*Presley*] and Chuck Berry.' (1968)

On closing down the Apple store in London's Baker Street, when thousands of pounds of clothing and goods were given away to passers-by: 'We didn't want to become classed as little Jewish businessmen.' (1968)

The original Beatles — for whom the fans screamed in 1963.
In 'The Magic Christian' (Commonwealth United, 1969) Ringo Starr played the part of a vagrant picked up in a London park by Peter Sellers.

Why he wears so many rings on his fingers: 'Because I can't get them all through my nose.' (1965)

On returning from the Maharishi's Himalayan meditation centre: 'It was just like Butlin's.'[5] (1968)

Beatles by others

Brian Epstein[6]: '. . . they are quite magnificent human beings, utterly honest, often irritating, but splendid citizens shining in a fairly ordinary, not very pleasing world.' (1964)

Marlene Dietrich: 'It was a joy to be with them. I adore these Beatles.' (1964)

Prince Philip: 'It seems to me these blokes are helping people to enjoy themselves.' (1965)

Perry Como: 'I think they're four youngsters who are lucky to have a lot of hair.' (1965)

Noël Coward: '. . . almost totally devoid of talent.' (1966)

Count Basie: 'They have their own department and they do it right.' (1966)

Richard Rodgers: 'I don't think there's anything creative or original about it. It's just loud. I think their music won't last.' (1966)

Harold Wilson, OBE, on why he recommended them for the MBE[7]: '. . . because of what they have done, to my knowledge, to reduce juvenile delinquency on Merseyside.' (1966)

Lord Bernstein: 'Only Hitler ever duplicated their power over crowds. I'm convinced they could sway a presidential election if they wanted to.' (1967)

Sir Malcolm Sargent said he was one of the few people in the world who had never heard a note of Beatles' music. (1967)

Arriving in Canada for a ten-day stay, John and Yoko invited Prime Minister Pierre Trudeau to join them in their seven-day bed-in for peace, and offered him acorns to plant for peace. 'I don't know about acorns', said Trudeau, 'but I'd like to see him if he's around. He's a good poet.' (1969)

Beatle facts

Their first regular club engagement was at the Cavern Club, 8 Mathew Street, Liverpool, from Jan. 1961 to Feb. 1962. They started on £5 ($14) a session and earned £300 ($840) for their last session there.

At the height of their group fame they received the highest fee ever paid to recording artists, $160,000 (£57,142), for their appearance at the William O'Shea Stadium, New York, on 15 Aug. 1965. They turned down an offer of $1,000,000 (£357,000) for a one-day two-appearance show at the Shea Stadium in 1967. Even larger offers for United States tours in 1969 and 1970 we also turned down.

Five Beatle numbers, *She Loves You, Twist and Shout, Can't Buy Me Love, I Want to Hold Your Hand,* and *Please, Please Me,* were simultaneous million-sellers in 1964 when they occupied the first five places in the US charts. At the same time they were first and second in the LP charts with *Meet the Beatles* and *Introducing the Beatles.* Total sales of Beatles records up to April 1969 were estimated at about 240,000,000, surpassing the previous world record total of Bing Crosby.

Up to April 1969 the Lennon-McCartney song-writing team had composed over 150 songs recorded by the Beatles. They had also composed 19 songs for other artists. In the same period over 1,000 different artists had recorded Lennon-McCartney songs, the most popular being *Yesterday* which was recorded by 119 singers or groups. A Beatles' album is an undertaking calling for repeated re-arrangements and re-takes, using as much as 500 hours of studio time and costing tens of thousands of pounds to produce.

The Beatles' experiments with drugs attracted much publicity and culminated in the so-called psychedelic period in which they produced the LP disc *Sgt. Pepper's Lonely Hearts Club Band.* Shortly after this they announced that they had discarded drugs and involved themselves in the cult of transcendental meditation. After their visit to India early in 1968 it was reported that they had abandoned this experiment too and gone back to Christianity.

[1] The Indian mystic preaching the cult of transcendental meditation. His fee was reported to be a week's salary. In the case of the Beatles this would amount to perhaps £20,000 ($48,000) each.
[2] Gautama Buddha (about 6th century BC), founder of the Buddhist religion.
[3] Krishna was the eighth incarnation in earthly form of the Hindu god Vishnu.
[4] Lysergic Acid Diethylamide, a drug originally extracted from the ergot, a rye fungus. LSD induces a psychic state in which the subject may feel he is watching himself and can relive feelings from childhood and infancy. It can be dangerous and should only be used under qualified medical advice and supervision.
[5] Low cost chain of coastal holiday camps.
[6] The Beatles' manager died aged 32 in 1967 after 'an incautious overdose' of sleeping pills. His net estate was £266,032 ($638,476).
[7] OBE is Officer (4th class) and MBE is member (5th class) of Britain's most junior order, that of the British Empire (instituted 1917).

LP RECORDINGS

Please Please Me (Parlophone PMC1202/PCS3042)
With the Beatles (Parlophone PMC1206/PCS3045)
A Hard Day's Night (Parlophone PMC1230/PCS3058)
Beatles for Sale (Parlophone PMC1240/PCS3062)
Help! (Parlophone PMC1255/PCS3071)
Rubber Soul (Parlophone PMC1267/PCS3075)
Revolver (Parlophone PMC7009/PCS7009)
A Beatles Collection of Oldies (Parlophone PMC7016/PCS7016)
Sgt. Pepper's Lonely Hearts Club Band (Parlophone PMC7027/PCS7027)
Long Tall Sally (Parlophone gep8913)
Hey Jude/Revolution (R5722)
The Beatles (double album) (Parlophone PMC or PCS7067/8)
Magical Mystery Tour (EMI MMT/SMMT –1)
Yellow Submarine (soundtrack) (Parlophone PCS7070/PMC7070)
Wonderwall (Apple SAPCOR1/APCOR1)
Two Virgins (John and Yoko) (SAPCOR2)
Life with the Lions – Unfinished Music No. 2 (John and Yoko) (ZAPPLE01)
Electronic Sound (George) (ZAPPLE02)
Abbey Road (Parlophone PCS7088)

FILMS

A Hard Day's Night (1964); all four starred.
Help! (1965); all four starred.
How I Won the War (1967); John appeared.
The Family Way (1967); Paul wrote the score.
Yellow Submarine (1968); all four appeared.
Candy (1969); Ringo appeared.
Wonderwall (1969); George wrote the score.
The Magic Christian (1969); Ringo starred.
Smiles (1969) ; John and Yoko starred

PLAY

In His Own Write (1968), an adaptation from John's two books *In His Own Write* (1964) and *A Spaniard in the Works* (1965)

TELEVISION

Magical Mystery Tour (1968); all four starred.
Rape (1969); produced by John and Yoko.

29

ENGLAND 3 GERMANY W. 2

GEOFF HURST

When he scored his third goal for England in the World Cup Final on 30 July 1966, Geoff Hurst joined the immortals of Association Football. No other player in history has scored three goals in a World Cup Final.

Full name Geoffrey Hurst.

Born Mon. 8 Dec. 1941, Ashton-under-Lyne, Lancashire, England.

Characteristics About 6′; about 189*lb.* (13*st.* 7*lb.*); dark brown hair; hazel eyes; non-smoker.

Married 1964 Judith Harries 2*d.*

The scoreboard at Wembley Stadium read England 3, West Germany 2. The remaining seconds of the 1966 World Cup Final were ticking remorselessly away with England, the host country, leading by a goal. Then came the perfect ace, the irreversible decider, the impeccable full point at the conclusion of a unique chapter in sports history. The last kick of the match, a left-footed volley, detonated

from a range of 25 yards, hurtled past the dazed West German goalkeeper, Hans Tilkowski. 'I knew', admitted Geoff Hurst, 'that I would never hit a better shot as long as I lived.' Had they been called upon to vote, the 96,924 live spectators and the 600,000,000 TV and sound radio audience must surely have agreed. For Geoff it completed a hat-trick of goals without precedent in the history of World Cup Finals. For England it clinched the World Cup for the first time. The British Press were understandably elated but the *mot juste* to sum it all up came from the pen of an American writer. 'Upper lips', he wrote succinctly, 'were limp'.

30

England team which won the World Cup Final in 1966.
k row, left to right: Harold Shepherdson (*Trainer*),
ert (Nobby) Stiles, Roger Hunt, Gordon Banks, John
cky) Charlton, George Cohen, Ramon (Ray) Wilson,
(now Sir) Alf Ramsey (Manager); *front row:* Martin
ers, Robert (Bobby) Moore (*Captain*), Alan Ball,
ert (Bobby) Charlton.

he World Cup was designed by the French sculptor,
l Lafleur. It was presented to FIFA (Fédération Inter-
onale de Football Association) by Jules Rimet
73–1956), Honorary President of FIFA (1921–54).
Cup is of solid gold and cost 50,000 francs (about
0 or $1,600) in 1930. It is now said to be worth about
00 ($7,200).

World Cup Winners

Year	Venue	Winners	Runners-Up	Score
1930	Montevideo	Uruguay	Argentina	4–2
1934	Rome	Italy	Czechoslovakia	2–1
1938	Paris	Italy	Hungary	4–2
1950	Rio de Janeiro	Uruguay	Brazil	2–1
1954	Berne	West Germany	Hungary	3–2
1958	Stockholm	Brazil	Sweden	5–2
1962	Santiago	Brazil	Czechoslovakia	3–1
1966	London	England	West Germany	4–2

Leading Goalscorers in World Cup Finals

r	Player	Goals
6	Geoff Hurst (England)	3
4	Helmut Rahn (Germany)	2
8	Edson Arantes do Nascimento 'Pelé' (Brazil)	2
8	Edvaldo Isidro Neto 'Vava' (Brazil)	2
	(Vava also scored a goal in the 1962 Final)	

Leading Goalscorers in World Cup Final Series

Year	Player	Goals
1958	Just Fontaine (France)	13
1954	Sandor Kocsis (Hungary)	11
1966	'Eusebio' Ferreira da Silva (Portugal)	9
1930	Guillermo Stabile (Argentina)	8
1930	'Leonidas' da Silva (Brazil)	8
1950	Marques Ademir (Brazil)	7
1938	Gyula Szengeller (Hungary)	7
1954	Max Morlock (Germany)	6
1954	Erich Probst (Austria)	6
1958	Edson Arantes de Nascimento 'Pelé' (Brazil)	6
1958	Helmut Rahn (West Germany)	6
	(Rahn also scored 4 goals for Germany in the 1954 series)	

Recording
hlights from 21 Years of BBC's Sports Report (BBC
io Enterprises REC29M)
udes commentary on the 1966 World Cup Final.

Jack Nicklaus

Full name Jack William Nicklaus.

Born Sun. 21 Jan. 1940, Columbus, Ohio, USA.

Characteristics About 6'; about 210*lb.* (15*st.*); rusty-blond hair; blue eyes.

Married 1960 Barbara Bash 2*s.*

Bulking mightily on the golf courses of the pro circuit, the player variously dubbed 'The Golden Bear', 'Ohio Fats', and 'Blobbo' announced in 1962 the very laudable ambition: 'I want to be the best golfer the world has ever seen.' Only two years had elapsed before the pundits were ranking him as one of the half-dozen truly great players of the modern era, bringing him if not within sight of his objective, at least on to a higher plane than any other golfer had climbed in so short a period.

Nicklaus once shot a 66 while humming *Moon River* to himself. If the music of Henry Mancini helped him do so, it was purely incidental, for Jack has much more than gimmicks going for him. He has, among other things, a shrewd competitive philosophy. 'I have come to believe', he has said, 'that the player who most often ends up winning is the one who, in a sense, is least afraid of winning. He has learned the technique of being a winner.' Aside from being an accomplished winner, Nicklaus has the priceless knack of being able to unwind. His wife has reported: 'He's never on time for anything but golf. But that's his nature. Jack sleeps through an alarm and can fall asleep the minute he gets into an aeroplane, a car, or even a chair.'

A round of 69 over a course of 7,095 yards when he was only 13 demonstrated Jack's immense potential. He took his first amateur title, the Ohio Open, at 16. Always a big hitter himself, he does not advise the beginner to start slowly and build up: 'A youngster first trying golf will enjoy the game more if allowed to whale away at the ball, and he will be developing the muscles he needs to become a strong hitter. Once he has achieved distance, he can learn control while still hitting a long ball. Jack broke the PGA long-driving record with 341 yards in July 1963.

It was after the 1960 World Amateur Competition that Nicklaus received his first real prognosis of impending greatness. President Eisenhower told him: 'Mr Nicklaus, at the Augusta National Golf Club, as you know, we build bridges to commemorate the records set by top players in

Jack Nicklaus: 'The player who most often ends up winning is the one who, in a sense, is least afraid of winning.'

the Masters. The way you're going, perhaps we should stop building those bridges. You look like you'll beat all the marks.' The prophecy was fulfilled when Jack took the Masters in 1963 and again in 1965 with a record 271. On hand to comment was the old master himself, Bobby Jones: 'I have a natural aversion to superlatives', he told Nicklaus, 'but this was the greatest performance in all golfing history.' Gary Player thought Jack would win the Masters more times than anyone who ever lived: 'A guy like him comes to the last hole needing four to win. He'll just aim it down the centre and hit hell out of it. Wherever it goes he only has to hit a wedge to the green.' Nicklaus has said that 'The good thing about Augusta is that if you play reasonably well you do reasonably well. Less is left to chance.'

Jack has collected more than $100,000 a year in prize money since 1963. In 1964 he got half way to that figure in one giant stride, winning the $50,000 (£17,857) first prize in the televised *Big Three Golf* series against Arnold Palmer and Gary Player, an exhibition which British viewers later enjoyed. In 1967 Jack collected $100,000 (£35,700) in the space of 12 days by capturing the Westchester Classic and the World Series, each of which carried a

$50,000 prize. His annual income was then said to be nudging the million-dollar mark, including profits from endorsements, real estate, and Louisiana oil.

One of only four golfers in history to have won the four major titles,[1] Jack's competitive consistency owes a lot to his steadiness under pressure. 'At critical times a player feeling pressure should step back, take a long breath and enjoy the challenge, not evade it', he has advised. 'Properly controlled, this tension can actually help you to hit a better-than-usual shot.' He has the enviable capacity for getting right away from golf at times, settling instead for an afternoon's fishing or a quiet nap. His coolness paid dividends in 1962 when he beat Palmer to become, at 22, the youngest player since 1923 to win the American Open. Experts recalled that he had finished second in the US Open in 1960 while still an amateur. In 1967 Jack again ousted Arnie for his second US Open title, shooting in the process a five-under-par 275, a record for the 67-year-old event.

The perfectionist in Nicklaus found satisfaction, though only temporarily, when he collected his first Open Championship at Muirfield in 1966. 'I am always trying to improve my golf', he told reporters. 'There is always something new to try and I figure that the day I become satisfied with the way I am playing is the day I will be over the hill. If I'm not making progress I'm finished.'

In 1968 Nicklaus played a prominent part in the dispute between American tour professionals and the PGA which ended in the players being granted a four-man representation on the board governing tour policy.

---

[1] The only other golfers to have won the American PGA, the American Open, the Masters', and the British Open are Gene Sarazen, Ben Hogan, and Gary Player.

MAJOR GOLF TITLES

Year	Championship	Score	Prize £	$
1962	American Open, Oakmont, Pennsylvania.	283	5,357	15,000
1963	American PGA, Dallas, Texas.	279	4,643	13,000
1963	American Masters', Augusta, Georgia.	286	7,142	20,000
1965	American Masters', Augusta, Georgia.	271	7,142	20,000
1966	American Masters', Augusta, Georgia.	288	7,142	20,000
1966	The Open, Muirfield, Scotland.	282	2,100	5,880
1967	American Open, Baltusrol, New Jersey.	275	10,714	30,000

OTHER CHAMPIONSHIP & TOURNAMENT WINS

Year	Tournament	Score	Prize £	$
1962	World Series of Golf, Akron, Ohio (36 holes).	135	17,857	50,000
1962	Seattle, Washington Open.	265	1,535	4,300
1962	Portland, Oregon Open.	269	1,250	3,500
1963	Tournament of Champions, Las Vegas, Nevada.	273	4,643	13,000
1963	World Series of Golf, Akron, Ohio (36 holes).	140	17,857	50,000
1963	Sahara Invitational, Las Vegas, Nevada.	276	4,643	13,000
1963	Canada Cup individual winner, St Nom-La-Breteche, France.	237	1,000	2,800
1963	Palm Springs Classic, California (90 holes).	345	3,214	9,000
1964	Phoenix, Arizona Open.	271	2,680	7,500
1964	Tournament of Champions, Las Vegas, Nevada.	279	4,286	12,000
1964	Whitemarsh, Pennsylvania Open.	276	8,586	24,042
1964	Portland, Oregon Open.	275	2,070	5,800
1964	Canada Cup individual winner, Maui, Hawaii.	276	1,000	2,800
1965	Memphis, Tennessee Open.	271	3,214	9,000
1965	Thunderbird Classic, Harrison, New York.	270	7,142	20,000
1965	Portland, Oregon Open.	273	2,357	6,600
1965	Philadelphia Classic.	277	8,678	24,300
1966	Sahara Invitational, Las Vegas, Nevada.	282	7,142	20,000
1967	Bing Crosby Tournament, Pebble Beach, California.	284	5,714	16,000
1967	Western Open, Chicago, Illinois.	274	7,142	20,000
1967	Westchester Classic, Harrison, New York.	272	17,857	50,000
1967	World Series of Golf, Akron, Ohio (36 holes).	144	17,857	50,000
1967	Sahara Invitational, Las Vegas, Nevada.	270	7,142	20,000
1968	Western Open, Chicago, Illinois.	273	10,833	26,000
1968	American Golf Classic, Akron, Ohio.	280	10,416	25,000
1969	Andy Williams Open, San Diego, California.	284	12,500	30,000

Nicklaus also won the Australian Open in 1964 and 1968.

TEAM CHAMPIONSHIPS

Year	Trophy
1963	Canada Cup[1], St Nom-La-Breteche, France.
1964	Canada Cup[1], Maui, Hawaii.
1966	PGA National[1], Palm Beach Gardens, Florida.
1966	Canada Cup[1], Tokio, Japan.
1967	World Cup[1] (formerly Canada Cup), Mexico City.
1969	Ryder Cup, Royal Birkdale, Southport, England.

[1] With Arnold Palmer.

TOTAL GOLF EARNINGS

Year	£	$	Placed
1962	22,476	62,933	3
1963	36,750	102,903	2
1964	41,457	116,079	1
1965	55,123	154,346	1
1966	50,450	141,258	2
1967	75,538	211,566	1
1968	66,440	159,455	2

David Frost

Full name David Paradine Frost.

Born Fri. 7 April 1939, Tenterden, Kent, England.

Characteristics About 5′ 10″; about 182*lb.* (13*st.*); dark brown hair; brown eyes; indoor complexion; classless accent.

So far as this writer is aware the only occasion when an egg and spoon race was ever staged at White City Stadium was when David Frost hired Britain's largest track athletics arena in 1967 for a party.

There was more elbow room than at Battersea Fun Fair, scene of his 1966 bunfight. Three-legged races were run and gatecrashers were readily accommodated in the banked tiers of 35,000 seats which had once echoed to the cheers of Sydney Wooderson and Roger Bannister fans. Frost has his fans, too, millions of them. Malcolm Muggeridge waited until Leap Year (1968) before dubbing him 'the most valuable TV property extant' qualifying the accolade in the true Muggeridge

Prince Charles was interviewed by David Frost for the one-hour colour feature film 'A Prince for Wales' (Drummer Films) which included scenes from the Prince's Investiture on 1 July 1969. (See above)

manner by adding 'his very lack of talent makes him king of the telly'. And if 1,000 fan letters weekly are evidence in favour then Frost has certainly made it. He has been TV 'Personality of the Year', 'Show Business Personality of the Year', won the 1967 Richard Dimbleby Award and the Golden Rose at the Montreux TV Festival for his 1967 programme *Frost Over England*. There were incidental honours, too, Left and right: Prime Minister Harold Wilson accepted his invitation to breakfast and the *Evening Standard* ranked him the fourth best-dressed man ahead of Cary Grant and Lord Snowdon – a surprise this, even to David, who never pretended to be sartorially smooth.

Frost in fact never really pretended about anything. His colleagues are unanimous that he is as real off TV as on, never fails to remember a name, and has the rare capacity for retaining as willing associates seniors in the business over whose heads he has adroitly clambered.

boss who later worked for him. Paid £20 ($56) a week on Rediffusion's *This Week* in 1961, he got no closer to the viewers than voicing off-camera commentaries, the producer relegating him as 'totally unsuitable' to show his face on the box. That producer also worked for Frost later. Twelve months later the BBC were paying him £135 ($378) a week as linkman on *That Was the Week That Was* which lured an audience of 11,000,000 from their accustomed Saturday night booze-up to strain their eyes over *TW3*. The American version of *TW3* had him flying to the States twice a week, logging over 50 Atlantic flights in six months. Then he was on £600 ($1,680) a week as front man on *Not So Much a Programme More a Way of Life*. In 1966, having conquered almost every peak in the business, he nearly drowned in a swimming-bath mishap. Rescued by Peter Cook he survived for his 28th birthday and read his name in *Who's Who* (1967), easily the youngest TV personality

Above all, Frost never pretended about wanting to succeed. Someone remarked that if there were a World Government he would gladly accept nomination as President.

At Cambridge University he said he would run the Footlights and edit *Granta*. He did these things, boosting the paper's circulation by a judicious use of four-letter words while reading for the English tripos in his spare time. His days as a TV trainee were largely spent serving coffee to his

ever listed.

Frost somehow fits five hours' sleep into an effective 28-hour working day made possible by assiduous dovetailing and double-banking. He may have two or three working breakfasts, distributing the menu between as many hotels. Two simultaneous business conferences, Frost oscillating from room to room, may be kept on the boil. Motoring at 100-plus, the radio-telephone and a secretary are kept feverishly at work. His secretary has often flown

37

with him to the States to take a six-hour stint of dictation then caught the next flight home loaded with letters.

The glad hand of Frost which presses gifts from Asprey's on hundreds of guests at his parties also chips in munificently to Oxfam and other less-publicized charities. Though he has been known to keep a taxi waiting on the meter while being measured for a suit, and owns a £25,000 ($60,000) home in Knightsbridge, he is not given to wild extravagance and does not drink.

The question of how soon he became a millionaire is perhaps academic but in the meantime life has its compensations. His fee for four TV programmes in America in 1968 was £125,000 ($300,000). Then he won a 12-month contract for $1,000,000 (£416,666) to appear five times a week in New York starting in June 1969. He no longer has to hitch-hike 109 miles to visit his mother, nor, presumably, has he any regrets about turning down a £12-a-week offer to turn professional footballer.

T.V. PROGRAMMES

That Was the Week That Was (GB 1962–63, USA 1963–64)

Not So Much a Programme More a Way of Life (GB 1964–65)

The Frost Programme (GB 1966)

The Frost Report (GB 1966–67)

David Frost's Night Out in London (USA 1966–67)

Frost on Friday
Frost on Saturday } (GB 1968–69–70)
Frost on Sunday

The David Frost Show (USA 1969)

L. P. RECORDINGS

The Frost Report on Britain (Parlophone PMC7005)

The Frost Report on Everything (Pye NPL18199)

John Cleese (left) and Ronnie Corbett were regular members of David Frost's team in 1967 when his BBC programme, 'Frost Over England', won the Golden Rose at the Montreux TV Festival.

Rudolf Nureyev

Nureyev added a new role to his repertoire with Dame Margot Fonteyn in the Roland Petit ballet 'Paradise Lost' which had its world première at Covent Garden on 23 Feb. 1967.

Full name Rudolf Hametovich Nureyev.

Born Thurs. 17 March 1938, on a train near Irkutsk, Siberia, USSR (travelling to Vladivostock).

Characteristics About 5' 8"; about 160*lb* (11*st.* 6*lb.*); light brown hair (which he is reported to trim with toe-nail clippers); blue-grey eyes.

Labels like 'blond Beatle' are strictly one-dimensional in relation to Britain's principal dancer and one of the world's leading ballet artists. So are adjectives like off-beat, way-out, and bizarre. It takes much more than star quality and funny hats to create a dancer of distinction and more than fine artistry to make a Nureyev. Ballet is an art where more, perhaps, than any other, beauty 'lingers in the eye of the beholder'. One must go and see to understand.

39

Of Tartar parentage on both sides of his family, Nureyev was born on a train. His restless spirit was prompting him to find wider fields of expression long before he grew to international stature. The son of a soldier who despised the ballet, Rudolf joined the Kirov Ballet School at 17. 'Nine of us shared a room', he recalled. 'There were moments when I just could not stand the claustrophobia any longer. I'd belt out of the room to find a place by the road to sit and dream. Always the same dream – that someone would come along and take me away forever.'

It was when the Kirov were on tour in Paris in 1961 that Nureyev finally broke out. Escaping at Le Bourget airport while the troupe were about to embark for London he requested, and was granted, political asylum in France. 'My escape was not for any political reason', he was quoted as saying. And then, as though in contradiction: 'My art would have suffered in a country where anything other than the Kollectiv is taboo.' But he was scrupulous in acknowledging his debt to the Kirov: 'My contract stipulated that I should be ready to appear eight times in a month; but actually I never did appear more than three. This enables a dancer to approach a part more deliberately, to study and develop it deeply.' With the Kirov he once danced in the presence of Premier Nikita S. Khrushchev.

Nureyev made his London debut on 2 Nov. 1961 at a gala performance at the Royal Academy of Dancing in the *Black Swan* pas de deux. In early 1962 he made his first English appearance in a full-length production opposite Margot Fonteyn in *Giselle*. A month later he staged his American debut with Sonia Arova in *Don Quixote*.

By 1963 Nureyev was being compared with the legendary Polish dancer Vaslav Nijinsky (1890–1950). Allowing for the difficulty of comparing two artists so widely separated in time – Nijinsky last danced in 1919 – it is interesting to note the impressions of Tamara Karsavina who partnered Nijinsky and has seen them both in the part of Albrecht in *Giselle*. 'While Nureyev's dancing is superb', she commented, 'Nijinsky's interpretation of the role made a deeper impression on me. Nijinsky's acting was more poignant. We must remember, too, that most of Nijinsky's parts were created for him to bring into relief his special qualities. And, of course, Nijinsky is judged over the whole of his career while Nureyev is only just beginning.' In 1969 Nureyev had talks with the American producer, Harry Saltzman, about a film of Nijinsky's life.

Nureyev's appearances with Fonteyn have, of course, been among the highlights of his career. Dame Margot paid her tribute to him: 'He is so completely in the character of the ballet. It is very different dancing with Rudolf than with any other dancer. When I dance with him I see not Nureyev but the character of the ballet. I don't see, as I do with others, a man I know and talk to every day. He is how I would like to be, and he makes it easier for me to dance as I wish.' The Fonteyn-Nureyev partnership had its warmest-ever reception at the Vienna Staatsoper where, after a performance of *Swan Lake* in 1964, they advanced for the record number of 89 curtain calls. They also starred together memorably in the films *Romeo and Juliet* and *Swan Lake*.

Rudolf has said that his ideal is for each performance to be a first performance, both for himself and for the audience. His approach is not geared to rigid concepts of technique: 'To me a work of art is something alive. To be true to the spirit is, to my mind, much more important than to be what is called correct; for that, in fact, may be less correct, in that it is false to the original idea.'

Faithful to his belief that 'the true artist

40

Repertoire

Antigone
Aurora's Wedding
La Bayadère
Birthday Offering
Black Swan
Le Corsaire
Diversions
Don Quixote
Esmerelda
Flower Festival in Genzano
Gayenah
Giselle
Hamlet
Images of Love
The Jazz Calendar
Le Jeune Homme et la Mort
Laurencia
Marguerite and Armand
The Nutcracker
Paradise Lost
Pelléas et Mélisande
Poème d'Ecstase
Poème Tragique
Prince Igor
Raymonda
Romeo and Juliet
The Sleeping Beauty
The Song of the Earth
Les Sylphides
Symphonic Variations
Swan Lake
Tancredi
Taras Bulba

Films
A Leap by the Soul (pre 1960)
Swan Lake (1965)
Romeo and Juliet (1966)

should always be ahead of his time', Nureyev has not restricted himself to the classical ballets. He expressed his admiration for *West Side Story* and showed himself to be perfectly at home in Frederick Ashton's *The Jazz Calendar*.

This readiness to embrace popular themes may, perhaps, account for the outburst attributed to George Balanchine, Master of the New York City Ballet, who was quoted in 1967 as saying: 'Rudolf Nureyev is the Brigitte Bardot of the ballet. He does what the public wants. I respect him very much as a dancer, but I regret what he is doing. His steps are boring and his music is bad.'

Nureyev can easily afford to ignore such grumbles. He has a £45,000 ($108,000) home near Richmond Park in South-West London and a £30,000 ($72,000) villa near Monte Carlo. His collection of several thousand discs, ranging from Bach to Peggy Lee, help to beguile the hours of leisure and he is prone to holding costly long-distance talks by telephone with his friends around the world. At other times his Tartar heritage takes over and he roams the streets alone at night.

Full name Rodney George Laver (known as 'Rocket').

Born Tues. 9 Aug. 1938, Rockhampton, Queensland, Australia.

Characteristics About 5′ 8½″; about 150*lb.* (10*st.* 10*lb.*); shirt measurements: chest 40″, waist 31″; pulse rate under 65; left-handed; red hair; blue eyes; freckled face.

Married 1966 Mary 1*s.*

Rod Laver

If it can be said that all sports have something in common it is, perhaps, that champions are in a minority. In sports of individual, as opposed to team, prowess they are in a minority of one. In the case of Rod Laver the exclusivity is something more for when in 1969 he won the four major singles titles of tennis (Australian, French, Wimbledon, and United States) for the second time, he achieved what no other player in tennis history had done before. His rejection of Jack Kramer's 1961 offer to turn pro for $33,600 (£12,000) had left the door open for him to win the 'grand slam' for the first time in 1962 when he was the only man since Don Budge (USA) in 1938 to capture all four in a single season.

Rod was raised on a farm in Gladstone, Queensland, a State more noted for the breeding of sheep than tennis stars. Coached by the Australian team manager, Harry Hopman, he won his first trophy at 14 and took the US Junior Championship in 1956, the year of his first appearance at Wimbledon. Reaching the final in four successive years, he was runner-up in 1959–60 and wore the coveted singles crown in 1961–62. His superiority over all-comers was instanced by the ease with which he disposed of his chief rivals; in 1961 Chuck McKinley (USA) went down in straight sets in only 55 minutes. After his first showing in the Davis Cup (the 'Holy Grail' of lawn tennis) in 1959, Rod's Davis Cup record was almost flawless: he lost only one set during Australia's winning streak of 1960–61–62.

Sometimes accused of looking bored on court, Laver in fact masks an intense concentration behind his poker face. He brings a wide range of strokes to his game and can deliver an overhead backhand shot, which few champions have used aggressively, with almost as much force as a forehand smash. His over-developed left arm, one-third as big again as his right, is immensely durable: he combats tennis elbow with his own portable hydroculator, a wrap-around device that

Left:

When Rod Laver won the Wimbledon singles title in 1969, he became the first man to win Wimbledon four times since Tony Wilding in 1910–13.

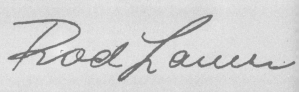

MAJOR TITLES

Year	Championship	Runner-Up	Score
1960	Australian	Neale Fraser (Australia)	5–7, 3–6, 6–3, 8–6, 8–6
1961	Wimbledon	Chuck McKinley (USA)	6–3, 6–1, 6–4
1962	Australian	Roy Emerson (Australia)	8–6, 0–6, 6–4, 6–4
1962	French	Roy Emerson (Australia)	3–6, 2–6, 6–3, 9–7, 6–2
1962	Wimbledon	Martin Mulligan (Australia)	6–2, 6–2, 6–1
1962	United States	Roy Emerson (Australia)	6–2, 6–4, 5–7, 6–4
1968	Wimbledon[1]	Tony Roche (Australia)	6–3, 6–4, 6–2
1969	Australian	Andres Gimeno (Spain)	6–3, 6–4, 7–5
1969	French	Ken Rosewall (Australia)	6–4, 6–3, 6–4
1969	Wimbledon[2]	John Newcombe (Australia)	6–4, 5–7, 6–4, 6–4
1969	United States[3]	Tony Roche (Australia)	7–9, 6–1, 6–2, 6–2

[1] Prize £2,000 ($4,800).　[2] Prize £3,000 ($7,200).　[3] Prize $16,000 (£6,666).

gives deep heat treatment and eases the tension from his racket arm. In 1969 he was using four Dunlop Maxply Fort laminated ash and beech rackets, with calf leather grips, and fine sheep-gut, strung to a tension of 58 pounds compared with the more normal 60–65 pounds.

Having turned professional in Dec. 1962, Rocket found the game tougher with the stakes higher, losing repeatedly to fellow-Aussies Lew Hoad and Ken Rosewall in 1963. But things were all different in 1964 when he took the United States Professional Grass Court Championship, beating Pancho Gonzales, and also the London Indoor Championship for the first of four successive years. In 1967 he became the first pro to win at Wimbledon, winning the BBC-2 Tournament for £3,000 (now $7,200) from Ken Rosewall. At the time he was quoted as saying: 'I guess it would be hard to find someone loving their work as much as I do.' He also felt more at home as a pro: 'As an amateur you feel guilty, at least I did,

getting paid and pretending not to.'

The advent of Open Wimbledon in 1968 saw Rod regain the title which he relinquished in 1963, raising the question of how many times he might have won Wimbledon had he been eligible in the intervening years. Another Wimbledon singles title in 1969 made him the first man since Tony Wilding (Australia) in 1910–13 to win four. Financially, he moved into the sports tycoon category. At the Madison Square Garden Tournament in May 1969 he collected $15,000 (£6,250). His five-year contract with the International Pro Tennis Association guarantees him a basic $100,000 (£41,600) a year until 1972 but his overall earnings, including endorsements, probably enable him to multiply that sum by three. In 1969 he was under contract to the Dunlop Rubber Company who first employed him as a clerk when he left school. Rocket's fellow-pro, Tony Roche, has confirmed that 'becoming world champion hasn't changed his make-up in any way.'

EL CORDOBES

Full name Manuel Benítez. The professional name El Cordobés, meaning the 'man from Córdoba' was first used in 1960. He has also been given the nickname 'El Beatle', pronounced 'Beatley', due to his length of hair.

Born Mon. 4 May 1936, Cala Ancha, Palma del Rio, Andalusia, Spain.

Characteristics About 5′ 9″; about 140*lb.* (10*st.*); dark brown hair and eyes; bears the scars of 21 wounds on his body; the combined length of his scars equals three times his waist measurement.

Among members of that exclusive band of humans who never feel themselves to be fully alive unless flirting with death, the world's top *matador* and best-paid entertainer ranks recklessly high. 'I love bulls', he has claimed, 'they are the *caballeros* of the animal kingdom.' The protestation was not made the day he received the final rites of Holy Church after being gored three times in the groin in Granada. But nobody who has seen him tossed like a rag-doll on the horns of rampaging bulls thinks he was indulging in an idle play of words when he said: 'I have no fear of death. What I fear is life.'

Manual Benítez was one year old when his father died in the Civil War. His mother died soon after. Hungry, he stole, and spent three months in prison. He endured a spell as a bricklayer's apprentice at 30 pesetas a day. At night he crept into private paddocks to try his hand at cow-fighting. The experience convinced him he was destined for finer things than hired

labour. He decided to be a *torero* but admitted that he would not have made the move for a sport like boxing which he deemed 'pretty ignorant, a sport of fools. Sooner than box I would have gone on being a labourer's apprentice.'

It was in 1956 that Benítez made his first appearance in the Plaza de Toros in Madrid, leaping uninvited into the arena from his seat in the stands. He was badly gored before police carried him off, then contrived an extension of his stay in the relatively well-fed comfort of the prison hospital by aggravating his wounds. Still judging it better to be a bullfighter than to load bricks, he took his *novillero* (novitiate) in 1959.

Thus 'out of necessity, out of ambition' El Cordobés grew to be a national figure, already wealthy by 1960, long before graduating to a fully-fledged *matador* on 12 Oct. 1963. His fame and wealth inflated until in 1965 he was earning at the rate of £7,000 ($19,600) a fight, accumulating in the year a total sum of over $2,000,000 (£714,000). Ten *paso dobles* were composed in his honour, 300 poems were dedicated to him, and 150 letters reached him daily, most of them with propositions of love without strings from devoted feminine admirers. His six cars and his private aircraft expedited his movements between his Madrid apartment, his 450-acre *hacienda* in Andalusia, his various other farms, and his frequent bullring engagements. Brands of wine, cigars, and assorted merchandise

45

were named after him. His construction company was thriving and his seven-storey hotel proudly 'overlooked the jail where once he languished at Córdoba. In 1968 his fortune was estimated at about $8,300,000 (£3,458,000). *En route* to all this he collected, incidentally, the Spanish award of 'Best Actor' for his performance in the film *Apprendiendo a Morir* (*Apprenticeship for Death*) (1962).

Launched on the fuller life, El Cordobés turned his thoughts to education for the first time long after he had earned his first million. Watching a blast-off from Cape Kennedy on TV he was enthralled to discover that the world is round, a fact previously unknown to him.

Though he has killed over 1,200 bulls[1], 221 in 1965, a record 64 in a single month that year, El Cordobés does not hold with cruelty. 'Look, it hurts me to see animals die. Once when I was hungry I stole a chicken and killed it but it made me shudder to kill it. I turned my head away when I killed it and then I lost my appetite.'

On the finer points of bullfighting he does not please the purists. Indeed, Picasso said he would not paint his portrait for all the money in the world. Being less an artist than an entertainer, he lacks, perhaps, the refinement and aesthetic capacity of such immortals as Juan Belmonte (1892–1962) and Victoriano de la Serna who admitted that a well-executed pass provoked orgasm. 'They must have been drunk' was the comment of El Cordobés. He has, however, showed his respect for past heroes. He revived Manolete's[2] custom of opening cases of whisky or cognac for his admirers and, in 1962, when he had contracts for 120 fights, stopped when he had equalled Belmonte's record of 109 *corridas* in a season[3].

In 1964 it was calculated that of the 125 major *matadors* in action since 1700, the number killed in the bullring was 42. The expectation of survival was thus 66 per cent or three to one. Of those who did live to enjoy retirement, Belmonte was gored over 50 times. El Cordobés has been ripped, gashed, and otherwise mutilated on the razor-sharp horns of bulls over 20 times. His nearest brush with eternity was when his femoral artery was missed by five millimetres – about a quarter of an inch. The moment of crunch was witnessed by 20,000,000 nail-biting TV spectators in 1964.

In the winter of 1967 El Cordobés announced his retirement only to reconsider when apprised of the grievous losses that restaurant owners, ticket touts, and other parasites of his deadly art would suffer. The Press, according to custom receiving up to $3,000 (£1,250) in bribes before a major *corrida*, complained loudest. After averaging 100 fights a year for three years he faced up to a further mortal stint on the fearful treadmill.

But the signs in 1969 were that he might come in for an unexpected reprieve. The decline of bullfighting as an art, lamented by the purists for some years, has been accompanied by a slump in standards of breeding. Under-developed bulls with blunted horns destined for the tourist trade have made life in the bullring less lethal. Impresarios, moreover, have been paying lesser *matadors* reduced fees in return for block contracts. And El Cordobés was never a man to be impressed either by mini-bulls or mini-fees.

[1] The record total of bulls killed stands to the credit of Rafael Molina 'Lagartijo' (1841–1900) who accounted for 4,867 bulls. He survived to enjoy retirement.

[2] Real name Manuel Rodríguez (1917–47), killed in the bullring.

[3] Carlos Arruza (born 1920) fought 112 *corridas* in 1945 but four of these were in Mexico. He had also intended to stop short of the record but lost count.

Julie Andrews

Full name Julia Elizabeth Wells (adopted her step-father's name, Andrews).

Born 06.00 hours, Tues. 1 Oct. 1935, Rodney House Maternity Home, Walton-on-Thames, Surrey, England.

Characteristics About 5′ 7″; about 120*lb.* (8*st.* 8*lb.*); blue eyes; light brown hair; retroussé nose; slightly bandy legs; size eight shoes.

Married 1959 Tony Walton (div. 1968) 1*d.*

Julie played the title role in 'Star!' (20th Century-Fox, 1968) which was based on the life of Gertrude Lawrence (1901–52). In it she sang 16 musical numbers, appeared in 143 scenes, made 114 wardrobe changes, and learned foot-juggling for the acrobatic takes.

The columnist who wrote: 'She's the kind of girl that you could take home to Mother. Providing, of course, that you can trust Dad', was indulging in the short of circumlocution necessary to fill columns though strictly superfluous when discussing Julie Andrews. What he really meant was that people liked her. Stanley Holloway liked her: 'She is the utmost fun and an absolute young gentlewoman in the finest sense of the word.' Alfred Hitchcock liked her too:

47

'She is one of those people whose strength and talent comes across on the screen.' And Richard Burton raved: 'Every man I know who knows her is a little in love with her.'

Julie showed right from the outset that she was a fine example of Nature's unpredictability. As a small girl she had to wear braces on her teeth and was given special exercises to correct a squint in her right eye. Then it was found that her voice had a four-octave range. 'It was thin, reedy, but very powerful', she has recalled. 'My parents carted me off to a throat specialist who discovered that I had an adult larynx.' The potentialities of this phenomenon were recognized and Julie began singing lessons at the age of eight. At 12 she was seen at the London Hippodrome in *Starlight Roof* with Vic Oliver and sang an astoundingly mature *Polonaise*. In her teens she was able to hit the F above top C. An obvious candidate for pantomime, she was invited at 16 by Emile Littler to be principal girl in *Aladdin*. By then she was so tall that the principal boy had to wear four-inch heels. In 1953 she played the title role in *Cinderella* at the Palladium and a year later made her New York debut in *The Boy Friend*.

Julie became an international star in *My Fair Lady* which opened on 15 March 1956 at the Mark Hellinger Theatre on Broadway and ran for a record 2,717 performances until Sept. 1962. Undeterred by director Moss Hart's comment that she played 'like a girl guide' in rehearsals, Julie studied Cockney under an American professor of phonetics and then brought what many critics thought was the authentic touch to the part of Eliza, the girl whom the author, George Bernard Shaw, had specified in his original stage directions for *Pygmalion* should be 'perhaps 18, perhaps 20, hardly older'. Said Julie: 'I think I learned more about show business during the run of *My Fair Lady* than in anything

else I've done. I was never really sure, on any given night, that I had enough strength to do the whole thing flat out.' The show had another record run of 2,281 performances at Drury Lane, London, and grossed a total of $66,250,000 (£23,630,000) from all productions. The *My Fair Lady* LP disc with the original theatre cast, including Rex Harrison and Stanley Holloway, sold over 6,000,000 copies.

Never one to shirk the hard work, Julie played in the stage version of *Camelot* (1960) while pregnant. Her leading man, Richard Burton, commented: 'She is among my three favourite co-stars, the others being E. Taylor and P. O'Toole.' The popularity of *Camelot*, which ran on into 1962, was also reflected in sales of the LP disc, another million-seller.

If it can be said that Julie ever had a setback it was when Audrey Hepburn was preferred for the film version of *My Fair Lady* but, characteristically, she took it in good part. 'One of the best things that ever happened to me', she remarked philo-

Julie Andrews will play opposite Rock Hudson in 'Darling Lili', due for release by Paramount in 1970.

sophically. 'It made it possible for me to do *Mary Poppins* and *The Americanization of Emily*.' The first of these films made her a screen star of the top rank and won Julie an 'Oscar' as the best actress of 1964. And once again the LP disc sold millions. The part in the celebrated Walt Disney film was almost made to measure for Julie as her father confirmed in saying of the 'Oscar': 'I don't think she was acting when she got that – Julie played herself in *Mary Poppins* and *The Sound of Music*.' *Sound* proved, if possible, even more popular than the others[1], earning Julie $225,000 (£80,000) and, of course, the LP disc was a runaway success, selling 7,000,000 copies.

Between other commitments Julie won two 'Emmys' and a Peabody Award in 1965 for her TV show and even found time to visit a psychiatrist five times a week: 'It's done me the world of good. . . . I suppose a lot of the trouble came from that early background when my parents were divorced. Anyway I got into such a muddle that I wanted to get it straight. I'm still in a muddle but at least I know why.'

With 143 scenes to act, over 100 costume changes, and 16 numbers to sing, Julie was not exaggerating when she said that her part in *Star!* was a 'bigger challenge than any other role I've played.' The film story of Gertrude Lawrence (1901–52) on which *Star!* is based was directed by Robert Wise who also directed *The Sound of Music*. 'Julie', he was quoted as saying, 'has a very great sincerity and genuineness which I think comes through in all the parts she plays.'

Earning at the rate of $1,000,000 (£416,666) a picture, Julie has homes in Hollywood, Switzerland, and Alderney in the Channel Islands. There is something of the fairy-tale quality about her favourite investment – an avocado pear and macadamia nut orchard in Hawaii.

---

[1] This film had a most unusual attendance record: a Mrs Myra Franklin of Cardiff, South Wales, claimed to have seen it 864 times.

Films

Mary Poppins (1964)
The Sound of Music (1965)
The Americanization of Emily (1965)
Hawaii (1966)
Torn Curtain (1966)
Thoroughly Modern Millie (1967)
Star! (1968)
Darling Lili (1970)

LP Recordings

Broadway's Fair Julie (CBS BPG 62018/SBPG62018)
Heartrending Ballads and Raucous Ditties (CBS BPG62405 SBPG62405)
A Christmas Treasure (RCA Victor RB6689/2B6689)
My Fair Lady (Original New York Cast) (CBS agg20023/5)
My Fair Lady (Original Drury Lane Cast) (CBS BRG70005/SBRG70005)
The Sound of Music (RCA Victor RB6616/SB6616)
Mary Poppins (Buena Vista BV4026/BVS4026)
Thoroughly Modern Millie (soundtrack) (Brunswick LAR8685/STA8685)
Star! (Stateside SL10233/SSL10233)

SOPHIA LOREN

Sophia as she will appear in the forthcoming MGM release 'Ghost Italian Style'.

Full name Sophia Loren née Sofia Scicolone.

Born Thurs. 20 Sept. 1934, Pozzuoli, Naples, Italy.

Characteristics About 5′ 8″; about 134*lb.* (9*st.* 8*lb.*); bust 38″; waist 24″; hips 38″; almond eyes; olive skin; reddish-brown hair.

Married 1957 (by proxy) Carlo Ponti[1]; 1966 (in person) Carlo Ponti 1*s.*

[1] The Mexico marriage was annulled in 1967. After a five-year trial Sophia and Ponti were acquitted of bigamy in July 1968. Under Italian law Ponti is still technically married to his first wife because divorce is not recognized in Italy.

It is one of the paradoxes of war that the avenging hand of conquest can quickly turn to acts of warm compassion. So it was that Sub-Lt. Alec Guinness, RN, found time when serving in the Allied invasion force at Anzio near Naples in 1943 to hand out bars of chocolate to hungry children waiting at the quayside. His deed was not forgotten. In 1963 when filming *The Fall of the Roman Empire* he was told by his co-star, Sophia Loren: 'I was one of those children.' Recalled Sir Alec: 'After that we got on famously.'

Sophia remembered the hard times in Naples: 'I never had a childhood. When I'm making a film and have to appear sad in a scene, I go back to my memories.' She is alleged to have said that 'being beautiful is no handicap, so long as you don't think too much about it'. Whether or not the matter has ruled her thoughts, nobody would claim that Sophia Loren's beauty has been a handicap. Known when small as *Stuzzicadenti* (tooth-pick) owing to her skinny form, she filled out rewardingly and won a beauty contest at 15. Her mother, who was once placed first out of 350 in a contest to find a double for Greta Garbo, shared her meagre weekly wage packet of $33 (£12) when they worked together as extras in *Quo Vadis* (1950). She had bit parts in 27 films before reaching international stardom.

It was producer Carlo Ponti who lent her the confidence to see herself as a star and he helped her into her first starring part in *Africa Under the Sea* (1952). Said

After two miscarriages, Sophia Loren gave birth by Caesarian section to a son, Carlo Ponti Jr. (weight 7lb. 12oz.), on Sun. 29 Dec. 1968. To mark her gratitude she said she would donate $1,000,000 (£416,666) for a new obstetrical clinic in Geneva.

Sophia Loren with her mother and sister Maria, wife of jazz pianist Romano Mussolini, son of the Duce.

Ponti: 'I saw in Sophia a vitality, a sensitivity, a sense of rhythm that no actor's studio can teach. She was not an actress, she was an artist.'

Seen with him constantly, she was asked in 1954 about her future marriage plans. 'I shall marry the man of my life in three years', she predicted. 'His name is written on a piece of paper enclosed in a bottle and the bottle itself is deposited in a safe. If after that date I am not married I will reveal the name.' True to her belief that 'Real love is an act of reciprocal gratitude that develops slowly', Sophia married Ponti (born 11 Dec. 1913), who is 21 years older than her and six inches shorter, by proxy in Juárez, Mexico, in 1957. 'I married an older man because I had always been insecure in the past. A younger man cannot give the same feeling of security to a woman who has never been lucky enough to have it. Anyone who marries for sex or passion is immature.' But the Mexico marriage was not accepted as valid in Italy and it was not until 1966 that they were married in a civil ceremony at Sèvres, near Paris, Ponti bestowing on Sophia an 87-carat emerald.

Miss Loren, who has described herself as 'a unity of many irregularities', makes no very elaborate beauty preparations. She wears little foundation, even on the set, and below the eyes uses only lipstick and powder. The eyes merit special treatment: 'I outline each hair in the eyebrow individually with a pencil. And of course I do the lashes and the make-up on the eyelid.' This operation takes 15 minutes. She keeps her smoking down to 10 a day and after a 14-hour day filming likes to sleep with

51

plastic earplugs. 'Diets I never do. Sometimes if I want to lose two pounds I just stop eating for a day. That is all.' Food is one of her hobbies and provides terms of endearment for her husband. Says Ponti: 'For dear she calls me *polpettone* (meat loaf), or for very dear *peperone* (pepper). But when she loves me most she calls me *suppli* (fried rice ball with *mozzarrella* cheese).'

The high point of Sophia Loren's career was the 'Oscar' for her part in *Two Women*, the first instance in the history of the award of an actress in a non-English-speaking role being so honoured. *The Black Orchid*, in which she starred with Anthony Quinn, won the Venice Festival Award.

A star in the real sense, there is no doubt that Sophia is universally loved by those who have met and worked with her. Frank Sinatra thought that: 'Nothing better has been made since Venus.' Vittorio de Sica, who directed her in *Bocaccio '70*, said: 'In spite of having the usual womanly defects, she is the only really spiritually honest woman I've ever met.' Charlie Chaplin, her 77-year-old director in *A Countess from Hong Kong*, sighed: 'Ah, if only I were 60.'

'I'll never wear a mini-skirt because I feel this new fashion destroys, in part, the feminine mystique. Mystery is a woman's strongest weapon. Nowadays, a man can see practically all of a woman in one glance. It's like swallowing a meal in one mouthful. Nothing remains to be enjoyed.'

'Only a moron can be happy always. Happiness isn't the object. It's accepting all experience – bad and good. It's taking risks, trying to achieve more than you think you can.'

'When I die I will go straight to paradise and it will be like my home and the gardens in the hills outside Rome.'

52

FILMS

Cuori Sul Mare (1949)
Il Voto (1950)
Era Lui, Si! Si! (1951)
Il Sogno di Zorro (1951)
E'Arrivato l'Accordatore (1951)
La Tratta Delle Bianchi (1952)
La Favorita (1952)
Africa Sotto i Mari (1952)
Aida (1953)
Carosello Napoletano (1953)
Ci Troviamo in Galleria (1953)
La Domenica Della Buona Gente (1953)
Un Giorno in Pretura (1953)
Il Paese dei Campanelli (1954)
Tempi Nostri (1954)
Due Notti con Cleopatra (1954)
Pellegrini d'Amore (1954)
Miseria e Nobilita (1954)
Attila (1954)
The Gold of Naples (1954)
Woman of the River (1954)
Too Bad She's Bad (1955)
The Miller's Wife (1955)
Scandal in Sorrento (1955)
Bread, Love and ... (1955)
Lucky to be a Woman (1955)
The Pride and the Passion (1957)
Boy on a Dolphin (1957)
Legend of the Lost (1957)
Desire Under the Elms (1958)
The Key (1958)
Houseboat (1958)
The Black Orchid (1959)
That Kind of Woman (1959)
Heller in Pink Tights (1960)
A Breath of Scandal (1961)
Two Women (1961)
The Millionairess (1961)
El Cid (1961)
Bocaccio 70 (1962)
The Condemned of Altona (1962)
Madame Sans Gene (1962)
Five Miles to Midnight (1963)
Yesterday, Today and Tomorrow
The Fall of the Roman Empire (1964)
Marriage Italian Style (1964)
Operation Crossbow (1965)
Judith (1965)
Arabesque (1966)
A Countess from Hong Kong (1967)
The Best House in Naples (1968)
More Than A Miracle (1969)
Cinderella Italian Style (1969)
Ghost Italian Style (1969)
The Sunflower (1970)

TELEVISION

With Love ... From Sophia (1967)

LP RECORDINGS

Peter and Sophia
(with Peter Sellers)
(Parlophone PMC1131/ PCS3102)

Full name
Elvis Aaron Presley.

Born
Tues. 8 Jan. 1935,
Tulepo, Mississippi,
USA.

Characteristics
About 6′ 1′′; about
185*lb.* (13*st.* 2*lb.*);
brown hair; blue eyes.

Married
1967 Priscilla Beaulieu
1*d.*

Elvis shook his snake-hips coast-to-coast when he appeared in his own NBC-TV Colour Spectacular in Jan. 1969.

ELVIS PRESLEY

'I like to "send" my fans. Even if they rip my clothes and skin – and that happens in nine places out of ten I hit – it really makes you feel good.' Reluctant though they might be to share the sensation, there are multitudes who appreciate the sentiment voiced by pop music's most adulated idol. The former truck-driver whose discs were at number one for 25 weeks in 1956 and 24 weeks in 1957 granted the fans who kept him there his wholehearted approbation: 'I don't know what I represent to them but I gets lonesome without their hollerin', he breathed. No less eloquent was the 'Minstrel of Moan' when he noticed a group of fans collecting dust off his car in envelopes. Those privileged to be within earshot caught the words: 'Crazy, man. Everything sure is c-r-a-z-y!' Mild disapproval was reserved for those responsible for his soubriquet: 'I don't like them to call me "Elvis the Pelvis". It is the most childish expression I have ever heard from an adult.' He has recognized, too, that notoriety has its hazards, as when he had this accidental brush with an old friend: 'I sat down with one girl I'd known a long time back home in Memphis, and sort of rested my head on her shoulder. . . . She sued me when the picture was printed.' Colonel Parker, his manager, settled out of court for $5,000 (£1,785).

The sacroiliac gyrations, as much in the act as the guitar and soulful vocalizing, are not what people have claimed them to be: 'People claim I do bumps and grinds. Why, I never did a bump or grind in my life. I've been to the burlesque show. I know what bumps and grinds are. I couldn't live with myself if I did.' Questioned about the

FILMS

Love Me Tender (1956)	Kissin' Cousins (1964)
Loving You (1957)	Girl Happy (1965)
King Creole (1958)	Tickle Me (1965)
Jailhouse Rock (1958)	Harum Scarum (1965)
Flaming Star (1960)	Frankie and Johnny (1965)
G.I. Blues (1960)	Paradise Hawaiian Style (1966)
Wild in the Country (1961)	Spinout (Californian Holiday) (1966)
Blue Hawaii (1961)	Easy Come, Easy Go (1967)
Girls! Girls! Girls! (1962)	Double Trouble (1967)
Follow that Dream (1962)	Clambake (1968)
Kid Galahad (1962)	Speedway (1968)
Fun in Acapulco (1963)	Stay Away, Joe (1968)
It Happened at the World's Fair (1964)	That Jack Valentine (1969)
Roustabout (1964)	Live a Little, Love a Little (1969)
	Charro (1969)
	The Trouble With Girls and How to Get Into It (1969)
	Change of Habit (filming 1969)

Elvis in an unaccustomed role as manager of a travelling chautauqua company, bringing entertainment to the Midwest in the Roaring 'Twenties. The film had the prolix title 'The Trouble With Girls and How To Get Into It' (MGM 1969).

LP Recordings (RCA Victor)

Elvis' Golden Records (RB16069)
Elvis – Rock 'n' Roll No. 2 (RD7528/SF7528)
Girls! Girls! Girls! (RD7534/SF7534)
It Happened at the World's Fair (RD7565)
Fun in Acapulco (RD7609/SF7609)
Elvis' Golden Records – Volume III
(RD7630/SF7630)
Kissin' Cousins (RD7645/SF7645)
Roustabout (RD7678/SF7678)
Girl Happy (RD7714/SF7714)
Flaming Star and Summer Kisses (RD7723)
Elvis for Everyone (RD7752/SF7752)
Harem Holiday (RD7767/SF7767)
Frankie and Johnny (RD7793/SF7793)
Paradise, Hawaiian Style (RD7810/SF7810)
Californian Holiday (RD7820/SF7820)
How Great Thou Art (RD7867/SF7867)

Double Trouble (RD7892/SF7892)
Clambake (RD7917/SF7917)
Elvis' Golden Records – Volume IV
(RD7924/SF7924)
Speedway (RD7957/SF7957)
Elvis' Christmas Album (RD27052)
King Creole (RD27088)
Elvis (RD27120)
A Date With Elvis (RD27128)
Elvis' Golden Records Volume II (RD27159)
Elvis is Back (RD27171/SF5060)
G.I. Blues (RD27192/SF5078)
His Hand in Mine (RD27211/SF5094)
Something for Everybody (RD27224/SF5106)
Blue Hawaii (RD27238/SF5115)
Pot Luck (RD27265/SF5135)
Flaming Star (INTS 1012)

sex element in his act, he explained: 'I don't see anything wrong with it. I just act the way I feel. . . . Without my left leg I'd be dead.'

Elvis was one of identical twins; his brother died aged two months. 'They say', Elvis pointed out, 'that when one twin dies, the other grows up with all the quality of the other. . . . If I did, then I'm lucky.' His luck and his talent brought him an income from record royalties and films reported in 1966 to be $6,000,000 (£2,140,000) a year. But he has insisted: 'I don't regard money or position as important. But I can never forget the longing to be someone. I guess if you are poor, you always think bigger and want more than those who have everything when they are born.'

The first of Presley's million-selling discs, *Heartbreak Hotel* backed with *I Was the One*, was released in 1956. In that year he achieved the sales in one year of 10,000,000 discs and earned over $1,000,000 (£357,000). His biggest seller was *It's Now or Never* which circulated over 9,000,000 discs. Total sales of his discs have been estimated at about 200,000,000. Apart from Presley's profits from all this, business on the side was brisk. Among the

assorted brands of merchandise offered by agents trading on the Presley cult is a tasty item called Hounds-Dog-Orange lipstick. These bring him in another $3,000,000 (£1,250,000) a year.

The year 1956 was also the take-off point for Presley's worldwide presentation as a motion picture star in *Love Me Tender*. Like several other films he starred in, it carried the title of a million-selling disc. The film *G.I. Blues* was released to coincide with his service in West Germany with the US army which, contrary to the gloomy forecasts of the prophets, did nothing to diminish his popularity. The fans now collected dust from his combat boots. It was during his period in uniform that he met his future wife, Priscilla. He also cost the United States Treasury $500,000 (£178,500) in lost tax.

Bing Crosby was quoted in 1957 as saying: 'Presley has a good beat and he sings in time, but he needs more training and diversified material. . . . He's a good-looking kid.' Cecil B. de Mille commended him warmly: 'I have always found him to be off stage an attractive, modest, unassuming, pleasant young man.' What they might have said had they known that Elvis was going to be as big as ever in 1969 cannot be conjectured. Making four motion pictures a year at $1,000,000 (£416,666) apiece, he runs a Rolls-Royce, a gold-plated Cadillac, owns a colonial-style mansion near Nashville, Tennessee, and has a dozen muscular bodyguards.

BRIGITTE BARDOT

Full name
Brigitte Bardot.

Born
Fri. 28 Sept. 1934, Paris, France.

Characteristics
About 5′ 6″; about 121*lb.* (8*st.* 9*lb.*); bust 35½″; waist 18″; hips 36″; hair originally brunette but usually dyed blonde; brown eyes.

Married
(1) 1952 Roger Vadim (div.).
(2) 1959 Jacques Charrier (div.) 1*s.*
(3) 1966 Gunther Sachs von Opel. (Miss Bardot was quoted in Dec. 1968 as saying that her marriage was 'over'.)

'I try to do my best, to be always prepared, but I am not an actress. Lady Macbeth does not interest me. I am just Brigitte Bardot. In the movies or out, I do not think I will ever be anything else.' The product of France most apt to cause stiff upper lips to relax the world over could have offered no more comforting reassurance to her fans, convinced as they may be that being Bardot is a loftier vocation than being an actress. But, however that may be, there is still the compelling evidence of Georges Simenon, author of the Maigret novels, who has said: 'The wealth of Brigitte Bardot resides solely in her talents as an actress.' Stephen Boyd, who enjoyed closer proximity to her in *Shalako*, commented: 'There's a great deal of the child-woman in her, but she is also a very exotic woman.'

Brigitte first showed her legs in ballet school but turned to drama and won an excellency award from the Paris *Conservatoire* at 13, demonstrating early promise of becoming something more than just a sex

57

Brigitte Bardot au naturelle.

to be courageous and stubborn. He kept telling me that I would be the impossible dream of married men.' The publicity campaign which followed her marriage to Vadim led to big parts in 10 films including *And God Created Woman* which grossed $8,500,000 (£3,036,000) throughout the world.

In 1959 Bardot became the highest-paid star in French entertainment. Bardolatrie in Paris reached such heights that in one month a major store sold 8,000 Bardot kerchiefs and 3,500 gingham dresses similar to the one she wore at her wedding to Jacques Charrier. Called on to endorse the 'Lovable' bra she waxed lyrical: 'A bra is like lipstick. No woman who values her looks should be seen without either.' The year 1959 also heralded a turning point in the Bardot approach to her public image: 'I am going to be a girl without anything unhealthy or equivocal about her, and I am going to be good if it kills me. I want to be cute and tender and warm, in the hope that people will forget the idea that I am a brainless, bosomy girl.'

The beauty preparations of the Gallic world's leading beauty normally take only five minutes and no more than half an hour even when she is working. 'The eyes are the most important', she has said, and she uses a greasy black pencil to outline them. She brushes her teeth three times a day; her hair, which receives 100 strokes of a brush daily, undergoes a dry shampoo once a week and a normal shampoo once every 15 days.

On her marriage to Gunther Sachs in 1966 the spirit moved Brigitte to rapture: 'I have never known a man like him. I feel mad, serene, wonderstruck. I have arrived at the end of a long journey.' Sachs, too, was in elevated mood: 'Since knowing Brigitte', he enthused, 'I have the feeling I can succeed at anything.' Two months later she went on record with: 'Love is the greatest illusion. At the instant that you

symbol. 'When I was 15 I was seeking something', she has recalled. 'Not just excitement – I don't know what it was. Perhaps a fulfilment of myself.' She had only to wait three years until fulfilment arrived in the person of Roger Vadim, her first spouse and the architect of her film career. 'I owe everything to Vadim', she admitted. 'He alone knew how to guide me, sustain me, console me, and teach me

seem to share the world with someone else you are in fact completely alone. . . . It is one of the supreme experiences yet it has nothing to do with marriage or children or washing the dishes.'

After more than a decade at the top, Bardot found fresh impetus in 1967 from the assurance that even President de Gaulle was a fan. 'What you do is very good', he told her, 'there's always something memorable in it. . . . I like *Viva Maria* very much.' The film depicted an attack by Latin American rebels on an imaginary outpost of the British Empire.

Never prominent as a vocalist, Brigitte made an impression on the cognoscenti with her New Year TV cabaret spot in 1968. Alluding, perhaps, to the effects of too much Christmas fare, she rendered the number *I Feel Strange Desires Creeping Up the Back of My Kidneys*.

'For a man to please me I have to feel attracted by him, and he has to be simple in every circumstance.'

'Sex is the first attraction. After that if I still feel affection I know it is love. Only then do I make the distinction.'

'Nobody has any security in loving me. . . . Sometimes eight days is too long to be faithful.'

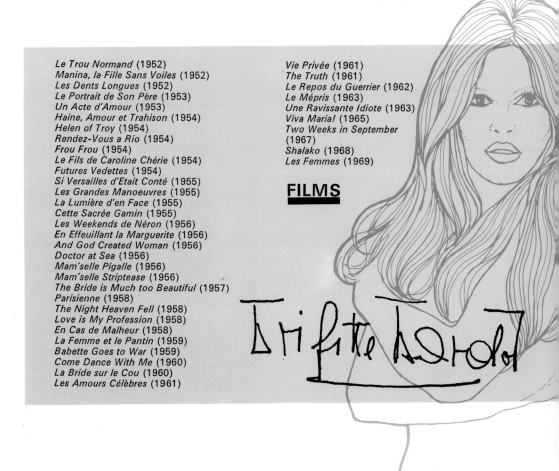

Le Trou Normand (1952)
Manina, la Fille Sans Voiles (1952)
Les Dents Longues (1952)
Le Portrait de Son Père (1953)
Un Acte d'Amour (1953)
Haine, Amour et Trahison (1954)
Helen of Troy (1954)
Rendez-Vous a Rio (1954)
Frou Frou (1954)
Le Fils de Caroline Chérie (1954)
Futures Vedettes (1954)
Si Versailles d'Etait Conté (1955)
Les Grandes Manoeuvres (1955)
La Lumière d'en Face (1955)
Cette Sacrée Gamin (1955)
Les Weekends de Néron (1956)
En Effeuillant la Marguerite (1956)
And God Created Woman (1956)
Doctor at Sea (1956)
Mam'selle Pigalle (1956)
Mam'selle Striptease (1956)
The Bride is Much too Beautiful (1957)
Parisienne (1958)
The Night Heaven Fell (1958)
Love is My Profession (1958)
En Cas de Malheur (1958)
La Femme et le Pantin (1959)
Babette Goes to War (1959)
Come Dance With Me (1960)
La Bride sur le Cou (1960)
Les Amours Célèbres (1961)

Vie Privée (1961)
The Truth (1961)
Le Repos du Guerrier (1962)
Le Mépris (1963)
Une Ravissante Idiote (1963)
Viva Maria! (1965)
Two Weeks in September (1967)
Shalako (1968)
Les Femmes (1969)

FILMS

ELIZABETH TAYLOR

Full name	Elizabeth Rosemund Taylor.
Born	Wed. 17 Feb. 1932, Hampstead, London, NW, England.

Characteristics

about 5′ 4½″; about 108*lb.* (7*st.* 10*lb.*) in 1952; about 130*lb.* (9*st.* 4*lb.*) in 1967 when she was quoted as saying: 'A woman can be big and still be sexy.' Six inches of her spine are fused following operations for slipped disc; a tracheotomy scar can be seen on her neck. In 1967 her waist, measurement unspecified, was reported to be insured for £650,000 (now $1,560,000). She has very dark brown hair, violet eyes, curly double eyelashes, and over 100 wigs and hairpieces.

Married	1	1950 Conrad Hilton Jr (div. 1951) (died 1969).
	2	1952 Michael Wilding (div. 1957) 2*s.*
	3	1957 Mike Todd (killed in an air crash 1958) 1*d.*
	4	1959 Eddie Fisher (div. 1964).
	5	1964 Richard Burton. ('I can't have any more of my own. I'd like to have lots of them by Richard, and it is very sad.') 1 adopted *d.*

Elizabeth Taylor as she appeared in 'Who's Afraid of Virginia Woolf?' (Warner Brothers, 1965). Her performance won her an 'Oscar' as best screen actress of 1966.

The film actress described by Richard Burton as 'a legend in her own lifetime' was aged twelve when she started building the legend with her first starring role in *National Velvet*, and nineteen when she earned the unanimous praise of the critics for her part in *A Place in the Sun*. Since then she had enjoyed, without pause, 'a place in the sun' matched by few celebrities in the history of cinema, including the distinction of having the greatest earnings from one film of any star, with at least $3,000,000 (£1,071,000) from *Cleopatra*.

In 1959 George Sanders wrote with scant regard for the facts: 'Elizabeth Taylor shares her ravishing beauty like a true patron of the poor with those who have none.' He might with greater accuracy have alluded to her marital career as providing a series of take-off points for much of the publicity surrounding her name. Richard Burton sorted out the men from the boys in his wife's nuptial 'Who Was Who' when he opined that 'apart from Mike Todd and myself, of course, she hasn't had any real men in her life'. Of those who failed to qualify as 'real men', Conrad Hilton Jr faded out after eight months, Michael Wilding gave her two sons and 'the darkest sapphire to match your eyes', and Eddie Fisher, who first developed a crush when he saw her in *National Velvet*, was heart-broken. 'I know I am not the great love in

Liz Taylor was at the centre of her own galaxy at the Palazzo Rezzonico, Venice, in 1967. Guests paid £80 ($192) a head to attend a charity masked ball. Flood victims benefited by £33,000 ($79,200).

LIZ TAYLOR

Elizabeth's life, but she is the great love in mine', he confessed.

The ebullient Todd ran up a monthly telephone bill of $2,000 (£700) courting her with the genial approbation of Wilding. Liz digs me deep', declared Todd. 'It's, chemistry . . . she's the realest dame that ever was.' She was, soon, one of the most bejewelled as he loaded with, among other baubels, a £33,000 ($92,400) diamond ring, a £32,000 ($89,600) diamond bracelet, and an £11,000 ($30,800) pearl ring. Liz said of him: 'It's nice to be married to someone who thinks I have a brain.'

The depredations to her health which accompanied these marriages and the bereavement of Mike Todd's tragic death in an air-crash compiled a catalogue of misfortune that only a star of rare courage could have endured. Surviving slipped disc, tachycarditis, pneumonia, meningism, and twenty-three operations, she emerged to scale fresh heights of film fame. Her box-office drawing power burgeoned hugely, reaching a pinnacle in *Cleopatra*, the setting for her affair with Richard Burton.

At first Burton's reaction to the proximity of the screen's leading beauty was disappointing: 'Elizabeth isn't particularly attractive', he complained. 'She has the shape of a Welsh village girl. Her legs are really quite stumpy. Her chest isn't anything extraordinary.' Hounded by the Press, he went further: 'I love Liz but marriage is out. Liz and I aren't made for marriage.' Marriage, notwithstanding, came about, and the teasing sometimes continued. While filming *The Taming of the Shrew*, in which Liz was required to gain weight for the part of Kate, Burton (Petruchio) ridiculed her fat stomach. Replied she: 'In Egypt they *adore* it. The trouble is all my films are banned in Egypt, so they never get to see it.'[1] Also appearing in bit parts in *The Taming of the Shrew* were Elizabeth's sons by Michael Wilding, Michael (born 6 Jan. 1953) and Christopher (born 27 Feb. 1955).

Marriage to Burton had inspired an unexceptionable avowal from Liz: 'My best feature is my grey hairs; I have them all named; they're all called Burton.' He had begun to speak of her in terms of appreciation: 'Elizabeth has taught me most of what I know about acting for the screen. Above all, she's taught me to take it seriously instead of just doing it for the money.' While filming *The Comedians*, Burton referred to the torrid love scenes he enacted with Liz: 'I couldn't have done them with any other actress. It never mattered to me before, but now it does. I just don't enjoy kissing other ladies any more.' He confirmed, too, that she is totally unlike her screen image: 'It's really a strange irony of life that Elizabeth is always cast as the "scarlet woman". Actually, she is one of those rare actresses whose family comes first. I don't know any movie star who is more devoted to her children than Elizabeth.'

Despite this evident domesticity, Liz

---

[1] The ban was imposed because Miss Taylor once purchased a large number of Israeli government bonds.

managed to stay at the summit of screen attainment, winning a second 'Oscar' for her performance opposite Richard in *Who's Afraid of Virginia Woolf?* She values this more than the 'Oscar' awarded for *Butterfield 8* which she admitted was partly a gesture prompted by her nearly fatal illness.

Of course, money is no longer an urgent incentive for Elizabeth Taylor Burton. Though she allows herself routine extravagances like hairdo's at Alexandre of Paris at $350 (£146) a time, and has sufficient collateral – 'I shampoo my diamonds once a week' – to make this possible for life, her career is now, she has said, subordinate to his: 'Richard's career is really more important than mine. He will, being a man, act longer than I do. I am not really a very ambitious person, you know. I've been in too many bad films to keep any burning drive alive.'

Despite this, she continues to make good films and to profit from them. The Burtons have two homes in Mexico, one in Ireland, extensive acres in the Canary Islands, and other homes in Switzerland and in Sardinia where their 279-ton $250,000 (£106,000) fourteen-berth yacht *Kalizma* is often moored. They spent as much again refitting the vessel which is equipped with waterproof carpets on account of their four dogs. In 1967 Burton gave Liz a twin-jet Hawker Siddeley executive aircraft – down payment $1,000,000 (now £416,666) – which they call *The Elizabeth.* For her thirty-fifth birthday he gave her an emerald and diamond necklace valued at between £150,000 ($360,000) and £200,000 ($480,000) with a pendant worth a further £60,000 ($144,000). In 1968 he bought her the 33.19-carat Krupp diamond for $305,000 (£127,083), a record price for a diamond ring. She reciprocated by presenting him with a $500,000 (£208,333) helicopter. Their other investments include a share in Harlech TV (Wales) and a fashion boutique in Paris.

Elizabeth Taylor met Richard Burton when filming 'Cleopatra' (20th Century-Fox, 1963). He came to regard her as 'the greatest living actress'.

Films

Lassie Come Home (1943)
Jane Eyre (1944)
The White Cliffs of Dover (1944)
National Velvet (1945)
The Rich Full Life (1947)
Life with Father (1947)
Courage of Lassie (1946)
A Date with Judy (1948)
Julia Misbehaves (1948)
Little Women (1949)
Conspirator (1949)
The Big Hangover (1950)
Father of the Bride (1950)
Father's Little Dividend (1951)
A Place in the Sun (1951)

The Light Fantastic (1952)
Ivanhoe (1953)
The Girl Who Had Everything (1953)
Rhapsody (1954)
Elephant Walk (1954)
Beau Brummell (1954)
The Last Time I Saw Paris (1955)
Giant (1956)
Raintree County (1958)
Cat on a Hot Tin Roof (1958)
Suddenly Last Summer (1960)
Butterfield 8 (1961)
Cleopatra (1963)
The VIPs (1963)
The Sandpiper (1965)

Who's Afraid of Virginia Woolf? (1966)
The Taming of the Shrew (1967)
Reflections in a Golden Eye (1967)
The Comedians (1967)
Dr Faustus (1967)
Boom! (1969)
Secret Ceremony (1969)
The Only Game in Town (1969)

Stage Appearance
Dr Faustus (1966)

LP Recording
The Taming of the Shrew (soundtrack)
(RCA Victor RB6711)

SEAN CONNERY

Full name Thomas Connery
(Sean Connery first used in 1953).

Born Mon. 25 Aug. 1930, 166 Fountain-bridge, Edinburgh, Scotland.

Characteristics 6′ 2″; about 196*lb.* (14*st.*); tailor's measurements: chest 46″, waist 33″, hips 42″; brown hair and eyes, wears a hair-piece; scar on right cheek with 30 stitches.

Married 1962 Diane Cilento 1*s.* (Miss Cilento has 1*d.* by previous marriage).

In 1899 the learned Austrian psychologist, Professor Doctor Sigmund Freud, pro-pounded that 'dreams often reveal them-selves without any disguise as the fulfil-ments of wishes.' Had Freud lived to observe the cult of 007 he might scarcely have raised an eyebrow to note the onset of a trend corresponding so closely to his theory. For the bourgeois, the untravelled, and the domesticated, the fantasy of jetting as James Bond to win the favours of the fair and vanquish the ungodly would clearly bring fulfilment. Yet to Sean Connery, the man who escalated from milkman to millionaire via the image of 007, such fantasies are plain bunk: 'I don't suppose I'd like Bond if I met him', he has remarked. 'He's not my kind of chap at all.' He has explained the Bond mania in this way: 'Fleming invented him after the

Sean Connery's fifth and last James Bond film was 'You Only Live Twice' (United Artists, 1967). One of his 'lives' was with Akiko Wakabayashi who survived this episode only to die of poison.

65

'For me, playing James Bond is like playing Macbeth in the theatre ... if I hadn't acted Shakespeare, Pirandello, Euripides ... I should never have managed to play James Bond.'

war when people were hungry for luxury. . . . And a character jumping in and out of bed all the time – you can see how that would catch on in a drab place like England.' Nor does he see Bond as a scion of sophistication: '. . . remove the exotic touches and what have you got? A dull, prosaic English policeman.'

Thomas Connery's early life was acutely deficient in exotic touches. He delivered newspapers, became a part-time milkman at 15s. ($3) a week in 1943, heaved sacks of coal when he grew bigger, and even tried his hand at polishing coffins. Then his interest in body-building opened up fresh horizons as a lifeguard at the local swimming-bath and as bouncer at a dance-hall. The well-stacked physique won a bronze medal in his class in a body-building contest at the Scala Theatre in London only a few steps from the West End cinemas where his name would one day appear in lights.

Connery's enthusiasm for fitness and sports could have taken him on quite a different course had he not opted for the stage. A part as an extra in *Glorious Days* in Edinburgh at 22 gave him his first taste of the footlights and he liked that better than golf or football, either of which might have given him a professional outlet. While working at Manchester he met Matt Busby, manager of Manchester United, who recalled: 'He did some training with us at the time and, in fact, had some football ability.' Rumours that Busby made him an offer are not true so the question of whether Connery could have served better in a forward line than in a chorus line is purely hypothetical. He got the part of Lieutenant Buzz Adams in the London musical, *South Pacific* (1953), and in this show he used the name Sean Connery for the first time. It was the year in which Ian Fleming wrote his first Bond novel, *Casino Royale*.

Skilful work with camera and lighting

allied to diligent use of scissors in the cutting-room transformed the film Bond into a two-fisted tornado, equally devastating when cramped in a railway sleeping-berth as when poised on a roof-top. What made it slightly more credible was that Connery actually had some ring experience while serving in the Merchant Navy. His shoulders not only filled out a well-tailored suit, they packed a useful punch and this was in evidence in Connery's first TV appearance in *Requiem for a Heavyweight* (1957). Among those watching who discerned something more than a good repertory actor was Terence Young, later director of several Bond films.

Connery now broke into motion pictures decisively and had several workmanlike parts under his belt before production of the Bond films was planned. Ian Fleming, author of the Bond novels, thought a relatively unknown actor should fill the role and producers Harry Saltzman and Albert 'Cubby' Broccoli came round to his view. Among the candidates considered were Trevor Howard, Richard Burton, James Mason, and Peter Finch. Connery was invited to do a screen test and declined. They took him anyway.

In more ways than one Connery was made to measure for 007. His build and looks corresponded to the Fleming plan, his age was right, and when in 1963 he won £10,700 ($29,960) at roulette in one night, even those who had not seen him in *Dr No* recognized aptitude for the part. Even Connery's golf handicap (14 in 1966) was within striking distance of Bond's (handicap 9).

Except in the case of *Casino Royale* in which Sean Connery did not star, the Bond films all followed the original Fleming story recognizably. Connery himself helped Terence Young to insert one or two humorous touches where they felt Fleming's text needed a lift. One of them, perhaps, was the casual aside: 'I think he got the point', dropped by Bond as he impaled the villain with his harpoon-gun in *Thunderball*.

Among the ladies who have known him well, Honor Blackman (Pussygalore in *Goldfinger*) said: 'I think Sean is a dish.' Shirley Eaton, who 'died' in a coat of gold paint in *Goldfinger*, said: 'I've had a lot of partners but I've never had a colleague as easy and generous as Sean Connery.' And Sean's grandmother was quoted as saying that he had not changed much 'since the time I used to push him in a pram'.

Departing from the Bond scene after his fifth 007 film, Connery announced in 1969 plans to go into politics as a member of the Scottish Nationalist Party, and embarked on his first Shakespeare film, *Macbeth*.

Asked what was his secret: 'Enjoying at least 60 per cent of your work. If you don't enjoy acting that much, life is monotonous and routine.'

Getting away from the James Bond type-casting, Connery squired Brigitte Bardot in 'Shalako' (Anglo-Amalgamated, 1968).

THE BOND FILMS with Sean Connery

Dr. No (1963)

From Russia With Love (1964)

Goldfinger (1965)

Thunderball (1966)

You Only Live Twice (1967)

TELEVISION

Requiem for a Heavyweight (1957)

Anna Karenina (1961)

Macneil (1969)

Male of the Species (1969)

CONNERY ON RECORD

Prokofiev: *Peter and the Wolf*

(Decca PFS 4104/LK 4801)

OTHER FILMS

No Road Back (1955)

Action of the Tiger (1956)

Timelock (1956)

Hell Drivers (1957)

Another Time, Another Place (1958)

Tarzan's Greatest Adventure (1959)

Darby O'Gill and the Little People (1959)

The Frightened City (1960)

On the Fiddle (1961)

Marnie (1964)

Woman of Straw (1964)

Operation Snafu (1964)

The Hill (1965)

A Fine Madness (1966)

Shalako (1968)

The Molly Maquires (1968)

The Longest Day (1969)

The Red Tent (1969)

Macbeth (1969)

ORIGINAL SOUNDTRACKS

Dr No (United Artists ULP1097/SULP1097/UEP1010)

From Russia With Love
(United Artists ULP1052/SULP1052/UEP1011)

Goldfinger (United Artists ULP1076/UEP1012)

Thunderball (United Artists ULP1110/SULP1110)

You Only Live Twice
(United Artists ULP1171/SULP1171)

Sean Connery's successor as James Bond was George Lazenby, seen here in the line of duty with nine girls in the sixth Bond film, 'On Her Majesty's Secret Service' (United Artists, 1969). Lazenby (born 5 Sept. 1939 at Goulburn, Australia) is 6 feet 2 inches tall and has yellow-brown eyes. He first made his name as an international male model, notably in the 'Big Fry' TV commercial.

ARNOLD PALMER

Full name	Arnold Daniel Palmer.

Born	Tues. 10 Sept. 1929, Latrobe, Pennsylvania, USA.

Characteristics
about 5′ 10½″; about 190*lb.* (13*st.* 8*lb.*); dark brown hair; brown eyes.

Married	1954 Winnie Walzer 2*d.*

Just how big a business the sport of professional golf has become was apparent when Arnold Palmer wrote a cheque for $800,000 (£285,714) and took delivery of a new six-seater jet runabout. 'In the long run buying a Commander jet is cheaper than renting one', he explained in 1966. 'I reckon I do maybe 40,000 miles of travelling from one tournament to another around the country, and jet travel is the quickest and the most comfortable way to

69

get around.' Palmer moved around the pro circuit triumphantly, building a reputation second perhaps to none in the history of the game. The fans who followed his progress came to be known as 'Arnie's Army' as they rooted for him in thousands at every tee and green. Among other triumphs they watched him win the American Masters' four times, more often than any other golfer in history.

Arnie is the son of a golf pro and though he started to practise his swing at the age of five his first real incentive was presented in 1954 when he met his future wife. Needing cash he played for a bet: Palmer to lose $100 for every stroke he scored over 80 or win $100 for every stroke under 72. He shot 68 and was rich enough to buy an engagement ring. Already US Amateur Champion, he turned pro and eloped with his fiancée to get married. He only had one set of golf clubs and a secondhand trailer to live in but Palmer had a motto. His wife's name is Winnie which he shortened to 'Win'. That is what Palmer the golf pro proceeded to do.

One of the leading exponents of the power game, Palmer has recommended the beginner to try for distance from the outset: 'Too many players learn a controlled swing first, then try to increase their distance and they can't. As a result, a lot of players don't hit the ball hard enough and never will.' He has emphasized, however, that power divorced from control makes for wild inaccuracy: 'The head of the club travels at a speed of from 85 to 110 mph as it comes through the ball. The speed of the ball as it leaves the tee is between 140 and 180 mph. . . . With such velocities . . . it is no wonder that a ball can fly so far out of whack if the swing isn't right.' He prefers the 1.62-inch British ball to the 1.68-inch American ball: 'Distancewise the small ball comes out on top every time. It can be hit farther through the air and I find it will roll farther, even on a wet course.'

Arnold's putting is probably his major golf asset. Jack Nicklaus said: 'Arnie wins because he is the best; he expects to make every putt and sees no reason why he should not win every tournament he plays in.' Bobby Jones also praised this department of his game: 'If I had a hard putt to make I'd rather have Arnold working on it than any other golfer I've seen.' More recently Gary Player hailed him as 'the best putter I have ever seen in my life'. Palmer used to play an indoor putting game which he thinks helped to promote his efficiency on the green: 'When Dow Finsterwald and I travelled together', he recalled, 'we would set up a dime on the floor and see if we could get the ball to sit on top of it.' One good shot in a hundred, he reckoned, was pretty good, 'but if you can stop that ball within inches of that dime, then you've got the kind of putting that will win matches.'

An ambassador of golf in many parts of the world, Palmer's message has been transmitted to golf addicts everywhere through his taped TV shows *Challenge Golf* and *Big Three Golf* and he has appeared on the small screen repeatedly as a celebrity. On Bob Hope's show in 1963 he even succeeded in scoring a laugh off the

Arnold Palmer was once described by Gary Player as 'the best putter I have ever seen in my life'.   71

master funnyman. One gag went like this. Hope: 'What do you think of my swing?' Palmer: 'I've seen better swings in a condemned playground.'

The punch in Palmer's golf is to a large extent a built-in commodity: his hands can crumple a beer-can like tissue-paper. And he has grasped the importance of good physical maintenance. 'A man's body is like a tractor', he has said, utilizing the language of the countryside where he grew up. 'Keep it in shape and it will be service-able for years.'

Arnie's extraordinary consistency has proved his point about fitness. Only superlative physical condition could have enabled him to sustain the high-quality skills necessary to stay at the top on the gruelling pro circuit for over thirteen years. Apart from over sixty wins in official events he has placed second about forty times. In addition he played up to twenty exhibitions a year. His endurance has earned him the unofficial title of one of the best finishers in the game. The average of his last-round scores in tournaments from 1955 to 1966 was a staggering 69.88. His best eighteen-hole round is 62 which he scored on three separate occasions. His first professional tour victory, the Cana-dian Open in 1955, produced his finest seventy-two-hole score of 265 (64, 67, 64, 70). In the period 1955 to 1966 he scored in the 60s in 425 rounds.

In 1963 Palmer became the first golfer to top $100,000 in a year with official tour earnings of $128,230 (£45,800). His total official earnings reached $1,000,000 (now £416,666) on 17 Sept. 1968 making him golf's first official millionaire. In addition his business enterprizes have prospered and diversified, being controlled by about fourteen companies concerned with golf clothing and equipment, real estate, music, dry-cleaning, after-shave lotion, deodor-ants, soft drinks, candy, and power tools. With all this going for him, his annual total individual income has been over the million-dollar mark since 1961.

MAJOR GOLF TITLES

Year	Championship	Score	Prize £	$
1958	American Masters', Augusta, Georgia	284	4,018	11,250
1960	American Masters', Augusta, Georgia	282	6,250	17,500
1960	American Open, Denver, Colorado	280	5,143	14,400
1961	The Open, Royal Birkdale, Southport, England	284	1,400	3,920
1962	American Masters', Augusta, Georgia	280	7,142	20,000
1962	The Open, Troon, Scotland	276	1,500	3,200
1964	American Masters', Augusta, Georgia	276	7,142	20,000

OTHER CHAMPIONSHIP AND TOURNAMENT WINS

Year	Tournament	Score	Prize £	Prize $
1955	Canadian Open, Toronto	265	857	2,400
1956	Panama Open	283	714	2,000
1956	Colombia Open	280	643	1,800
1956	Insurance City Open, Wethersfield, Connecticut	274	1,428	4,000
1956	Eastern Open, Baltimore, Maryland	277	1,357	3,800
1957	Houston, Texas Open	279	2,680	7,500
1957	Azalea Open, Wilmington, North Carolina	282	607	1,700
1957	Rubber City Open, Akron, Ohio	272	1,000	2,800
1957	San Diego, California Open	271	1,000	2,800
1958	St Petersburg, Florida Open	276	714	2,000
1958	Pepsi Open, East Norwich, Long Island	273	3,214	9,000
1959	Thunderbird Invitational, Palm Springs, California	266	536	1,500
1959	Oklahoma City Open	273	1,250	3,500
1959	West Palm Beach, Florida Open	281	714	2,000
1960	Palm Springs Desert Classic, California (90 holes)	338	4,286	12,000
1960	Texas Open, San Antonio	276	1,000	2,800
1960	Baton Rouge, Louisiana Open	279	714	2,000
1960	Pensacola, Florida Open	273	714	2,000
1960	Insurance City Open, Wethersfield, Connecticut	270	1,250	3,500
1960	Mobile, Alabama Open	274	714	2,000
1961	San Diego, California Open	271	1,000	2,800
1961	Phoenix, Arizona Open	270	1,535	4,300
1961	Baton Rouge, Louisiana Open	266	1,000	2,800
1961	Texas Open, San Antonio	270	1,535	4,300
1961	Western Open, Grand Rapids, Michigan	271	1,786	5,000
1962	Palm Springs Golf Classic, California (90 holes)	342	1,893	5,300
1962	Phoenix, Arizona Open	269	1,893	5,300
1962	Texas Open, San Antonio	273	1,535	4,300
1962	Tournament of Champions, Las Vegas, Nevada	276	3,928	11,000
1962	Colonial National Invitation, Fort Worth, Texas	281	2,500	7,000
1962	American Golf Classic, Akron, Ohio	276	3,214	9,000
1963	Los Angeles Open	274	3,214	9,000
1963	Phoenix, Arizona Open	273	1,893	5,300
1963	Pensacola, Florida Open	273	1,250	3,500
1963	Thunderbird Classic, Harrison, New York	277	8,928	25,000
1963	Cleveland, Ohio Open	273	7,857	22,000
1963	Western Open, Chicago, Illinois	280	3,928	11,000
1963	Whitemarsh, Pennsylvania Open	281	9,285	26,000
1963	Wills Masters', Sydney, Australia	285	800	2,240
1964	Oklahoma City Open	277	2,070	5,800
1964	Piccadilly World Match Play, Wentworth, Surrey, England	2 & 1	5,000	14,000
1965	Tournament of Champions, Las Vegas, Nevada	277	5,000	14,000
1966	Los Angeles Open	273	3,928	11,000
1966	Tournament of Champions, Las Vegas, Nevada	283	7,142	20,000
1966	Australia Open, Brisbane	276	640	1,790
1966	Houston Champions International, Texas	275	7,500	21,002
1967	Los Angeles Open	269	7,142	20,000
1967	Tucson, Arizona Open	273	4,286	12,000
1967	American Golf Classic, Akron, Ohio	276	7,142	20,000
1967	Thunderbird Classic, Clifton, New Jersey	283	10,714	30,000
1967	Piccadilly World Match Play, Wentworth, Surrey, England	by 1 hole	5,000	14,000
1967	World Cup individual winner, Mexico City	276	1,000	2,800
1968	Bob Hope Desert Classic, Palm Springs, California (90 holes)	348	8,333	20,000
1968	Kemper Open, Sutton, Massachusetts	276	12,500	30,000

TEAM CHAMPIONSHIPS

Year	Trophy
1960	Canada Cup, Portmarnock, Ireland
1961	Ryder Cup, Lytham St Anne's, England
1962	Canada Cup[1], Buenos Aires, Argentina
1963	Ryder Cup, Atlanta, Georgia
1963	Canada Cup, St Nom-La-Breteche, France
1964	Canada Cup[2], Maui, Hawaii
1965	Ryder Cup, Royal Birkdale, England
1966	PGA National[2], Palm Beach Gardens, Florida
1966	Canada Cup[2], Tokio, Japan
1967	World Cup[2] (formerly Canada Cup), Mexico City

VARDON TROPHY

Year	Average
1961	69,859
1962	70.271
1964	70,010
1967	70.188

TOTAL GOLF EARNINGS

Year	£	$	Placed
1955	2,936	8,226	–
1956	7,158	20,044	19
1957	11,323	31,704	5
1958	16,288	45,608	1
1959	13,812	38,675	5
1960	28,917	80,968	1
1961	23,215	65,002	2
1962	29,448	82,456	1
1963	46,726	30,835	1
1964	41,460	116,089	2
1965	29,535	82,700	10
1966	55,167	154,468	3
1967	75,165	210,464	2
1968	47,750	114,602	7

[1] With Sam Snead   [2] With Jack Nicklaus

HSH PRINCESS GRACE OF MONACO

Full name Grace of Monaco (née Grace Patricia Kelly).

Born Tues. 12 Nov. 1929, Philadelphia, Pennsylvania, USA.
Characteristics About 5′ 7″; about 115*lb.* (8*st.* 3*lb.*) in 1955; blonde hair; blue eyes.

Married two ceremonies, 18 and 19 April 1956 to HSH Prince Rainier III of Monaco (Louis Henri Maxence Bertrand, *born* Thurs. 31 May 1923).

The Royal Children Prince Albert Alexandre Louis Pierre (*born* Fri. 14 March 1958); Princess Caroline Louise Marguerite (*born* Wed. 23 Jan. 1957); Princess Stephanie Marie Elizabeth (*born* Mon. 1 Feb. 1965).

At 8.00 every morning, Her Serene Highness Princess Grace butters the toast for the Royal Family breakfast taken in the company of her husband, Prince Rainier, and their three children. It is an ordinary occasion in the castle at Monaco, a fortress rebuilt by the Genoese in 1215.

HSH Princess Grace serenely formal with HSH Prince Rainier of Monaco.

Within its ancient walls breakfast is presided over by a lady whose career might be described as one of the more extraordinary real-life fairy stories of the 20th century.

One of the more surprized witnesses of his daughter's rise to Royalty by way of film fame was Princess Grace's father, John Kelly, the 1920 Olympic single and double sculls champion. 'I can't believe it,' he was quoted as saying. 'Of the four children, she's the last one I'd expected to support me in my old age.' Not that old age threatened him with undue exigency. He built his multi-million-dollar construction business from a $7,000 (£1,750) loan from his brother. Kelly Sr. later had the satisfaction of seeing his son, Jack Jr., win the Henley Diamond Sculls in 1947 and 1949, an event from which he had been barred because his then occupation as a 'working man' disqualified him under the amateur rules.

Grace's ambition to be a film actress probably began to take shape at the age of seven when Douglas Fairbanks Jr. visited her parents' home. 'He kissed me goodnight,' she recalled. 'I was never going to wash again.' Her stage debut took place in *The Father* on Broadway in 1949 with

Raymond Massey. In 1952 she scored an international hit with her part in the outstanding Western, *High Noon*, with Gary Cooper. Then in 1954, still a relative newcomer to films, she won an 'Oscar' for her role in *The Country Girl*. Bing Crosby, her co-star, expressed his respect for her: 'She has a good mind, a sense of humour, and is considerate of those around her. She worked her head off to get the performance the director wanted from her.'

Bing was not the only one to appreciate her talents as this anecdote proves. Getting into a cab once in New York, she was told by the driver: 'Lady, you look a *lot* like Grace Kelly.' Just before she got out, he added: 'Oh, one more thing. Actually, you're a lot prettier than Grace Kelly ever was.'

Her box-office appeal at this time was such that although she was under contract to MGM, she was borrowed by other studios for a reported fee of $50,000 (£17,860). In *Rear Window* she starred with James Stewart who found her 'easy to play to. You can see her thinking the way she's supposed to think in the role. You know she's listening and not just for the cues. Some actresses don't think and don't listen.' William Holden, her co-star in *Bridges of Toko-ri*, was likewise edified: 'With some actresses you have to keep snapping them to attention like a puppy. Grace is always concentrating. In fact she sometimes keeps *you* on the track.' In 1957 Grace broke new ground with the release of the million-selling disc *True Love*, one of the numbers composed by Cole Porter for the film *High Society*.

The film she enjoyed most – 'When I was a child I wanted to work for the FBI' – was perhaps *To Catch a Thief*. Her co-star, Cary Grant, commented after she retired from the screen to marry a year later: 'In show business the thing to do is to get out at the top as Grace Kelly did. She couldn't have done any more, so she quit. After all, what could she have become? Only an older actress, not a better one.' The publicity surrounding her marriage inevitably gave rise to speculation about a film comeback and in 1962 a provisional agreement was reached with Alfred Hitchcock to star in the film *Marnie* for a reported fee of $1,000,000 (£357,000) plus a share of the profits. The money was to go to some of the charities in which

FILMS
Fourteen Hours (1952)
High Noon (1952)
The Country Girl (1953)
Dial M for Murder (1954)
Rear Window (1954)
Bridges of Toko-ri (1955)
To Catch a Thief (1955)
The Swan (1956)
High Society (1957)
To Be Continued (1952)

STAGE APPEARANCES
The Father (1949)

TELEVISION
Over 50 plays on live TV (1949–53)

LP RECORDING
High Society (Capitol LCT6116/SLCT6116)

Grace Kelly with her partners in song, Bing Crosby and Frank Sinatra, in 'High Society' (MGM, 1956). Her recording with Bing Crosby of 'True Love' from this film was her first and only million-selling disc.

Princess Grace was and still is actively interested. But this plan did not follow through and Tippi Hendred starred opposite Sean Connery in *Marnie*.

Grace was introduced to her future husband, Prince Rainier, by Pierre Galante, editor of *Paris Match*. News of her impending marriage galvanized Monaco businessmen into taking out insurance policies as a safeguard against the contingency that she might fail to produce a male heir. In that event Monaco would, on the death of Prince Rainier, become part of France, making its citizens liable to far less attractive rates of tax. They breathed a loyal sigh of relief when Prince Albert Alexandre was born on 14 March 1958.

One of Princess Grace's funniest experiences occurred when she was expecting Princess Caroline. She was out shopping on a religious holiday when she was approached by an Italian woman who, in keeping with an ancient custom, rubbed Princess Grace's tummy and wished her good luck. Not many months later the Princess was able to report: 'The most exciting day of my life wasn't the day I got the "Oscar". It was the day when Caroline, for the first time, began to walk and she took seven small steps by herself, one after the other, before she reached me, throwing herself into my arms. She had a weight problem after the birth of a baby because the Princess breast-fed her babies for at least two months.

Princess Grace's daily round of official functions keeps her in close touch with many aspects of the life of the Principality. She has a special interest in the Red Cross, the Garden Club which she founded, and, of course, in the Princess Grace Hospital. But she still finds time for an occasional outing by herself. Prince Rainier has confirmed that 'the Princess carries her own money when she goes shopping'.

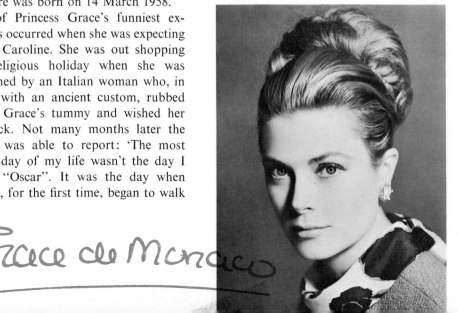

Gina Lollobrigida

Full name Luigina Lollobrigida.

Born Wed. 4 July 1928, Subiaco, Sabine Hills, about 40 miles from Rome, Italy.

Characteristics About 5′ 5″; about 120*lb.* (8*st.* 8*lb.*); bust 36″; waist 22″; hips 35″; black hair; dark brown eyes.

Married 1950 Drago Milko Skofic (div. 1968) 1*s.*

Skofic obtained an Austrian divorce. In 1969, when he married the Viennese soprano, Ute von Aichbichler, a legal dispute arose because under Italian law he was still married to Gina.

From time to time the name and public image of a celebrity become so engraved in the popular mind as to warrant incorporation into the language of the day. Mae West's figure furnished the pretext for an entry in *The Concise Oxford Dictionary*[1], ensuring for Miss West a more enduring currency as a proper noun than as a slightly improper screen symbol. A quarter of a century later, the anatomy of Gina Lollobrigida did a similar service for the French language, the word *Lollobrigidienne*, according to a recent French dictionary, being 'Used by artists to describe rolling landscape, or by surveyors, etc., for a hilly terrain.'

In court on charges of outraging the public morals in the film *The Dolls*, Italy's 'Queen of Contours' expressed a demure and reasoned defence:[2] 'The theatre has always been full of daring performers since Grecian times – even the great Greta Garbo, who undressed more than today's actresses without creating a scandal.' La Lollo might have claimed with truth that even fully clothed she shed a radiance many a film fan has happily paid to see. Producer Sir Carol Read said: 'Gina's face is like a bright light. When she appears on a darkened set, it is

Gina was 41, and still beautiful, when she appeared in 'Buona Sera, Mrs Campbell' (United Artists, 1969).

as if someone has switched on a powerful arc lamp.' Burt Lancaster, who starred with her in *Trapeze*, said: 'I consider her the most beautiful woman in the world.' Sam Rayburn (1882–1961), former Speaker of the US House of Representatives, told her: 'I've never crossed the ocean but since I've seen you I might.'

Harsh necessity forced the teenage Luigina into the life of an actress. As the Allied forces advanced through Italy in 1944, RAF bombers destroyed her father's home and furniture factory. 'We lost everything. We were penniless,' she recalled. 'I made up my mind to win fame and fortune so I could give my family a fresh start.'

Fortune favoured her as soon as her gifts were identified at Hollywood. The two 'Bread' films established Gina as an international star: *Bread, Love, and Dreams* for which she was paid $48,000 (£17,140), and *Bread, Love, and Jealousy* for which she asked, and received, double that sum. When producer Harold Hecht asked her what she hoped to make in films she replied: 'a million dollars American'. In time she was seen as a rival to the top American sex symbols. Her meeting with Marilyn Monroe was the occasion for a frank exchange of views. 'They call me the Lollobrigida of America,' began Monroe. 'They call me the Marilyn Monroe of Italy,' responded Lollo diplomatically. Humphrey Bogart, who met in her in *Beat the Devil*, was explicit: 'She was the most woman I'd seen for a long time – made Marilyn Monroe look like Shirley Temple.'

The emoluments of notoriety did not entirely reconcile Gina to the ballyhoo that goes with it. 'When I am with people

[1] The entry reads: 'Airman's life-jacket. [person]'

[2] It was reported from Rome in April 1967 that Lollo had been granted a pardon for this offence under a general amnesty.

I am always watched and I can't get used to this kind of thing – that they look at me as a chimpanzee at a zoo. Some nights when I cannot sleep, I have the feeling of being in bed without anything on, and the people look at me. This is awful'. The encroachments of work on her private life proved tedious too: 'If I'd realized the demands of fame on my private life, I wonder whether I'd have fought so hard for it.'

That she succeeded so well in becoming famous has been a matter for high-level approbation. President Dwight D. Eisenhower proclaimed: 'You are the incarnation of the Italian cinema,' while Marshal Tito was sufficiently edified to announce that 'Gina Lollobrigida is the modern Italian who has made the greatest impression on me.' Bob Hope, unhampered

by the exigencies of protocol, spoke more specifically of her charms: 'I stood there enthralled as her dark lustrous eyes gazed into mine, while her long eyelashes dusted the dandruff from my lapel. Gazing raptly at Gina's loveliness, I suddenly knew why pizza had become Italy's second most popular dish.'

The 'dish' was still high on the popular menu in 1968 when Gina appeared at a party in Rome wearing a garland of diamond flowers reported to be worth $2,000,000 (£833,333). She was quoted as saying at 39: 'I look better now than before. All kinds of people tell me the same thing . . . so I think it must be true.'

'I've found that Americans talk more and do less about sex than men of any other nationality.'

Films

Aquila Nera (1946)	Le Infedeli (1952)
L'Elisir d'Amore (1946)	Beat the Devil (1952)
Lucia di Lammermoor (1946)	Il Maestro di Don Giovanni (1952)
A Man About the House (1947)	Bread, Love, and Dreams (1952)
Il Segreto di Don Giovanni (1947)	La Romana (1954)
Il Delitto di Giovanni Episcopo (1947)	Le Grand Jeu (1954)
La Danse de Mort (1947)	Bread, Love, and Jealousy (1954)
Follie Per l'Opera (1947)	La Donna Più Bella del Mondo (1955)
I Pagliacci (1948)	Trapeze (1955)
Campane a Martello (1948)	The Hunchback of Notre Dame (1956)
A Tale of Five Women (1949)	Anna of Brooklyn (1958)
Anselmo Ha Fretta, o La Sposa Non Puo Attendere (1949)	La Loi (1958)
	Solomon and Sheba (1959)
Miss Italia (1950)	Never So Few (1959)
Cuori Senza Frontiere (1950)	Come September (1961)
Vita da Cani (1950)	Go Naked in the World (1961)
Alina (1950)	Woman of Straw (1964)
La Città si Difende (1951)	Strange Bedfellows (1965)
Enrico Caruso (1951)	Four Kinds of Love (The Dolls) (1965)
Achtung, Banditi! (1951)	Hotel Paradiso (1966)
Fanfan la Tulipe (1951)	Death Has Laid an Egg (1967)
Amor non ho! . . . Pero! . . . Pero! (1951)	Buona Sera Mrs Campbell (1969)
Altri Tempo (1952)	Stuntman (1969)
Les Belles de Nuit (1952)	The Private Navy of Sgt. O'Farrell (1969)
Moglie per Una Notte (1952)	That Wonderful November (1969)
La Provinciale (1952)	

Gina Lollobrigida as the Royal Seductress in 'Solomon and Sheba' (United Artists, 1959).

SAMMY DAVIS JR

Full Name
Sammy Davis.

Born
Tues. 8 Dec. 1925, New York City, USA.

Characteristics
About 5′ 6″; about 124lb. (8st. 12lb.); black hair; brown eyes; blind in the left eye.

Married
(1) 1958 Loray White (div. 1959).
(2) 1961 Mai Britt (div. 1968) 1d. 2 adopted s.

The second Mrs Davis was awarded $3,000 (£1,251) a month alimony.

In a business where gifted performers are often lost in the crowd, any artist who can act, sing, dance, project a brace of images, and play the piano, drums, vibraphone, trumpet, and bass, is not likely to require the services of a talent scout. If the man in question is Sammy Davis, the hypothesis leaps into iridescent life and the onlooker is left limp in contemplation of such a feast of facilities.

Sammy first toddled on stage in the family vaudeville act at the age of four. His aptitude for the light fantastic owes something to the hours he spent watching Bill 'Bojangles' Robinson, once the world's finest tap dancer. The rest is a compound of over 35 years in the business and a compulsive urge to go through life like a sort of one-man combo: 'I've got to have total involvement. I've always done two things at once. I've worked at Las Vegas and commuted to Los Angeles for a movie.'

A certain pre-conscious inspiredness has enabled Sammy to take off other people almost at will: 'I never studied anything I do', he has claimed. 'I just wake up in the morning thinking it would be good to do Bing Crosby, and I can do him.' He once 'did' Nat King Cole on a radio

81

programme. Nat was listening at the time and remarked to his wife: 'Gee, honey, I don't recall recording that number!' In his own style, Sammy has hit the top on disc with the million-selling *What Kind of Fool Am I* (1962) from the musical show *Stop the World – I Want to Get Off* (1961). It was recorded for Reprise, the firm started by Frank Sinatra. Said Frankie: 'Sammy represents to me the finest traditions in our business. His talents are so staggering that each time I see him I experience a greater thrill.'

The gifts of Sammy Davis were almost lost to the public when, in 1954, he was involved in a motor collision which cost him the sight of his left eye. 'God must have had his arms around me. He really did or I would have been killed. I understand there was an identical accident in Oregon . . . and everybody in both cars was killed instantly.' Ten well-wishers offered their corneas for transplantation and the manufacturers of the Cadillac re-designed their steering wheel.

Two-dimensional vision has not prevented Sammy becoming one of the fastest non-professional draws in America. He carries a gun, on licence, and favours the James Bond type Beretta. Sammy is a great Ian Fleming fan and was gratified to hear that Fleming was sufficiently an admirer of his to say that when he died he hoped to come back as Sammy Davis, because of his great zest for life.

Sammy's conversion to the Jewish faith enabled him to refer to himself as 'a one-eyed Jewish Negro'. He explained: 'I wanted to be a Jew because I wanted to become part of a 5,000-year history and hold on to something not just material which would give me the strength to turn the other cheek.'

His marriage to the Swedish actress, Mai Britt, aroused sour comment in some American newspapers who quoted him as saying he didn't mind if they had polka-dot children. He wrote later: 'Nobody in England got the idea that I didn't care if I had polka-dot children. Only in my homeland were the readers offered that choice piece of dishonesty.' Mai shared his interests in riding, music, movies, and TV. The Davis family had two adopted children and one of their own. 'My youngsters are having the childhood I never had and that pleasures me,' wrote Sammy. 'I mean for them to have the education I never had, and that excites me. I never had a day of school. I hope my children never miss a day of school.'

With the capacity to earn as much as $100,000 (£41,666) a week, Sammy has taken obvious delights in giving: 'When I was booked into the Copa in New York, I bought a pack of cigarettes and left the girl change for a $20 bill. I wanted to do that because once I went in there as a nobody and they put me on the side.' On a visit to Hong Kong he heard that Frank Sinatra had ordered 15 suits there and promptly said 'treble it'. On that trip his largesse to his entourage reached regal proportions: 'I bought a miniature television, tape-recorder, and camera for everyone with me and you know what I had to pay in Customs, over £1,100. They had to delay the plane take-off, not because they were searching through the stuff, just so they could read all the forms I'd had to fill in.'

All this, however, was small potatoes compared with the handouts Sammy has lavished on the Civil Rights movement in America. Appearing on the BBC *24 Hours* Programme in London in 1968 he said: 'I have given over a million and a half dollars to Civil Rights – but it's not enough.' He also contributed £5,000 ($12,000) to the Black Power movement in England.

FILMS

Anna Lucasta (1959)
Oceans 11 (1960)
Pepe (1960)
Porgy and Bess (1961)
Sergeants Three (1962)
The Threepenny Opera (1963)
Robin and the Seven Hoods (1964)
A Man Called Adam (1966)
Salt and Pepper (1968)
Sweet Charity (1969)
One More Time (1969)
Yes I Can (1970)

LP RECORDINGS

The Wham of Sam (Reprise R2003)
Mr Entertainment (Brunswick LAT8384)
Sammy Belts the Best of Broadway
(Reprise R2010/R9-2010)
Hit Songs from 'Stop the World I Want to Get Off' (Reprise R30002)
Spectacular (Reprise R6033)
At the Cocoanut Grove (Reprise R6063/1/2/3)
Sammy Salutes the London Palladium
(Reprise R6095/R9-6095)
Treasury of Golden Hits (Reprise R6096)
Sammy on Broadway (Reprise R300026)
Nat King Cole Song Book (Reprise R6164)
Sammy Davis Show (Reprise R6188)
That's All (Reprise RLP6237-1/2 and
RSLP6237-1/2)
Golden Boy (Capitol W2124/SW2124)
Sammy Davis Jr's Greatest Hits
(Reprise RLP6291)
Lonely is the Name
(Reprise RLP6308/RSLP6308)
Sweet Charity (MCA MUCS133)
*Sammy Davis Jr Sings the Complete
'Dr Doolittle'* (Reprise RLP6264)
Sammy Davis Jr (Reprise RSLP6324)

Left:
Sammy Davis came out all psychedelic as Big Daddy in 'Sweet Charity' (Universal Pictures, 1969). In this scene he sang 'The Rhythm of Life'. Shirley MacLaine took the role of Charity Hope Valentine. Holding her hand in this number was John McMartin as Oscar.

When Durham, a second class County, played the Australians in 1938 they were informed by the insurance company providing cover for the match that they could be issued with two alternative policies, one for £1,000 ($4,000) if Don

Si Donal BRADMA

Full name Donald George Bradman, Kt (1949).

Born Thurs 27 Aug. 1908, Cootamundra, New South Wales, Australia.

Characteristics about 5′ 8″; about 144*lb.* (10*st.* 4*lb.*) when playing Test cricket; fair hair; blue eyes.

Married 1932 Jessie Menzies.

Bradman played and one for £800 ($3,200) if he did not. Such was the drawing power of the cricketer who, in the judgement of Sir Jack Hobbs (1882–1964), was 'above everybody as far as scoring runs is concerned. Whatever odds there may be on any other player getting a score, those odds are increased by 50 per cent when Don walks to the crease.'

Statistics supporting the verdict of Hobbs are conclusive. Bradman scored 6,996 runs, including a world Test record 29 centuries in 52 Tests for Australia (1928–48) at a world record average of 99.94. His average of 95.14 for his complete career of 338 innings (1927–49) is a world record. He scored the highest

English seasonal average of 115.66 for 26 innings played in 1938. He hit the fastest Test 200 on record – 90 minutes – against England at Leeds in 1930 and the same innings, totalling 334, is a record score for Australia against England. He amassed 309 of those runs on the first day, the highest ever individual score in a single day's Test cricket. Sir Learie (now Lord) Constantine described that innings as 'the masterpiece' in his memory of first-class cricket. Bradman's total of 974 runs in the 1930 Test series is the biggest individual aggregate in a Test rubber. On average Bradman hit a century every three innings throughout his career, compiling a total of 117 centuries. He hit

Don Bradman needed only one more boundary to make a Test batting average of 100. His world record average was 99.94 in 52 Tests for Australia (1928-48)

Bradman himself said that: 'McCabe's[1] innings of 232 at Nottingham in the first Test in 1938 was the greatest I ever saw or ever hope to see.' He listed the greatest Tests he played in as follows: (1) Leeds, 1938, (2) Melbourne, 1932–33, (3) Lord's, 1930, (4) Nottingham, 1934, (5) Sydney, 1947, (6) Leeds, 1948.

From 1936 to 1948 while Bradman was Captain, Australia never lost a Test rubber. As skipper he had a sharp eye for the morale of his team and expected them to be conscious of their responsibility. He had fairly straightforward views on what was required of a good batsman: 'Given normal physical attributes, the man who scores most runs will be the one who most often plays the right stroke off the right ball, and that, of course, must be allied to judgement and concentration.' He emphasized that a batsman has less than a second to see the ball and decide what to do. Bradman developed his exceptional eye as a boy when he used to play a golf ball on the rebound off a corrugated wall for hours on end, using a cricket stump instead of a bat. On bowling his observations were again simple: 'From my experience I should think all great bowlers have had one characteristic, namely: they were predominantly attacking bowlers who made the stumps their prime objective.'

C. B. Fry wrote in 1939: 'W. G. Grace had more power than the other three put together, and one stroke for every

six double centuries in a single season (1930), a record in first-class cricket. His highest score in an over was 30 (4, 6, 6, 4, 6, 4) at Folkestone in 1934.

---

[1] Stanley McCabe, nicknamed 'Napper' because he looked like Napoleon, played in 39 Tests for Australia. He was killed in a cliff fall in 1968 aged 58.

ball the bowler could bowl; Victor Trumper had the greatest charm and two strokes for every ball; Ranjitsinhji had the greatest finesse and three strokes to every ball; Don Bradman has the highest number of runs and has strokes of his own which the other three had not; he may be briefly scheduled as a phenomenon.' Denis Compton, writing in 1958, brought a different perspective to bear: 'Sir Don Bradman was probably the greatest batsman ever, but I don't think I'm being disrespectful to his genius if I say that against the type of bowling bowled today he would have been lucky to get 170 runs in a day's cricket . . .'

For comparison with modern professional rewards, Bradman's best offer was £1,000 a week plus fares for himself and family to fulfil a proposed engagement in South Africa. His testimonial match raised £9,342 in 1949.

Perhaps the finest testimonial to Bradman as a cricketer and as a person came from the former Australian Premier, Sir Robert Menzies, who referred to him in his memoirs in 1967 as 'the master batsman, the superb Captain, the very able man of many talents . . .'

Bradman's 29 Test Centuries

Year	Venue	Australia Against	Score
1928–29	Melbourne	England	112
1928–29	Melbourne	England	123
1930	Nottingham	England	131
1930	Lord's, London	England	254
1930	Leeds	England	334
1930	Oval, London	England	232
1930–31	Brisbane	West Indies	223
1930–31	Melbourne	West Indies	152
1931–32	Brisbane	South Africa	226
1931–32	Sydney	South Africa	112
1931–32	Melbourne	South Africa	167
1931–32	Adelaide	South Africa	299*
1932–33	Melbourne	England	103*
1934	Leeds	England	304
1934	Oval, London	England	244
1936–37	Melbourne	England	270
1936–37	Adelaide	England	212
1936–37	Melbourne	England	169
1938	Nottingham	England	144*
1938	Lord's, London	England	102*
1938	Leeds	England	103
1946–47	Brisbane	England	187
1946–47	Sydney	England	234
1947–48	Adelaide	India	201
1947–48	Brisbane	India	185
1947–48	Melbourne	India	132
1947–48	Melbourne	India	127*
1948	Nottingham	England	138
1948	Leeds	England	173*

Complete Batting Record in Test Cricket

Tests	Innings	Not Outs	Runs	Highest	Centuries	Average
52	80	10	6996	334	29	99.94

Complete Career Batting Record

Innings	Not Outs	Runs	Highest	Centuries	Average
338	43	28,067	452*	117	95.14

* Not out

Dr Christiaan Barnard

Full Name
Christiaan Neethling Barnard

Born
Wed. 8 Oct. 1922, Beauford West, South Africa

Characteristics
About 5′ 11″; dark brown hair and eyes

Married
1948 Aletta Gertruida 'Louwtjie' Louw. 1*s.* 1*d.* (div. 1969)
reported engaged to Barbara Zoellner, Oct. 1969

'When I was admitted to hospital a year ago I could scarcely lift a finger. I was gasping for breath, choking almost. Death would have been welcome.' The words of Philip Blaiberg, 58, who believed after his operation in 1968 that he would live to see 70, is the finest tribute yet paid to the work of Professor Christiaan Barnard, the man who performed the world's first heart transplant operation.[1] Barnard's first attempt at what has been called the 'ultimate operation' was on 3 Dec. 1967 when Louis Washkansky, 55, received the heart of 25-year-old Denise Ann Darvall but survived only 18 days before dying of double pneumonia. Not discouraged, Barnard and his team at the Groote Schuur Hospital in Cape Town operated on Blaiberg on 2 Jan. 1968, transplanting the heart of Clive Haupt, 24, a Coloured donor.[2] The major steps in the five-hour operation, expressed simply for the layman, were as follows:

1. The recipient's chest was opened.
2. The donor's chest was opened and his heart connected to a heart-lung machine.
3. The donor's heart was excised and examined. Found to be normal, it was placed in a cooling solution.
4. The donor's heart was transferred to the operating room and connected to a heart-lung machine.
5. The recipient's heart was excised.
6. The donor's heart was transferred to the recipient and sutured in place.
7. Re-warming of the heart was commenced and electrodes placed against the heart walls caused it to start beating again.
8. The heart was disconnected from the heart-lung machine and the patient's chest closed.

The total expenditure on this operation was about £15,000 ($36,000). Blaiberg made a swift recovery and was able to resume marital relations with his wife only 20 days after the operation.

Dr Barnard was quoted in an interview as saying that the surgical technique required no change and that research would have to be concentrated on post-operative care and the improvement of methods of immuno-suppression, that is, the drugs used to block the body's mechanism which would otherwise cause the heart to be rejected. He added that organ banks should be established so that donor

---

[1] The first attempt at transplant occurred in 1771 when the Scottish surgeon John Hunter (1728–93) took a sound tooth from a person's head and inserted it into a cock's comb.

[2] Blaiberg, who died on 17 Aug. 1969, was then the longest-surviving heart transplant patient at 594 days.

Dr Christiaan Barnard's first heart transplant case was Philip Blaiberg.

hearts could be available when required, rather than waiting for a donor to die. Discussing the possibility that animal hearts might be used, he said that the best would be 'that of a primate – an ape or a baboon, but their hearts are too small. The best animal that is in many cases most suitable for human use is the pig, because the anatomy is very similar.'

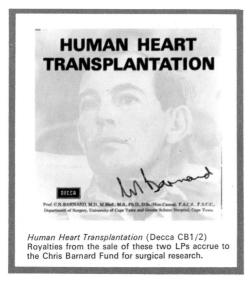

Human Heart Transplantation (Decca CB1/2) Royalties from the sale of these two LPs accrue to the Chris Barnard Fund for surgical research.

The son of a missionary, Christiaan Barnard is one of a highly successful and creative family. His daughter is a famous water-skier. His brother, Marius, is a member of his team at the Groote Schuur Hospital. Another brother, Johannes, has several inventions patented. Barnard graduated in 1946 at the University of Cape Town and, after post-graduate studies at the University of Minnesota, emerged as a Master of Surgery and Doctor of Philosophy. He has originated surgical techniques for the treatment of congenital heart lesions and for the correction of a heart disease known as Ebstein's Anomaly. He once operated on 49 dogs in an unsuccessful attempt to solve a problem connected with intestinal abnormality in the new-born. At the 50th operation he hit on the answer. Possessed of immense powers of industry and perseverance, Barnard, with his team, had performed over 1,000 open-heart operations before the first heart transplant. His 'Barnard Valve', developed at the Groote Schuur Hospital, is in universal use today.

Following his worldwide acclaim for the first successful heart transplant, Barnard travelled to Europe, South America, and elsewhere on lecture tours and made a strong impression on televiewers in Britain with his directness and good humour. In Rome he was received by Pope Paul VI who told him: 'I bless your achievement and I invite you to proceed along the same road, doing good as you have up to now'.

RICHARD

BURTON

Full name Richard Walter Jenkins (the name Burton was taken from a schoolteacher friend).

Born Tues. 10 Nov. 1925, Pontrhydfen, South Wales.

Characteristics About 5′ 11″; about 165*lb.* (11*st.* 11*lb.*); chest 42″; light brown hair; green eyes; a very tough beard which cuts his make-up man, flying up in his face when he trims it.

Married (1) 1949 Sybil Williams (div. 1963) 2*d.*; (2) 1964 Elizabeth Taylor.

In entertainment as in other fields of popular acclaim the surest sign of eminence is the regularity with which a star is quoted or mis-quoted. The truth, disguised in words that Bowdler[1] might have envied, gives fame an image which the owner often fails to recognize. In this sense it seems no more than vaguely possible that Richard Burton ever really said, as quoted: 'By heaven I'm going to be the greatest actor or what's the use of acting?'

Burton was a lusty Petruchio to Elizabeth Taylor's Katharina in 'The Taming of the Shrew' (Columbia, 1967).

Brought to London as a boy by Emlyn Williams, Burton made his stage debut in *Druid's Rest*. After war service in the RAF he broke into motion pictures and shortly won the commendation of the critics for his starring role, opposite Olivia de Havilland, in *My Cousin Rachel* in 1952. In 1960, the year the American Broadcasting Company signed him as narrator in the series televising Churchill's memoirs, Burton played King Arthur in *Camelot*, winning the New York Drama Critics Award for 1961. 'One song in *Camelot*' he said, 'takes more than one speech in Shakespeare. Singing-breathing is different from talking-breathing, it uses more lung-power.' The show ran into 1962 and was the subject of a million-selling LP disc.

Burton's skill owes as much to instinctive taste as to professional competence: 'I can't act with a person unless I'm powerfully, sexually interested.' His leading ladies have not always proved equal to this prerequisite. 'One heroine – I simply can't tell you who she was – had a mouth like the

Grand Canyon. Kissing her was like taking a deep dive into space,' he complained. According to Gina Lollobrigida, 'as manly off screen as on', Burton does not rate physique an important ingredient of his success: 'I've got a body like an abandoned dressing-room. When I took my clothes off to appear in bathing trunks in *The Night of the Iguana*, strong men laughed and strangers kissed each other.' His preparations for *Becket* included a friendly agreement with Peter O'Toole that they would not drink for ten days. The truce lasted for five days. 'Well, three days later we hadn't been to bed – we had to do the scene where the king has to put the archbishop's ring on Becket's finger. Try doing *that* when you've been sloshed for three days', he challenged.

The lure of Hollywood – he liked 'every dollar of it' – proved irresistible to Burton and it was there that he first met Elizabeth Taylor in 1952. Their affair was not to blossom until 1961 on the set of *Cleopatra*. 'I did not tame Elizabeth,' he pointed out. 'She came, she saw, and I conquered.' She also helped to elevate him into the top money bracket. In *Cleopatra* he earned a reported £117,000 ($327,600). Then came *The Night of the Iguana*: £165,000 ($462,000); *The Spy Who Came in From the Cold*: £250,000 ($700,000); and *The Sandpiper*: $1,000,000 (£357,000). In 1966 he stated: 'I now get more money for a film than Liz does; not in cash, but I get a bigger percentage of the profits.' That year they were reported to have earned $3,000,000 (£1,071,000) between them and that was the sum they contributed to the production of the potentially less profitable *Taming of the Shrew*. The film turned out to be so lucrative that Burton felt moved to give Liz a jet runabout (*see page* 64). Then the producer of *Boom!* announced he was giving them a white Rolls-Royce. Asked why, he replied: 'Because that seems to be the only colour

they haven't got.' In 1969 it was reported that Liz and Burton were now asking $1,250,000 (£520,833) a film and that Burton had ordered a $5,000,000 (£2,083,333) 117-seat Boeing 737 because the smaller jet could not accommodate all their luggage.

Those who felt that Burton might be destined for the same matrimonial exit as three previous husbands have the word of Liz that things are cosy between them. 'If you ever get killed or die before me,' she told him, 'I'll never speak to you again.' She has said that he has 'a softness of soul' and 'remembers almost everything ever said to him.' Asked whether playing opposite him in the squalid domestic in-fighting of *Who's Afraid of Virginia Woolf?* had affected their private lives, Burton thought not: 'Elizabeth and I both thought we might carry it home with us, but we never did, though it might have been different if we'd had to do it on the stage every night instead of in a film studio.'

Working with his wife has enhanced Burton's respect for her talents. He has rated her the greatest living actress and accepts her advice, particularly in matters of on-camera technique: 'You've got to be very careful, as she explained to me, when your face is going to be 38 feet high, depending on the size of your face, and 30 feet wide. I mean, you've got to be very careful how massively you register any emotions.'

'Acting is like being in the infantry. There are long stretches of boredom and a few peaks of excitement.'

'Monogamy is one of man's greatest inventions.'

'We Welshmen are all Puritans from way back. That enables us to see the error of our ways, even while we're indulging them. I now call myself a daytime atheist – but, by jingo, I get tremors at night.'

---

[1] Thomas Bowdler (1754–1825) editor of expurgated works of Shakespeare for 'family' consumption.

FILMS

The Last Days of Dolwyn (1948)
Now Barabbas Was a Robber (1949)
Waterfront (1950)
The Woman With No Name 1951)
Green Grow the Rushes (1951)
My Cousin Rachel (1952)
The Desert Rats (1953)
The Robe (1954)
Prince of Players (1955)
The Rains of Ranchipur (1956)
Alexander the Great (1956)

Sea Wife (1957)
Bitter Victory (1958)
Look Back in Anger (1959)
The Bramble Bush (1960)
Cleopatra (1963)
The VIPs (1963)
Becket (1964)
The Night of the Iguana (1964)
The Spy Who Came in From the Cold (1965)
The Sandpiper (1965)
Who's Afraid of Virginia Woolf? (1966)

The Taming of the Shrew (1967)
Dr Faustus (1967)
The Comedians (1967)
Candy (1968)
Boom! (1968)
Where Eagles Dare (1969)
Laughter in the Dark (1969)
Staircase (1969)
The Longest Day (1969)
Anne of the Thousand Days (1970)

STAGE APPEARANCES

Druid's Rest (1943–44)
Measure for Measure (1944)
Castle Anna (1949)
The Lady's Not for Burning (1950)
The Boy With a Cart (1950)
A Phoenix Too Frequent (1950)
Legend of Lovers (1952)
Montserrat (1953)

Old Vic
- Hamlet (1953–54)
- King John (1955)
- Twelfth Night (1955)
- Coriolanus (1955)
- The Tempest (1955)
- Henry V (1955)
- Othello (1956)

New York
- Time Remembered (1957)
- Camelot (1960)
- Hamlet (1964)
- Dr Faustus (1966)

LP RECORDINGS

Coriolanus (Caedmon SRS226/SRS-M-226)
Hamlet (CBS SBRG72259/BRG72259)
The Taming of the Shrew (soundtrack) (RCA Victor RB6711)
The Rape of Lucrece (Caedmon SRS-M-239)
Becket (RCA Victor RD7679)
Dr Faustus (HMV ASD2270/ALP2270)
Under Milk Wood (Argo RG21–22)
A Selection from the Works of Dylan Thomas (Argo RG43)
Poems of Coleridge (Argo RG438)
Poems of Thomas Hardy (Caedmon TC1140)
Camelot (CBS BRG70009/SBRG70009)

Burton played a bibulous Professor McPhisto in 'Candy' (Selmur Pictures, 1968). The part of his chauffeur, Zero, was taken by Sugar Ray Robinson, former world welter and middleweight boxing champion.

Burton as Henry VII in 'Anne of the Thousand Days' (Universal Pictures, 1970) based on the play by Maxwell Anderson.

Maria Callas

Maria Callas received the tribute of her co-stars Tito Gobi (left) and Renato Cioni after her Royal Gala performance of Tosca at Covent Garden in 1965.

Full name Cecilia Sophia Anna Maria Meneghini, née Kalogeropoulos (her parents changed their name to Callas by deed poll in about 1926).

Born Tues. 4 Dec. 1923 (during a snow storm), New York City, USA.

Characteristics About 5′ 8″; about 135*lb.* (9*st.* 9*lb.*) slimmed from 210*lb.* (15*st.*); black hair (sometimes dyed blonde); dark eyes; very short-sighted, wore contact lenses on stage.

Married 1949 Giovanni Batista Meneghini (annullment proceedings reported in 1966).

Standards of operatic genius do not permit of accurate or precise appraisal. So it is that the view of one critic after the famed soprano's Covent Garden debut in 1952 that she was '. . . the greatest singer, male or female, since Nordica' may not be taken too literally.[1] Critics have, on occasion, been less lyrical and Miss Callas accordingly reserves a healthy antagonism towards them. 'As long as I hear them stirring and hissing like snakes out there, I know I'm on top,' she once stated. 'If I'd heard nothing from my enemies, I'd know I was slipping.' It may have been a slippery patch that bedevilled her performance of *Norma* at New York in 1956 when, atypically it should be emphasized, a bouquet of carrots and onions thudded on stage.

Miss Callas won a scholarship at 13 to the Royal Conservatory in Athens and made her debut at 16 at the Royal Theatre there in *Boccaccio*. She made her first important appearance, the lead in *Tosca*,

[1] Lilian Nordica (1859-1914), the American singer.

Maria Callas

when aged 18 in 1941. Though she displayed a marked precocity, instanced by the ability to learn the most difficult opera in eight days, she does not recommend the singer to start performing too young. 'There must be a law against forcing children to perform at an early age. Children should have a wonderful childhood. They should not be given too much responsibility.' She has opined that the best results can only follow a careful grounding: 'Too many singers are unprepared, too interested in quick money, and a quick success.' I believe in preparation and I believe, too, in waiting for things. They happen much sooner if you are not in a big rush.'

Among other things, a close study of instrumental technique has persuaded Miss Callas that the voice is a sublime musical instrument: 'Singing is not only a vocal display. We singers are the first instrument of the orchestra.' She has preserved an almost reverential approach to singing: 'You hear a piece of music . . . and you make love to it, you purify it, you beautify it. It is this which drives you forward, or pulls you; it is this which makes great musicians of all kinds.'

Callas has admitted she suffered the pangs of anticipation familiar to all artists. 'Before I sing I know nothing; it's panic, for I do not remember anything and I feel quite lost. I do not even know with what gestures I should begin. Until I go on the stage, then everything comes pouring out, the music, words, gestures, everything.' The dramatic side of her performance is spontaneous: 'My gestures are never premeditated . . . They are linked with one's colleagues, with the music, with the way you've moved before: one gesture is born from another like the remarks in a conversation . . . There are millions of tiny considerations which make up the beauty of a performance, and they must be the authentic product of the moment.' Authenticity was unexpectedly reinforced by actuality when, in a 1964 rehearsal of *Tosca* at Covent Garden, the Divina's wig caught fire on a stage candle. Still giving forth with the high notes, she beat out the blaze with the gallant aid of the attentive Scarpai, played by Tito Gobbi.

Temperament, the prerogative of the star soprano, has propelled Miss Callas into strife on occasion. For those intent on avoiding a clash of personalities, her warning note has been: 'I like respect. I respect others. They must respect me. When they don't – that's when my temperament comes out.' Tension arose at the Metropolitan Opera House, New York, in 1958 when she refused to alternate two performances of the light opera *La Traviata* with two performances of the much heavier theme of Verdi's *Macbeth*. Her contract was terminated forthwith. In 1956 she was sued by her ex-agent for ten per cent of her earnings since 1947, claimed by him for her alleged failure to meet contractual obligations. The dispute was settled out of court in 1957 for an undisclosed amount.

Miss Callas is estimated to have earned more than $100,000 (now £41,666) a year from appearances and record royalties and to have maintained a wardrobe including 25 fur coats, 40 suits, 150 pairs of shoes, 200 dresses, and 300 hats. When she was told once that she earned more than the

96

then President of the United States, she retorted: 'Let *him* sing then.' But, according to her mother's book, Callas is reluctant to share her wealth with anybody, including relations. When the 54-year-old lady wrote asking for an allowance of $100 (£35) a month in 1952, her daughter wrote back: 'You are a young woman, and you can work. If you can't earn enough to live on throw yourself out of the window.'

Aristotle Onassis was quoted as both admitting and categorically denying in Nov. 1967 that he had married Maria Callas. On 20 Oct. 1968 he married Mrs Jacqueline Kennedy.

The end of her ten-year association with Aristotle Onassis, on his marriage to Mrs Jacqueline Kennedy, gave Callas an incentive to come back to professional singing. It was reported in 1969 that she was engaged in making her first film, *Medea*, in a non-operatic role, and that she planned to return to the stage in a production of *Traviata* at the Paris Opera in Feb. 1970.

L.P RECORDINGS

(Releases March 1966–March 1969)
Beethoven: *Arias* (World Record Club T690)
Bellini: *I Puritani, Sonnambula*; Milan La Scala Orchestra
(Columbia 33CX1540)
Bellini: *I Puritani* (complete); Milan La Scala Orchestra
(Columbia CX1058/60)
Bellini: *Norma* (complete); Milan La Scala Orchestra
(Columbia SAX2412/4 and CX1766/8)
Berlioz: *Le Damnation de Faust* (excerpts); Paris
Conservatoire Orchestra
(Columbia SAX2503/33CX1858)
Bizet: *Carmen* (complete); French National Opera
Orchestra (HMV Angel SAN140/2 and AN140/2)
Bizet: *Carmen* (excerpts); French National Radio
Orchestra (Columbia SAX2401/33CX1771)
Bizet: *Pecheurs des Perles* (excerpts); Paris Conservatoire
Orchestra (Columbia SAX2503/33CX1858)
Charpentier: *Louise* (excerpts); French National Radio
Orchestra (Columbia SAX2401/33CX1771)
Cherubini: *Medea* (excerpts); Milan La Scala Orchestra
(Columbia 33CX1540)
Donizetti: *Anna Bolona*, etc. (World Record Club T591)
Donizetti: *La Figlia del Reggimento*, etc. (excerpts)
Paris Conservatoire Orchestra
(Columbia SAX1564/33CX1923)
Donizetti: *Lucia di Lammermoor* (complete);
Philharmonia Orchestra
(Columbia SAX2316/7 and CX1723/4)
Gluck: *Iphigenie en Tauride*; Paris Conservatoire
Orchestra (Columbia SAX2503/33CX1858)
Gluck: *Orphee et Eurydice*; *Alceste*; French National
Radio Orchestra (Columbia SAX2401/33CX1771)
Gounod: *Romeo et Juliette*; French National Radio
Orchestra (Columbia SAX2401/33CX1771)
Leoncavallo: *I Pagliacci* (complete); Milan La Scala
Orchestra (Columbia CXS1211/CX1212)
Mascagni: *Cavalleria Rusticana*; Milan La Scala
Orchestra (Columbia CXS1182/CX1183)
Massenet: *Le Cid* (excerpts); French National Radio
Orchestra (Columbia SAX2401/33CX1771)
Massenet: *Manon Werther* (excerpts); Paris
Conservatoire Orchestra
(Columbia SAX2503/33CX1858)
Mozart: *Arias* (World Record Club T690)
Ponchielli: *La Gioconda*
(World Record Club OC190/1/2)
Ponchielli: *La Gioconda* (highlights)
(World Record Club OH193)
Puccini: *La Boheme* (complete); Milan La Scala
Orchestra (Columbia CX1464/5)
Puccini: *Madame Butterfly* (complete); Milan La Scala
Orchestra (Columbia CX1296/8)
Puccini: *Manon Lescaut* (complete); Milan La Scala
Orchestra (Columbia CX1583/5)
Puccini: *Tosca* (complete); Paris Conservatoire Orchestra
(HMV Angel SAN149/50 and AN149/50)
Puccini: *Tosca* (complete); Milan La Scala Orchestra
(Columbia CX1094/5)
Puccini: *Opera Excerpts* (Columbia 33CX1204)
Rossini: *La Cenerentola* etc. (excerpts); Paris
Conservatoire Orchestra
(Columbia SAX1564/33CX1923)
Rossini: *Il Barbiere di Siviglia*; Philharmonia Orchestra
(Columbia SAX2266/8 and CX1507/9)
Saint-Saens: *Samson et Delila*; French National Radio
Orchestra (Columbia SAX2401/33CX1771)
Spontini: *La Vestale*; Milan La Scala Orchestra
(Columbia 33CX1540)
Thomas: *Mignon*; French National Radio Orchestra
(Columbia SAX2401/33CX1771)
Verdi: *Aida* (complete); Milan La Scala Orchestra
(Columbia CX1318/20)
Verdi: *Un Ballo in Maschera* (complete); Milan La Scala
Orchestra (Columbia CX1472/4)
Verdi: *Rigoletto* (complete); Milan La Scala Orchestra
(Columbia CXS1324 and 1325/6)
Verdi: *Il Trovatore* (complete); Milan La Scala Orchestra
(Columbia CXS1483 and 1484/5)
Verdi: Excerpts including *Aida* (Columbia 33CX1725)
Verdi: *Verdi Heroines* (World Record Club T633)

FILM

Medea (1969)

PETER USTINOV

If it were true that the discoveries of modern science had shed no light on cosmic truths propounded by philosophers of ancient times, the world would have no further use for thinkers. But happily our age is blessed with minds which soar above mere occult utterance or a study of the pigeons in Trafalgar Square. From one such mind, untrammelled by the vain or trivial, important words have emanated:

'A gentleman of considerable weight makes by far the very best mate.'

Opinions harnessed to the author's bulk are bound to gather impetus and Ustinov, the 240-pound cosmopolite, can hardly be ignored. Substantially endowed, the playwright, actor, producer, film, television, and recording star and author has the universal merit, beyond self-praise, that people like him. And if individual reference is required, that conspicuous co-endomorph Robert Morley, star of the Ustinov play *Halfway Up the Tree*, has generously supplied one: 'I do like appearing in a play by an author as distinguished as myself.'[1] Morley, however, does not appear in Madame Tussaud's waxworks in London where Peter Ustinov was measured for eyeballs in 1962: 'It tickled like mad', he remarked. 'I had to concentrate on a spot on the wall to stop myself giggling.'

After schooling at Westminster, Ustinov joined Aylesbury Repertory Company at fifty shillings a week. He made his first

[1] According to the somatotype system of classifying human physique, an endomorph is one with a tendency to globularity. Morley weighs at least as much as Ustinov.

Right: *Peter Ustinov cheek-by-jowl with the many-headed bronze of himself by Enzo Piazotta.*

Full name Peter Alexander von Ustinow (shortened to Ustinov).

Born Sat. 16 April 1921, Swiss Cottage, London, England.

Characteristics About 6′; about 252*lb.* (18*st.*); light brown hair; grey eyes.

Married (1) 1940 Isolde Denham (div. 1950) 1*d.*; (2) 1954 Mrs Suzanne la Flèche (née Cloutier) 1*s.* 2*d.*

London stage appearance in his own sketch *The Bishop of Limpopoland* in 1939 and his film debut in 1941 as a schoolboy in the Will Hay film *The Goose Steps Out*. His mother, Nadia Benois, the artist, designed the set for his first play, *The House of Regrets*, staged just before Peter was drafted in World War II.

His mother also helped to mitigate the hardships of army life when Peter was serving in North Africa, sending supplies of toilet paper via diplomatic bag which was conveyed to 6411623 Private Ustinov by courtesy of a Cuban Minister on his way to military conferences with General Dwight D. Eisenhower. Private Ustinov did not have any pretensions to military prowess but won some reflected glory by serving as batman to the genial Colonel David Niven. Army life provided some useful insights which came out in the film *The Way Ahead*, starring Niven, which Peter co-scripted, and in *Private Angelo* for which he also wrote the script.

Recognition of Ustinov's talents came from many directions in the early 'fifties. There was steep 'promotion' for the ex-Private to Emperor when he played the part of Nero in the film *Quo Vadis*. 'In a studio canteen,' he reported cheerfully, 'I always get better service when I am playing an Emperor than when I am playing a member of the proletariat.' On the stage his *Love of Four Colonels* won the New York Critics' Circle Award and the Donaldson Award as the best foreign play of 1951. In the same year *The Moment of Truth* proved a commercial flop though he rated it the best play he ever wrote.

Recuperating from slipped disc, Ustinov won 'Tony' Awards for Best Play and Best Performance in *Romanoff and Juliet* which he played in New York in 1957 when his TV debut as Dr Johnson earned him an 'Emmy'. Then on the big screen he collected 'Oscars' for his supporting roles in both *Spartacus* and *Topkapi*.

Ustinov's French-Canadian wife, Suzanne, a former model and actress, met him before he became really famous. She

PLAYS
House of Regrets (1942)
Blow Your Own Trumpet (1943)
Beyond (1943)
The Banbury Nose (1944)
The Tragedy of Good Intentions (1945)
The Indifferent Shepherd (1948)
Frenzy (1948)
The Man in the Raincoat (1949)
The Love of Four Colonels (1951)
The Moment of Truth (1951)
High Balcony (1952)
No Sign of the Dove (1953)
The Empty Chair (1956)
Romanoff and Juliet (1956)
Photo Finish (1961)
The Life in My Hands (1963)
Halfway Up the Tree (1968)
The Passion According to Pontius Pilate (1968)
The Unknown Soldier and His Wife (1968)

REVUES AND SKETCHES
The Bishop of Limpopoland (1939)
Diversion (1941)
Diversion No. 2 (1942)

MAJOR TV PARTS
Omnibus (*Dr. Johnson*) (1957)
Barefoot in Athens (1968)
Portrait of a Master Entertainer (1969)

STAGE APPEARANCES
The Wood Demon (1938)
The Bishop of Limpopoland (1939)
Swinging the Gate (1940)
Diversion (1941)
The Wood Demon (1946)
Crime and Punishment (1946)
Frenzy (1948)
Love in Albania (1949)
The Love of Four Colonels (1951)
The Unknown Soldier and His Wife (1968)

FILM SCRIPTS
The Way Ahead (1944), co-author.
School for Secrets (1946)
Vice Versa (1947)
Private Angelo (1949)
Romanoff and Juliet (1961)
Billy Budd (1962)
Lady L (1965)

LP RECORDINGS
Peter Ustinov Reads Cautionary Verse
(Argo RG599)
The Two Peters (with Peter Sellers)
(Parlophone GEP8853)
The Theatre Today (with others)
(Argo RG279)
The Many Voices of Peter Ustinov
(BBC Radio Enterprises REB26m)
Blackbeard's Ghost (Music for Pleasure
MFP1249)

said: 'He has this terrible inferiority complex . . . He doesn't think that women or men can be attracted to him because he is fat and ugly.' She has reported that he methodically reads the *Encyclopedia Britannica* in bed, writes almost anywhere – in the bathroom or lying on the floor, and is 'the most humble man I have ever met'. Their former Chelsea address in London was once the home of the Victorian actress Dame Ellen Terry (1848–1928) and of Dr Thomas Augustine Arne (1710–1778) composer of *Rule Britannia.*

Of mixed Russian, German, Spanish, Italian, French, and Ethiopian descent, Ustinov speaks six languages and several dialects. His great-great-great grandfather was musical director of the St Petersburg Imperial Theatre in the 18th century, which may have helped when he produced Mozart's *The Magic Flute* at Hamburg in 1968.

In 'Viva Max!' (Commonwealth United, 1969) Ustinov played the preposterous Colonel Max who, in this fictionalized episode from United States history, succeeded in re-capturing the Alamo.

'Beware politicians! They only reached the top because they had no qualifications to detain them at the bottom!'

'I believe there are too many exceptions to every rule in the world to make any rule valid.'

On being elected Rector of Dundee University in 1968: 'Is it not our solemn duty, with all our jocularity and horseplay and noise, to ensure that never will there be a risk that the shy thought, shyly expressed by a shy man, will be shouted down or be carried away on a wave of indiscriminate militancy? For that shy thought may be the most valuable of the lot.'

'Nobody who is lucky enough to know success can avoid exciting envy, nor can he fully enjoy success unless he has tasted failure.'

'We are living in an age when it's all strip and no tease.' (1969).

FILM APPEARANCES

The Goose Steps Out (1941)
One of Our Aircraft is Missing (1942)
Let the People Sing (1942)
Private Angelo (1949)
Quo Vadis? (1950)
Odette (1950)
Hotel Sahara (1950)
Beau Brummell (1954)
The Egyptian (1954)
We're No Angels (1954)
Lola Montez (1955)
An Angel Flew Over Brooklyn (1957)
The Spies (1957)
Spartacus (1960)
The Sundowners (1960)
Romanoff and Juliet (1961)
Billy Budd (1962)
Topkapi (1964)
John Goldfarb, Please Come Home (1964)
The Comedians (1967)
Blackbeard's Ghost (1967)
Hot Millions (1968)
Viva Max! (1969)

SIR EDMUNI

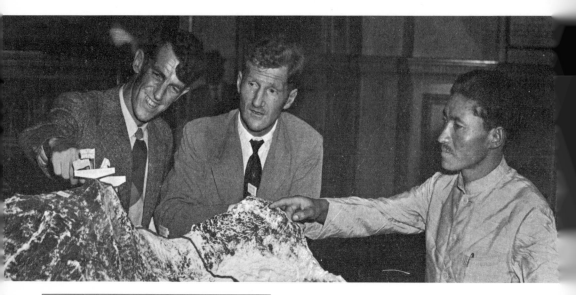

Full name Edmund Percival Hillary, KBE (1953).

Born Sun. 20 July 1919, Auckland, New Zealand.

Characteristics About 6′3″; dark hair and eyes.

Married 1953 Louise Rose 1s. 2d.

Within weeks of his first ascent of Mount Everest in 1953 Sir Edmund Hillary gave a talk with Sir John (now Lord) Hunt and Sherpa Tenzing at the Royal Geographical Society in London.

'In consultation with Hillary and Evans, I've decided to stand Hillary and Tenzing ready to go up to Camp VII tomorrow . . . They will have to get this route through [*sic*] and come back as soon as possible. I chose these two as they were the last in the assault programme and because they are the strongest.' So wrote Sir John (now Lord) Hunt in his diary on 20 May 1953. Hillary's impressions on approaching the summit of Mount Everest[1] at 11.30 hours on 29 May are recorded in his book *High Adventure*: 'I waved Tenzing up to me. A few more whacks of the ice-axe, a few very weary steps, and we were on the summit of Everest.' Prince Philip later told the climbers that his most unforgettable experience was 'when I heard of the ascent of Everest on the day of the Coronation.' The question of who actually stepped on the summit first was answered by Tenzing in his biography *Man of Everest*: 'The rope that joined us was 30 feet long, but I held most of it in loops in my hand, so that there was only about six feet between us . . . We went on slowly, steadily. And then we were there. Hillary stepped on top first. And I stepped up after him.' Hillary also noted: 'I didn't worry about getting Tenzing to take a photograph of me – as far as I knew he had never taken a photograph before and the summit of Everest was hardly the place to show him.' It was a beautiful day with a moderate wind.

Speaking in London at the Everest

[1] Named after Sir George Everest (1790–1866) formerly Surveyor-General of India.

HILLARY

Dinner given by members of both Houses of Parliament on 23 July 1953, Hillary revealed that his first words on getting to the top were: 'Well, I'm glad we've found it.' His first words to Lowe on coming down were: 'Well, we've knocked the bastard off!' He also revealed that Hillary and Tenzing felt very drunk in the last stages of the assault. The 'big black bottle' containing their last reserves of oxygen would not open because Lowe, who had brought it up, had gone down with the spanner in his pocket. Asked about the possibility of reaching the summit of Everest without oxygen Hillary has said: '. . . with a proper programme of acclimatization it should be possible to get men to the top and without oxygen. We might have to use gas for heavy work in setting up high-altitudes camps, but . . . two men – excused from the work of making camp – could succeed.'

The first human to ascend the world's highest peak[1] (29,028 feet) is also reputed to be the world's greatest apiarist. Helena Rubinstein reported that she flew to New Zealand to consult Sir Edmund about royal jelly which she was investigating as a possible beauty preparation. Hillary advised: 'By all means, eat honey, Madame. You will derive much energy from it. But forget the myth of its rejuvenating or beautifying purposes. That's strictly for the bees. Not all the apiarists in New Zealand could produce more than a few pounds of royal jelly in a year, and you would need tons of it to supply a mass market with an effective cream.'

Asked what he would do about the 'Abominable Snowman', Hillary said in 1960: 'My personal inclination would be to let the creature go. I think there is precious little in civilization to appeal to a Yeti, anyway.' Two years later, having made a Himalayan expedition with the express purpose of investigating the mysterious creature, he reported: 'Pleasant though they felt it would be to believe in the existence of the Yeti, when faced with the universal collapse of the main evidence in support of this creature the members of my expedition – doctors, scientists, zoologists, and mountaineers alike, could not in all conscience view it as more than a fascinating fairy tale . . .'

Sir Edmund has not been content to rest on past laurels. In 1957 he drove a tractor across the South Pole to meet Sir Vivian Fuchs, and in 1967 climbed Mount Herschel (11,000 feet) in Antarctica before trekking to the Pole once again. He has acted as consultant to a mail order firm in Chicago selling camping and outdoor equipment. More important, he has been responsible for the introduction of several new schools together with other benefits in Nepal, scene of his Himalayan conquest.

[1] By 1965 a total of 24 climbers, including Hillary and Tenzing, had conquered Everest.

103

Dame

Margo Fonteyn

Full name   Margot Fonteyn de Arias, née Margaret Hookham, DBE (1956). Changed her name to Margot Fontes (her mother's maiden name), then to Fonteyn.

Born   Sun. 18 May 1919 at Reigate, Surrey, England.

Characteristics   About 5′ 4″; about 112*lb*. (*8st.*); dark brown hair; brown eyes; nose altered to its present shape.

Married   1955 Dr Roberto Emilio Arias.

The greatest ballerina of her era born outside Russia, since 1954 President of the Royal Academy of Dancing, Dame Margot occupies a transcendent place in the world of ballet. Tamara Karsavina has spoken of her 'artistic logic' while Dame Ninette de Valois has testified that 'Everything about her is in complete proportion and such people have a very wide range of expression. Her talents are tremendously diffused.'

Margaret Hookham passed Grade I

One of Fonteyn's more scintillating roles with Nureyev has been in 'Le Corsaire' pas de deux.

One of Fonteyn's more scintillating roles with Nureyev has been in 'Le Corsaire' pas de deux.

from a dancing school at Ealing in London at the age of five, entered the Sadler's Wells Ballet School and made her debut as Snowflake in *Casse-Noisette* in 1934. She has acknowledged the influence of Alicia Markova in her career, and in perfecting such roles as that of *Giselle*, which she has said 'is a test part for ballerinas' she was helped enormously by her partnership with Robert Helpmann. 'He is such an innate person of the theatre that the experience of working with him proved invaluable.' Dancing with Helpmann during World War II, she did much to promote the popularity of the ballet in England.

Fonteyn, like all great artists, developed and refined her art through long and arduous discipline: 'I am sure if everyone knew how physically cruel dancing is, nobody would watch – only those people who enjoy bullfights.' The dancer she implies, must have a high level of contentment: '. . . the technique of ballet dancing is so exacting that it is almost impossible to give a really flawless performance, and slight mishaps – probably imperceptible to the onlooker – assume exaggerated importance in the mind of the artist when they occur.'

Though *Giselle* is a favourite with Fonteyn, she has a wide repertoire including the parts of Mazurka in *Les Sylphides*, Cygnet and Odette in *Le Lac des Cygnes*, Love in *Orpheus and Eurydice*, Ophelia in *Hamlet*, Swanilda in *Coppelia*, *The Sleeping Beauty*, *Cinderella*, the title role in *Sylvia* with Michael Somes, *The Firebird*, the Ballerina in *Petrouchka* and many others. She has toured the United States several times as well as many parts of Europe. She loves the classical roles: 'I think we in Sadlers Wells are very lucky to have the opportunity to dance the great ballets in their entirety.'

On the art of remembering a choreography she has said: 'I find it is the automatic association in one's mind of the movement with the music which makes it so easy to remember any number of ballets which may be in the repertoire at the same time.' In 1966 Fonteyn was seen in the space of two weeks dancing four separate roles – *Ondine*, *Cinderella*, *Giselle*, and *The Sleeping Beauty* – demonstrating

HM The Queen was present at a gala performance of 'Pelléas et Mélisande' at Covent Garden on 26 March 1969 marking Dame Margot's 35th anniversary with the Royal Ballet. Fonteyn and Nureyev danced the principal roles.

her incomparable range when in her 48th year.

Fonteyn's partnership with Rudolph Nureyev (*see page* 39) has been the leading box-office attraction in world ballet. She has said of Nureyev: 'I can still become fascinated if I catch sight out of the corner of my eye of the way in which Rudolf will place his foot on the stage.' Nureyev's tribute to Fonteyn distills the rare virtues seen in her miraculous artistry: 'There is an absolute musical quality in her beautiful body and phrasing. For me, she represents eternal youth. I have not met any dancer who has her femininity.'

Marriage to Dr Roberto Arias in 1955 gave rise to a significant change in Fonteyn's attitude to her work: 'I would give it all up if my husband asked me to,' she was quoted as saying. 'I have never been particularly dedicated, to tell you the truth. If you value your marriage you should put it before everything else.'

In 1964 Arias was attacked by a former political colleague after he had been elected to Panama's National Assembly. Four bullets struck him in the neck and spine. Though still gravely handicapped and confined to a wheelchair, Arias stood for the National Assembly in 1968 and won a seat. However he was forced into exile again early in 1969 and returned to London.

'Each good performance means the audience will come expecting a bit more next time. That's a tremendous responsibility. In the end it's like carrying the earth.'

REPERTOIRE

Apparitions
Le Baiser de la Fée
Ballet Impérial
Birthday Offering
Carnaval
Cinderella
Comus
Coppélia
Le Corsaire
Dante's Sonata
Daphnis and Chloe
Les Demoiselles de la Nuit
Don Juan
Don Quixote
The Entry of Madame Butterfly
Facade
The Fairy Queen
The Firebird
Giselle
Hamlet
The Haunted Ballroom
Homage to the Queen
Horoscope
The Judgement of Paris
The Lord of Burleigh
Mam'zelle Augot
Marguerite and Armand

Night Shadow
Nocturne
Nutcracker
Ondine
Orpheus and Eurydice
Paradise Lost
Pelléas et Mélisande
La Peri
Petrouchka
Pomona
The Quest
The Rake's Progress
Les Rendezvous
Rio Grande
Scènes de Ballet
Les Sirènes
The Sleeping Beauty
Le Spectre de la Rose
Swan Lake
Sylvia
Les Sylphides
Symphonic Variations
Three-Cornered Hat
Tiresias
The Wanderer
A Wedding Bouquet
The Wise Virgins

FILMS

Ondine (early 1960s)
An Evening with the Royal Ballet (1963)
Swan Lake (1967)
Romeo and Juliet (1966)
Margot Fonteyn (biographical film with Viktor Rona on TV) (1969)

'... the left hand must find its way unerringly

Yehudi Menuhi

ions and sub-divisions of a space which varies as does a slide-rule.'

On 25 Nov. 1927, an 11-year-old virtuoso made his debut at the Carnegie Hall with the New York Philharmonic Orchestra. Clad in velvet breeches and exercizing the practised authority of a soloist of four years' experience, he rendered a Beethoven sonata with a poise and maturity that sent the critics into raptures and reduced women in the audience to tears. But adulation was not new to him even then. When he was only seven a woman had come up to him after a concert at San Francisco, embraced him and gushed: 'You are better than Paganini – much, much better.' Calmly the boy wiped the kisses off his cheek and replied: 'Ah, so you have *heard* Paganini?'[1]

The precocity of genius, noted in many great musicians, was explained by Menuhin's father in terms of inner tranquillity: 'I believe ability or genius is but the absence of friction in the human organism.

[1] Niccoló Paganini (1782–1840) the Italian virtuoso. He published compositions so difficult that he alone could play them and astounded his audiences by his skill at playing on the fourth string only. In 1968 Menuhin became the first violinist since Paganini to be measured for Tussaud's waxworks, London.

Full name Yehudi Menuhin (Yehudi in Hebrew means 'the Jew').

Born Sat. 22 April 1916, New York, USA.

Characteristics About 5′ 7″; about 150lb. (10*st.* 10*lb.*); light brown hair; blue eyes.

Married
(1) 1938 Nola Nicholas (div. 1947) 1*s.* 1*d.*
(2) 1947 Diana Gould 2*s.*

There is nothing for Yehudi to overcome in his mastery of his violin.' Yehudi recalled that as a child he had 'no dreams of becoming a famous violinist, or even making music my career. I just played because I wanted to, because the music within me impelled me to.' He had announced his intention of taking up the violin on the eve of his fourth birthday. His teacher was Georges Enesco (1881–

109

1955) and he was influenced by Fritz Kreisler (1875–1962).

By 1929 Menuhin was on his travels touring Europe. Albert Einstein heard his Berlin debut and told him that his performance had proved to him that there was a God in heaven. George Bernard Shaw was compelled to reach a similar conclusion when Menuhin appeared in London in 1929: 'Listening to such an artist like Yehudi makes even an atheist believe in God.' At a banquet in Menuhin's honour at Leipzig in 1931 the Vice-President of the German Republic said: 'This is the very first time in my life, and I am sure in the lives of all those present, that we really and actually came into contact with God's greatest phenomenon of Nature, the greatest genius of music that probably ever lived on earth.'

In the 'thirties Menuhin continued to play his celestial music on tours of the United States, Germany, France, England, Italy, Austria, and Holland. In 1935–36 he went farther afield, visiting Australia, Africa, and Asia, giving 110 concerts in 63 cities in the space of 15 months. The strain made a short retirement necessary but during World War II he was again on his travels and his violin earned over $5,000,000 (£1,250,000) for various benefits. During his tour of India in 1952–53 he raised about £28,000 ($78,000) for famine relief. On that occasion he engaged in a head-standing contest with the Prime Minister, Jawaharlal Nehru, with Mrs Indira Gandhi (later to become Prime Minister) an interested onlooker. Nehru was adjudged the winner. Menuhin is a devotee of yoga and the head-stand occupies 15–20 minutes of his day. 'I find that this discipline of mind and body a great benefit both to my general health and to my mental outlook,' he has said. 'I am sure that if everyone were to practise these exercises of the wise men of the East, half of their troubles would be soothed away,

and they would become more carefree.'

Menuhin has expressed the opinion that the technique of playing the violin is more exacting than that of the piano: 'Not only does the violinist handle the strings at both ends, but the instrument itself must be held in a way that it at one and the same time firm and free. In order to select the notes, the left hand must find its way unerringly over divisions and sub-divisions of a space which varies as does a slide rule.' Apart from these intricacies the violinist must have a phenomenal memory and Menuhin's vast repertoire has given rise to compliments on his exceptional ability to retain music. He has admitted that he cannot be com-

pared with such people as Arturo Toscanini (1867–1957) who could memorize an entire symphonic score at a single reading. 'Musical memory', Menuhin has said, 'consists of several distinct kinds of retentiveness, not one of which is in itself miraculous, but does become so when reinforced by the other kinds. They are the memory of the mind, the eye, and the fingers.' He also has the memory to speak or write eight languages.

Menuhin has several valuable violins. The best known is probably the 'Prince Khevenhueller' which was made by Antonio Stradivari when at the height of his powers, aged about 90, in 1733. A wealthy American, who had paid $60,000 (£15,000) for it in 1928, gave it to Menuhin. It is now estimated to be worth very much more. Another of his violins was made by Joseph del Guarnieri in 1742.

In 1944 the famous composer, Bela Bartok (1881–1945), dedicated a violin sonata to him. When Menuhin played it Bartok said: 'I thought music was played like that long after the composer was dead.' Since 1944 the Maestro has crossed the Atlantic well over 50 times and on 13 Dec. 1967 he appeared at the Menuhin Gala Concert in New York celebrating the 40th anniversary of his boyhood debut there.

LP RECORDINGS

(Releases March 1966–June 1969)

Bach: *Concerto for Flute, Violin, Harpsichord, and Strings*
(HMV ASD2267/ALP2267)
Bach: *Violin Concerti in A Minor and E; 2-Violin Concerto*
(HMV ASD346/ALP1760)
Bartok: *Concerto for Violin and Orchestra No. 2*
(HMV ASD2281/ALP2281)
Bartok: *Rhapsodies Nos. 1 and 2* (HMV ASD2449)
Beethoven: *Violin Concerto in D Major*
(HMV ASD264/ALP1568)
Beethoven: *Romances* (HMV ASD618/ALP1070)
Beethoven: *Concerto for Violin and Orchestra in D*
(HMV ASD2285/ALP2285)
Beethoven: *Piano Trio No. 4 in D* (HMV ASD2259/ALP2259)
Berg: *Violin Concerto* (HMV ASD2449)
Berlioz: *Romance, Reverie, et Caprice*
(HMV ASD618/ALP2070)
Brahms: *Horn Trio in E Flat* (HMV ASD2354)
Bruch: *Violin Concerto No. 1* (HMV ASD334/ALP1669)
Chausson: *Poeme* (HMV ASD618/ALP1070)
Elgar: *Violin Concerto* (HMV ASD2259/ALP2259)
Enesco: *Sonata No. 3; Indian Music* (HMV ASD2294)
Handel: *Concertos for Oboe and Strings Nos. 1, 2, and 3*
(HMV ASD500/ALP1949)
Handel: *Concerti Grossi* (World Record Club T817)
Handel: *Organ Concertos Nos. 1, 13, and 14* (HMV ASD2352)
Handel: *Organ Concertos Nos. 4, 6, 8, and 10* (HMV ASD2443)
Lalo: *Symphonie Espagnole* (HMV ASD290/ALP1571)
Mendelssohn: *Violin Concerto* (HMV ASD334/ALP1669)
Miscellaneous: *Excerpts from various recordings since 1931*
(HMV HQM1018)
Miscellaneous: *Instruments of the Orchestra* (instructional)
(HMV SMF2092)
Mozart: *Sinfonia Concertante* (HMV ASD567/ALP2017)
Mozart: *Violin Concertos Nos. 3 and 5*
(HMV ASD473/ALP1905)
Nielsen: *Concerto for Violin and Orchestra*
(Music for Pleasure MFP2079)
Purcell: *Trio Sonatas 1, 6, 8; Pavan in C Minor; Fantasias 1, 4, 5, 8; Fantasia on One Note* (HMV ASD635/ALP2088)
Saint-Saens: *Introduction and Rondo Capriccioso*
(HMV ASD290/ALP1571)
Schubert: *Symphonies Nos. 1 and 3* (HMV ASD2426)
Schubert: *Symphonies Nos. 4 and 5* (HMV ASD2478)
Wieniawski: *Legende* (HMV ASD618/ALP1070)

Yehudi Menuhin at rehearsal for his 50th Birthday Concert at the Royal Festival Hall in 1967 with his sisters, Yaltah and Hephzibah, and his son, Jeremy, who made his debut as a concert pianist on that occasion.

111

HAROLD WILSON

Full name James Harold Wilson, OBE (1945), (PC 1947).

Born Sat. 11 March 1916 at 4 Warneford Road, Linthwaite, Huddersfield, Yorkshire, England.

Characteristics About 5′ 9″; compact physique, tending to portliness; pale blue eyes; fined £2 ($8) for speeding in 1948 and gave up cigarettes for a pipe that year; shaved off his moustache in 1950.

Married 1940 Gladys Mary Baldwin 2s.

One of the tenser exchanges overheard in the Corridors of Power during the month of April 1954 – a piece of verbal mayhem not, of course, recorded in *Hansard* – occurred following the resignation from the Shadow Cabinet of the left-wing Member for Ebbw Vale, Aneurin 'Nye' Bevan (1897–1960). Under the rules, the vacancy was due to be filled by Harold Wilson, runner-up in the ballot held at the beginning of the session. But since Wilson, hitherto regarded as a 'Bevanite', did not wish to accept without Bevan's approval, the matter was referred for consultation and it fell to Richard Crossman, later to join the Cabinet in Wilson's Government, to act as intermediary. When Crossman approached Bevan for his formal nod, the answer, contrary to some if not all expectations, was an emphatic negative. According to Hugh (later Lord) Dalton[1] (1887–1962), himself a former Labour Chancellor of the Exchequer, the conversation went something like this. Crossman: 'So you regard Harold as expendable?' Bevan: 'Yes, and you too.' Wilson himself rounded off the proceedings in a subsequent comment, declaring that he was never a 'Bevanite' and that there was never really such a thing as 'Bevanism'. Fate further confounded the terse predictions of 1954, for the untimely deaths both of Bevan and of Hugh Gaitskell (1906–63), whom Lord Attlee said 'would have made a very good Prime Minister', smoothed the path to Leadership of the Labour Party of a man primarily known as an astute economist, or in the plainer jargon of the percipient Bevan: '. . . all bloody facts, no bloody vision.'

Discarding his earliest ambition to be an undertaker, the boy who at 48 was to become the youngest Premier since Lord Rosebery[2], first trod the road to Westminster at the tender age of eight. Taken to London for the day in the sidecar of his father's motorcycle, he had tea in the ABC cafe near Westminster Bridge, paid three pence to squint through a pavement telescope at the House of Commons, and was snapped by his proud parent on the steps of his future official residence at 10 Downing Street.

At university Wilson was well compensated for his failure to win an athletics 'blue'. As a graduate of Jesus College, Oxford, loaded with donnish honours, he applied for deferment at age 23 from service in the armed forces in World War II to be appointed Director of Economics and Statistics at the Ministry of Fuel and Power. His diligence was recognized by the award of a Civil OBE and in 1948 he was promoted to the Front Bench as President of the Board of Trade in Clement Attlee's Government. At 31 he was the youngest Cabinet Minister of the century.

Once rated by Sir William Beveridge[3] the ablest research student he ever had, Wilson brought vestiges of optimism to his view of the economic scene. 'Against the background of world economics', he predicted in the House of Commons on 20 Oct. 1949, 'the development of Commonwealth territories might in 10 or 15 years, prove to be the most important event of the present century. Given time, it might well revolutionize the world economic position and balance of trade.'

In Opposition his combative energy was displayed in vigorous bouts of infighting as when he castigated Duncan Sandys over the Blue Streak missile

---

[1] Dalton wrote in his memoirs: 'Some Pressmen claimed to have heard me describe him (Wilson) as "Nye's little dog".' The epithet was revived on 2 March 1967 when Wilson, as Prime Minister, rebuked left-wing rebels at a private meeting of the Parliamentary Labour Party saying: 'A dog is allowed one bite. After that a dog becomes vicious and there is more than the possibility that the licence will not be renewed.'

[2] 5th Earl of Rosebery (1847-1929), Liberal Prime Minister (1894-95).

[3] Sir William Henry (later Lord) Beveridge (1879-1963), author of *Social Insurance and Allied Services* (1942), known as the 'Beveridge Report', which was the blueprint of the Welfare State promulgated by the 1945 Labour Government under Clement Attlee.

A future Prime Minister of England posed on the doorstep of 10 Downing Street in 1925. In residence next door at the time was Winston Churchill, Chancellor of the Exchequer.

project: 'We all know why Blue Streak was kept on. It was to save the Minister of Defence's face. We are, in fact, looking at the most expensive face in history. Helen of Troy's face, it is true, launched a thousand ships, but at least they were operational.' The interplay of verbal missiles between Wilson and Prime Minister Harold Macmillan reached a frenzied pitch in July 1961 when Wilson accused Mac of 'degrading, debasing, and debauching our national life by preaching a gospel of free-for-all . . .' But the Tory Harold's disarming humour evened the score. He blandly dispelled a persistent rumour that the Member for Huyton had been so poor as a boy that he went to school without any boots. 'If Harold Wilson ever went to school without any boots', murmured Mac, 'it was only because he was too big for them.'

Aneurin Bevan had once predicted: 'If I were to make all the flamboyant speeches and Harold were to ask all the questions we would have Churchill out in a month.' More than a decade of Tory rule later, the 46th (and 3rd Labour[1]) Prime Minister took office on 16 Oct. 1964, displacing Macmillan's successor, Sir Alec Douglas-Home. A man of simple tastes – 'I must be the only Prime Minister who cleans his own shoes' – he lunched for the first time at Downing Street on fish fingers, cooked according to the instructions set out on the frozen food package which was delivered to Whitehall by official limousine. The new Premier professed an unconcern

for outward signs which did not tally with the pipe-smoking image he sedulously cultivated in public: 'I am one of those old-fashioned people who believe that the last word on the question of image is that which every man learns each morning in front of the shaving mirror.' He had, none the less, to suffer the embarrassment of hearing himself identified more than once by tongue-tied speakers at functions as: 'The Prime Minister, the Right Honourable Harold Macmillan.'

From the very outset a vociferous antagonist of Britain's application to join the European Economic Community, first announced by Macmillan on 31 July 1961, Wilson in power about-faced to the view that membership was a priority yet failed in successive attempts to gain admission to the Common Market. On other matters of high policy he proved equally ambivalent. In Opposition his cry had been that Britain's premature withdrawal from South-East Asia was 'the surest prescription for a nuclear holocaust'. On his visit to America in July 1966 he emphasized: 'We have a world role to play both in foreign policy and defence. We will not turn ourselves into little Englanders or even little Europeans.' But this stance was abruptly reversed in 1967 when Wilson stated that Britain no longer had any special relationship with the United States. His Eastern promise lapsed in January 1968

[1] The two previous Labour Prime Ministers were James Ramsey Macdonald (1866-1937), Prime Minister (1924 and 1931-35 Coalition), and Clement Attlee (1883-1967) Prime Minister (1945-1951)

when the withdrawal of British forces East of Suez was brought forward by four years to 1971.

Wilson's plans for a dynamic economy rested heavily on repeated assurances, the latest by Lord Chalfont on 17 Nov. 1967, that devaluation was no remedy for the nation's economic ills. On 18 Nov. 1967 Wilson announced devaluation of the £ sterling by 14.3 per cent to $2.40. It was the third devaluation in three Labour Governments.[1] The Tory view of Labour was expressed by Sir Alec Douglas-Home who said: 'On the record of promise and performance, no one can any longer believe anything that the Prime Minister or his Ministers say.' The Labour perspective was epitomized by Richard Crossman who described devaluation and East of Suez withdrawal as 'giant strides towards the historic mission of British Socialism'.

The Labour Government's standing reached an even deeper abyss with the resignation of Wilson's Deputy, Foreign Secretary George Brown, on 15 March 1968 because of 'the way this Government is run and the manner in which we reach our decisions'. A Gallup Poll in May 1968 found that Wilson's popularity was at a lower level than that of Neville Chamberlain[2] in 1940.

About Freddie Trueman, the England Test cricketer: 'the greatest living York-

[1] Ramsey Macdonald took the £ off the gold standard in 1931; Clement Attlee devalued the £ from $4.03 to $2.80 in 1949.
[2] Arthur Neville Chamberlain (1869-1940), Prime Minister (1937-40).

shireman . . . When I'm at the dispatch box I pray to send them down as fast and straight as Freddie Trueman.'

At an election meeting in Slough in 1966 a schoolboy hit Wilson in the eye with a stink bomb. Remarked the Premier: 'With that aim he should be in the England cricket team, but he should stick to a cricket ball.'

'I do feel that morality is too often judged purely in terms of personal morality. Actions or inactions that lead to mass unemployment and poverty are much more criminal than personal weakness, for example in the field of drink or even of sex.'

'Every individual is responsible to himself and to his Maker for what he is, and at the end of the day one has got to hope that his Maker either doesn't read the whole of the British national Press, or, if he does, that he's fairly generous in his interpretation.' (1969)

Mr Wilson alluded in a speech on 10 March 1969 to 'the divine doctrine that all men were created equal . . .' No Biblical source exists for this belief which probably originated in the writings of Jean-Jacques Rousseau (1712-78) who wrote in his *Du Contrat Social* that 'all men were born free and equal'. Another possible source is the original draft for the American *Declaration of Independence* by Thomas Jefferson (1743-1826): 'We hold these truths to be sacred and undeniable; that all men are created equal and independent . . .'

Left:
The Queen receiving the Prime Minister, on one of his routine visits, in the Audience Room at Buckingham Palace.

Right:
A hypothetical vote for the Premier from Beatle John Lennon at the Variety Club of Great Britain Show Business Awards luncheon in 1964. George Harrison stood by.

115

Harold

IMPORTANT ACTS OF THE WILSON ADMINISTRATION

DATE EFFECTIVE	LEGISLATION
31 July 1964	Zambia (formerly Northern Rhodesia) Independence Act.
9 Nov. 1965	Murder (Abolition of the Death Penalty) Act.[1]
8 Dec. 1965	Race Relations Act.
17 Dec. 1965	Gambia Independence Act.
26 May 1966	Guyana (formerly British Guiana) Independence Act.
12 Aug. 1966	Prices and Incomes Act.
30 Sept. 1966	Botswana Independence Act (formerly Bechuanaland).
4 Oct. 1966	Lesotho Independence Act. (formerly Basutoland)
30 Nov. 1966	Barbados Independence Act.
28 Jan. 1967	NHS Family Planning Act.
16 Feb. 1967	West Indies Act.
23 March 1967	Road Safety Act ('Breathalyser').
14 July 1967	Prices and Incomes Act.
July 1967	Decimal Currency Act (effective 15 Feb. 1971).
27 July 1967	Sexual Offences Act ('Consenting Males').
27 Oct. 1967	Abortion Act[2].
29 Feb. 1968	Mauritius Independence Act.
8 March 1968	Commonwealth Immigrants Act.
27 April 1968	Abortion Act.
26 July 1968	Swaziland Independence Act.
26 July 1968	Finance Act (including 103 per cent tax on 'unearned' income).
27 Oct. 1968	British Standard Time Act.
1 April 1969	Pensions (Increase) Act.

[1] According to Home Office figures released on 22 Feb. 1969 there were 53 murders in the three years before suspension. In the three years following suspension there were 120 murders for which the death penalty would previously have been applied.

[2] Up to April 1969 about 35,000 abortions had been performed under this act in Britain of which about 21,000 were carried out under the NHS.

The Prime Minister's Salary

Year	£	$
Pre-1920	MP's salary only (£400)	
1920	5,000	20,000
1937	10,000[1]	40,000
1957	10,750[1]	30,100
1964	14,000[1]	39,200

Wilson told the House of Commons on 14 July 1969 that his salary of £14,000 was now worth £11,970 ($28,728), a $14\frac{1}{2}$ per cent depreciation.

[1] £4,000 allowable as expenses. Also £750 deductible as expenses on salary as an MP.

FRANK SINATRA

*Frank Sinatra: 'There are so many people to thank along the way –
song writers, directors, conductors, arrangers, musicians . . . if you
can't make it with that kind of help, you've gotta be real stupid.'*

Full name Francis Albert Sinatra.

Born Sun. 12 Dec. 1915, 414 Monroe Street,
Hoboken, New Jersey, USA.

Characteristics About 5′ 7″; about 138lb.
(9st. 12lb.); dark brown hair (owns about 60
hairpieces); blue eyes; scars at left side of
neck due to forceps delivery at birth; rejected
for military service due to a hole in his left ear
drum.

Married (1) 1939 Nancy Barbato (div. 1951[1])
1s. 2d.; (2) 1951 Ava Gardner (div. 1957);
(3) 1966 Mia Farrow (div. 1968).

[1] Under the divorce settlement the first Mrs Sinatra got custody of
the three children, one-third of his income up to $50,000
(£17,857) a year and ten per cent thereafter.

It is said that Sammy Davis Jr. once made casual reference to the fact that there were only two boys left who were not the boy next door – Cary Grant and Frank Sinatra. The boy named second has plainly come a long way to earn the Davis hallmark of exclusivity. He once delivered newspapers for the *Jersey Observer* and according to Bing Crosby was so weedy as a child that 'when he went to school he didn't dare turn sideways for fear that teacher would mark him absent'. Bob Hope confirmed this when he alluded to Sinatra as 'my favourite three-iron'. But spare physique did not prevent the lad from Hoboken from heavyweight stature in the world of show business and industry. Sometime owner of a private airline, film company, record business, radio stations and missile parts firm, he engages a personal staff of over 75 and earns an estimated income from all sources of between three and four million dollars a year. His holdings in Warner Brothers-Seven Arts and Reprise Records were sold in 1969 for $30,000,000 (£12,500,000). His homes in Palm Springs, New York, Miami, Paris, and London ensure that on his travels he can usually dispense with hotel reservations.

The voice upon which all this was built was the product of overtime dedication. He has recalled that to make his voice work in the same ways as a trombone or violin – playing the voice like those instruments – he tried to develop extraordinary breath control. 'I began swimming every chance I got . . . I worked out on the track – running one lap, trotting the next.' Always he paid meticulous attention to detail: 'I used to listen to Jascha Heifetz a great deal, and the way he phrased affected my thinking. I found that sustaining the voice in song can be likened to the way Heifetz uses the bow, the way he draws across the strings.'

Sinatra earned his first break as a crooner with the Harry James orchestra at $75 (£19) a week in 1939. Shortly after, he went over to Tommy Dorsey at double the salary and was the vocalist on the million-selling Dorsey disc *There are Such Things* (1942). This number was later selected for the million-selling LP album *60 Years of Music America Loves Best* (1959). Frankie became the idol of the bobby-soxers, one of whom was in the habit of rushing into restaurants where he had eaten his breakfast in order to bolt down the remains of his cereal.

Sinatra's success in the record business can be measured in terms of a pile of discs over 35 miles high. 'There are so many people to thank along the way – song writers, directors, conductors, arrangers, musicians . . . If you can't make it with that kind of help, you've gotta be real stupid,' he has declared. In recording sessions, he is acutely conscientious about his product: 'Somewhere in my subconscious there is the constant alarm that rings, telling me that what we're putting on tape is going to be around for a lotta, lotta years.' Nelson Riddle, who provided the backing for many of his hit numbers, has confirmed that 'He's stimulating to work with. You have to be right on your mettle all the time.' Gina Lollobrigida saw him as a once-and-for-all artist: 'He is fantastic; he likes to do everything right first time. One take – and that's it, even with his singing. He sings a song once, and that is the end of it.'

Sinatra made his film debut with Tommy Dorsey in *Las Vegas Nights* (1941). In 1953 he won an 'Oscar' for his supporting role in 'From Here to Eternity. Grace Kelly, who starred with him in *High Society*, reported that 'Frank has a sweetness and charm as a person and actor which is very endearing'. Sophia Loren, who met him on the set of *The Pride and the Passion*, said that she 'detected no sign of the supposedly hardened woman-

Sinatra's third wife was born Maria Farrow on 10 Jan. 1945, the daughter of actress Maureen O'Sullivan. Mia has fair hair, blue eyes, and is about 5' 5½" and 7st. or 98lb. In Oct. 1969 it was reported that she was expecting a baby by conductor Andre Previn.

FRANK

chaser, the flighty egomaniac, the bad-tempered bully'.

Sinatra divorced and was divorced by his first wife, Nancy, and followed this with a stormy marriage to Ava Gardner who claimed: 'All I ever got out of any of my marriages was the two years Artie Shaw financed on the analyst's couch.' But he is reported to maintain a tranquil rapport with both his ex-wives. 'I'm supposed to have a PhD on the subject of women, but the truth is I've flunked more often than not. I'm very fond of women: I admire women. But like all men, I don't understand them.' That was his 1965 perspective, a year before he married his third wife, Mia Farrow (*see picture at left*), who quit her $2,800 (£1,000) a-week job in the TV series *Peyton Place* to get her hair cut by his barber and marry him. Said Mia: 'When I met Frank on the set of his film *Von Ryan's Express* I had not heard one of his records: you don't get much chance to listen to the radio in a convent. We were just in love.' She was to divorce him 25 months later, denying that he had made a $1,000,000 (£416,666) settlement in her favour.

Sinatra has been described as living a full day, and often, night: 'I'm for anything that gets you through the night, be it prayer, tranquilizers, or a bottle of Jack Daniel.' Generous to profusion, he discarded a habit of giving away $250 cigarette lighters in favour of $1,000 wristwatches. But beyond mere personal extravagance, he has exerted himself in various good causes. His world tour in 1961 raised over $1,000,000 (£357,000) for children's charities. He has been generous, too, to others in his profession and once rated Tony Bennett 'the best singer in the business, the best exponent of a song'.

Bing Crosby observed of Sinatra: 'If he likes you he'll do anything for you, but if he doesn't he can be the most ornery cuss you've ever known.' Nancy Sinatra, the subject of his early hit number *Nancy with the Laughing Face* (1944), had the last word on Daddy when she said: 'He's better than anybody else, or at least they think he is, and he has to live up to it.' But living up to it does not include suffering intrusion, as people have been reminded when arriving at one of his homes. A sign outside the door says: 'If you haven't been invited, you better have a damn good reason for ringing this bell.'

FILMS

1941	*Las Vegas Nights*
1942	*Ship Ahoy*
1943	*Reveille With Beverly*
1944	*Higher and Higher*
1944	*Step Lively*
1945	*Anchors Aweigh*
1945	*The House I Live In*
1946	*Till the Clouds Roll By*
1947	*It Happened in Brooklyn*
1948	*The Kissing Bandit*
1948	*The Miracle of the Bells*
1949	*Take Me Out to the Ball Game (Everybody's Cheering)*
1949	*On the Town*
1951	*Double Dynamite*
1952	*Meet Danny Wilson*
1953	*From Here to Eternity*
1954	*Suddenly*
1955	*Young at Heart*
1955	*Not As a Stranger*
1955	*Guys and Dolls*
1955	*The Tender Trap*
1956	*The Man With the Golden Arm*
1956	*High Society*
1956	*Johnny Concho*
1957	*The Joker is Wild*
1957	*The Pride and the Passion*
1957	*Pal Joey*
1958	*Kings Go Forth*
1959	*Some Came Running*
1959	*A Hole in the Head*
1959	*Never So Few*
1960	*Can-Can*
1960	*Oceans 11*
1960	*Pepe*
1961	*The Devil at Four O'Clock*
1962	*Sergeants Three*
1962	*The Manchurian Candidate*
1963	*Come Blow Your Horn*
1963	*Four for Texas*
1964	*Robin and the Seven Hoods*
1965	*None but the Brave*
1965	*Von Ryan's Express*
1965	*Marriage on the Rocks*
1966	*Cast a Giant Shadow*
1966	*Assault on a Queen*
1967	*The Naked Runner*
1967	*Tony Rome*
1968	*The Detective*
1969	*The Lady in Cement*
1970	*Amigos*

Nancy Sandra Sinatra (born 8 June 1940) became a top recording star with the golden disc 'These Boots Are Made for Walkin'' (1966). In 1968 she filed a $3,500,000 (about £1,458,000) law suit against the Goodyear Tyre and Rubber Company for allegedly adapting the number for a TV commercial.

LP RECORDINGS
CAPITOL LABEL

High Society (sound track) (LCT6116/SLCT6116)
Songs for Swingin' Lovers (LCT6106/TA-W-653)
This is Sinatra (LCT6123)
A Swingin' Affair (LCT6154)
A Jolly Christmas from Frank Sinatra (LCT6168)
Come Fly With Me (LCT6154)
Swing Easy (W587)
Nice 'N Easy (W1417/SW1417)
Sinatra's Swingin' Session (W1491/SW1491)
Come Swing With Me (W1594/SW1594)
London by Night (T20389)
Point of No Return (W1676/SW1676)
The Great Years, Volume 1 (W1-1762) Pocket Album
The Great Years, Volume 2 (W2-1762) sold as one
The Great Years, Volume 3 (W3-1762) package.
My Funny Valentine (T10577)
The Connoisseurs' Sinatra (T20734/TA-T20734)
Sinatra for the Sophisticated (T20757)
The Movie Songs (T2700/ST2700)
The Best of Frank Sinatra (T21140/ST21140)

OTHER LABELS

Frank Sinatra's Greatest Hits – The Early Years (2 LPs) (CBS BPG66201)
Frank Sinatra (Reprise RLP1022/RSLP1022)
Romantic Songs from the Early Years (Hallmark HM500)
Have Yourself a Merry Little Christmas (Hallmark HM521)
Frank Sinatra's Greatest Hits (Reprise RLP1025/RSLP1025)
Essential Frank Sinatra (3 Records) (Polydor-International 63172/3/4)
Francis A. Sinatra and Edward K. Ellington (Reprise RLP1024/RSLP1024)
Something Stupid (with Nancy Sinatra) (Reprise rep30082)
Cycles (Reprise RLP1027/RSLP1027)
My Way (Reprise RLP1029/RSLP1029)
When Your Lover Has Gone (World Record Club T611)
September Song (World Record Club T635)
Love and Things (World Record Club T706)
No One Cares (World Record Club T868)
Sunday and Every Day (Music for Pleasure MFP1324)
A Man Alone (Reprise RLP1030/RSLP1030)

Rex Harrison

Full name Reginald Carey Harrison.

Born Thurs. 5 March 1908, Liverpool, England.

Characteristics About 6′ 1″; about 168*lb.* (12*st.*); dark brown hair; blue eyes; wears a hairpiece.

Married (1) 1934 Collette Thomas (div.) 1*s.*; (2) 1943 Lilli Palmer (div. 1957) 1*s.*; (3) 1957 Kay Kendall (died 1959); (4) 1962 Rachel Roberts.

Visitors to the enchanting village of Portofino on the Gulf of Genoa can tell at a glance when the local mandarin is in residence. They can also discern that he is not an Italian. For except when his wife has boldly hoisted the red dragon of Wales, the flag of St George flutters expatriotically over the home of Rex Harrison.[1] It is a refinement worthy of a man who has earned the approbation of Noël Coward himself: 'After *me*, dear boy, you're the best light comedian in the world.' Harrison may not, in fact, have seriously contributed to the myth which caricatured the English as dressing immaculately for dinner to the beat of native tomtoms in the equatorial jungle. But he has never failed to live up to the criterion of his second wife, Lilli Palmer: 'He's a man's man, an Englishman.'

What constitutes an 'Englishman' is a matter Englishmen have sedulously refrained from specifying, preferring to allow the onlooker to form his own unprejudiced conclusion. Some years before Rex Harrison was born, H. H. Asquith[2] composed his celebrated aphorism about 'a tranquil consciousness of effortless superiority'. He then referred exclusively to those educated, like himself, at Balliol College, Oxford. Harrison was educated at Liverpool but this does not preclude the use of words like 'tranquil' and 'effortless' about him. Even when he says or does very little, he says or does it very well indeed. Furthermore he is reported to have earned $1,000,000 (£416,666) a picture, which certainly suggests 'superiority'.

What he has termed a 'useful backlog' of experience was Rex's lot in provincial repertory from the 'twenties when he made his stage debut: 'That taught me how to pitch my voice and the need for timing.'

[1] Reports have not confirmed whether Harrison adheres to correct usage: the flag should be hoisted at dawn and lowered at sunset.

[2] Herbert Henry Asquith, 1st Earl of Oxford and Asquith, Liberal Prime Minister (1908-16).

Rex Harrison was urbanity itself when he talked to the rhinoceros in 'Dr Dolittle' (20th Century-Fox, 1968). One take of the film was ruined when the parrot screamed 'cut'.

It was uphill work and unrewarding but with charm, a monocle, and staying power he forged ahead. When World War II claimed his services as a radar instructor he was known as a seasoned though not distinguished stage and screen performer.

His American film debut in *Anna and the King of Siam* was Harrison's first real hit. Ineffably regal in the oriental manner as King Mongkut, he impressed the critics by stealing thunder from Anna played by Irene Dunne. 'I could leave Rex Harrison in England and become the King,' he remarked, effectively altering his speech, demeanour, and gait for the demanding role. Later when Yul Brynner played the King in the stage musical version of this story, Rex cabled magnanimously: 'The King is dead. Long live the King!'

With rising fame, Harrison was courted by the columnists but managed to arch their backs with the bland detachment that now became his hallmark. They paid him off in prose but failed to slow his progress. In *Anne of the Thousand Days* he gave them something to digest. Harrison was laid low by cramps and an X-ray revealed that his stomach, gnawed by tension, had contracted to the size of a man's fist. The truth was out, they gloated. The man was human after all!

In *My Fair Lady* England's man of manners climbed the peak of stage attainment. Among the first night audience Charles Laughton gushed his praise: 'In all my theatre experience I have seen only a handful of performances to match Rex's. He makes every man in the audience laugh at himself, and every woman laugh at the man beside her.' Stanley Holloway later wrote his tribute: 'As a performer I respect and admire Rex tremendously. I think he has few peers as a light comedian . . . I found it both a pleasure and a privilege to star with him.' With the award

of an 'Oscar' as best actor in the film version of *My Fair Lady* Harrison scaled another summit and records were established for attendances and LP disc sales (*see page* 48). The latter, incidentally, made Rex the first non-singer to produce a million-selling disc. His expertise in talk-singing was passed on to Richard Burton for his part in *Camelot*.

By now the name of Harrison was more than just a household word. His sister had married David Maxwell Fyfe, 1st Earl of Kilmuir, former Lord Chancellor of England. His son by Lilli Palmer, Noël Harrison, was twice a member of Great Britain's Olympic ski team (1952–56). He sang the ballad *Windmills of Your Mind* which won an 'Oscar' as Best Song in a 1968 motion picture; it was heard in *The Thomas Crown Affair*. Noël also starred in the popular TV series *The Girl from Uncle*. Rex's fourth wife, Rachel Roberts, was nominated for an 'Oscar' in the film *Saturday Night, Sunday Morning*. He met her in the play *Platonov*, where nightly she repeated words which surely found their mark: 'Smoke me to the end . . . like a cigarette.'

In recent years an Honorary Citizen of Portofino, entitled on occasion to wear the Mayoral chain, Harrison can view at ease his Villa San Genesio; his private vineyard; his orange, lemon, fig, and cherry trees; his Welsh wife; his English flag. The prospect might, in sum, evoke the question: 'What more, Oh King, can life possibly hold in store?' But life, it happened, had not exhausted all the possibilities. Wealth, fame, tranquillity were his yet still he lacked some special mark of exclusivity not enjoyed by other stars.

The occasion for his elevation came in 1968. Recording for posterity the names of people also present at the premiere of *Dr Dolittle*, a caption in *The Times* blandly noted: 'the Queen is introduced to Rex Harrison'.

Films

The School for Scandal
The Great Game
Get Your Man
All at Sea
School for Husbands
Men are not Gods
1936 Storm in a Teacup
1937 St Martin's Lane
1938 The Citadel
1939 Ten Days in Paris
      (Missing Ten Days)
1940 Sidewalks of London
1940 Night Train to Munich
      (Night Train)
1941 Major Barbara
1942 Continental Express
1944 Blithe Spirit
1944 I Live in Grosvenor Square
      (A Yank in London)
1945 The Rake's Progress
      (Notorious Gentleman)
1946 Anna and the King of Siam
1947 The Ghost and Mrs Muir
1947 The Foxes of Harrow
1948 Escape
1948 Unfaithfully Yours
1951 The Long Dark Hall
1952 The Four Poster
1954 King Richard and the Crusaders
1955 The Constant Husband
1958 The Reluctant Debutante
1960 Midnight Lace
1961 The Happy Thieves
1963 Cleopatra
1964 My Fair Lady
1965 The Yellow Rolls Royce
1965 The Agony and the Ecstasy
1967 Honey Pot
1967 Dr Dolittle
1968 A Flea in Her Ear
1969 The Battle of Britain
1969 Staircase
      The Right Honourable Gentleman
      (filming 1969)

Stage Appearances

1924	Thirty Minutes in a Street
1925–30	Charley's Aunt
1925–30	Potiphar's Wife
1925–30	Alibi
1925–30	The Chinese Bungalow
1925–30	A Cup of Kindness
1931	Getting George Married
1931	After All
1932	The Ninth Man
1932	Other Men's Wives
1932	For the Love of Mike
1933	Another Language
1933–34	Road House
1933–34	Mother of Pearl
1934	No Way Back
1934	Our Mutual Father
1934	Anthony and Anna
1935	Man of Yesterday
1935	Short Story
1935	Charity Begins
1936	Sweet Aloes
1936	Heroes Don't Care
1936–38	French Without Tears
1939	Design for Living
1940–41	No Time for Comedy
1948	Anne of the Thousand Days
1950	The Cocktail Party
1951	Bell, Book, and Candle
1952	Venus Observed
1953	The Love of Four Colonels
1956	My Fair Lady
1959	The Fighting Cock
1960	Platonov
1961	August for the People
1969	The Lionel Touch

LP Recordings

Much Ado About Nothing (Caedmon SRS-M-206)
My Fair Lady (Original New York cast) (CBS agg20023/5)
My Fair Lady (Drury Lane cast) (CBS BRG70005/SBRG70005)
Dr Dolittle (Stateside SL10214/SSL10214)

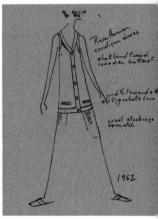

Above:
In 'Staircase' (20th Century-Fox, 1969), Harrison partnered Richard Burton in the role of a homosexual hairdresser. He was reported as saying: 'It really is the most satisfying thing I've ever done.'

Right:
Rex Harrison's penchant for cardigans inspired Mary Quant to design this mini-dress in 1962.

Full name Laurence Kerr Olivier, Kt (1947).

Born Wed. 22 May 1907, Dorking, Surrey, England.

Characteristics About 5′ 10½″; about 175*lb.* (12*st.* 7*lb.*); brown hair; blue eyes.

Married (1) 1930 Jill Esmond (div. 1940) 1*s.*; (2) 1940 Vivien Leigh (div. 1960, died 1967); (3) 1961 Joan Plowright 1*s.* 2*d.*

Of those equipped with both the memory and the authority to pronounce an opinion on the career of Britain's foremost man of the theatre, nobody is better placed than Noël Coward in whose play, *Private Lives*, Olivier acted in 1930. 'I believe Laurence Olivier to be the greatest actor of our time,' said Coward in a 1966 interview, adding: 'His greatness as a tragedian has been an accepted fact now for many years.' Just how many years is difficult to calculate but it is known that in 1917, when Olivier was just 10, Ellen Terry[1] said of him: 'The boy who plays the part of Brutus is already a great actor.' In the intervening half-century, Olivier's portrayal of characters from the plays of Shakespeare have formed the major, if not the only, aspect of his classic contribution to both stage and screen entertainment. His faith in Shakespeare is understandably complete: 'In an age of splintering values there is a steady public will to keep Shakespeare alive. The actors like to play Shakespeare because his is the most challenging drama. The directors want to produce him

In 'The Battle of Britain' (Spitfire Productions, 1969) Sir Laurence played Air Chief Marshal Sir Hugh (later Lord) Dowding, the first Commander-in-Chief of RAF Fighter Command.

[1] Dame Ellen Terry (1848-1928), one of the most famous Victorian actresses and an ancestress of Sir John Gielgud.

and the public believe in Shakespeare because he is part of their life.'

Olivier first played Shakespeare at Stratford-on-Avon in 1922 when, at the age of 15, he appeared as Katherine in *The Taming of the Shrew*. In the ensuing years his performances consistently inspired the warmest tributes, not only from Press and public, but from Olivier's most distinguished theatrical contemporaries. John Gielgud, who in 1935 alternated with him as Romeo and Mercutio in *Romeo and Juliet*, recalled: 'Larry had a great advantage over me in his commanding vitality, striking looks, brilliant humour, and passionate directness ... His love scenes were instantly real and tender, and his tragic gift profoundly touching.' Coward has described his Macbeth at Stratford as 'one of the greatest performances I ever saw on the stage,' while Sir Cedric Hardwicke thought that his Richard III and Oedipus are 'among the greatest performances I have seen'. Vivien Leigh said: 'I saw him about 15 times in *Hamlet* and thought "That's the greatest actor in the world." '

Part of his greatness has consisted in his versatility, which has enabled him to project himself with equal facility as Sir Toby Belch in *Twelfth Night*, as Iago in *Othello*, or as Archie Rice in *The Entertainer*. This capacity to master parts ranging from the tragic to the comic singles out Olivier as unique in the firmament of thespians. Noël Coward contrasted his Macbeth with his Mr

Puff in *The Critic* which, he said: 'was one of the most brilliant, light, soufflé performances that I have ever seen – incomparable technique.'

After a German film debut in *The Temporary Widow*, Olivier went to Hollywood and played in *Too Many Crooks* (1930). There was a brief setback when Greta Garbo rejected him as her co-star in *Queen Christina* (1933), but this was offset by a starring role opposite Gertrude Lawrence in *No Funny Business* (1933).

In films it was again Shakespeare who was to provide the finest vehicle for his talent. Cecil B. de Mille had contemplated casting Rufolf Valentino as Romeo in 1922 but abandoned the idea. 'The public had to wait for Sir Laurence Olivier', he wrote, 'before being ready for Shakespeare on the screen.' Olivier's first film Shakespeare was *As You Like It* (1937). In 1946 he played, produced, and directed *Henry V*, an achievement which won him the New York Film Critics Award. Then in 1948 his dazzling success in *Hamlet* secured him both the International Grand Prix and the coveted 'Oscar' as best actor. Other major citations to his name were the British Film Academy Award for *Richard III* (1956) and, in quite a different field, his 'Emmy' for the part of Strickland in Somerset Maugham's *The Moon and Sixpence* on American TV in 1960.

In discussing the craftmanship which goes into great theatre, Peter Ustinov has given an excellent sketch of the methods used by Olivier in preparing for the stage:

'He's a character actor with the face of a leading man. He sets up the externals for the role he is going to play, whatever it is – the kind of house such a man would live in, the kind of clothes he would wear, that sort of thing – and then he begins to work out the kind of man who would live that way. Also, he has a thing about noses. Along with everything else, he tries to figure out what kind of nose the character would have.'

With less relevance, but with intriguing perspicacity, Salvador Dali, who was once commissioned to paint Sir Laurence's portrait, observed his duality in a typical Dalian fantasy: 'He is two-faced, a split personality, an ideal subject to express the meteorology of the rhinoceros.'

'What you need in your make-up as an actor is observation, intuition. Put at its most high-falutin', the actor is important as the illuminator of the human heart – as important as the psychiatrist, or the doctor, or the minister if you like.'

Sir Laurence had emerged from a rapturously applauded performance of *Othello* and locked himself gloomily in his dressing room. Fellow actors asked him what was wrong: 'I know it was great, damn it,' he retorted, 'but I don't know how I did it so how can I do it again?'

STAGE APPEARANCES

Year	Play	Year	Play
1922	The Taming of the Shrew	1945	Henry IV, Part I (Old Vic)
1924	Byron	1945	Henry IV, Part II (Old Vic)
1925	Henry IV, Part II	1945	Oedipus Rex (Old Vic)
1925	Henry VIII	1945	The Critic (Old Vic)
1925	The Cenci	1945	Peer Gynt
1926–28	Something to Talk About	1945	Arms and the Man
1926–28	Uncle Vanya	1945	Richard III
1926–28	All's Well that Ends Well	1946	Oedipus Rex (NY)
1926–28	She Stoops to Conquer	1946	The Critic (NY)
1926–28	The Farmer's Wife	1946	Peer Gynt (NY)
1928	The Adding Machine	1946	Arms and the Man (NY)
1928	Macbeth	1946	Richard III (NY)
1928	Back to Methusaleh	1946	King Lear (Old Vic)
1928	Harold	1948	The School for Scandal
1928	Taming of the Shrew		(Old Vic) (Australia and NZ)
1928	Bird in Hand	1948	Richard III (Old Vic)
1928	Journey's End	1948	The Skin of our Teeth
1929	Beau Geste		(Old Vic)
1929	The Circle of Chalk	1949	Richard III (Old Vic)
1929	Paris Bound	1949	The School for Scandal
1929	The Stranger Within		(Old Vic) (Australia and NZ)
1929	Murder on the Second Floor	1949	Antigone (Old Vic)
1930	The Last Enemy	1950	Venus Observed
1930	After All	1951	Antony and Cleopatra
1930	Private Lives	1951	Caesar and Cleopatra (NY)
1931	Private Lives (NY)	1953	The Sleeping Prince
1933	Rats of Norway	1955	Macbeth (Stratford)
1933	The Green Bay Tree (NY)	1955	Titus Andronicus (Stratford)
1934	Biography	1955	Twelfth Night (Stratford)
1934	Queen of Scots	1957	The Entertainer
1934	Theatre Royal	1957	Titus Andronicus (Europe)
1935	Ringmaster	1958	The Entertainer (NY)
1935	Golden Arrow	1959	Coriolanus (Stratford)
1935	Romeo and Juliet	1960	Rhinoceros
1936	Bees on the Boatdeck	1960	Becket (NY)
1937	Hamlet (Old Vic)	1961	Becket (NY)
1937	Twelfth Night (Old Vic)	1962	Semi-Detached
1937	Henry V (Old Vic)	1962	Uncle Vanya
1937	Macbeth (Old Vic)	1962	The Broken Heart
1937	Hamlet (Elsinore) (Old Vic)	1963	The Recruiting Officer (National)
1938	Othello (Old Vic)	1963	Uncle Vanya (National)
1938	The King of Nowhere (Old Vic)	1964	The Master Builder (National)
1938	Coriolanus (Old Vic)	1964	Othello (National)
1939	No Time for Comedy (NY)	1965	Love for Love (National)
1940	Romeo and Juliet (NY)	1967	Dance of Death (National)
1944	Peer Gynt (Old Vic)	1969	Home and Beauty (National)
1944	Arms and the Man (Old Vic)	1970	The Merchant of Venice
1944	Richard III (Old Vic)		
1944	Uncle Vanya (Europe) (Old Vic)		

FILMS

Year	Film		Year	Film
1930	Too Many Crooks		1959	The Devil's Disciple
1931	Friends and Lovers		1960	The Entertainer
1932	Perfect Understanding		1960	Spartacus
1933	No Funny Business		1963	Term of Trial
1937	As You Like It		1965	Bunny Lake is Missing
1937	Fire Over England		1966	Othello
1938	The Divorce of Lady X		1967	Khartoum
1939	Wuthering Heights		1968	Romeo and Juliet, spoke prologue and epilogue only.
1939	Twenty-One Days			
1939	Q Planes		1969	Oh! What a Lovely War
1940	Rebecca		1969	The Shoes of the Fisherman
1940	Pride and Prejudice		1969	The Battle of Britain
1941	That Hamilton Woman (Lady Hamilton)		1969	Dance of Death
				David Copperfield (filming 1969)
1942	49th Parallel			Three Sisters (filming 1969)
1946	Henry V			
1948	Hamlet			**Television**
1952	The Beggar's Opera		1958	John Gabriel Borkman
1952	Carrie		1960	The Moon and Sixpence
1956	Richard III		1961	The Power and the Glory
1958	The Prince and the Showgirl		1963	Uncle Vanya

LP Recordings

Uncle Vanya (Philips AL3448–9)
Othello (Argo ZNF4/NF4)
Hamlet (RCA Victor RB16144)
Henry V (RCA Victor RB16144)
Homage to T. S. Eliot (HMV CLP1924)
Sir Laurence Olivier Reads from the Psalms (Music for Pleasure MFP1136)
Homage to Shakespeare (with others) (Argo ZNF4)

Olivier played a tight-lipped Soviet Premier in the film of Morris West's novel, 'The Shoes of the Fisherman' (MGM, 1968). Anthony Quinn played Kiril Lakota.

SALVADOR DALI

Full name Salvador Felipe Jacinto Dali.

Born Wed. 11 May 1904, Figueras, Upper Catalonia, Spain.

Characteristics About 5′ 10″; black hair; piercing dark eyes; reported in 1967 to be going bald, shaving off his moustache, and acquiring a wig.

Married 1935 Gala Elena Diaronoff.

Moustachios atwirl, the century's most controversial artist proclaimed in 1945: 'Since 1929 I have had a very clear consciousness of my genius, and I confess that this condition, ever more deeply rooted in my mind, has never excited in me emotions of the kind called sublime. Nevertheless, I must admit that it occasionally affords me an extremely pleasurable sensation.' Dali, on his own analysis, ranks fifth among the greatest artists of all time, after Jan Vermeer (1632–75), Sanzio Raphael (1483–1520), Diego Velasquez (1599–1660), and Leonardo da Vinci (1452–1519). With Picasso sixth on the list, the deduction that Dali deems himself the greatest of the last 300 years is inescapable. Picasso's comment on this order of precedence is not on record but he has been quoted as comparing Dali's mind with a 'ceaselessly turning outboard motor'.

Whatever the validity of his self-elevation among the immortals, there is no doubt that Dali always aimed high: 'At the age of six I wanted to be a cook. At seven I wanted to be Napoleon. And my ambition has been growing steadily ever since.' Educated at Barcelona and at the Academy of Fine Arts in Madrid, from which he was expelled, Dali was originally a Cubist,[1] then transferred his attention to Surrealism,[2] only to abandon it owing to its implied Marxism. He produced two Surrealist films, *Le Chien Andalou* (*The Andalusian Dog*) (1929) and *L'Age d'Or* (*The Golden Age*) (1931), the latter causing such a stir that it was closed down by Paris police. His first one-man show was mounted at Paris in 1929.

Dali's ideas always challenged the imagination of his audience even if they failed, at times, to grasp their trend: 'My whole ambition in the pictorial domain,' he has explained, 'is to materialize the images of concrete irrationality with the most imperialist fury of precision.' Probably his most important painting is *Christ of St John of the Cross*.

The man who once delivered a lecture on a hot summer's afternoon wearing a diver's suit, a dagger at his belt, carrying a billiard cue, and leading a pair of Russian wolf hounds, earned the respect of no less a thinker than Sigmund Freud: 'I was inclined to look upon Surrealists, who have apparently chosen me as their patron saint, as absolute . . . cranks. The young Spaniard, however, with his candid fanatical eyes and his undeniable technical mastery, has made me reconsider my opinion,' wrote Freud in 1938.

Dali's experiments in search of artistic truth have had a uniquely bizarre quality: 'I used to balance two broiled chops on my

[1] Cubism is a style of art in which objects are so represented as to give the effect of an assemblage of geometrical figures.
[2] Surrealism is a 20th century movement in art and literature expressing the subsonscious mind by means of images in sequences or associations such as may occur in dreams.

wife's shoulders, and then by observing the movement of tiny shadows produced by the accident of the meat on the flesh of the woman I love while the sun was setting, I was finally able to attain images sufficiently livid and appetizing for exhibition in New York.' A champion of fashion, Dali was never more creative than in his projected design for a shoe: 'Provided with certain elastic qualities, it will have the form of a rhineceros' horn and will correspond to both the biological and aesthetic needs to give women a new tremulous, airy gait.' His scheme for Helena Rubinstein's New York apartment – 'I will design a fountain spouting from a grand piano. It will hang from the ceiling and never be played' – singled him out as an interior decorator of rare taste, even if the idea was never actually accepted. More suitable was his enormous stuffed bear in shocking pink with drawers in its stomach which he offered to Elsa Schiaparelli. He proved discriminating in his choice of gifts for Mia Farrow, selecting an owl, some parts of a frog, and fragments of rock said to be from the moon. Questioned as to the authenticity of the 'moon matter', Mia said: 'I believe him. If he says so, it is true. Dali brought me out. He taught me the world is what you make of it.'

Dali's observations on political topics have not always commanded such ready credence. 'I cannot understand why toilet manufacturers do not put concealed bombs in the flushing compartments of their products which would explode the moment certain politicians pulled the chain,' was one distinctive proposal. Others were probably made in the years 1952–63 when the pages of his *Diary of a Genius* remained blank because: 'Democratic societies are unfit for the publication of such thunderous revelations as I am in the habit of making.' In the meantime, for the benefit of those still baffled by the under-lying implications of his published theories

he has offered this clue: 'The only difference between myself and a madman is that I am not mad. I am able to distinguish between the dream and the real world.'

'Life would be practically impossible on the globe if two or three hundred Dalis existed, but do not be frightened, this can never be!'

Asked about his work: 'I am a bad painter, but if it is compared with my contemporaries, it is of great quality. I am not good but they are worse.' (1966).

132

RICHARD M. NIXON

Full name Richard Milhous Nixon.

Born Thurs. 9 Jan. 1913, Yorba Linda, California, USA.

Characteristics About 5′ 11½″; about 175*lb.* (12*st.* 7*lb.*); brown hair and eyes; scar on left side of scalp from forehead to neck.

Married 1940 Thelma Catherine Patricia Ryan 2*d.*

Whatever Richard M. Nixon may achieve in power, it could already be said of him in 1969 that no President in United States history had closer brushes with destiny before finally assuming the supreme burden of office. Three times, in 1955, 1956, and 1957, the illness and near demise of Dwight D. Eisenhower made necessary the delegation of authority and posed the risk that Vice-President Nixon might have to take the Presidential oath. In each case he proved himself equal to the emergency, earning Ike's bouquet as 'the most valuable member of my team'. In 1960, as the Republican Presidential candidate, he came within an eyelash of the summit, carrying 26 States to John F. Kennedy's 23, but losing on a smaller total of electoral votes (303–220).

Richard M. Nixon held his first Press Conference as President in the White House on 27 Jan. 1969. He promised 'new approaches' in domestic policy and 'new directions and tactics' to settle problems in Vietnam and the Middle East.

Though some hinted that Ike's tardiness to declare himself was a factor in Nixon's defeat, others heaped the blame on the Soviet Premier, Nikita S. Khrushchev, who made the believe-it-or-not claim that it was his refusal to release the U-2 pilot, Gary

133

Powers, at Nixon's request which swung the ballot, costing Dick 200,000 votes. However, Khrushchev's attitude may have been influenced by the recollection, still recent in his mind, of Vice-President Nixon's visit to Moscow in 1959. The pair met at the US exhibition where, in a demonstration-model American home, they became involved in what became known as the 'kitchen debate', Khrushchev cutting a rather clumsy figure in the verbal exchanges.

There was no hesitation by Eisenhower in 1969. The old soldier had the satisfaction, within weeks of his death, of seeing his former understudy elected President on 5 Nov. 1969 with 43.6 per cent of the popular votes to Hubert H. Humphrey's 43.2 per cent. Nixon, who carried 32 States, took office on 20 Jan. 1969.

The 37th President[1] is of Irish ancestry. His mother, a Quaker, used the traditional 'thee' and 'thou' in conversation. Young Dick helped in his father's grocery store and petrol station during his college years at Whittier, California, before graduating with honours from Duke University Law School in 1937. In the same year he met his future wife, proposing to her the first time they met. She accepted three years later.

Nixon served as an aviation ground officer in the South Pacific during World War II and was demobilized with the rank of lieutenant-commander. Elected to the House of Representatives from California in 1946, he helped to draft the Taft-Hartley Labour Relations Act in 1947 and was co-author of the Mundt-Nixon Communist Control Bill in 1948, two years before winning election to the US Senate. He was a member of the House Un-American Activities Committee which secured the conviction of Alger Hiss. Always an advocate of the hard line against Communism, Nixon wrote in his book, *Six Crises* (1962), that those who represent the United States must recognize 'that we will be doomed to defeat in the world struggle unless we are willing to risk as much to defend freedom as the communists are willing to risk to destroy it'.

However, the capacity for compromise is not lacking in Nixon's make-up. He

134

has recalled with pride that in his early years in law practice he proved most skilful at the unlucrative work of reconciling petitioners for divorce. A visitor to 56 countries when Vice-President, and many more since then, he has declared himself to be a 'whole-worlder'. His policy on Vietnam called for a new diplomacy 'that looks past Vietnam to the prevention of future wars and to enlisting other nations more fully in their own defence'.

In domestic affairs Nixon has emphasized his resolve to uphold law and order: 'Dissent is a necessary ingredient of change, but in a system of government that provides for peaceful change, there is no cause which justifies resort to violence.' He has also confirmed that private enterprise is 'the greatest engine of progress ever developed in the history of man'.

'The first responsibility of leadership is to gain mastery over events, and to shape the future in the image of our hopes.'

[1] Actually the 36th President because Grover Cleveland was in office on two separate occasions (1885-89 and 1893-97) and is listed in works of reference as both the 22nd and 24th President.

President's Salary

Year	$	£
1789	25,000	6,250
1873	50,000	12,500
1906	50,000[1]	12,500
1909	75,000[1]	18,750
1948	75,000[2]	18,750
1949	100,000[3]	46,666
1969	200,000[3] [4]	83,333

[1] Plus $25,000 (£6,250) travelling expenses.
[2] Plus $40,000 (£10,000) travelling expenses.
[3] Plus $50,000 (£17,857) official expenses and $40,000 (£14,285) travelling expenses.
[4] Net salary after tax is about $78,000 (£32,500).

Aristotle Onassis

Full name Aristotle Socrates Onassis.

Born Sat. 20 Jan. 1906, Smyrna, now Izmir, Turkey[1].

Characteristics About 5′ 5″; steel grey hair; dark brown eyes; heavy smoker; suffers from insomnia.

Married
(1) 1946 Athina 'Tina' Livanos[2] (div. 1960) 1*s*. 1*d*.
(2) 1968 Mrs Jacqueline Kennedy.

[1] His passport records, erroneously, that he was born on 21 Sept. 1900 at Salonika, Greece.
[2] Married the Marquess of Blandford in 1961.

'If you haven't made a million by the time you're 21, you don't stand much of a chance of making the grade.' As a criterion of success, this one attributed to Aristotle Onassis might seem just too severe were it not for his own example which has proved that such miracles are not out of reach. Emigrating to the Argentine from his native Greece at the age of 16 with $250 (then about £62), he set himself a 21-hour working day for the first year. At night a telephonist, he built up a tobacco business by day which by the age of 23 had made him a dollar millionaire. Today his wealth

Onassis shook a leg at Venice in 1967. Shaking with him in a see-through dress was Gina Lollobrigida.

has been calculated to grow at the rate of about £2,000 ($4,800) an hour round the clock.

With immense industry, a working knowledge of seven languages, and unquenchable optimism, Onassis has displayed an uncanny instinct for grasping commercial opportunity as the pendulum of chance swings upward. One of his boldest enterprizes was the purchase in 1946 of 20 United States Government surplus oil tankers. This transaction cost him a fine of $7,000,000 (£2,500,000) because the best American legal brains had advised him his purchase was in keeping with the conditions of sale, namely that the vessels should be owned by an American company, but it transpired that his advice had been misguided. Moreover it happened that the lawyer on whose advice he had acted later became head of the US Department of Justice and prosecuted him for conspiracy. More trouble loomed, for an indemnity of $8,000,000 (£2,860,000) was payable in the event that Onassis failed to build more ships of equivalent tonnage to his original purchase, to be operated by American companies. As the demand for

137

tankers did not then justify such an outlay, Onassis agreed to pay the indemnity only to be offered instead by the US Government a loan of $14,000,000 (£5,000,000) to enable him to proceed with the programme of shipbuilding.

In 1954 Onassis acquired a 40 per cent interest in the Société des Bains de Mer at Monte Carlo which controlled the Casino, five hotels, and other properties in the principality of Monaco. His holding later increased to 520,000 of the million shares in the SBM for which he paid between seven and 14 shillings each. In 1963 the Monaco National Council turned down a price of £7 ($19.60) a share which he asked for the surrender of his controlling interest. In 1967 he parted with his stake in consideration of a reported payment of £3,000,000 ($8,400,000) and abandoned his hope of maintaining Monaco as a millionaire's playground. Said Prince Rainier of Monaco: 'I want a clientele of people from the upper middle class who have a holiday budget and who like to amuse and enjoy themselves.'

Onassis was said in 1968 to have an interest in 85 companies in 10 countries with an estimated value of about $500,000,000 (£283,333,333), a figure said to represent the insurance value of his merchant fleet of over 100 cargo ships and

tankers. He has homes in Paris, Athens, and Buenos Aires, and owns the 500-acre island Skorpiós off the Western coast of Greece which cost him about $3,000,000 (£1,071,000) in 1962 and which he has developed for a further outlay of that order. His private DC-6 84-seat airliner belongs to Olympic Airways in which he holds a concession not due to expire until 2006. His 1,700-ton yacht *Christina*, named after his daughter, has a crew of 50, eight speedboats, a five-seat amphibian aircraft, 42 telephone extensions, and a swimming pool. It was reported to be worth at least $5,000,000 (£2,833,333) in 1968. The vessel has provided Mediterranean holidays for many of his friends including Maria Callas, John F. Kennedy, and Sir Winston Churchill one of whose paintings, a gift to the shipping magnate, is on board *Christina* as is the priceless *Madonna and Angel* by El Greco.

Despite all this Onassis does not regard himself as a rich man without qualification. 'Mr Getty,' he has pointed out,' is in a rich man's business ... He produces oil and controls it from the source to the consumer. All I do is to carry it, like a man in the station who carries your luggage. I am a porter ...' On the Onassis bookshelf rests a book entitled *How to be Rich*. Its author is ... J. Paul Getty.

Onassis married Jackie Kennedy on 20 Oct. 1968 on his own island, Skorpios. His wedding present to her was a ruby and diamond ring with matching earrings reported to be worth about $1,200,000 (£500,000). Six months later he presented her with a villa near the Temple of Poseidon on the Aegean Sea, overlooking the Gulf of Salonika.

MARLENE DIETRICH

Full name Maria Magdalena von Losch Dietrich.

Born Tues. 27 Dec. 1904[1], Berlin, Germany.

Characteristics About 5′ 5″; about 120*lb.* (8*st.* 8*lb.*); bust 36″; waist 24″; hips 36″; red-golden hair; blue eyes.

Married 1924 Rudolf Sieber 1*d.*

[1] Some sources give 27 Oct. or 27 Nov. Others give the year of birth as 1900, 1901, or 1902.

Personifying most men's idea of sultry sex-appeal well into her sixties, the world's most glamorous grandmother is also possibly the most tactful: 'In general,' she has said, 'men are better people than women. They have stronger characters, better brains, and are not so muddled in their thinking.' Her advice to women is that they should never give so much of themselves as to bore men. 'It is the same with acting. Each man, or woman . . . should be able to find in the actress the thing he or she most desires and still be left with the promise that they will find something new and exciting every time they see her again.' Millions would testify that Miss Dietrich does as she says, nor would they quarrel with her claim: 'I give the audience what they want. In my case it is beauty.'

Marlene has said that: 'A film star's

Marlene gave the veterans glamour when she appeared at the 21st El Alamein reunion at the Royal Albert Hall in 1963.

139

career must necessarily be brief. It can only last as long as one's youth lasts, and one's youth fades quicker on the screen than on the stage.' Her own career has flown in the face of this rule. Her first important film, *The Blue Angel*, was released in Berlin in 1930. Of her early American films, *Morocco* with Gary Cooper, and *Blonde Venus* with Cary Grant were hits. After *Shanghai Express* she became Hollywood's highest paid actress at $125,000 (£31,250) a picture. In *Golden Earrings* with Ray Milland she showed herself to be far from faded at 45. In 1959 she signed a three-year contract for $2,000,000 (£714,000) by Revlon to talk about aids to beauty on TV.

Those who have met her in the flesh have been unanimous about the charms of Dietrich. Ernest Hemingway wrote: 'Even if she had only her voice she could break your heart. But she also has that beautiful body and that timeless loveliness of face.' Cecil Beaton observed: 'She is not very animated but the camera is somehow able to register every nuance of expression. Indeed, her face makes love to the camera, and she appears on film as one of the most striking women of our day.' And Maurice Chevalier, who had no reason to exaggerate, found her 'a woman of great intelligence and sensitivity, spiritual, kind, amusingly and charmingly unpredictable in her moods.'

A German by birth, Marlene emigrated to the US in 1930 and became an American citizen in 1934, resisting all attempts by Hitler to make her return to Nazi Germany. 'I sometimes wonder if I might have been the one person in the world who could have prevented the war and saved millions of lives,' she has said. 'It troubles me a lot, and I'll never stop worrying about it.' The anxieties of war surrounded her in a very personal way: 'Can anyone imagine the conflict one feels when one's own mother is hourly threat-

ened by American bombers, and still one has to hope the Germans will not win this war?' Her own contribution to victory, entertaining the troops, was rewarded with the Medal of Freedom, the US State Department's highest civilian award. 'But while one department of the government was giving me medals,' she later reported, 'another was suing me for back taxes.'

In cabaret, Miss Dietrich has been the apogee of night-club glamour. Three apparently transparent gowns, on which 15 seamstresses had worked for three months stitching in 600 rhinestones at a dollar apiece, created a furore in 1954. 'The news pictures of my Las Vegas dress were misleading,' she explained. 'It was not transparent; those flashbulb shots, they shoot right through the dress. They could shoot through a black sweater.' In 1948 she commented on a nude statue over a shop in New York. 'Sometimes I wonder about this American morality. That statue hasn't even got panties on, but if I so much as show the top of my stockings they slap me down? She has opined: 'Sex – in America an obsession. In other parts of the world a fact.'

Miss Dietrich is not at heart a career woman. 'I have no ambition,' she has claimed. 'I work because I need money. I wish I did not have to work. I lead a full life; not working would give me more time for it.' She has enlightened views on money: 'It *does* bring happiness, if used wisely, and don't let anyone tell you it doesn't. If I had lots of money, I'd fill hundreds of boats with food for Europe's starving children. That would bring happiness to them – and me.' Marlene has no make-up man, no secrets about beauty, and no superimposed devices to disguise the alleged onset of old-age. Her legs were once insured for a reported £175,000 (now $420,000) and according to reliable reports she is still anatomically 'all there'. What is more, she despises diets. 'Women only grow old when they are idle', she has said. 'To use the hands is important and it's what I like to do because you get results – cleaning the house, doing the walls, taking care of the kids.' Though she has patronized Chanel and Balenciaga she has admitted that fashion bores her. She has been bored too by Hollywood and by people who talk about her 'legend'. Her home is in New York and her main interest is her grandchildren.

Other great contemporaries have spoken warmly of Dietrich. Noël Coward, an old friend, has said: 'Marlene is a realist and a clown.' Richard Burton has been more forthcoming, describing her '. . . in a curious way like a skeleton risen from the grave, face bones barely covering the makeup . . . Beautiful and extraordinary. Besides, she cooks well.'

LP Recordings

Dietrich Returns to Germany (HMV CLP1659)
Marlene Returns to Germany (HMV 7eg8844)
Die Neue Marlene (*The New Marlene*)
(HMV CLP1885)
Dietrich in Rio (CBS-Realm RM52007/
SRM52007)
The Legendary Marlene Dietrich
(Music for Pleasure MFP1172)

Films

The Great Baritone (1924)
Manon Lescaut (1926)
Wenn Ein Weit den Weg Verhurt (1926)
Gefahren der Brautzeit (1926)
Sein Grosster Bluff (1927)
Ich Kusse Ihre Hand, Madame
(*I Kiss Your Little Hand, Madam*) (1929)
Prinzess in Olala (*The Art of Love*) (1929)
Die Frau Nach der Man Sich Sehut
(*Three Loves*) (1929)
Das Schiff der Verlorenen
(*Le Navire des Hommes Perdus*) (1929)
Liebesnachte (1929)
Der Blaue Engle (*The Blue Angel*) (1930)
Morocco (1931)
Dishonoured (1931)
Blonde Venus (1932)
Shanghai Express (1932)
Song of Songs (1933)
The Scarlet Empress (1935)
The Devil is a Woman (1936)
Desire (1936)
The Garden of Allah (1936)
Knight Without Armour (1937)
Angel (1937)
Destry Rides Again (1939)
Seven Sinners (1946)
The Flame of New Orleans (1941)
Manpower (1941)
The Spoilers (1942)
The Lady is Willing (1942)
Pittsburgh (1942)
Follow the Boys (1944)
Kismet (1944)
Martin Roumagnac (1946)
Golden Earrings (1947)
A Foreign Affair (1948)
Stage Fright (1950)
No Highway (1951)
Rancho Notorious (1952)
Around the World in 80 Days (1956)
The Monte Carlo Story (1956)
Witness for the Prosecution (1957)
Touch of Evil (1958)
Judgement at Nuremberg (1961)
Black Fox (1962)

Bing Crosby

Bing: the nodules on his larynx served him well.

Full name Harry Lillis Crosby. (Nicknamed 'Bing' in childhood because he resembled a comic strip character called Bingo.)

Born Mon. 2 May 1904, Tacoma, Washington, USA.

Characteristics About 5' 8"; about 175*lb.* (12*st.* 7*lb.*); brown hair; blue eyes.

Married
(1) 1930 Dixie Lee (real name Wilma Winnifred Wyatt) (died 1952) 4*s.*
(2) 1957 Kathryn Grant 2*s.* 1*d.*

Over 30 years ago, a young American with a casual air and nodules on his larynx entered a Bing Crosby Imitation Contest. The judges, hearing aids tuned, placed him third. The alias under which he entered is not on record but his professional name was Bing Crosby, a star already well on his way to earning his brother Bob's tribute: 'He rolled uphill to success that's all.' Success can be briefly scheduled as a host of friends, a fortune estimated in 1966 at between £20,000,000 and £25,000,000 (then $56,000,000 and $70,000,000), and disc sales topping 200,000,000, the highest ever by a recording artist until The Beatles surpassed this total in 1967. His disc of Irving Berlin's *White Christmas*, first heard in the film *Holiday Inn* (1942), had sold 29,000,000 by 1968. The nodules, once insured for a large sum, served him well, so well in fact that Bob Hope remarked: 'Bing doesn't pay taxes. He just calls up the Treasury and asks them how much they need.'[1]

The neatest description of the most-heard voice in the history of popular music came from Louis Armstrong: 'Bing's voice has a mellow quality. It's like gold being poured out of a cup.' Said Satchmo: 'Every record he makes I buy.' Bing himself has revealed: 'My notion was to make a sound which resembled the human voice with a bubble in it.' He explained: 'A crooner gets his quota of sentimentality with half his natural voice. That's a great saving. I don't like to work.' Bing acknowledged his debt to the Paul Whiteman band with whom he sang back in the thirties: 'If I have any ability as a song stylist or have made out musically, it's largely because of the association I found while working with that band.' And, he pointed out that, like all craftsmen, he served an apprenticeship: 'Frank Sinatra, Perry Como, all of us learned as we came along to work in sketches with comedians, with girls, how to time jokes.' Coupled with all this Bing mastered the art of relaxation. Danny Kaye has said: 'He has one of the most amazing talents for making hard work look easy.'

Bing's film debut was in *King of Jazz* (1930). His career ran up against an early hazard in 1932 when his ears were thought to be too large for photogeneity, but the problem did not defeat the resourcefulness of Hollywood: 'When I went to work in *The Big Broadcast* ... they insisted on gluing them back against my head with spirit gum ... I looked streamlined, like a whippet dashing after a bunny.'

It was in films that his gag-alliance with Bob Hope won global popularity. Of this happy partnership Bing has said: 'America really is the land of opportunity. Look at

us. Where else could a piece of spaghetti and a meat ball wind up with so much gravy.' The Hope-Crosby 'feud' was not a planned vendetta, Bing has admitted. 'It was a thing we fell into. It grew out of the fact that when we appeared on each other's radio programme and in the 'Road' pictures, it seemed easier for our writers to write abusive dialogue than any other kind.'

Bing won an 'Oscar' for his performance in *Going My Way*. His many fans will remember him especially in *The Bells of St. Mary's* with Ingrid Bergman, and in *The Country Girl* with Grace Kelly. *High Society* in which they starred together again along with Frank Sinatra featured the ballad *True Love* which was to become Grace's first million-selling disc and Bing's 22nd in 1957; his first was *Sweet Leilani*, a number from the film *Waikiki Wedding* (1937). On 9 June 1960 the Hollywood Chamber of Commerce awarded Bing a platinum disc to mark his 200,000,000th record sold from 2,600 recorded titles. In 1963 he contributed to the million-selling LP disc *All-Star Festival*, the profits of which went to the United Nations High Commission for Refugees.

Outside of the recording and film studios, Bing has been a regular sports fan and gave his name to the annual Bing Crosby national golf tournament: 'Golf has provided the relaxation that has kept my batteries charged when I put too heavy a load on them.' He is also proficient with rod and line: '. . . my personal nomination for the greatest thrill of them all is to fish a good trout stream – a stream in which there is plenty of room in which to throw a dry fly.' He makes sure of his facilities by owning his own trout streams. He is also a racehorse owner and here again circumstantial testimony is furnished by Bob Hope: 'I put two dollars on one of Bing's horses and the horse balanced the two dollars on his nose all the way around.

[1] As joint owners of several Texas oilwells, Hope and Crosby both make substantial contributions to the tax man.

Bing has the only horses I've ever seen that can start from a kneeling position.'

One of the few stars of his vintage to go over big on television, Bing has offered this advice to those who have that ambition: 'Anybody who allows himself to appear in television once a week is out of his mind . . . Exposure like that will devour him. It's not a question of becoming physically tired: it's a question of audiences becoming so used to his every gesture, his every nuance, his every tone, that even if they love him they're not interested any more.'

Looking back on a long and varied career in show business Bing is not sure he would have succeeded in the modern environment:

'If I had to start again I'd be worried. I don't see how I ever could do it today. You have to be well managed and well exploited to get anywhere. But I'd sure try, because I love the business. I'd choose the same route but I'm not sure I'd arrive at the same destination.'

Bing won an 'Oscar' for his performance in Going My Way (Paramount, 1944) with Barry Fitzgerald. His Holiness Pope Pius XII wrote saying how much he liked it.

Films

1940	Road to Singapore
1941	Road to Zanzibar
1942	Road to Morocco
1946	Road to Utopia
1948	Road to Rio
1953	Road to Bali
1962	Road to Hong Kong

THE 'ROAD' FILMS

1930	King of Jazz
	The Big Broadcast of 1932
	The Big Broadcast of 1937
1936	Anything Goes
1937	Pennies from Heaven
1937	Rhythm on the Range
1940	If I Had My Way
1941	Birth of the Blues
1942	Holiday Inn
1943	Dixie
1944	Going My Way
1945	Duffy's Tavern
1945	The Bells of St. Mary's
1946	Blue Skies
1949	A Yankee at King Arthur's Court
1950	Mr Music
1951	Here Comes the Groom
1954	The Country Girl
1956	White Christmas
1956	High Society
1958	Man on Fire
1959	Say One for Me
1960	High Time

OTHER FILMS

The Early 30s, Volume 1 (Decca AH40)
The Early 30s, Volume 2 (Decca AH88)
When Irish Eyes Are Smiling (MCA MUP323)
Christmas Around the World (MCA MUP329)
Merry Christmas (MCA MUP328)
Beloved Hymns (Ace of Hearts AH145)
Bing – Rare Style (Ace of Hearts AH164)
Crosby Classics (Hallmark HM520)
Bing Crosby in Hollywood, 1930–34 (2 LPs) (66206)
Bing and Louis (with Louis Armstrong)
          (Music for Pleasure MFP1209)
That Travelin' Two Beat (with Rosemary Clooney)
          (World Record Club T652)
The Great Country Hits (World Record Club T833)
Bing Crosby Story, Volume 1 (2 LPs)
          (Polydor-International 66210)
Thoroughly Modern Bing (Stateside SL10257/SSL10257)
Hey Jude! Hey Bing! (London SHU8391/HAU8391)

SIR JOHN GIELGUD

Full name Arthur John Gielgud Kt (1953).

Born Thurs. 14 April 1904, London, England.

Characteristics About 5′ 11″; about 154*lb.* (11*st.*); light brown hair; blue eyes.

Gielgud as Count Berchtold in 'Oh! What a Lovely War' (Paramount, 1969), a film which rated almost exclusively good notices.

'Of all the arts, I think, acting must be the least concrete, the most solitary.' As one who has occupied a lonely eminence in his profession over a long period, Sir John Gielgud is one of very few qualified to voice this verdict. Descended from a famous Polish actress on his father's side and from the Victorian actress Dame Ellen Terry (1848–1928) on his mother's, Gielgud began acting at school and made his first public appearance as a spearholder

in *Henry V* at London's Old Vic Theatre in 1921. His first speaking part was in *The Wheel* (1922), and his first Shakespearian part as Romeo in 1924 but he confessed he 'made an awful mess of it'.

Well grounded in the school of repertory, Gielgud's stage apprenticeship was served under true professionals. 'I imitated all the actors I admired when I was young' he has recalled, 'particularly Claude Rains,[1] who was my teacher at dramatic school. I admired him very much . . . And then I understudied him. I also understudied Noël Coward, whom I felt I had to imitate because he was so individual in his style.' The play in which he understudied and later replaced Coward was *The Vortex* (1925). He again followed Coward in *The Constant Nymph* in 1927. His first outstanding Shakespearian success was in *Richard of Bordeaux* (1933).

Actor, manager, and director, Gielgud is without doubt one of the most articulate authorities in expounding the secrets of his art. Samples of his wisdom are: 'To me acting is the art of impersonating an author's character so as to translate it into living form upon the stage. To do this, the actor must develop sensitivity but not self-indulgence; a strong temperament governed by self-discipline, and a flexibility for using every quality of voice, bodily movement, recollection, and imagination at his command'; and: 'A long run, with continuous good houses, gives the actor confidence and sureness in his technique; he is able to try many different ways of timing, to study the details of tone and inflection, to watch his mannerisms, and to develop a capacity for give-and-take acting with his partners.' His advice to the young actor is: 'Develop a thick skin for listening to adverse criticism, and a tolerance of your colleagues, even when you feel sure they may be wrong.'

President of the Shakespeare Reading Society since 1958, Sir John has, apart from other things, a universal reputation for his recitals. Richard Burton has said: 'He's the best bloody verse actor in the world. You can't speak in brutal prose when Sir John's speaking.' Gielgud has explained that 'Good verse-speaking is rather like swimming. If you surrender to the water it keeps you up, but if you fight you drown. The phrasing and rhythm and pace should support the speaker just as water does a swimmer, and should be handled with the same skill, ease, and pace.'

One of the outstanding Shakespearian actors of the century – his Hamlet, a role he has played over 500 times, has been

[1] Claude Rains (1889-1967) starred in film versions of *Caesar and Cleopatra* and *Lawrence of Arabia* among many others.

compared with that of every great actor since David Garrick (1717–79) – Gielgud has extolled the enduring qualities of Shakespeare: 'There are answers in this man to every contemporary question. There is religion without dogma; humour without facetiousness; tragedy without grotesque horrors, and a simplicity and knowledge of human nature unsurpassed.' Elizabeth Taylor once asked Sir John if he would teach her how to play Shakespeare. His reply: 'But of course, my dear – so long as you teach me how to play Tennessee Williams.'

In films, Gielgud made his debut in the days of silent pictures. His first 'talkie' was *Insult* (1932). In 1937 he was directed by Alfred Hitchcock in *Secret Agent*, the film of Somerset Maugham's novel *Ashendan* (1928). One of his most brilliant screen performances was as Disraeli in *The Prime Minister* (1940). As Cassius in *Julius Caesar* (1952) he excelled in a part which he had already made his own on the stage. In 1957 he appeared as Mr Moulton Barrett in *The Barretts of Wimpole Street*.

Among the many who have made known their esteem for Sir John Gielgud is Sir Laurence Olivier who, as long ago as 1935, alternated with him in the roles of Romeo and Mercutio in *Romeo and Juliet*. Said Sir Laurence: 'I have admired John Gielgud all my life with complete devotion. have never thought of myself as quite the I same sort of actor. I have always thought we were reverses of the same coin: John all spirituality, all beauty, all abstract things; and myself all earth, all blood, everything to do with humanity, if you like the baser part of humanity.'

'Acting is pretence, but it is also an art. It may convey poetry, realism, or always must be interpretative except in the case of clowns and improvisators. Therefore, the dramatic truth is the most important thing for an actor to find in a first-class text.'

Sir John Gielgud played Louis VII in 'Becket' (Paramount, 1964) with Richard Burton in the title role.

STAGE APPEARANCES

The Insect Play
Robert E. Lee } (1923)
Charley's Aunt
Romeo and Juliet (1924)
The Orphan
The Vortex
The Cherry Orchard
The Seagull } (1925)
Gloriana
L'Ecole des Cocottes
The Tempest
The Three Sisters
Katerina } (1926)
The Constant Nymph
The Great God Brown (1927)
The Constant Nymph (1927)
The Patriot (NY)
Ghosts
Holding out the Apple
The Skull } (1928)
The Lady from Alfaqueque
Fortunato
Out of the Sea
Red Rust
The Lady with a Lamp
Red Sunday
Old
Vic { Romeo and Juliet
The Merchant of Venice
The Imaginary Invalid
Richard II
A Midsummer Night's Dream } (1929)
Julius Caesar
As You Like It
Androcles and the Lion
Macbeth
Hamlet
Old
Vic { Hamlet
The Importance of Being Earnest
Henry IV, Part I
The Tempest } (1930)
The Jealous Wife
Antony and Cleopatra
Old
Vic { Twelfth Night
Arms and the Man
Much Ado About Nothing } (1931)
King Lear
The Good Companions
Musical Chairs
Richard of Bordeaux (1932)
Richard of Bordeaux (1933)
The Maitlands (1934)
Hamlet (1934)
Noah (1935)
Romeo and Juliet (1935)
The Seagull (1936)
Hamlet (NY) (1936)
He Was Born Gay
Richard II } (1937)
The School for Scandal

Three Sisters
Merchant of Venice } (1938)
Dear Octopus
The Importance of Being Earnest (1939)
Hamlet (1939)
King Lear (Old Vic)
The Tempest (Old Vic)
ENSA
tour { Fumed Oak
Hands Across the Sea } (1940)
Swan Song
Dear Brutus (1941)
Macbeth (1942)
The Importance of Being Earnest (1942)
The Doctor's Dilemma (1943)
Love for Love (1943)
The Circle
Love for Love
Hamlet } (1944)
A Midsummer Night's Dream
The Duchess of Malfi
Hamlet (1945)
Blithe Spirit (1945)
Crime and Punishment (1946)
USA
and
Canada { Love for Love
The Importance of Being Earnest
Medea } (1947)
Crime and Punishment
The Return of the Prodigal (1948)
The Lady's Not for Burning (1949)
Stratford { Measure for Measure
Much Ado About Nothing
Julius Caesar } (1950)
King Lear
The Lady's Not for Burning (USA) (1950)
The Winter's Tale (1951)
Much Ado About Nothing (1952)
The Way of the World
Venice Preserv'd } (1953)
Richard III (Rhodesia)
A Day by the Sea
Much Ado About Nothing (1955)
King Lear (1955)
Nude With Violin (1956)
The Tempest (Stratford and London 1957)
The Potting Shed (1958)
Henry VIII (Old Vic and Paris 1958)
The Ages of Man (1959)
The Last Joke (1960)
Othello (Stratford 1961)
The Cherry Orchard (1961)
The School for Scandal (USA 1962)
The Ides of March (1963)
Tiny Alice (1964)
Ivanov (GB 1965, USA 1966)
Tartouffe (National 1967)
Oedipus (National 1967)
40 Years On (1968)

Films

1930 (about)	*Clue of the New Pin*	1967	*Falstaff*
1932	*Insult*	1968	*Sebastian*
1932	*The Good Companions*	1968	*The Charge of the Light Brigade*
1937	*Secret Agent*	1968	*The Shoes of the Fisherman*
1940	*The Prime Minister*	1969	*Oh! What a Lovely War*
1952	*Julius Caesar*	1969	*Julius Caesar*
1955	*Richard III*		
1956	*Around the World in 80 Days*		**Television**
1957	*The Barretts of Wimpole Street*	1966	*Conflict*
1957	*St Joan*	1966	*The Mayfly and the Frog*
1964	*Becket*	1966	*Alice in Wonderland*
1965	*The Loved One*	1967	*From Chekhov With Love*
1966	*Chimes at Midnight*	1968	*St. Joan*
		1969	*Conversation at Night*

LP Recordings

One Man in His Time (Philips ABL3331)

Ages of Man (Philips ABL3269)

Poems of Edith Sitwell (RCA Victor SB6657/RB6657)

As You Like It (RCA Victor SB6740/RB6740)

Hamlet (excerpts) (CBS SBRG72259/BRG72259)

King Lear (RCA Victor SB6740/RB6740)

Measure for Measure (Caedmon SRS-M-204)

The Merchant of Venice (RCA Victor SB6740/RB6740)

A Midsummer Night's Dream (RCA Victor SB6740/RB6740)

Othello (Argo ZRG5289/RG5289)

Richard II (Caedmon SRS216/SRS-M-216)

Romeo and Juliet (RCA Victor SB6740/RB6740)

Shakespeare's Sonnets (2 records) (Caedmon SRS-M-241)

Becket (RCA Victor RD7679)

The Importance of Being Earnest (Music for Pleasure MFP2123/4)

Julius Caesar (Music for Pleasure MFP2122)

40 Years On (original cast recording) (Decca SKL4987/LK4987)

Homage to Shakespeare (with others) (Argo ZNF4)

John Gielgud

STILL PRODUCTIONS LTD.
PRESENT

JOHN GIELGUD   ALAN BENNETT

AND
THE ORIGINAL WEST END CAST
IN
ALAN BENNETT'S

40 YEARS ON

DIRECTED BY
PATRICK GARLAND
MUSIC ARRANGED AND DIRECTED BY CARL DAVIS
ENTIRE PRODUCTION SUPERVISED BY TOBY ROWLAND   DECCA

CARY GRANT

Full name
Alexander Archibald Leach (his screen name, Cary Grant, became his legal name in 1942 when he became an American citizen).

Born
Mon. 18 Jan. 1904, Bristol, England.

Characteristics
About 6′ 1″; about 180*lb.* (12*st.* 12*lb.*); dark brown hair; brown eyes; cleft chin; never used stage make-up; used a sun-lamp to keep his tan in winter; broke his nose in a motor accident in 1968.

Married
(1) 1934 Virginia Cherril (div. 1935).
(2) 1942 Barbara Hutton (div. 1945).
(3) 1949 Betsy Drake (div. 1962).
(4) 1965 Dyan Cannon (div. 1968) 1*d*.

[1] The fourth Mrs Grant received a settlement of $57,000 (£23,750) plus $24,000 (£10,000) a year maintenance.

About to face the cameras in the film *She Done Him Wrong* (1933), Mae West was captivated by the limber gait of 'a sensational-looking young man' walking along the Hollywood studio street. As no leading man was yet cast, she insisted on having him. The film was shot without a re-take in 18 days and Cary Grant was *en route* to screen immortality. A succession of parts opposite the movie stars of the thirties elevated him to a special niche in the box office ratings and by 1940 he was wealthy enough to donate his fee of $125,000 (£31,250) from *Philadelphia Story* to British War Relief.

The stealthy tread that transported Grant's elegance across the movie screens of the world was both natural and man-made. As a child in England, Archie Leach had been shy and afraid of heights: 'Since then I have attempted gradually to overcome my fear,' he has said. 'Even by learning, years later, to walk on stilts in a theatrical troupe specializing in panto-mime and acrobatics.' The training served him well on location for the film *To Catch a Thief* when he was required by Alfred Hitchcock to race over the sloping roof-tops of four-storey Riviera villas, with no safety nets below. 'I've always felt queasily uncertain whether or not Hitchcock was pleased to see me survive each day's work,' he commented. 'I can only hope it was as great a relief to him as it was a disappoint-ment.'

But pigeon-toed poise is not all that fitted Cary Grant like a well-oiled com-ponent into the familiar romantic-comedy roles. A famous director was once quoted as saying: 'Some men squeeze a line to death; Cary tickles it into life.' While tickling it, he remained shrewdly conscious of the fundamentals of audience psycho-logy: 'The best way to get the sympathy of an audience is to get yourself into a jam and let them help you wangle your way out of it. A kindly chuckle is the actor's

152

Audrey Hepburn was Cary Grant's co-star in 'Charade' (Universal, 1964). Cary's memorable performance included taking a shower while wearing a drip-dry suit.

best old-age insurance.'

Grant has attributed his longevity in films to the technique noted by Mae West which, sparing of re-takes, saved money for his studio. His art is crystallized in this sketch of how to speak a line while drinking iced tea: 'If I bring the glass up too soon, I sound like a man hollering in a barrel. If I hold it up in front of my mouth, I spoil my expression. If I put it down too hard, I kill a couple of words on the sound track; if I don't, I make it seem unreal.' He also has to keep his head up

RANT

Cary Grant's last motion picture was 'Walk, Don't Run' (Columbia, 1966) in which he played a British industrialist visiting Tokyo who gets mixed up with the 1964 Olympic Games.

on account of his double chin.

Apart from the double chin, Cary succeeds in manifesting few symptoms of post-juvenile decline. A magazine editor, doubting from the evidence of photographs that he was, as reported, threescore years next birthday, once got in touch discreetly for the facts, cabling the economical message: 'How old Cary Grant?' The reply, only a shade more prolix, brought the glad tidings: 'Old Cary Grant fine. How you?'

It figures that the lean silhouette of over 30 years' screen photogeneity has a diet-free history. 'My close friends have named me "the scavenger" he once confided, 'because, after finishing every morsel of my own meal, I look around to purloin little delicacies they've left uneaten on their plates.'

Indelibly etched in the public mind as the nonpareil of polish and address, Grant holds the admiration even of fellow-luminaries, among them Sammy Davis Jr who classified him along with Frank Sinatra as one of the 'two boys left who are not the boy next door'. George Sanders, who does not live next door, was correspondingly un-neighbourly in his view of Grant, seeing him in real life as 'a prey to theosophical charlatans, socially insecure, and inclined to isolation'.

The imputation of financial insecurity is one that has never been levelled at Cary. It is claimed he could draw $1,000,000 a picture plus as much as 75 per cent of the profits. His own agent, he makes each film his outright property after seven years. His earnings from 1958 to 1966 alone were estimated to total over $12,000,000 (£4,285,700), making him the male actor with the highest income in that period. Though all this keeps him comfortably in Rolls-Royces and other necessary trivia, the tax drain is heavy. 'Out of each $100,000 I take home exactly $13,000,' he once complained, but added: 'Even at these bargain prices I like to work.' Not entirely resentful about his contribution to the Federal budget he suggested: 'I'd be happy if they'd invest the money in something useful, like having schoolteachers analysed so they could raise a generation of happy children who'd refuse to start World War III.'

Of the women who did not marry Cary Grant, Joan Crawford may not be the only one to claim: 'I just missed catching him as a husband.' Sophia Loren may well be the only one to have passed up the opportunity of becoming Mrs Grant. 'I knew he loved me,' she declared, 'and that if I chose to, I could marry him. I gave the prospect serious thought.' He gave her a gold chain. Of his wives, Betsy Drake, his co-star in *Every Girl Should Be Married* and *Room for One More*, made an important contribution to his well-being by teaching him self-hypnotism so that he could deaden his jaw for the dentist. Dyan Cannon presented him with a daughter, enabling him to make his first pronouncement on parenthood at age 62: 'I think having a child when you're older has its advantages. At my age I reckon I'm about ready for it. You're older but you're able to understand a child better because you know yourself.'

Cary Grant announced his retirement from motion pictures in 1969, stating that he would devote more time to the cosmetic firm, Faberge Incorporated, of which he is a director. There were no plans for naming cosmetics after him.

FILMS

This is the Night (1933)
Merrily We Go to – (1933)
Sinners in the Sun (1933)
Devil and the Deep (1933)
Blonde Venus (1933)
Hot Saturday (1933)
Madame Butterfly (1933)
She Done Him Wrong (1933)
The Woman Accused (1933)
The Eagle and the Hawk (1933)
Alice in Wonderland (1933)
Gambling Ship (1934)
I'm No Angel (1934)
Thirty-Day Princess (1934)
Born to be Bad (1934)
Kiss and Make Up (1935)
Ladies Should Listen (1935)
Enter Madame (1935)
The Last Outpost (1935)
Wings in the Dark (1936)
Sylvia Scarlett (1936)
Big Brown Eyes (1936)
Suzy (1937)
The Amazing Quest of Ernest Bliss (1937)
Wedding Present (1937)
For You Alone (1937)
Topper (1937)
The Toast of New York (1938)
The Awful Truth (1938)
Bringing Up Baby (1938)
Only Angels Have Wings (1939)
Free to Live (1939)
Gunga Din (1939)
In Name Only (1940)
My Favourite Wife (1940)
His Girl Friday (1940)

(1941) Philadelphia Story
(1941) The Tree of Liberty
(1941) Penny Serenade
(1942) Suspicion
(1943) The Talk of the Town
(1943) Once Upon a Honeymoon
(1943) Mr Lucky
(1944) Destination Tokyo
(1944) Once Upon a Time
(1945) Arsenic and Old Lace
(1945) None But the Lonely Heart
(1947) Night and Day
(1947) Notorious
(1947) The Bachelor and the Bobbysoxer (Bachelor Knight)
(1948) The Bishop's Wife
(1948) Every Girl Should be Married
(1948) Mr Blandings Builds His Dream House
(1949) I Was a Male War Bride
(1949) You Can't Sleep Here
(1951) Crisis
(1951) People Will Talk
(1952) Room for One More
(1952) Monkey Business
(1953) Dream Wife
(1955) To Catch a Thief
(1957) An Affair to Remember
(1958) Kiss Them for Me
(1958) Indiscreet
(1959) Houseboat
(1959) North by Northwest
(1959) Operation Petticoat
(1961) The Grass is Greener
(1962) That Touch of Mink
(1964) Father Goose
(1964) Charade
(1965) Walk, Don't Run

154

BOB HOPE

On one of his regular visits to England, Bob Hope gave a lift to 'Frost on Saturday' (London Weekend Television, 1968; repeated, 1969). When David Frost tried to draw him on serious topics, Hope steered the conversation round to his favourite subject — golf.

Full name Leslie Townes Hope.

Born Fri. 29 May 1903, Craigton Road, Eltham, Kent, England.

Characteristics About 5′ 11″; about 170*lb.* (12*st.* 2*lb.*); dark hair and eyes.

Married 1933 Dolores Reade 2*s.* 2*d.* (all adopted).

Hope and Crosby kept in touch with Dorothy Lamour in 'The Road to Hong Kong' (United Artists, 1962). The seven 'Road' films grossed $50,000,000 (now £20,833,333).

At the 38th annual 'Oscar' awards ceremony in Hollywood in 1966, the Academy of Motion Picture Arts and Sciences presented a new gold medal for 'unique and distinguished services to our industry'. The recipient, and master of ceremonies for the twelfth time, was Bob Hope, the man whom latter-day sociologists may well cite as the Englishman who did most to bring laughs to 20th-century America, and indeed to the entire English-speaking world. The honour was one of many dating back to 1949 when a Gallup poll published the popular verdict that he was the funniest comedian.

Hope's stock of gags, the product of 40 years' work and a phenomenal memory, are kept in a comprehensive filing system in a vault at one of his homes. He even has gags about the days, back in the 'twenties, when his professional repertoire was built around Charlie Chaplin imitations. Life in a third-rate Chicago boarding house was bleak. Moreover, he has recalled, 'the maid came in once a day to change the rats'. It was altogether a lean time for the man Bing Crosby was to name 'Robert Hope of the non-classic profile and unlissome mid-section'. He was $4,000 (£1,000) in debt, had holes in his shoes, and was subsisting on doughnuts and coffee. 'When I met a friend one day who bought me a luncheon featuring beefsteak I had forgotten whether you cut steak with a knife or drink it with a spoon.'

Bob's arrival in films ensured that he never had to fall back on doughnuts. The 'Road' series with Bing Crosby won him a wider international following and put him in demand during World War II as a Forces' favourite. Entertaining the troops in a hospital in Sicily he cracked: 'Fellas, the folks at home are having a terrible time about eggs. They can't get the powdered eggs at all. They've got to use the old-fashioned kind you break open.' His war tours to Africa, Alaska, the Aleutians, the Pacific, the United Kingdom, and elsewhere were probably the most extensive and frequent of any show business personality. John Steinbeck voiced the conviction of many when he said: 'It is impossible to see how he can do so much, cover so much ground, can work so hard, and can be so effective.'

Wars in Korea and Vietnam kept Bob on his travels annually. In 1962 he won Presidential commendation as 'America's most prized Ambassador of Good Will'. He was awarded a gold medal, voted by Congress and struck by the US mint. President John F. Kennedy, in a tape-recorded speech praising Bob's work entertaining servicemen abroad, suggested he made a 'Road to Washington' film. 'From my own experience,' said Kennedy, 'I can tell him it's not the easiest road to travel, but it will give him the chance to visit his money – at least what's left of it.' In 1963 when Bob was sick with an eye ailment, happily cured by means of laser-beam surgery, President Lyndon B. John-

son wrote him a personal note in hospital. In a nationwide TV programme in 1965, LBJ presented Bob with a plaque inscribed with the words: 'Thanks for the memory from a grateful nation.'

Once a prizefighter – 'They called me Rembrandt Hope, I spent so much time on the canvas' – Bob's enthusiasm for sports has made itself apparent in many ways. In 1946 he became part-owner of the Cleveland Indians baseball team. In 1952, with Bing Crosby, he pledged more than $1,000,000 (£357,000) to the US Olympic fund by staging a $14\frac{1}{2}$-hour coast-to-coast telethon. A good golfer[1] (about 10 handicap), he promotes the annual Bob Hope Desert Classic, proceeds from which are donated to the Eisenhower Medical Centre in Palm Springs, California. Bob gave land worth $500,000 (now £208,333) as a site for the centre. His charities run into millions but many of them are not publicized. In 1968 it was reported by *Fortune* magazine that he was one of the 66 Americans whose wealth amounted to $150,000,000 (£62,500,000) or more.

One of the tribulations of being a comedian is that fans always try to get in on the act. 'Because so many people have listened to me they think they have to tell me a joke. And I go along with it because otherwise you might snub somebody and then wonder later on "What did I do that for."' Bob's jokes are generally the product of teamwork. 'Even when I use my writers there are things we hammer out, then polish together . . . you get several slants on each gag, so you play around with them and select the one you want.' The question everybody would like to ask him is – can he do it without the gagwriters? Bing Crosby has supplied the necessary nod: 'Offstage no man alive makes me laugh more than old Scow Prow

[1] According to one report he has beaten Ben Hogan over nine holes and tied with Arnold Palmer. His repartee reinfoced his handicap.

Hope.' Jack Benny has explained his success like this: 'It's not just enough to get laughs. The audience has to love you, and Bob gets love as well as laughs from his audiences.'

'People who throw kisses are hopelessly lazy.'

On visiting the Lenin-Stalin mausoleum in Moscow: 'A great show but what do they do for an encore?'

On President de Gaulle: 'He thinks there just two kinds of people – those who believe in de Gaulle and atheists.'

BOB HOPE

THE 'ROAD' FILMS

Road to Singapore (1940)
Road to Zanzibar (1941)
Road to Morocco (1942)
Road to Utopia (1946)
Road to Rio (1948)
Road to Bali (1953)
Road to Hong Kong (1962)

OTHER FILMS

The Big Broadcast of 1938
Thanks for the Memory (1938)
The Cat and the Canary (1939)
The Ghost Breakers (1941)
Nothing but the Truth (1941)
My Favourite Blonde (1942)
Star-Spangled Rhythm (1943)
Monsieur Beaucaire (1946)
The Paleface (1948)
Here Come the Girls (1953)
Casanova (1954)
The Seven Little Foys (1955)
Beau James (1957)
Paris Holiday (1958)
Facts of Life (1961)
Critic's Choice (1962)
Call Me Bwana (1963)
A Global Affair (1963)
I'll Take Sweden (1965)
Boy, Did I Get a Wrong Number? (1966)
Eight on the Run (1968)
How to Commit Marriage (1968)
The Private Navy of Sgt. O'Farrell (1969)

SATCHMO

There is just two kinds of music – good and bad

Full name Daniel Louis Armstrong (Louis is pronounced 'Lewis'). (Nicknames: Dipper Mouth, Satchel Mouth, Satchmo, and Pops.)

Born Wed. 4 July 1900, James Alley, Back o' Town, New Orleans, Louisiana, USA.

Characteristics About 5' 7½"; normally about 187*lb*. (13*st*. 5*lb*.); reduced by 50*lb*. in 1968 with use of herbal laxatives; black hair, brown eyes.

Married
(1) 1917 Daisy Parker (div. 1917).
(2) 1924 Lilian Hardin (div. 1932)
(3)   Alpha Smith (div.).
(4) 1942 Lucille Wilson.

'Anybody in the world knows more about playin' that trumpet than Louis Armstrong—show him to me. And I'll show that doubter! I'll run 'im! And if I can't run 'im – Man, I'll sure talk him down!' Volunteers to be talked down by James 'Bunk' Johnson probably number very

few. And they would certainly be trampled underfoot in the crush of fans eager to be stood on their ear at the behest of the well-loved Satchmo.

'Jazz and I grew up side by side when we were poor' is the abridged version of Louis Armstrong's early life in music. Even when he had graduated from strumming a four-string guitar made of a cigar box and copper wire, he found that: 'For some time funerals gave me the only chance I had to blow my cornet.' For Louis, coming up the hard way included spells as milk roundsman, newspaper-seller, rag-and-bone man, and coalman: 'From seven in the morning to five in the evening I would haul coal at 15 cents per load. And I loved it. I was 15 years old, and I felt like a real man when I shovelled a ton of coal into my waggon ... The 75 cents I made in the day plus the dollar and

Satchmo

a quarter plus tips I made in the tonk added up.' At that time, he recalled 'playing in the honkey-tonk all night long, I split my lip wide open. Split my lip so bad in Memphis there's meat still missing. Happened many times . . . Blood all down my shirt . . . Only reason I got my lip is a salve I keep; draws tiredness out, keeps my lips strong.'

Louis first played with an organized group in Kid Ory's Band in 1917. By 1922 he had graduated to Joseph 'King' Oliver's band at Chicago, and by 1924 was heading his own bands, known as the 'Hot Five' and 'Hot Seven'. His first recording sessions were in 1923 when he made *Mabel's Dream*, *Southern Stomps*, *Riverside Blues*, *Canal Street Blues*, *China Blues*, and *Dipper Mouth Blues*. Other early numbers, including some of his own composition, were committed to wax in the 'twenties: *Rockin' Chair*, *Ol' Man Mose*, *Brother Bill*, *Sugar Foot Strut*, and *You Rascal You*, were among the favourites. Some of them have sold as collector's items for more than $20 (£8). His theme tunes have been *When It's Sleepy Time Down South* and *On the Sunny Side of the Street*.

Willie 'the Lion' Smith commented on Satchmo's craftsmanship and the groundwork on which he built up his instrumental virtuosity: 'He works like a horse, knows how to pace himself, and knows his chord construction.' It is said that Louis hardened his jaw muscles and developed his abdominal air pressure to a point where he could strike and hold high C longer than any other swing trumpeter. Smith cited an occasion at the Schiller in New Orleans when Louis, at his peak, took around 40 choruses of *The Sheikh of Araby*.

The fame of the man from New Orleans put him in demand on a wider national and international scale. In 1929 he played in the New York revue *Hot Chocolates* and in

160

1932 made his first appearance at the London Palladium, following it with a three-year tour of Europe.[1] He broke into films and entertained discerning audiences at Carnegie Hall, America's foremost concert venue. Everywhere the fans took in his zest and sincerity. 'Look, you don't pose never', he explained to one interviewer. 'That's the last thing you do, because the minute you do you're through as a jazz-man. Maybe not as a musician, but jazz is only what you are.' Italian fans bestowed a rare compliment on Louis for what *he* was. 'When we played at Milano', he recalled, 'after I finished my concert . . . I had to rush over to the La Scala and stand by those big cats like Verdi and Wagner . . . and take pictures, 'cause they figure our music's the same. We play them both from the heart.'

The voice of Louis was never his cardinal qualification for a place in jazz history but like his instrumental skill it just naturally appealed to his listeners. 'There was no genius in evolving my style of singing,' he admitted. 'It was just presence of mind. If you forgot a line you could always put another one in there easily.' Whatever the logic of this method the result was right: his first and only million-selling disc was a vocal – *Hello, Dolly* (1964)[2]. It was in the charts in the United States for 22 weeks.

Even Bing Crosby has admitted that he drew inspiration from Louis: '. . . there's a man I idolize as an entertainer. At home there are nights when I'll play a Satchmo record over and over. And I'm proud to confess that I've stolen a few notes from him.' Bing and Louis sang *Now You Has Jazz*, composed by Cole Porter for them, in the film *High Society*, and also teamed up for the long-time favourite *Gone Fishin'*.

It speaks volumes for the durability of Louis Armstrong that he made his first comeback as long ago as 1947 after he had disbanded his group. At that time he said:

'Some cats say Old Satchmo is old-fashioned, not modern enough. Why, man, most of the modern stuff I first heard in 1918. Ain't no music out of date as long as you play it perfect.' Asked how long he thinks he will last he promised: 'Right until I get to the Pearly Gates, I hope. I'm gonna blow a kiss to Gabriel.' On his visit to England in 1965, the subject of retirement was again gently broached. To the relief of his fans he growled: 'When the man upstairs says put down that horn, that's the day I'm through. Until then it's my pleasure to play for people.'

Money and acclaim never quite robbed the man from the New Orleans honkey-tonks of his innate honesty. Looking back on it all he shrugged: 'All this travelling around the world, meeting wonderful people, being high on the horse, all *grandioso* – it's nice – but I didn't suggest it. I would say it was all wished on me.'

When complimented on his appetite: 'Man that's just a synopsis.'

How to lose weight: 'All you have to do is give up food – and that's really nothin' after the taste is gone.'

'A lot of people live according to Hoyle, but Hoyle's dead. I live according to Louis Armstrong.'

'I just want to keep the horn in my chops 24 hours a day. Ain't much, Pops. But I ain't complainin'.'

---

[1] He made other tours to Europe in 1949, 1952, 1959, 1961, 1962 and 1965; the Nice Jazz festival welcomed him in 1948; in 1952 he toured Japan; in 1956 West Africa; in 1957 the West Indies; in 1961 Mexico and 19 African countries; in 1963 Australia, New Zealand, Hong Kong, Korea, Japan, and Hawaii; in 1964 Australia, New Zealand, Singapore, India, Japan, Formosa, and Okinawa. He was in England again in 1967 and 1968.

[2] Louis also contributed to the million-selling disc *All-Star Festival* (1963) profits of which went to the United Nations High Commission for Refugees.

FILMS

Pennies from Heaven (1936)
Going Places (1938)
Cabin in the Sky (1943)
Jam Session (1944)
Atlantic City (1944)
Pillow to Post (1945)
New Orleans (1947)
A Song is Born (1949)
The Strip (1951)
Glory Alley (1952)
The Glenn Miller Story (1954)
Artists and Models (1956)
High Society (1956)
Satchmo the Great (1957)
The Five Pennies (1959)
Paris Blues (1961)
Where the Boys meet the Girls (1965)
A Man called Adam (1966)
Hello, Dolly! (1969)

Louis and Barbra Streisand sang the title song in 'Hello Dolly!' (20th Century-Fox, 1969), said to have attracted 'the most glittering team of successful creators ever to be gathered together for a single filmed enterprise.'

LP RECORDINGS

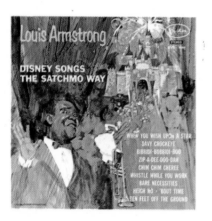

His Greatest Years, Volume 1 (Parlophone PMC1140)
His Greatest Years, Volume 2 (Parlophone PMC1142)
His Greatest Years, Volume 3 (Parlophone PMC1146)
His Greatest Years, Volume 4 (Parlophone PMC1150)
Jazz Classics (Ace of Hearts AH7)
New Orleans Nights (Ace of Hearts AH18)
King Louis (All Stars) (Brunswick LAT8508/ST8508)
Satchmo at Symphony Hall, Volume 1 (Ace of Hearts AH73)
Satchmo at Symphony Hall, Volume 2 (Ace of Hearts AH74)
Satchmo at Pasadena (Ace of Hearts AH79)
At the Crescendo, Volume 1 (Ace of Hearts AH81)
At the Crescendo, Volume 2 (Ace of Hearts AH82)
In the 30s, In the 40s (RCA Victor RD7706)
Armstrong Plays W. C. Handy (CBS-Realm RM52067)
Ambassador Satch (All Stars) (CBS BPG62302)
Louis Armstrong in New York (Reprise RLP8811)
Louis Armstrong Sings (Mercury 20083MCL/20083SMCL)
Singing Style of Louis Armstrong (Verve VSP7/8)
What a Wonderful World (Stateside SL10247/SSL10247)
Greatest Hits (CBS BPG63035)
Ella and Louis (Verve VSP19/20)
Satchmo Style (Parlophone PMC7045)
I Will Wait for You (MCA MUPS356/MUP356)
Town Hall Concert Plus (RCA Victor RD7659)
Disney Songs the Satchmo Way (Buena Vista BVS4044)
Bing and Louis (with Bing Crosby) (Music for Pleasure MFP1209)
Ella and Louis (with Ella Fitzgerald) (Music for Pleasure MFP1296)
Louis and the Big Bands 1928–30 (Parlophone PMC7074)

NOËL COWARD

Noel Coward
'As a man, my greatest single
achievement is simple enough.
I've kept my old friends.'

Full name Noël Pierce Coward.

Born Sat. 16 Dec. 1899, Teddington, Middlesex, England.

Characteristics About 5′ 11″; about 154*lb.* (11*st.*); dark brown hair; blue eyes.

Conscious worth – 'Let's face it. I'm tremendously gifted and there's no use pretending I'm not' – springs eternal in the breast of the man with over 40 years' attainment in the world of theare. Nor could anyone have imagined him genuinely exercized when he pondered: 'My only problem is how to apportion my many talents.' Sometimes, it is true, a share of glory has been allotted to lesser mortals. 'The American public's taste is impeccable. They like me,' was one such lapse. Another was when he assured Rex Harrison: 'After *me* you're the best light comedian in the world.' The height of self-appreciation was

scaled, tongue in cheek, when demonstrating his flashy new convertible to his neighbour, Ian Fleming. As they purred through a sleepy Jamaican hamlet, the resplendent vehicle roused a lounging bystander to exclaim: 'Jesus Christ! I wonder,' mused the driver with tranquil curiosity, 'how he knew.'

Few can remember a time when Noël Coward was not 'the Master'. Of those with longer memories, some may still be be alive who saw his first stage appearance in a children's fairy play *The Goldfish* (1911). The late Gertrude Lawrence (1901–52)[1] recalled a pantomime, *The Miracle*,

---

[1] Gertrude Lawrence partnered Coward in his plays *Private Lives, Tonight at 8.30,* and *Lady in the Dark* which ran to packed houses in the 'thirties. Their association was a feature of the film *Star!* (1968) with Julie Andrews playing the part of Gertie and Coward's godson Daniel Massey, son of Raymond Massey of the TV series *Dr Kildare,* portraying the part of Coward.

163

in which she appeared with him in 1912: 'We kids never knew Noël was a genius then. He was just a nice boy who ate peppermint candies and who shared them with us.' In World War I Coward made a humble start in motion pictures, collecting £1 a week for wheeling a barrow up and down a village street in *Hearts of the World* (1918). He had been discharged from the army after suffering concussion in a fall.

Coward's first important play was *The Vortex*, also his first to be produced both in London and New York. Sir John Gielgud, who understudied him in this play, has said that some of his lines are so characteristic that 'when once you have heard him deliver them, it is impossible to speak them without giving a poor imitation of him'. His most popular play was probably *Blithe Spirit* which ran in London for 1,997 performances. It was made into a film, screened on TV, and was also adapted for a musical on Broadway entitled *High Spirits*. Coward recorded in his autobiography that of all his shows *Bitter Sweet* gave him 'the greatest personal pleasure'. He also revealed that the waltz *I'll See You Again* 'dropped into my mind, whole and complete, during a twenty minutes' traffic block', while riding home in a taxi after a matinée.

Though it enabled him to indulge a taste for silk shirts and pyjamas, brilliant success never made Coward entirely indifferent to the critics: 'I think there is something slightly phoney in an actor or author who says he doesn't read notices. I always do. If they're bad I'm irritated. If good – very pleased. Neither emotion lasts for long.' The bland detachment was only slightly jarred when critics attacked a play for being 'too thin'. He replied: 'From now on I will write nothing but very fat plays for very fat critics.' The hostile reception accorded to his play *Sirocco* evoked more genuine indignation.

'As a general rule the most uppish people I have ever met have been those who have never achieved anything whatsoever.'

'Wit ought to be a glorious treat, like caviar; never spread it about like marmalade.'

'Work is more fun than fun.'

'Time has convinced me of one thing. Television is for appearing on, not looking at.'

'I had to send my tailcoat to the cleaners', he complained after irate members of the audience had spat on him at the stage door. Nasty letters left him 'amazed' that so many people had so much time to waste.

The author of over 40 plays and revues, Coward has offered realistic advice to the writer, maintaining that his first allegiance should not be to his political convictions or to his moral or social conscience but to his talent. He should bring to his work 'industry, economy of phrase, self-criticism, taste, selectivity, and enough technical ability to convey whatever he wishes to a large audience'. He has agreed with Somerset Maugham's dictum that a good story should have a beginning, a middle, and an end and that this 'applies even more sternly to playwriting'. The most important ingredients of a good play are life, death, food, sex, and money though not necessarily in that order.

Over 100 songs with lyrics composed and written by Coward have given rise to a lengthy discography. The inimitable *Mad Dogs and Englishmen*, from his revue *Words and Music*, is perhaps the most famous. He composed it in 1930 while motoring from Hanoi to Saigon and sang it both for Winston Churchill and Franklin D. Roosevelt at their personal request. *The Stately Homes of England* was first heard in his play *Operette* while another classic, *London Pride*, was contributed to the show *Up and Doing* (1940).

In addition to writing and appearing in plays and motion pictures, composing songs and writing lyrics, Coward found time to write two volumes of biography, one of poetry, a novel, a ballet, and several short stories. He also fitted in cabaret engagements in England and America earning as much as $30,000 (£10,714) a week in Las Vegas in 1955.

A tax exile from England for many years, Coward has made no bones about his distaste for the depredations of socialism:

'I have always believed more in quality than quantity, and nothing will convince me that the levelling of class and rank distinctions, and the contemptuous dismissal of breeding as an important factor of life, can lead to anything but a dismal mediocrity.' In 1968 he bought a home in Switzerland where he reported that he had 'a spectacular view overlooking an absolutely ravishing tax advantage'.

The Master has seldom been serious on record. One instance was when speaking at the Book and Author Luncheon at New York in 1961. 'Who can truly say,' he asked, 'that there is more truth in tears than laughter?' In a crowded career there has been little pause for the backward glance. But caught just once looking over his shoulder he was heard to say: 'As a man, my greatest single achievement is simple enough. I've kept my old friends'.

His friends have not been hesitant to express their admiration. Maurice Chevalier thought he typified sophistication: 'He is intelligent; he is also chichi. To me, he is a man who is always with the people of the smart set.' Sir Laurence Olivier conceded: 'I think Noël probably was the first man who took hold of me and made me use my silly little brain. He taxed me with his sharpness and shrewdness and his brilliance and his brain.' Terence Rattigan wrote: 'He is simply a phenomenon, and one that is unlikely to occur ever again in theatre history. Let us at least be grateful that it is our own epoch that the phenomenon so signally adorns.'

Noel Coward's Plays and Revues

(dates of first performance)
I'll Leave it to You (GB 1920, USA 1923)
The Better Half (1922)
The Young Idea (GB 1922–23, USA 1932)
London Calling! (1923)
The Vortex (GB 1924, USA 1925)
Hay Fever (GB, USA 1925)
On With the Dance (1925)
Fallen Angels (GB 1925, USA 1927)
Easy Virtue (USA 1925, GB 1926)
'This Was the Man' (USA 1926)
The Rat Trap (1926)
The Queen Was in the Parlour (GB 1926, USA 1929)
Sirocco (1927)
The Marquise (GB, USA 1927)
Home Chat (GB 1927, USA 1932)
This Year of Grace! (GB, USA 1928)
Bitter Sweet (GB, USA 1929)
Private Lives (GB 1930, USA 1931)
Some Other Private Lives (1930)
Cavalcade (1931)
Words and Music (1932)
Weatherwise (1932)
Design for Living (USA 1933, GB 1937)
Conversation Piece (GB, USA 1934)
Pointe Valaine (USA 1935, GB 1944)
⎰ *Tonight at 7.30* (1935)
⎱ *Tonight at 8.30* (GB, USA 1936)
— the same show: a collection of 10 one-act plays which
were combined in various groups to make three programmes
each of three plays:

⎧ *We Were Dancing*
⎪ *The Astonished Heart*
⎪ *'Red Peppers'*
⎪ *Hands Across the Sea*
⎨ *Fumed Oak*
⎪ *Shadow Play*
⎪ *Family Album*
⎪ *Star Chamber*
⎪ *Ways and Means*
⎩ *Still Life*

LP Recordings, Coward in perso

Noel Coward at Las Vegas (CBS BPG62426)
The Master Sings (Music for Pleasure MFP1111)
Noel and Gertie (HMV CLP1050)
The Critics (spoken word) (Ember SCEL906/CEL906)
The Theatre Today (spoken word, with others) (Argo RG279)

Operette (1938)
Set to Music (USA 1938)
Blithe Spirit (GB, USA 1946)
Present Laughter (GB 1942, USA 1946)
This Happy Breed (GB 1942, USA 1949)
Sigh No More (1945)
Pacific 1860 (1946)
Peace in Our Time (1947)
Ace of Clubs (1950)
Island Fling (*South Sea Bubble*) (USA 1951, GB 1956)
Relative Values (GB 1951, USA 1954)
Quadrille (GB 1952, USA 1954)
After the Ball (GB 1954, USA 1955)
Nude With Violin (1956)
Look After Lulu (1959)
London Morning (*Ballet*) (1959)
Waiting in the Wings (1960)
Sail Away (USA 1961, GB 1962)
The Girl Who Came to Supper (USA)
Suite in Three Keys (1966):
⎧ *Shadows of the Evening*
⎨ *Come Into the Garden Maud*
⎩ *Song of Twilight*

Adapted or Composite Versions of Earlier Plays

High Spirits (USA, GB 1964); musical version of *Blithe Spirit*)
Noel Coward's Sweet Potato (USA 1968); an anthology of
songs, sketches and plays of over 40 year
Mr and Mrs (1968); musical based on *Fumed Oak* and *Still Life*
from *Tonight at 8.3*

Other LP Recordings

High Spirits (Pye International NEP24196)
Joan Sutherland Sings the Songs of Noel Coward
(HMV CLP1050
Mr and Mrs (original cast recording) (CBS 70048)

NOËL

*Noel Coward on location during 19
with Elizabeth Taylor and Richa
Burton when filming Boor
(Universal) in Sardinia. The film w
based on the Tennessee Williams boo
The Milk Train Doesn't Stop Here A
More.*

Films and TV Productions of Coward's Plays and Revues

The Vortex (1924), filmed in 1928

Easy Virtue (1925), filmed in 1928

Hay Fever (1925), adapted for TV in 1968

The Queen Was in the Parlour (1926), filmed silent in 1926 and with sound in 1928 entitled *Tonight is Ours*

Bitter Sweet (1929), filmed in 1933 and 1944

Post-Mortem, written in 1930 but unproduced; adapted for TV in 1968

Private Lives (1930), filmed in 1932 and again in 1936 entitled *Les Amants Terribles*

Cavalcade (1931), filmed in 1932 and 1956, and adapted for TV in 1955

Design for Living (1933), filmed in 1933

Tonight at 8.30 (1935) gave rise to several films; *We Were Dancing* was filmed in 1942 and *The Astonished Heart* in 1950; the film *Meet Me Tonight* (1952) was based on three plays from *Tonight at 8.30* – 'Red Peppers', *Fumed Oak,* and *Ways and Means*; *Still Life* was filmed in 1945 entitled *Brief Encounter*; in 1954 'Red Peppers', *Still Life,* and *Shadow Play* were adapted for TV

Blithe Spirit (1941), filmed in 1945 and adapted for TV in 1956

Present Laughter (1942), adapted for TV in 1967

This Happy Breed (1942), filmed in 1943 and adapted for TV in 1956

Excerpts from seven plays: *Pacific 1860, Sigh No More, Bitter Sweet, This Year of Grace!, Private Lives, Conversation Piece,* and *Shadow Play,* were anthologised in a TV production entitled *Together With Music* in 1955

Films and TV Productions Based on Short Stories

The Kindness of Mrs Radcliffe (1939), adapted for TV in 1968

Star Quality (1951), adapted for TV in 1968

Mrs Capper's Birthday (1963), adapted for TV in 1968

Pretty Polly Barlow (1964), filmed as *Pretty Polly* in 1967 and adapted for TV in 1968

Bon Voyage (1967), adapted for TV in 1968

Stage Appearances

The Goldfish (1911)
The Great Name (1911)
Where the Rainbow Ends (1911)
An Autumn Idyll (1912)
The Miracle (1912)
Hannele (1913)
War in the Air (1913)
A Little Fowl Play (1913)
Peter Pan (1913)
Peter Pan (1915)
Where the Rainbow Ends (1915)
Charley's Aunt (1916)
The Light Blues (1916)
The Happy Family (1916)
The Saving Grace (1917)
Scandal (1918)
The Knight of the Burning Pestle (1919)
I'll Leave it to You (1920)
The Knight of the Burning Pestle (1920)
Polly with a Past (1921)
The Young Idea (1922)
The Young Idea (1923)
London Calling! (1923)
The Vortex (GB 1924)
The Vortex (USA 1925)
The Constant Nymph (1926)
The Second Man (1928)
This Year of Grace! (USA 1928)
Journey's End (Compere 1930)
Private Lives (1930)
Private Lives (USA 1931)
Design for Living (USA 1933)
Conversation Piece (1934)
Tonight at 7.30 (1935)
Tonight at 8.30 (GB, USA 1936)
Blithe Spirit (1942)
Present Laughter (1942)
This Happy Breed (1942)
Present Laughter (1943)
This Happy Breed (1943)
Sigh No More (1945)
Present Laughter (1947)
Joyeux Chagrins (Paris 1948)
The Apple Cart (1953)
Suite in Three Keys (1966)

Film Appearances

Hearts of the World (1918)
The Scoundrel (Miracle in 49th Street) (1935)
In Which We Serve (1943)
Brief Encounter (1945)
The Astonished Heart (1950)
Around the World in 80 Days (1956)
Our Man in Havanna (1960)
Surprise Package (1960)
Paris When it Sizzles (1964)
Bunny Lake is Missing (1965)
Boom! (1969)
The Italian Job (1969)

TV Appearances

Together With Music (1955)
Blithe Spirit (1956)
This Happy Breed (1956)
Androcles and the Lion (1967)

FRED ASTAIRE

Full name Fred Austerlitz.

Born Wed. 10 May 1899, Omaha, Nebraska, USA.

Characteristics About 5′ 9″; about 133*lb.* (9*st. 7lb.*); size 8½ shoes; brown hair and eyes.

Married 1933 Phyllis Livingstone (died 1954) 1*s.* 1*d.* (1 stepson by his wife's previous marriage).

There is no evidence that if you have toes that wiggle in your sleep you have the makings of a great dancer. Except that Fred Astaire's toes do and he is, according to Noël Coward: 'The greatest who ever lived – even greater than Nijinsky.'[1] Apart from this glowing testimonial, Coward also supplied the title of Fred's book *Steps in Time* which records his progress in show business from the bottom up: '... in Vaudeville, when we needed work, my sister and I were fired a number of times and once we were replaced by a dog act.' Adele and Fred were not utterly discouraged. They appeared in their first Broadway show, *Over the Top*, in 1917 and regularly thereafter until Adele retired in 1931. Their most famous show was probably George Gershwin's *Lady, Be Good!* which played in New York in 1924 and in London two years later. It was on the closing night of Gershwin's *Funny Face* that Adele met

Fred Astaire's feet were still twinkling at the age of 70 when he played the title role in 'Finian's Rainbow' (Warner Brothers–Seven Arts, 1969).

168

Lord Charles Cavendish, the English peer whom she was to marry. The Astaire duo's last appearance together was in *The Band Wagon* (1931).

Fred has explained his dancing virtuosity in terms not to be taken too literally by the average earthbound mortal: 'I like to keep my feet in the air and move around.' He has admitted that the academic aspect does not concern him: 'When you come to the evolution of the dance, its history and philosophy, I know as much about that as I do about how a television produces pictures – which is absolutely nothing.' He could, however, originate his own dances and often looked over a four-hour anthology of his dances before rehearsing in front of a mirror to get the routine fixed in his mind. 'Choreography for the camera', he has pointed out, 'requires 80 per cent brainwork and 20 per cent footwork.' Preparing for a musical show or film is 'like living in a sweatbox . . . I used to average eight months of work on a musical, rehearsing dance numbers for the first three.'

The report on Fred's first screen test noted: 'Can't act. Slightly bald. Can dance a little.' The qualifications proved more than adequate. Within 12 months of his teaming up with Ginger Rogers they had become the greatest money-making partnership in Hollywood and RKO Studios insured his legs for $1,000,000 (£250,000). The first of his nine pictures with Ginger was *Flying Down to Rio*.

Fred's legs hoofed hard and often in the 'thirties and 'forties. Bing Crosby reported that in *Holiday Inn* he 'danced himself so thin I could almost spit through him.' His weight dropped from 140 to 126 pounds (10 stone to 9 stone). 'When you're in a picture with Astaire', Bing warned, 'you've got rocks in your head if you do much dancing. He's so quick-footed and so light that it's impossible not to look like a hay-digger compared with him.'

When Gene Kelly broke an ankle in 1946, Fred made an unscheduled comeback from retirement for *Blue Skies*. This started him on another decade of dancing and a fresh series of partners to complete a career spanning over 40 years of the light fantastic. In 1949 he was awarded a special 'Oscar' for 'raising the standards of all musicals'.

The song-dance routines which featured in his shows and films made Fred famous also as a recording star and top composers wrote songs that will forever be linked

[1] Vaslav Fomich Nijinsky (1890-1950) the Russian ballet dancer.

with his name. The glamourous ballad *Dancing in the Dark* featured in the revue *The Band Wagon*. Cole Porter's *Night and Day* was in the film *Gay Divorcee* and the show *The Gay Divorce*. Irving Berlin wrote *Cheek to Cheek* sung by Fred in the film *Top Hat*; *Let's Face the Music and Dance* in the film *Follow the Fleet*; and *Change Partners* in the film *Carefree*. Berlin's music was the inspiration in two other great pictures: *Blue Skies* and *Easter Parade*, both of which had well-loved title songs. In *The Barkleys of Broadway* Fred sang Berlin's *It Only Happens When I Dance With You*. Jerome

Kern melodies in the film *Swing Time* furnished with more standard song hits, including *The Way You Look Tonight*, *Bojangles*, and *A Fine Romance*.

Fred's contributions to the national effort in World War II were considerable. The *Ziegfield Follies* netted 'many millions' in war bond sales in 1944–45. In 1942 he made 350 appearances at fund-raising shows in a two-week period. The marathon culminated in the sale of one of his well-worn pairs of tap shoes at a luncheon in Cleveland, Ohio for $100,000 (£25,000) in bonds. In addition the laces fetched $16,000 (£4,000).

Fred Astaire's dancing partner in 'You'll Never Get Rich' (1941) and 'You Were Never Lovelier' (1942) was Rita Hayworth.

Films and Dancing Partners

Dancing Lady (1933) with Joan Crawford.
Flying Down to Rio (1933)
The Gay Divorcee (1934)
Roberta (1935)   with Ginger Rogers.
Top Hat (1935)
Follow the Fleet (1936)
Swing Time (1936)
A Damsel in Distress (1937) with Joan Fontaine.
Shall We Dance (1937)
Carefree (1938)   with Ginger Rogers.
The Story of Vernon and Irene Castle (1939)
Broadway Melody of 1940 with Eleanor Powell.
Second Chorus (1940) with Paulette Goddard.
You'll Never Get Rich (1941) with Rita Hayworth.
Holiday Inn (1942) with Marjorie Reynolds.
You Were Never Lovelier (1942) with Rita Hayworth.
The Sky's the Limit (1943) with Joan Leslie.
Ziegfeld Follies (1944–45) with Lucille Bremer.
Blue Skies (1946) with Olga San Juan.
Easter Parade (1948) with Judy Garland.
The Barkleys of Broadway (1949) with Judy Garland.
Three Little Words (1950) with Vera Ellen.
Let's Dance (1950) with Betty Hutton.
Royal Wedding (1951) with Judy Garland.
Belle of New York (1952) with Vera Ellen.
The Band Wagon (1953) with Cyd Charisse.
Daddy Long Legs (1955) with Leslie Caron.
Funny Face (1956) with Audrey Hepburn.
Silk Stockings (1957) with Cyd Charisse.
An Evening with Fred Astaire (TV – 1958) with Barrie Chase.
On the Beach (1959)
Finian's Rainbow (1968) with Petula Clark.
Midas Run (1969)

Anticipating the time when his own perspiration and shoe-leather would be expended less prodigally, Fred started in 1947 a ballroom dancing business which had over 100 dance studios in operation by 1958. Though not a ballroom dancer – 'I don't enjoy dancing as a social pastime. Dancing is hard work for me' – Astaire has offered this tip for ballroom fans: 'When you're dancing with a lady, her dress immediately becomes *our* dress. We have to manage it, keep it out of our eyes, whirl it, and get it out of our way.'

At the age of 61, Fred explained his endless durability like this: 'Dancing makes you look young. I mean the very physical act of dancing is almost symbolic of youth. Right now there's no reason why I cannot continue dancing for years . . . Dancing keeps me in good shape all year around . . . I never diet and I hate calisthenics.' Following *Funny Face* with Audrey Hepburn, Fred turned to television and in the succeeding years won nine 'Emmy' Awards.

New York Shows

Over the Top (1917)
The Passing Show of 1918
Apple Blossoms (1919)
The Love Letter (1921)
For Goodness Sake (1922), in London as
Stop Flirting (1923).
The Bunch and Judy (1922)
Lady, Be Good! (1924), in London (1926).
Funny Face (1927), in London (1928).
Smiles (1930)
The Band Wagon (1931)
The Gay Divorce (1932), in London (1933).

LP Recordings

Three Evenings with Astaire (London HAA8225)
Band Wagon (1932) (RCA Victor RD7756)
Nothing Thrilled Us Half as Much (Columbia SX6059)
Fred Astaire Now (Ace of Hearts ZAHR171/AHR171)
Finian's Rainbow (Soundtrack) (Warner WFS2550)
Fred Astaire (28 titles) (Verve VSP23/24)
Band Wagon (RCA Victor INT1037)

Duke Ellington

Full name   Edward Kennedy Ellington.

Born   Sat. 29 April 1899, Washington, DC, USA.

Characteristics   About 5′ 11½″; about 192*lb.* (13*st.* 10*lb.*); black hair; brown eyes.

Married
(1) 1919 Edna Thompson (div. 1930) 1*s.*
(2) 1930 Mildred Dixon (div. 1939).
(3) 1939 Bea Ellis.

An Englishman boasting to an American about British Royalty was once stopped in his tracks with the unanswerable squelch that in the United States they had Count Basie, Earl Hines, Nat King Cole, and, above all, Duke Ellington. Setting aside the mild confusion of 'aristocracy' with 'royalty' few would question the assertion that the Duke has precedence among the senior citizens of 20th-century jazz music. Almost continuously for over 40 years the leader of the finest jazz ensemble in the world, he is acknowledged as the time's most accomplished composer and arranger of Negro folk music. He has written scores for Broadway shows and motion pictures, produced over 1,200 pieces of music, was once nominated for

Duke Ellington and his Orchestra recorded a special TV programme of jazz music in Coventry Cathedral, England in 1966. The concert included the first performance of his suite 'In the Beginning God'.

a Pulitzer Prize, and was elected to the *Down Beat* Hall of Fame in 1956.

Duke began taking piano lessons at seven but though he enjoyed them he never got on with practising: 'Before I knew it I would be fashioning a new melody and accompaniment instead of following the score.' At 13 he took a job as a soda jerk at an ice cream parlour where, incidentally, he acquired the name Duke: 'They called me that because I was so prideful of the stiff, starched uniform I used to wear.' In those surroundings he came up with his first composition, *The Soda Fountain Rag*, and played it at a local café in five different styles: straight, blues, foxtrot, waltz, and fast tempo stomp. 'They never knew it was the same piece. I was established . . . I had a repertoire.'

Forming his own jazz band in 1918, Ellington was engaged at New York's Cotton Club from 1927–32. He described their playing as 'stark, wild, and tense . . .' and they were not afraid of new effects. One day a trombonist turned up with a kitchen pot as a sliphorn. It sounded all right so Duke let him keep it until the group could afford 'a handsome gadget that gave him the same effect'.

Duke's first hit, one of his most important compositions, was *Mood Indigo* which was recorded in 1930 with the title *Dreamy Blues*. This became one of his theme tunes along with *East Street Toodle-oo* and *Take the 'A' Train*. The latter was one of the numbers selected for the million-selling album *60 Years of Music America Loves Best* (1959).

Experts have classified Ellington's work in eight different categories but they can be reduced to two main headings, basic Ellingtonia and what is called Jungle Jazz. Duke himself does not like the word jazz, preferring to be known as a composer of Negro folk music: 'I try to catch the character and mood and feeling of my people . . . I think the music of my race is something that is going to live.' He has admitted to drawing on every personal

which evolve rather than emerge spontaneously: 'One act of creation leads to another, and to that high plane where inspiration is encountered.'

Duke's first European tour took place in 1933, the band sailing only after he had overcome his fears about icebergs in the Atlantic. Another tour in 1939 spread the Ellington gospel to a wider and increasingly receptive audience, while in the post-war years at least seven European tours made his name familiar to successive generations of fans not born when he began composing. He carried out a US State Department tour of the Middle and Near East in 1963 and made other tours to Africa and Japan. His reputation was accorded academic recognition when he made his debut as a

experience and observation for his musical ideas: 'I remember once I wrote a 64-bar piece about a memory of when I was a little boy in bed and heard a man whistling on the street outside, his footsteps echoing away.' His ear is unfailingly sensitive to the sounds of the open air. Driving in Florida once before dawn he heard a bird call: 'Man it was sensational. I stopped to listen and repeat it to myself. I could use that.' He has described the musician's art as being 'the creation of musical flowers

Lecturer at the University of Cincinnati in 1966 and a year later when he was made an Honorary Doctor of Music by the University of Yale.

Duke's orchestra, originally a 14-piece ensemble, know him as a perfectionist but not a disciplinarian. He never uses a baton, pays his instrumentalists well, and is notoriously easy on advances: 'Why should I knock myself out in an argument about $15 when in the same time I can probably write a $1,500 song?' This is almost literally true because Duke has been known to write songs casually while riding in taxis or trains, a gift shared by Noël Coward and Cole Porter.

Duke's unofficial fan club includes nearly all the leading figures in the world of jazz and popular music. They recognize him as the greatest originator in his field – among other things he pioneered the wordless use of the voice as a musical instrumentation, not the only Ellington invention that has been widely admired and imitated.

His first wife, Edna, thought their son Mercer, who composed *Tonight I Shall Sleep* (1945) in collaboration with his father, a better musician than his father. She described him as 'a lonely man. He masks his emotions. Never wants you to know what he actually feels.' But his

e Ellington received the highest United States
ian award, the Presidential Medal of Freedom,
his 70th birthday, 29 April 1969. President
hard M. Nixon entertained him at the White
use and played 'Happy Birthday to You' on the piano.

associates revere him almost as a legend. Willie 'the Lion' Smith wrote that Duke was 'always a good-looking, well-mannered fellow: one of those guys, you see him, you like him right away.'

LP Recordings

Selections from Grieg (CBS BPG62056/SBPG62056)
The Indispensable Duke Ellington, Volume 1
(RCA Victor RD27258)
The Indispensable Duke Ellington, Volume 2
(RCA Victor RD27259)
Cotton Club Days, Volume 1 (Ace of Hearts AH23)
Cotton Club Days, Volume 2 (Ace of Hearts AH89)
Cotton Club Days, Volume 3 (Ace of Hearts AH166)
The Duke in Harlem (Ace of Hearts AH47)
Duke Ellington Plays (Capitol T477)
Ellington '65 (Reprise R6122/R9–6122)
Mary Poppins (Reprise R6164)
Ellington '66 (Reprise R6165)
Will the Big Bands Ever Come Back (Reprise R6168/R9–6168)
The Duke Steps Out (RCA Victor RD7731)
Concert in the Virgin Islands (Reprise R6185/R9–6185)
The Nutcracker Suite (CBS BPG62030/SBPG62030)
Piano in the Foreground (CBS BPG62204/SBPG62204)
Duke Ellington Presents (Ember CJS813)
It's Duke Ellington and His Orchestra (Ember FA2036)
Rare Duke Ellington Masterpieces (Verve VLP9)
The Great Big Bands (Capitol T20808)
The Ellington Era 1927–40 (CBS BPG66302) (3 LPs)
Duke Ellington's Greatest Hits (Reprise RLP6234/RSLP6234)
Duke Ellington's Concert of Sacred Music
(RCA Victor RD7811/RM52310)
Pretty Woman (RCA Victor RD7942)
And His Mother Called Him Bill (RCA Victor SF7964)
Back to Back and Side by Side (with Johnny Hodges)
(Verve VSP11/12)
Johnny Come Lately (RCA Victor RD7888)
Duke Ellington's Far East Suite (RCA Victor RD7894/SF7894)
Duke Ellington at the Cote d'Azur (Verve VLP9170/SVLP9170)
Soul Call (Verve VLP9197/SVLP9197)
Such Sweet Thunder (CBS Realm RM52421)
Best of Duke Ellington (World Record Club T708)
The Popular Duke Ellington (RCA Victor SF7835/RD7835)
At His Very Best (RCA Victor RD27133)
Francis A. Sinatra and Edward K. Ellington
(Reprise RLP1024/RSLP1024)
North of the Border in Canada (MCA MUPS372)
Cottontail (with Billy Strayhorn) (Riverside 673019)

THE EARL OF AVON

Anthony Eden (now Lord Avon) was Under-Secretary of State for Foreign Affairs (1931–33), Lord Privy Seal (1934–35), Minister Without Portfolio for League of Nations Affairs (1935), Secretary of State for Foreign Affairs (1935–38, 1940–45, and 1951–55), Secretary of State for War (1940), and Prime Minister (1955–57). He was Conservative MP for Warwick and Leamington (1923–57).

In March 1918, at the village of La Fère on the River Oise in France, a German corporal (Iron Cross, Second Class) went into action in the last major offensive of World War I. Near by, a young English Adjutant (Military Cross[1]) rallied his troops to withstand the brutal shock of an assault in which the Allied troops were outnumbered by ten to one. Neither the German corporal, destined to be Chancellor of the Third Reich, nor the English officer, later Prime Minister of England, were aware how close they came to a physical confrontation which might have deflected the course of history, until 1935, when they were neighbours at a Berlin banquet (*see page 179*). Anthony Eden (now Lord Avon) has described this meeting in his memoirs: 'It emerged we must have been opposite each other . . . Together we drew a map on the back of a dinner card, which I still possess, signed by both of us, Hitler marking in some places and I in others. The corporal on the German side had as clear a recollection of place names and dispositions as the young staff officer, as I had then just become, on the British.'

Eden commenced his parliamentary career in 1923, delivering his maiden speech in the House of Commons on 19 Feb. 1924 in the debate on air strength: 'It is a natural temptation for members opposite,' he said, 'whose views on defence were fairly well known during the years of the war, to adopt the attitude of that very useful animal, the terrier, and roll on their backs and wave their paws in the air with a pathetic expression. That is not the line by which we can insure this country against attack from the air.'

Eden was only 34 when he became a junior Minister in the Coalition Government under Ramsey Macdonald.[2] Harold Macmillan, another young Conservative of the day, wrote a glowing account of his colleague's stature in parliament: 'Eden's position, first as Under-Secretary for Foreign Affairs and then as Lord Privy Seal, was commanding. His fine war record, his charm, his versatility, his pre-eminence in debate: all these made him an outstanding figure.'

Eden was one of the leading protagonists of a policy of preparedness against the Nazi threat, not then widely recognized by members of the government. In a speech at Bradford in 1935 he warned: 'There is a spirit of violence abroad in Europe today which bodes ill for the future unless all the restraining and responsible influences in humanity are brought to bear to check it.' Eden's influence in this period was such that when he resigned as Foreign Secretary over Neville Chamberlain's policy of appeasement on 20 Feb. 1938, it caused Winston Churchill a sleepless night. 'There seemed one strong young figure', wrote Churchill, 'standing up against the long, dismal, drawling tides of drift and surrender, of wrong measurements and feeble impulses. My conduct of affairs would have been different from his in various ways; but he seemed to me at this moment to embody the life-hope of the British nation.'

Described by Lord Beaverbrook as 'the most popular member of the War Cabinet', Eden was Churchill's right-hand man and was nominated as successor to the Premier-

ship in June 1942 when Churchill visited President Franklin D. Roosevelt. 'In case of my death on this journey I am about to undertake', wrote the Prime Minister to King George VI, 'I avail myself of Your Majesty's gracious permission to advise that you should entrust the formation of a new government to Mr Anthony Eden . . . who is in my mind the outstanding Minister . . . who, I am sure, will be found capable of conducting Your Majesty's affairs with the resolution, experience, and capacity which these grievous times require.' So much was Eden the acknowledged authority on Foreign Affairs after Churchill himself that in 1945, Clement Attlee, then Prime Minister, automatically suggested after the Potsdam Conference that a message be sent to 'the Prime Minister and Mr Eden'.

On 6 April 1955 Eden was elected Leader of the Conservative Party and became the 43rd Prime Minister on the resignation of Churchill. The man he defeated, R. A. (now Lord) Butler, said: 'I am perfectly clear that he has three qualities for leadership. The first is courage; the second is integrity; the third is flair.' All these qualities were evident in Eden's handling of the Soviet leaders, Nikolai Bulganin and Nikita S. Khrushchev, when they visited England in 1956. Said Khrushchev: 'I have great confidence in Eden, I have great confidence in Selwyn Lloyd, and I have great confidence in Butler; I am sure they are all anxious for peace, and I think we are beginning to understand each other.' Before returning to Moscow, Khrushchev was positively benign: 'Bulganin can vote Labour if he likes but I'm going to vote Conservative.'

Eden thus made his first contribution as Premier to the period of 'peaceful co-existence' but the Suez crisis was to undo much of his work in relaxing tensions

[1] Awarded on 5 June 1917 for rescuing his sergeant in circumstances of particular gallantry.
[2] James Ramsey Macdonald (1866-1937), Prime Minister (1924 and 1929-31, then 1931-35 Coalition).

between East and West. The Prime Minister who had lost a brother killed in World War I and a son killed in World War II was faced with a decision the consequences of which might, in the view of some observers, have precipitated World War III. In his broadcast on 8 Aug. 1956 following the seizure of the Suez Canal[3] by Colonel Nasser, Eden said: 'Our quarrel is not with Egypt, still less with the Arab world; it is with Colonel Nasser . . . we all know this is how Fascist governments behave, and we remember . . . what the cost can be in giving in to Fascism.'

British armed intervention in Egypt was preceded by an Israeli attack against Egypt on 20 Oct. 1956 provoked by the Arab pact which threatened Israel's security. Following the rejection of a Franco-British ultimatum to Israel and Egypt to cease operations, Allied air strikes against Egypt commenced on 31 Oct. and on 5 Nov. British and French paratroops landed on Egypt. Said Eden: 'We have stepped in because the UN could not do so in time.' Sir Winston Churchill endorsed the action: 'Not for the first time, we have acted independently for the common good.' Khrushchev, himself the architect of policies directed at fomenting unrest in the Middle East, synthetically denounced the attack as 'piratic' and hailed Nasser as 'the hero of his nation and our sympathies are on his side'. Eden's reply to this was: 'For a country to enslave Hungary[4] and at the same time lecture us for our action in Egypt is nauseating hypocrisy.' Meanwhile, at Nasser's order, Cairo radio sent a message to the people of Port Said: 'The enemy who subjugated us for so many years is now in your hands. Kill any number[5] you want.' The brief action terminated after the UN had ordered a ceasefire on 6 Nov. and agreed to provide an emergency force. Britain complied with the UN's demand for withdrawal on 24 Nov.

Among those who criticized Eden's Suez action, Butler said later: 'I admired Eden's courage in attempting to save the canal, because I thought from my knowledge of Disraeli[6] and the old history of the canal, that it was vital to British interests.' Hugh Gaitskell, Leader of the Labour Party, who had earlier compared Nasser with Hitler, said the action had done 'irreparable harm to the prestige and reputation of our country'. India's Prime Minister, Jawaharlal Nehru who, according to some sources, had encouraged Nasser to nationalize the Suez Canal, exploded: 'In all my experience of foreign affairs I am not aware of a grosser case of naked aggression.' Nehru's own intervention in Kashmir (*see page*) was not a distant memory. Harold Macmillan, then a member of Eden's Cabinet, said: 'There are times in a man's life when he has to make bold decisions. History alone will prove whether what we did was right or wrong.'

After Eden's retirement due to ill health, the incoming Premier, Harold Macmillan, spoke in the House of Commons on 22 Jan. 1957: 'Throughout his whole political life he has shown on many occasions rare courage. He has always done what he thought was right, and we can pay no greater tribute to any man.' Gaitskell referred to Eden as 'an outstandingly gifted Parliamentarian'. He added: 'Out of the many successful international negotiations which he conducted, two comparatively recent ones come at once to our minds – his recent achievement in bringing about the Paris agreements[7] within a few weeks of the collapse of the European Defence Community project, and his successful handling of the Geneva negotiations on Indo-China.'[8]

The Suez affair again came into the news with the Arab-Israeli war of 1967 when the former Australian Premier, Sir Robert Menzies, wrote in his book *Afternoon Light*: 'I know that it has become fashionable to condemn Anthony Eden, to say that he ruined his great and deserved reputation as Foreign Secretary of Great Britain by his "inept" handling of the Suez crisis. Of all the politicians now surviving this event, I should be the last to adopt this fashion for I still think he was right.'

'Nothing is more important in politics than to distinguish appearance from reality.'

'There are occasions in diplomacy when to reach for the better is to lose the good.'

'Neutrality is not a crime, it is a risk. Indo-China could be an example where neutrality could also be a way through to peace.' (1966)

[3] In 1854 the French former diplomat, Ferdinand de Lesseps (1805-94), was authorized by the Wali of Egypt to form the *Compagnie Universelle du Canal Maritime de Suez* for the purpose of constructing a waterway linking the Mediterranean Sea and the Gulf of Suez. The 104-mile Suez Canal was opened on 17 Nov. 1869. The Company's 99-year concession was due to expire in 1968.

[4] Total lives lost in the Soviet suppression of the Hungarian revolution of October 1956 were about 32,000 (25,000 Hungarians and 7,000 Soviet soldiers killed).

[5] British and French forces lost 32 men killed; Egypt lost 650 killed in Port Said and about 100 killed in Port Fuad.

[6] Benjamin Disraeli, 1st Earl of Beaconsfield (1804-81), Prime Minister (1868 and 1874-80). Disraeli purchased about 44 per cent of the shares in the Suez Canal Company in 1875. Britain supplied over 50 per cent of the total traffic through the Canal, five times more than the next biggest users, the Dutch. The canal shortened the sea route from Europe to India by 5,000 miles.

[7] By the London and Paris agreements of 5 May 1955, the German Federal Republic attained sovereignty and entered NATO.

[8] Eden played a leading role in drafting the terms of the armistice, signed at Geneva on 21 July 1954, ending the 7½-year civil war in Vietnam.

Full name Robert Anthony Eden, 1st Earl of Avon (1961), KG (1954), MC (1917), (PC 1934).

Born Sat. 12 June 1897, Windlestone, Durham, England.

Characteristics Just over 6′; dark brown hair; blue eyes.

Married
(1) 1923 Beatrice Helen Beckett (div. 1950, died 1957) 2s.
(2) 1952 Clarissa Anne Spencer Churchill.

There were no smiles for the camera when Anthony Eden dined with Hitler in 1935.

It has sometimes been observed that the finest products of Scotland are exclusively for export. In this distinctive category may be mentioned one American on the moon (*see page*), six 20th-century Prime Ministers of England, and Sir Robert Menzies, who served as Prime Minister of Australia twice as long as any other man and has not refrained from stating that he is 'a reasonably bigoted descendant of the Scottish race'.

Bob Menzies was the grandson of a goldminer who lost his job because he organized a union. When he was only nine a phrenologist felt the bumps on his head and declared: 'This boy will make a successful barrister and public speaker.' In the fourth grade at Jeparit School, the headmaster gave him a book for coming top and told him: 'Robert,

you might be Prime Minister of Australia one of these days.' Bob finished his school education at the head of the Victorian State scholarship list and went on to take first-class honours in Law at the University of Melbourne. Called to the Bar in 1918, he built up a lucrative practice worth £10,000 ($40,000) a year by 1928 when he decided to enter politics. He was elected to the Victorian Legislative Council in a by-election when only 33 and then became Australia's youngest King's Counsel only a year later.

In debate he quickly won a reputation for incisiveness and attack. When the Minister of Education enforced his argument in favour of a large appropriation for works with a threat to resign, Menzies said: 'The real question we are discussing, Mr Premier, is whether we are prepared to spend £400,000 of the State's money to keep the Minister in Parliament.' In public he scored no less effectively, especially when given a lead. A woman once shouted

Sir Robert Menzies

Full name Robert Gordon Menzies, KT (1963), CH (1951), QC (1929), (PC 1937). Menzies is pronounced 'Menzees' in Australia, 'Mingies' in Scotland.

Born Thurs. 20 Dec. 1894, Jeparit, Victoria, Australia.

Characteristics About 6′ 2″; about 250*lb.* (17*st.* 12*lb.*); originally black hair; hat size 7½; enjoys wines and cigars.

Married 1920 Pattie Maie Lecknie 2*s.* 1*d.*

180

Sir Robert Menzies was Attorney-General, Commonwealth of Australia (1934–39); Treasurer 1939–40); Minister for Trade and Customs (1940); Minister for Co-ordination of Defence (1939–41); Minister for Information and for Munitions (1940); Prime Minister (1939–41 and 1940–66); also Minister for External Affairs (1960–61).

out from his audience: 'I wouldn't vote for you if you were the Archangel Gabriel.' Murmured Menzies, courteously: 'Madam, if I were the Archangel Gabriel, I'm afraid you wouldn't be in my constituency.' To hecklers of the male sex he was less gallant. 'Tell us all you know, Bob, it won't take long,' called one would-be wag. 'I'll tell you all we both know', rapped Bob, 'it won't take any longer.'

Menzies was Deputy-Premier, Attorney-General, and Minister for Railways in Victoria from 1932 to 1934 when he entered Federal politics, successfully contesting the seat of Kooyong as a member of the new United Australia Party (UAP), the forerunner of the Liberal Party which he later helped to form in 1944. As Federal Attorney-General he acquired the nickname 'Pig-Iron Bob' after a dispute in 1938 about cargoes of pig-iron destined for Japan under government contract led to strikes in Port Kembla.

A supporter of Neville Chamberlain's 1938 policy of appeasement in Europe, Menzies was none the less ready, after his appointment as Prime Minister in 1939, to lead Australia into World War II at the side of Great Britain. When he resigned in 1941, Winston Churchill thought the Australian government was weakened 'by the loss of its ablest figure'. He wrote a personal note to Menzies saying: 'I am the gainer by our personal friendship.'

In 1947 Menzies stated that it is 'loyalty to a common Crown which marks out the relation between the British Dominions as being different from any other association now to be found in the world.' During his marathon Premiership (1949–66) he remained a staunch Commonwealth man but drew Australia more into the world orbit through a closer alignment with America. This was cemented by the ANZUS Pact, signed on 1 Sept. 1951, a military alliance between Australia, New Zealand, and the United States. Menzies made himself respected at the United Nations, even trading quips with Nikita S. Khrushchev, the Soviet Premier, who looked him up and down and said that 'for an Imperialist, you are not a bad specimen'. Bob retorted that as a Communist he improved on closer inspection. Strongly anti-Communist, Menzies supported British action in Suez (*see page* 179), and authorized the assignment of an Australian battalion to South Vietnam, stating on 7 June 1965 that most Australians were in favour of what the Americans were doing in Vietnam because they feared that 'if the Communists won in Vietnam the whole world would be endangered.'

Menzies received many tributes from world statesmen. Sir Anthony Eden (now Lord Avon) wrote in his memoirs: 'Menzies shows his legal training in the lucidity of his mind and a penetrating intelligence. His statesmenship is something more. He has an instinct for great affairs and he cannot tolerate humbug.' He was described by Harold Wilson as 'cast in the same mould as Sir Winston Churchill', a compliment Sir Robert would cherish for in his own memoirs he had recorded his admiration for Churchill, noting: 'I know that I can be accused of a sort of hero-worship; and if so I will plead guilty.' President Lyndon B. Johnson sent a personal note to Menzies on his retirement as Prime Minister saying that he had been 'the trusted colleague of four American Presidents' and 'a statesman of freedom'.

'Democracy's true glory is not the achievement of a uniform mediocrity or of a spirit of dependence on government, but the encouragement of talent and initiative, the elevation of the individual, the giving of opportunity to all who have the inherent quality to seize it.'

NIKITA

'We will in my life time rul

'. . . none of this would have happened if a couple of writers had been shot in time', remarked the Soviet leader as he completed the task of crushing the 1956 Hungarian revolution.[1] Fond of quoting the old adage, 'In a fight don't stop to choose your cudgels', the former herdsman, metal worker, and miner started life labouring among the masses. In America in 1959, he revealed that his grandfather had been 'an illiterate peasant serf. He was the landlord's property and could be sold or even, as was often the case, traded for a dog.' Nikita Sergeyevich was a peg above this and what is more he had a pious upbringing. 'Khrushchev was once an altar boy', revealed Dwight D. Eisenhower; 'he told me that as a youth he won prizes for excellence in religious education and ritual. But to become a dedicated Communist he had to become an atheist.'

Surviving an attempt on his life in 1939[2], Khrushchev graduated through the echelons of Communist Party power by

Full name Nikita Sergeyevich Khrushchev.
Born Tues. 17 April 1894, Kalinovka, Kursk, USSR.
Characteristics About 5′ 3″; about 215*lb.* (15*st.* 5*lb.*); blue eyes; gold teeth; artificial steel jawbone.
Married
(1) 1915 Galina (died 1921) (1*s.* killed in World War II) 1*d.*
(2) 1924 Nina Petrovna 1*s.* 2*d.*

methods appropriate to the enterprise, 'We are men of lofty morals', he pronounced at a Moscow press conference in 1960, 'and we believe that our kind of morality will come to prevail not only in the socialist lands but throughout the world.' Those present who were conversant not only with the facts of the 1956 Hungarian blood-bath but also the mass murder of 10,000 prisoners in the Ukraine in 1937–39, may have hoped earnestly that his forecast would not materialise.

A disciple of Stalin, whose image he at first extolled and later vilified, Khrushchev was not trusted by the man he hoped to

KRUSHCHEV

minded, articulate, hard-reasoning spokesman for a system in which he thoroughly believed and in which he was thoroughly versed'. Eisenhower wrote: 'There was no denying that he was an interesting man . . . He was shrewd, tough, and coldly deliberate, even when he was pretending to be consumed with anger. Certainly he was ruthless. In personal conversations he was blunt but witty; he laughed often and seemed devoted to his family'. He also noted that the Khrushchev of the tea table was scarcely recognizable to people who knew him at conference. A graphic personal sketch was provided by Milovan Djilas, former Vice-President of Yugoslavia, who noted that Mr K. was 'Rather short and stocky, but brisk and agile; he was strongly hewn and of one piece. He more or less bolted down impressive quantities of food – as though wishing to spare his artificial steel jawbone.'

Despite his public threat of 17 Nov. 1956 aimed at the West – 'History is on our side. We will bury you' – Khrushchev sometimes appeared jovially informal in public, achieving a semblance of departure from the bleaker aspects of the Communist image. At a meeting of Labour leaders in San Francisco in 1959 he gave a burlesque demonstration of his idea of the Can-Can, which he had seen on the set of the film of that title starring Shirley MacLaine at Hollywood. 'This is what you call freedom – freedom for girls to show their backsides', he bawled. 'To us it's pornography. The culture of people who want pornography. It's Capitalism that makes the girls that way'. Asked if there should be a law about this, the Hero of the Soviet Union asserted: 'There should be a law prohibiting the girls from showing their backsides, a moral law'. Bob Hope suggested that Mr K. should visit Disneyland but the Los Angeles security police would not allow it. Hope reported: 'We quickly found out why Mr K. is known as the

succeed. Shortly before his death, Stalin told Georgi Malenkov: 'Cut excessive drinking of wine, otherwise sink to the level of Bulganin and Khrushchev and gradually become a will-less tool of Molotov.' He added: 'See that Khrushchev is Secretary-General of the Party but be on your guard. You have the better brain of the two, you can also be decisive and stubborn.' Khrushchev duly became Secretary-General in 1953, succeeding Nikolai Bulganin as Chairman of the Council of Ministers in 1958. Bulganin had taken the chair from Malenkov[3] in 1955 and during his tenure operated a kind of tandem leadership with Khrushchev in the period 1955–58, when they were commonly referred to by the Western Press as Mr B. and Mr K.

Khrushchev commanded the respect of all the Western leaders who met him. Lord Avon found him 'extremely well-informed and of a very retentive memory'. President John F. Kennedy thought him a 'tough-

"fastest mouth alive". He took off on a 10-minute talk about the capitalist plot against his visiting Disneyland. Personally, I think they should have let him go to Disneyland – after all, he missed Congress.' Bob paid a further gratuitous compliment to the Soviet leader, stating that 'the workers love Khrushchev very much. He hasn't got an enemy in the entire country. Quite a few under it.'

Khrushchev's bellicosity was seen at full fury during Harold Macmillan's speech at the United Nations in 1960 when the Soviet Premier thumped so heavily on his desk with both fists 'that Mac, interrupted several times in mid-sentence, was obliged to ask the Assembly: 'Can anybody translate that?' On that occasion, Khrushchev actually removed his shoes the better to slam his disapproval on the table. When the American U-2 reconnaisance aircraft was shot down over Soviet territory in May 1960, Khrushchev's rage was vivid: 'If anyone hits me on the left cheek, I would hit him on the right one, and so hard it would knock his head off', he yelled. Commenting on the gold watches and rings carried by the American flyer by way of emergency currency, he gibed: 'Perhaps the pilot should have flown higher – to Mars, and was preparing to seduce Martian women.'[4]

In his policy of de-Stalinization (see page 281) and his expressed view that the Lenin dictum 'wars are inevitable' was no longer valid, Khrushchev took the sting out of his harsher verbal attacks on the West. But the new line was to bring him under fire from Mao Tse-tung who did not join the campaign to damn Stalin. 'In what position does Khrushchev, who participated in the leadership of the Party and the State during Stalin's period, place himself when he beats his breast, pounds the table, and shouts abuse of Stalin at the top of his voice?' asked Mao. 'In the position of an accomplice to a "murderer"

or a "bandit"? Or in the same position as a "fool" or an "idiot"?' In 1962 when, under pressure from President Kennedy, Khrushchev agreed to dismantle his missile bases in Cuba (see page 278), Mao denounced him for 'adventurism' and 'capitulationism'. By April 1964 Khrushchev had reached the conclusion that China's policies were formed by men 'who want to bring Stalin's corpse back to life, who do not rely on Marxism-Leninism, who want to rely on the axe and the knife.' A few days later he accused China of 'slipping into a quagmire of Trotskyism and big-China chauvinism.' Within months, Mao answered with a full-length publication entitled *On Khrushchev's Phoney Communism and Its Historical Lessons for the World* in which he wrote that Khrushchev 'serves both the interests of the handful of members of the privileged bourgeois stratum in his own country and those of foreign imperialism and reaction.'

On 15 Oct. 1964 Khrushchev was replaced as Secretary-General of the Communist Party by Leonid Ilyich Brezhnev (*born* 19 Dec. 1906), and as Chairman of the Council of Ministers by Alexei Nikolaevich Kosygin (*born* 20 Feb. 1904), the reason for his dismissal being given as 'advanced age and deterioration of health'. In a Kremlin speech on 6 Nov. 1964 presumed to refer to Khrushchev, Brezhnev said: 'Experience has shown . . . that wherever the scientific approach is replaced by subjectivism and arbitrary decisions, failure is certain and mistakes are inevitable.' In a radio and television broadcast on 18 Oct. 1964, President Lyndon B. Johnson spoke favourably of the outgoing Soviet Premier: '. . . he learned from his mistakes and was not blind to realities. . . . He joined in the "hot line" which can help prevent war by accident. He agreed that space can be kept free of nuclear weapons. In these actions he demonstrated good sense and sober judgement.' The Communist Party Central Committee, however, was less generous. Its 50th Anniversary Statement published in 1967 made no mention of Khrushchev whatsoever. The ex-Premier lives in his dacha outside Moscow but maintains residence in the city with an apartment so that he can cast his vote at elections for the sole candidate, Alexei N. Kosygin.

'We will in my lifetime, rule the world by invitation.'

'Do not believe we have forgotten Marx, Engels, and Lenin. They will not be forgotten until shrimp learn to sing.'

'Those who wait for the Soviety Union to abandon Communism will wait until a shrimp learns to whistle.'

'Rock-and-roll music and outlandish fashions of dress can never, of course, be the main interests in life of young people. They can only appeal to those who are not quite right in the head.'

President John F. Kennedy once told the story of how a Russian had been apprehended for running through the Kremlin shouting: 'Khrushchev is a fool . . .' The man was sentenced to 23 years in prison, three for insulting the Party Secretary and 20 for revealing a state secret.

[1] The cost of lives was 25,000 Hungarians and 7,000 Soviet soldiers killed. On 16 Feb. 1957 the Hungarian Foreign Ministry announced that 196,000 Hungarians had fled the country since 23 Oct. 1956.

[2] A bomb thrown into a railway compartment in which he was travelling killed three other passengers.

[3] Georgi Maximilianovich Malenkov (born 8 Jan. 1902) was Chairman of the Council of Ministers (1953–55). According to Sir William Hayter, British Ambassador in Moscow (1953–57), he was a small, dark man with sleek hair and a smooth, sallow skin. There was something creepy about his appearance, like a eunuch, though he could produce a charming smile. He was quick, clever, and subtle . . .' In 1957, Malenkov was appointed Manager of the Ust-Kamenogorsk Hydro-Electric Station.

[4] In a televised interview released in 1967 Khrushchev alleged that by declining the request of the Republican Presidential Candidate, Richard M. Nixon, for the release of the pilot, Gary Powers, he deprived Nixon of 200,000 votes. As a result Khrushchev claimed credit for Kennedy's election as President.

The Soviet Premier captured the spirit of Capitalism when he visited Hollywood in 1959. Shirley MacLaine showed her paces.

According to 'Debrett's Peerage, Baronetage, Knightage, and Companionage' (1967), Khrushchev was descended from a Pole named Jan Khrushch ('Beetle') who went to Moscow in 1493. His Coat of Arms was said to have been a golden salamander rampant amidst flames gules, on a field argent (sic).

185

Jack Benny

Full name Benjamin Kubelsky.

Born Wed. 14 Feb. 1894, Waukegan, Illinois, USA.

Characteristics About 5′ 9″; about 150*lb.* (10*st.* 10*lb.*); brown hair; blue eyes.

Married 1927 Mary Livingstone 1*d.* (adopted).

In 'A Guide for the Married Man' (20th Century-Fox, 1967), Jack Benny received guidance from Virginia Wood as Bubbles.

Rumour has it that early on in the 20th century a holdup man challenged Jack Benny with the menacing formula 'Your money or your life.' There was a lengthy pause for reflection before Hollywood's thriftiest millionaire came up with a reply that might even have stopped Dick Turpin in his tracks – 'I'm thinking it over.' Many years later Benny showed that his sense of values was in no way impaired as he explained to his audience at the 1965 Royal Command Variety Performance in London: 'I had a choice of either doing this show or making a donation, and I didn't want to kill an image.' The Benny image is one that a lot of people are happy to see stay alive. Danny Kaye has rated him one of the three outstanding comics of our time: 'Bob Hope is the best story-teller, Jack Benny is the best situation comedian, and Charlie Chaplin the best pantomimic.' Bob Hope also rated Benny in the highest bracket maintaining that, among other things, he long preceded Sir Francis Chichester in circumnavigating the globe. Moreover, said Hope, Benny 'did it in a rowboat, on his honeymoon'.

Though he says his father gave him a monkey wrench along with a violin, advising him that plumbing was a good trade, Benjamin Kubelsky was always in show business. He started at 15 as a violinist in the local theatre orchestra and graduated at 17 to a Vaudeville show called *From Grand Opera to Ragtime* at his hometown of Waukegan, Illinois, before World War I. Today he is the town's most celebrated citizen and the Junior High School is named after him. The violin got into his act when he discovered that it was the ideal foil for his dry, straight-faced brand of humour. 'I found out that when you're holding a fiddle your talk sounds impromptu – you know, the fiddler who's just stood up to say a few words before he fiddles. That was my crutch, the fiddle.'

Benny's first film appearance was in *Hollywood Ice Revue* (1928) but his real break came when he entered radio with Ed Sullivan in 1932. His radio spot became so much a habit with listeners that when President Franklin D. Roosevelt made an important national speech to clash with his programme, Benny had more than double his rating. By 1941 he was reported to be earning $350,000 (£87,500) a year from radio, and regular film contracts brought in at least another $200,000 (£50,000) a year. He was voted the best radio comedian by *Motion Picture Daily* in 1951-54.

Whether or not golf has anything to do with Jack's impeccable gag-delivery, he has said that 'the timing of a joke is very much like the timing of a golf swing . . . if you make any kind of timing mistake in telling a joke, you have lost anywhere from 25 to 50 per cent of the laugh.' Though he has been seen on golf courses recently, the rumour that Jack gave up golf for reasons of economy because he had lost his only golf ball persisted. They were confirmed by Bob Hope at the 1967 Royal Command Performance: 'Benny did lose his golf ball – the string broke.'

Jack's shows owe a lot to his four scriptwriters, all of them many years on his team, and also to a kind of spontaneous evolution: 'You don't plan anything . . . Something gets started on one show and you keep it on for the next show or for three shows in a row because it got laughs. And then just by accident, it becomes a characterization.'

In 1958 Benny ended 26 successful years in radio and promptly showed he was quite in his element on TV, winning an 'Emmy' for his *Jack Benny Show* in 1959. He signed a three-year contract with CBS for $3,000,000 (£1,071,000), and by way of patriotic gesture, sent President John F. Kennedy a money clip with a $1 bill in it. Kennedy later had occasion to thank

Jack Benny demonstrated the senior citizen' look when he met Danny Thomas at a Hollywood dinner. Just how senior he is has been a matter for conjecture.

FILMS

Hollywood Ice Revue (1928)
The Medicine Man (1930)
Transatlantic Merry-Go-Round (1935)
It's In the Air (1936)
Broadway Melody of 1936
The Big Broadcast of 1937
Artists and Models (1938)
Stranded in Paris (1939)
Man About Town (1939)
Buck Benny Rides Again (1940)
Charley's American Aunt (1941)
Love Thy Neighbour (1941)
George Washington Slept Here (1942)
To Be or Not to Be (1942)
The Meanest Man in the World (1943)
The Fifth Chair (It's in the Bag) (1945)
The Horn Blows at Midnight (1945)
Somebody Loves Me (1953)
Beau James (1957)
It's a Mad Mad Mad Mad World (1963)
A Guide for the Married Man (1967)

Benny 'for helping an older man'. Meanwhile his violin was performing even greater acts of munificence. By 1963 he had played with 30 symphony orchestras, sometimes accompanied by Jascha Heifetz, and had raised $3,300,000 (£1,178,500) for musical and other charities. Apart from golf, the fiddle is his favourite recreation – he owns a $25,000 (£10,417) Stradivarius – and once borrowed the home of Kirk Douglas for a holiday, passing the entire three weeks playing the violin.

As long ago as 1954 when he was 60, Jack Benny was handing out guidance on how to avoid being 40. 'When in the company of younger people', he said, 'ask their advice on everything. Pretty soon they'll begin to believe they're older than you are.' Another tip from his fund of experience was: 'Avoid reminiscing about the past. If the name Lincoln should come up in your conversation, be sure that it's the car you're talking about and not the President.' In 1963 he appeared on Broadway in *Life Begins at 39*. The audience, some of whom might have remembered his last appearance there in 1931, witnessed the Benny thriftmanship in full freeze when, with his arms around singer Jane Morgan, he was seen to scrutinize her ring through a jeweller's magnifying glass. Still riding economically in a Rolls-Royce in 1966, he confided to an interviewer: 'The best party I ever threw was in an automat in New York. It was so *cheap*, I can't tell you. And I made $3.70 on the empties.'

'People laugh at me because I'm demonstrating all the qualities they're afraid to admit they possess.'

'Humour never changes. There are new comedians, that's all.'

'There are enough basic concepts in life to poke fun at. Funny things happen to us all the time. The comedian or comedy writer must be alert to these, remember them and invent variations on them. If a gag is hurtful, I don't need it.'

'I don't ever want to retire. I would think about giving it up if I can't make people laugh as I used to.'

188

Harold Macmillan

Harold Macmillan was Minister of Housing and Local Government (1951–54), Minister of Defence (1954–55), Secretary of State for Foreign Affairs (1955), Chancellor of the Exchequer (1955–57), and Prime Minister (1957–63). He was Conservative MP for Stockton-on-Tees (1924–29 and 1931–45) and for Bromley (1945–64).

Lying wounded in No Man's Land during World War I, the young Grenadier Guards officer quietly read a pocket edition of Homer while waiting to be rescued.[1] His unruffled stoicism matched the unflappable image of the man who, as the 44th Prime Minister, remarked: 'Indeed, let us be frank about it, most of our people have never had it so good.'[2] This apparently ambiguous comment was recalled so often by would-be critics – Harold Wilson actually thought it won a General Election for the Conservative Party – that Macmillan made a point of referring to it in his Guildhall speech in London on 13

Nov. 1961, some four years after the original utterance. 'One often regrets impromptu remarks,' he said, 'but I do not regret that one. What I do regret is that time and time again, people have taken it out of its context. For I was not making a boast but giving a warning. We had then, as we have now, a state of prosperity such as has never been in my lifetime. My point was – and I say it again – that the indispensable condition for the prosperity of all sections of the community and for none more than the old people, is the control of inflation.'

A reputation among those who did not

189

know him for condescension, even grandeur, did not fairly belong to one of the less Tory of Conservative Premiers. In 1964 he declined an Earldom, the Order of the Garter, and the French *Legion d'Honneur* and, when the publishers of *Burke's Landed Gentry* sent him a biographical questionnaire, returned the blank form with the comment: 'I don't believe I want my name alongside those who exploited my crofter ancestors.' In fact, beneath the bland demeanour there lurked a highly sensitive nature. 'I have hardly ever had to make an important speech without feeling violently sick most of the day before', he recorded in his memoirs. 'The House of Commons or the platform

At Eton, Harold Macmillan was a member of the 'Wall Game' team which scored a goal in 1909, one of only two such occasions in the history of the game which goes back over 140 years.

190

were equally bad; and even at the end of seven years' Premiership I had the same anticipation about Parliamentary Questions as men feel before a race or a battle.'

Macmillan graduated with first-class honours from Balliol College, Oxford, alma mater of H. H. Asquith, Prime Minister (1908–16), who was once reputed to have observed that Balliol men 'have a tranquil consciousness of effortless superiority'. It happened that Macmillan held the longest unbroken tenure of the Premiership (six years, nine months) since Asquith (eight years, eight months).

Early political life has its ups and downs for the future 'Supermac'. As he wrote to President Dwight D. Eisenhower years later: 'In my first constituency, in Teesside, I fought six elections – I lost three and won three. I remember very well that when one lost one was apt to say how tiresome and foolish all this business of counting noses was: when one won, of course, one felt convinced of the soundness of public opinion.' A publisher by profession,[3] Macmillan was one of a group of young Conservatives, described by Winston Churchill as 'the inheritors of Tory Democracy', who entered Parliament in 1924. Ramsey Macdonald,[4] then Leader of the Opposition, tried to induce them to join the Labour Party but Mac, in his maiden speech, firmly rejected the idea: '. . . if he thinks that we are either so young or so inexperienced as to be caught by a trap so clumsy as his, it shows that he totally misunderstands the moral principles and ideals of democratic Toryism.' The same day, Mac voiced his support of the budget launched by Churchill, then Chancellor of the Exchequer, introducing contributory old-age pensions. In the years to come he was to earn praise from Churchill as 'a man of fearless intelligence' who, like himself, 'had violently criticized the rejoicings which followed Munich'.

Macmillan first exercised political power

as Resident Minister for the Central Mediterranean (1943–44) during World War II. He was commended by most of the service chiefs with whom he worked. General Dwight D. Eisenhower wrote: 'From the start I found him more than competent; my high opinion of him had been frequently expressed in later years, publicly and privately.' Field-Marshal Alexander found him 'a delightful companion who was both wise in advice and always amusing; a man of great intellect, morally and physically brave, but far too reserved to show these admirable qualities outwardly.' General de Gaulle referred in his diary to Mac's 'lofty soul, his clear mind ... he had all my esteem'.

As Minister of Housing in the second Churchill administration, Macmillan carried through a housing programme which, according to the former Labour Chancellor, Hugh Dalton, 'led the way towards the "affluent society" '. Mac's slogan was: 'Housing is not a question of Conservatism or Socialism. It is a question of humanity.' As Chancellor of the Exchequer in Sir Anthony Eden's government, he was responsible for the issue of Premium Savings Bonds, unkindly labelled a 'squalid raffle' by Harold Wilson. Said Macmillan: 'This is an encouragement to the practice of saving and thrift by those members of the community who are not attracted by the reward of interest, but do respond to the incentive of fortune.' The 'Macmillan Bonds' were to become the second most popular method of saving after Life and Endowment Assurance.

Within weeks of succeeding Eden as Premier on 10 Jan. 1957, Macmillan journeyed to Bermuda for the first of his conferences with President Eisenhower. The policy of 'interdependence' with America which he cultivated in talks with Ike was further pursued in meetings with President John F. Kennedy, culminating in the Nassau Pact on 21 Dec. 1962

which pledged that American and British atomic weapons and military units would contribute to a 'multilateral NATO force ... in the closest consultation with other NATO allies.'

Mac also strove for a *détente* between East and West, visiting Russia in 1959 when, despite the ultimate stalemate in talks, he had the satisfaction of hearing Nikita S. Khrushchev admit that his visit was 'a thaw in the cold war'. Doffing his Russian hat, Mac re-visited Eisenhower and secured, at the Camp David Declaration of 29 March 1960, a nuclear moratorium. The discontinuation of nuclear tests was again a major topic when Mac met Kennedy at Bermuda on 21–22 Dec. 1961 and the US President, in a personal letter written shortly after the ratification of the Nuclear Test Ban Treaty on 8 Oct. 1963, lauded the British Premier's part in

Full name
Maurice Harold Macmillan (PC 1942).

Born
Sat. 10 Feb. 1894, 52 Cadogan Place, London SW1, England.

Characteristics
About 6'; about 165*lb.* (11*st.* 11*lb.*); dark brown hair; brown eyes.

Married
1920 Lady Dorothy Evelyn Cavendish (died 1966) 1*s.* 3*d.*

Mac

Harold Macmillan (signature)

this historic achievement; 'History will eventually record your indispensable role in bringing about the limitation of nuclear testing', wrote JFK, 'but I cannot let this moment pass without expressing to you my own keen appreciation of your signal contribution to world peace.' This achievement of Macmillan's was further praised by the late President's brother, Robert F. Kennedy, in a BBC-TV interview in 1968.

On 3 Feb. 1960, Macmillan made his famous speech before the South African parliament, the opening words of which were to supply the title for his memoirs: 'The wind of change is blowing through this continent and, whether we like it or not, this growth of national consciousness is a political fact. We must all accept it as a fact, and our national policies must take account of it.' South Africa's policy of 'apartheid', incompatible with continued membership of the Commonwealth, led to her decision not to re-apply for that status in 1961. However, the voluntary continuance within the British family of many nations shortly to attain independence was the vindication of Macmillan's theme.[5] He had reported to the House of Commons, following his 1958 visit to India and Pakistan, that it was 'profoundly moving to feel that these great countries with their immense populations, so different in creed, colour, tradition, and history, should now be free and willing partners with the old Commonwealth countries . . .

the best of the old Empire is continuing into the new Commonwealth.'

The former diplomat, Sir Harold Nicolson (1886–1968), while admitting that he 'hated' the Tories, rated Macmillan the politician of his acquaintance who served Britain best in peacetime: 'He has many fine qualities,' commented Sir Harold, 'probity, courage, patience, and judgement. He is absolutely fearless about facing and coming to terms with unpleasant realities.' Harold Wilson thought his adversary was 'The cleverest politician of our age. An adept politician, not a statesman, not a great Prime Minister.' But Wilson also noted Mac's 'traditional parliamentary generosity,' and conceded 'he's a sportsman—that's what I like about him.'

'Politics is like drink; when you once take to it you can't keep away from it.'

'The art of politics is making angles into curves.'

'Socialist finance is that of the bucket-shop, the confidence man, and the three-card trickster.'

'Great things are made out of poverty as well as out of wealth.'

Mr Macmillan was a regular viewer of the _Forsyte Saga_ TV series. He was overheard to say in his club in 1968: 'Soames is a man after my own heart.'

---

[1] Macmillan had previously been wounded twice. On this occasion, at the Battle of the Somme in Sept. 1916, he suffered a broken pelvis which kept him out of action till the end of the war. The wound has caused him pain and a shuffling gait ever since.

[2] President Lyndon B. Johnson revived this theme in a speech in Washington on 25 March 1968 when he said: 'I am not saying we never had it so good – but that's the truth isn't it.'

[3] Macmillan heads the family firm at 4 Little Essex, London WC2. His mother persuaded the firm to buy the rights of Margaret Mitchell's Pulitzer Prize-winning novel _Gone With the Wind_ (1936).

[4] James Ramsey Macdonald (1866-1937), Prime Minister (1924 and 1931-35).

[5] During or soon after Macmillan's Premiership, the following Commonwealth countries attained independence: Ghana, formerly Gold Coast (6 March 1957); West Malaysia, formerly the States of Malaya (31 Aug. 1957); Cyprus (16 Aug. 1960); Nigeria (1 Oct. 1960); Sierra Leone (27 April 1961); Tanzania, formerly Tanganyika (9 Dec. 1961); Jamaica (6 Aug. 1962); Trinidad and Tobago (31 Aug. 1962); Uganda (9 Oct. 1962); Zanzibar (9 Dec. 1963), joined the United Republic of Tanzania 29 Oct. 1964; Malawi, formerly Nyasaland (6 July 1964); Zambia, formerly Northern Rhodesia (24 Oct. 1964).

GENERAL CHARLES DE GAULLE

'De Gaulle is not of
the left. Nor of the
right. Nor of the
centre. De Gaulle
is above.'

Full name Charles André Joseph Marie de Gaulle.

Born Sat. 22 Nov. 1890, Lille, France.

Characteristics About 6′ 4″; brown hair; brown eyes; suffers from arthritis and mild diabetes.

Married 1921 Yvonne Charlotte Anne-Marie Vendroux 1*s*. 1*d*. *(1 daughter died)*

'. . . perhaps it is my mission to represent in the history of our country its last upsurge towards the lofty heights. Perhaps it is my lot to have written the last pages in the book of our greatness.' The words epitomize what many conceive to be the destiny of the man of whom Winston Churchill said in the House of Commons: '. . . he stood forth as the first eminent Frenchman to face the common foe in what seemed to be the hour of ruin of his country, and possibly of ours.'

World War II was not the first time de Gaulle had stood forth against the common foe. In World War I he was left for dead on the battlefield of Verdun. Severely wounded with a bayonet through his leg, his head ripped by shrapnel, he was picked up by a German patrol. 'I realized', wrote de Gaulle in his memoirs, 'that these men who were now saving my life were those who, only a little time before, in the hand-to-hand struggle, were trying desperately to kill me.' An order carrying with it the Cross of the *Légion d'Honneur* was issued, posthumously as was then thought, by General Pétain on 2 March

1916. The citation read: 'Captain de Gaulle, commanding a company, reputed for his high intellectual and moral qualities, at a moment when his battalion was decimated under fire of a ferocious bombardment, and when the enemy was investing his company on all sides, carried his men into a furious attack and fierce hand-to-hand assault, the only solution which he judged to be compatible with his sentiments of military honour. He is an officer without equal in every respect.' Despite five attempts, de Gaulle's conspicuous height prevented him from escaping from German imprisonment.

As Chief of the Free French in World War II after the fall of France, de Gaulle sent a stirring message of hope to his people in occupied France. Transmitted by the BBC on 18 June 1940, it contained these historic words: 'I tell you that nothing is lost for France. The very same means that conquered us can be used to give us one day the victory. For France is not alone! She is not alone! She is not alone!' In London, the towering French leader, who had been known as 'Long Asparagus' when a cadet in military academy, soon won a reputation for intransigence. 'He had to be rude to the British', wrote Churchill, 'to prove to French eyes that he was not a British puppet. He certainly carried out this policy with perseverance.' Clement (later Lord) Attlee recalled that he 'wasn't awfully sensible in dealing with other

DE GAULLE

Frenchmen, he didn't work happily with other people in exile, and he wasn't very wise in his dealings with us or the American government.' General Dwight D. Eisenhower wrote: 'I personally liked General de Gaulle, as I recognized in him many fine qualities. We felt, however, that these qualities were marred by hyper-sensitiveness and an extraordinary stubbornness in matters which appeared inconsequential to us.' Eisenhower told one interviewer that 'he and I were never Charles and Ike – never – not like with Winston, for example. Winston and I – why, we were just as warm, personal friends as we could be under the circumstances. De Gaulle was never that.' Harold Macmillan met de Gaulle in North Africa in 1943 and wrote: 'He is by nature an autocrat. Just like Louis XIV or Napoleon. He thinks in his heart that he should command and all others should obey him ... But I had no doubt at all of his greatness or of the opportunities which lay before him.' Sir Anthony Eden (later Lord Avon) was one of the few prominent figures during World War II who spoke with almost unqualified approval of the French leader: 'I had the most sincere admiration for this great Frenchman's qualities. To know him was to understand how exaggerated was the picture, often created of him in the public mind, of arrogance and even majesty. This facilely mistook the man ... His selflessness made it possible for him to keep the flame of France alive when in

political or diplomatic hands it must have flickered out.'

De Gaulle's resentment at his subordinate role in the war came to the boil in November 1944 when Churchill was cheered through the streets of liberated Paris by half a million Frenchmen. 'The imbeciles! The cretins!' exclaimed de Gaulle to a friend. 'Just look at that: the mob acclaiming that old brigand.'

After the war de Gaulle was the founder of the 'Rassemblement du Peuple Francais' in 1947. 'It is not tolerable, it is not possible', he said, 'that from so much death, so much sacrifice and ruin, so much heroism, a greater and better humanity shall not emerge.' Still reluctant to acknowledge the heroism of those who had made possible the restoration of democratic government in France, he delayed until 1958 before presenting Churchill with the Medal of Liberation.

After a period in retirement he returned to public life in 1958 allaying suspicions as to his motives with well-chosen words: 'I am a man who belongs to no one and therefore who belongs to everybody ... Can anyone believe that at the age of 67 I am going to begin the career of a dictator?' But there were those who still had doubts as to his aptitude for the task. Reviewing one of his books, Attlee wrote: 'General de Gaulle is a very good soldier and a very bad politician.' De Gaulle wrote to him: 'I have come to the conclusion that politics are too serious a

195

General de Gaulle paid tribute to a great English-man in 1958. Embracing Sir Winston on both cheeks, he decorated him with the Medal of Liberation.

matter to be left to the politicians.'

The West German Chancellor, Konrad Adenauer, developed a high regard for the man who was once a prisoner of the Germans. After their meeting on 14 September 1958 he said: 'General de Gaulle was very frank, and I found him to be a completely different man from the one presented to us in recent weeks by the German Press, and not only by the German Press . . . He is not a nationalist. He showed a perfect understanding of the international situation and the importance of French-German relations.' Rapport was maintained with Adenauer's successor, Ludwig Erhard, who was assured by de Gaulle in 1964: 'Our two countries, if they stick together, can bring the English to their knees.' Uneasiness over the spirit of de Gaulle's resolute interception of British attempts to enter the European Economic Community was redoubled in January 1967 when Paul-Henri Spaak[1],

196

one of the architects of the Common Market, accused the French President of being 'Machiavellian and immoral', and attacked his 'destructive work' . . . 'his disconcerting faculty of adaptation' . . . 'his desire to accede to greatness, his resentments, his refusal to accept what has been done without him, and the feeling that he has of his superiority.' Baroness Asquith[2] (1887-1969), in a TV interview in Paris in December 1967, underlined the flaw in de Gaulle's attitude. Recalling that Churchill had in 1940 offered indissoluble union between England and France, she pointed out that no mention had then been made of France's economic weaknesses. The offer was welcomed by de Gaulle but could not be implemented because occupied France had no government.

Across the Atlantic, de Gaulle made strategic preludes. President John F. Kennedy found him 'a wise counsellor for the future and an informative guide to the history he has helped to make'. Kennedy's awakening to the truth came in 1963 when de Gaulle rejected the Nuclear Test Ban Treaty. 'Charles de Gaulle will be remembered for one thing only', said JFK, 'his refusal to take that treaty.' President (then Senator) Lyndon B. Johnson first met him at a NATO meeting in 1960 and told a reporter: 'I discovered that de Gaulle and I are exactly the same height, which permits us to see eye to eye.' But Johnson too grew disillusioned as France fell out of step with every major US policy. By 1967 matters had reached a gaping misalignment as de Gaulle withdrew militarily from NATO, invited Soviet troops to train in France, made his rallying call to French Canadians, and uttered the lofty supposition: 'Ah if only I were President of the United States.'

Several attempts to assassinate de Gaulle have proved, even without the historic evidence of Verdun, that he has a charmed life.[3] His narrowest escape was on 22

August 1962 when a crossfire of at least 150 bullets failed to find their mark. Stepping unscratched from his shattered car, he brushed the broken glass from his suit and remarked calmly to his guard: 'This is getting to be dangerous. Fortunately these gentlemen are poor shots.' Under the surgeon's knife he has been scarcely less composed. About to undergo, with reluctance, the anaesthetic for a major abdominal operation in 1964, aged nearly 74, he told the surgeon: 'I warn you, if I die I'll come back and haunt you.' Asked by the doctor if he feared death, he roared: 'Good God, how can you be so dense? I fear not death. I fear only sleep. I want to know what is happening.'

De Gaulle's courage never commanded more admiration than during the 'revolution' of May 1968. Students and workers, who may have forgotten that before he came to power in 1958 France was 'the sick man of Europe', staged a series of strikes and demonstrations which in a fortnight reduced the nation to virtual paralysis. Brushing aside the 'de Gaulle must go' chorus-makers, he secured the allegiance of his army commanders, decreed a General Election, and made known his will in a stirring TV broadcast. 'The Republic will not abdicate', he thundered. 'The people will get a grip on themselves again. Progress, independence, and peace will prevail along with liberty.' His warning that France was threatened by 'the power of totalitarian Communism' added weight to his message. In the General Election, the Gaullist Party was returned to power with the biggest absolute majority in the history of the French Republic.

But even this proved transitory. On 28 April 1969 de Gaulle was obliged to 'lay down the functions of Head of State' after 53.07 per cent of voters declared against him in the referendum proposing reforms in the Senate and regional councils.

'I should not be a Gaullist myself were I not obliged to take into account a phenomenon which takes command over me and which I cannot always explain to myself: the phenomenon of de Gaulle.'

'So long as Britain opts for the Welfare State, she can be counted out of world affairs.'

About the French: *'It is impossible in normal times to rally a nation that has 265 brands of cheese.'*

---

[1] Prime Minister of Belgium (1938-39 and 1947-49), and Secretary-General of NATO (1957-61).
[2] Daughter of Herbert Henry Asquith, 1st Earl of Oxford and Asquith (1852-1928), Prime Minister (1908-16).
[3] In Aug. 1944 shortly after the liberation of Paris, a sniper's bullet missed him at Notre Dame in Paris. On 8 Sept. 1961 an 80-pound plastic bomb rocked his car from the roadside at Pont-sur-Seine as he drove from his country home to Paris. On 22 Aug. 1962 a group of 15 assailants sprayed his car with at least 150 bullets at Petit Clamart, a Paris suburb. The ringleader, Lieutenant-Colonel Jean-Marie Bastien-Thiry, who had only recently been decorated by de Gaulle with the Cross of the Legion of Honour, was executed on 11 March 1963. Three other assailants are still at large including Georges Watin, a marksman, who was revealed to have been implicated in a further plot against de Gaulle's life at the Paris Military Academy on 15 Feb. 1963. This was forestalled.

J Paul Getty

The vast majority of citizens will certainly never amass the kind of wealth that would make the adage 'If you can count your money you don't have a billion dollars' assume any practical significance. Mr Getty, who can't, has never given any official corroboration to attempts to compute his riches. He has, however, been quoted as saying: 'I don't know of anybody who could sell out for more than I could', a claim that has so far remained unchallenged.

Getty started out drilling for oil in Oklahoma on a budget of $100 (£25) a month in 1914. He spudded his first oil well in 1916, made $40,000 (£10,000) in his first year in business, and $1,000,000 (£250,000) in the next two. He used an old Model-T Ford as his executive headquarters, negotiating contracts and sometimes even sleeping in the front seat. On occasions, he worked round several clocks without a break. In 1924 he retired from business to enjoy his wealth but came back through boredom two years later. He had climbed to multi-millionaire status long before his wealthy father died in 1930 leaving him a token $500,000 (£125,000).

Today Getty owns or controls over 100 companies in five continents, with his main oil interests located in the United States, Italy, Denmark, and the Persian Gulf. Oil plus his art collections, his hotels in Manhattan and Acupulco, and other property, were the basis for *Fortune* magazine's 1968 evaluation of Getty's wealth. Computing a 'conservative' figure of $957,404,289 (nearly £400,000,000) and a 'liberal' figure of $1,338,417,316 (£557,850,000) as representing the value of his *visible* assets, *Fortune* arrived at a slightly higher total for Howard Hughes but confessed it was 'impossible to say which is richer'. It is also impossible to assess the value of Getty's *invisible* assets though they certainly dwarf those of Hughes. Proven oil reserves in the area of Getty's concession in the so-called Neutral Zone on the Persian Gulf alone are reported to exceed 13 billion barrels. Reckoned at a balance sheet figure of 75 cents a barrel these would be worth far more than the total of all his visible assets. Furthermore the discovery in 1967 of huge uranium deposits on his oil estates in Wyoming, USA, must add unimaginable sums to any hypothetical figure for his overall assets.

Getty can thus be described without too great a risk of exaggeration as 'the world's richest private citizen'. In addition he has the reported distinction, almost as

The world's richest private citizen, J. Paul Getty, took part in an egg-and-spoon race at his party for orphans in 1966.

rare as this professional one, of being the only amateur boxer ever to have knocked out Jack Dempsey. The two used to double-date as young men out in California. They were good friends but quarrelled only once – when they both wanted the same girl. Dempsey has been quoted as reporting the subsequent confrontation in these terms: 'Paul threw a feint with his right and knocked me senseless with a left uppercut, the first and only time I've ever been completely out in my life. It was a beautiful punch – one of my big surprises.' Getty would not confirm or deny the truth of this story when questioned in 1966. His comment was: 'The only way to knock out Jack Dempsey would be to hit him with an automobile going at 60 mph.'

Getting back to heavyweight finance, Getty maintains that the true investor succeeds by a cautious appraisal of all the factors, both underlying and on paper, that concern the enterprise in which investment is envisaged. 'My stock buying system is fairly simple he has divulged. 'I buy when other people are selling. I have always bought stocks at bargain prices.' He deprecates speculating on the margin and relies on long-term trends, ignoring periodical market tremors. His business logic, though impeccable, often infuriates

199

get-rich-quick aspirants who approach him for pointers, only to be told that there is no secret in sound investment and that real business fortunes are not made merely by dicing on the stock exchange.

Outside the boardroom, Getty enjoys a wide range of interests, speaks seven languages, and commands a considerable knowledge of art which, on occasion, he has put to profit. In 1938 he purchased for $38,000 (£9,500) the 11 feet by 24 feet Ardabil Persian Carpet, once described by the Muslims as 'too good for Christian eyes to gaze on'. He declined an offer of $250,000 for it from King Farouk and later donated it to the Los Angeles County Museum where it is now valued at over $1,000,000 (£416,666). In 1940 he picked up for a mere $250 (£62) a painting he thought might be a Raphael. It turned out to be Raphael's *Madonna di Loreto* (1508–09) and is now worth upwards of $1,000,000. His art collection – multi-million-dollar, of course – has mostly been donated to the Los Angeles County Museum and includes priceless tapestries and sculptures, works by Rubens, Gainsborough and other masters, and some of the famed Elgin Marbles.

Sometimes accused of meanness, Getty on principle declines to dispense charity in answer to begging letters. He receives requests for sums averaging between two and five million dollars a month: 'It would not take long to bankrupt myself and my companies at that rate', he has pointed out. His record for begging letters in a single day's post is $15,000,000 (£6,250,000). 'All my contributions are made to legitimate charities . . . and to these, my companies and I donate a million dollars or more each year.' On one occasion he was quoted as saying: 'I give away a third of my income and have done for years.'

In 1959 Getty moved from his suite in the Ritz Hotel in London and purchased for £150,000 ($420,000) Sutton Place in Surrey, built in 1523–30 by Sir Richard Weston, a favourite of King Henry VIII. 'I generally have a group of business associates with me and I have worked out that our combined hotel bills will be more than is required to run a stately home. If your name is Getty, you can't expect to live in a hotel for less than $100 a day.' The house-warming party at Sutton Place cost a reported £10,000 ($28,000).

The much-married oil magnate has stated: 'I blame my business interests for having married five times. A woman resents a man dedicated to his business. She, in fact, resents anything dedicated to anything but herself.'

'I always remember my father saying that a man's opinions are only as good as his information.'

'The rule which holds that what goes up must eventually come down applies on occasion to crude oil prices with as much validity as it does to tennis balls and slingshot pellets.'

'Culture is like fine wine that one drinks in the company of a beautiful woman. It should be sipped and savoured – never gulped.'

Full name   Jean Paul Getty.

Born   Thurs. 15 Dec. 1892, Minneapolis, Minnesota, USA.

Characteristics   About 5′ 11″; about 180*lb.* (12*st.* 12*lb.*); reddish hair; grey-blue eyes.

Married
(1) 1923 Jeannette Demont (div. 1925) 1*s.*
(2) 1926 Allene Ashby (div. 1928).
(3) 1928 Adolphine Helmle (div. 1932) 1*s.*
(4) 1932 Ann Rork (div. 1935) 2*s.*
(5) 1939 Louise Dudley Lynch (div.) 1*s.*

200

FIELD MARSHAL VISCOUNT MONTGOMERY OF ALAMEIN

Field-Marshal Viscount Montgomery of Alamein, of whom Churchill wrote : 'It may almost be said : "Before Alamein we never had a victory. After Alamein we never had a defeat." '

Full name Bernard Law Montgomery, 1st Viscount (1946), KG (1946), GCB (1945), DSO (1914).

Born Thurs. 17 Nov. 1887, London, England.

Characteristics About 5′ 8″; about 144*lb.* (10*st.* 4*lb.*); brown hair; blue-grey eyes.

Married 1927 Elizabeth Carver (died 1937) 1*s.*

On 23 Oct. 1942, the eve of one of the decisive battles of history, the Commander of the Eighth Army issued his orders of the day to the British and Commonwealth troops at El Alamein: '. . . let every officer and man enter the battle with a stout heart, and the determination to do his duty so long as he has breath in his body. AND LET NO MAN SURRENDER SO LONG AS HE IS UNWOUNDED AND CAN FIGHT.' Three weeks later, the man known affectionately to those serving under him as Monty, posted a further message summing up tersely the outcome of the events of the tumultuous period which intervened: 'I said that together we would hit the Germans and Italians for six right out of Africa. In three weeks we have completely smashed the German and Italian Army, and pushed the remnants out of Egypt, having advanced ourselves nearly 300 miles up to and beyond the

201

A facsimile of the autograph of Field-Marshal Erwin Rommel (1891–1944), Commander of Hitler's Afrika Corps, which was defeated in Nov. 1942 by the British Eighth Army under General Montgomery. The original of Rommel's autograph made $250 (£104) at an auction in New York in 1968.

frontier.' The job was completed in the manner confidently predicted by the General who once said: 'We soldiers don't make war. War is a continuation of diplomacy.[1] When they can't do any more, they ask the soldiers to get on with it.'

The qualities that contributed to the 'Montgomery Legend' have been acknowledged by some of his greatest military contemporaries. General Dwight D. Eisenhower thought he had no superior in two important characteristics: 'He quickly develops among the British enlisted men an intense devotion and admiration – the greatest personal asset a commander can possess . . . In the study of enemy positions and situations and in the combining of his own armour, artillery, and infantry to secure tactical success against the enemy he is careful, meticulous, and certain.' Field-Marshal Alexander thought him 'a first-class trainer and leader of troops on the battlefield, with a fine tactical sense. He knows how to win the loyalty of his men and has a great flair for raising morale. Alexander added in his memoirs: 'Personally, I owe Monty a lot – as we all do.' Lieutenant-General Sir Brian Horrocks[2] recorded that 'his knowledge of the personalities under his command was uncanny. Often he would ring me up and make the most searching enquiries about some young second-lieutenant whom he had noticed in training.' Horrocks added: 'He was obviously a complete master of his craft – the craft of war.' When Monty's book *A History of Warfare* was published in 1968 Field-Marshal Sir William Slim[3] added his tribute, calling him 'the most continuously successful General we've had since Wellington.[4] We owe him almost everything we can owe.'

Monty thought that high morale was the most important single factor in war: 'Without high morale no success can be achieved – however good may be the strategical or tactical plan, or anything else.' His definition of leadership was: 'The capacity and will to rally men and women to a common purpose and the character which inspires confidence.' He further considered that: 'To exercise high command successfully' a commander must have 'an infinite capacity for taking pains and for careful preparation; he must also have an inner conviction which, at times, will transcend reason.'

To those who served under him in the commissioned ranks, Monty will perhaps best be remembered by his conference technique, described by Horrocks as 'Monty's power of mass hypnosis'. At one important gathering of military brass he brought the company sharply to order with a glance of his eagle eye and this preliminary directive: 'I do not approve of smoking or coughing. For two minutes you may cough; thereafter coughing will cease for 20 minutes, when I shall allow another 60 seconds for coughing.' His aversion for tobacco was such that he once reprimanded Eisenhower, snapping: 'I don't permit smoking in my office.' He failed, however, to impress Churchill with his rule of life. 'I do not smoke or drink and I am 100 per cent fit,' he stated. The Prime Minister came back with the perfect squelch: 'I smoke and drink and I am 200 per cent fit.'

Less rigid was Monty's attitude to dress. Only once did he find it necessary to dictate a guideline. It was when he saw a soldier who was driving a lorry clad only in a top hat and otherwise naked. An order was promptly issued to the troops: 'Top hats will not be worn in the Eighth Army.'

The spare, erect figure topped usually by the uniform beret became so familiar a sight in time of war that British intelligence conceived the idea of using a decoy to confuse the enemy as to Allied intentions prior to the D-Day landings in Normandy in 1944. An actor, Major Clifton James, was trained for the role and studied Monty's mannerisms, perfecting his natural likeness to the point of having a plastic finger made to replace one of his own that had been blown off in action. One detail, requiring a last minute check from the man himself, was the question of his eating habits, known to be austere. The facts were relayed promptly from headquarters: 'Don't eat meat, fish, or eggs, and have porridge without milk or sugar.' James (alias Montgomery) flew to Gibraltar and the German High Command received, as planned, a red herring, after a Spanish double-agent had reported 'Monty's' presence in that sector.

The political leaders under whom Monty served have been warm in their testimony about him. Clement (later Lord) Attlee, Prime Minister in the closing stages of the war, said: 'Lord Montgomery is a most attractive character, a brilliant leader, a generous friend. He is not afraid to admit where he made errors. He has perhaps the defects of his qualities. He is inclined, perhaps, to be a little too cocksure.' Churchill, too, weighed in with his tribute: 'this vehement and formidable General – a Cromwellian figure – austere, severe, accomplished, tireless – his life given to the study of war, who has attracted to himself in an extraordinary degree the confidence and devotion of the Army.'

[1] Probably from an aphorism of General Karl von Clausewitz (1780-1831), the Prussian military author, who wrote: 'War is nothing more than a continuation of politics by other means.' The saying has also been adopted by Mao Tse-tung (*see page* 229)
[2] Horrocks commanded 10 Corps in Egypt and Africa and 9 Corps in Tunis.
[3] Slim commanded the 10th Infantry Brigade in the Sudan and Eritrea; the 10th Indian Division in Syria, Persia, and Iraq; the 1st Burma Corps in Burma; and was C.-in-C. Allied Land Forces in South East Asia (1945-46).
[4] Field-Marshal the Duke of Wellington (1769-1852), victor of the Battle of Waterloo in 1815.

Montgomery of Alamein
F·M.

203

Charlie Chaplin, the 'immortal tramp' of silent films. One of his early films, 'The Bond' (1918), was purchased by the BBC for a TV re-run in 1969.

Opposite page:
The Chaplin Coat of Arms: Gules a fesse nebulee or, between six billets argent.

Full name
Charles Spencer Chaplin.

Born
Tues. 16 April 1889, 3 Pownall Terrace, Kennington, London SE11, England.

Characteristics
About 5′ 5″; originally dark brown hair; blue eyes; left-handed.

Married
(1) 1918 Mildred Harris (div. 1920) 1*s*. (died in infancy).
(2) 1924 Lolita McMurry (Lita Grey) (div. 1927) 2*s*. (Charles Chaplin Jr. died in 1968).
(3) 1936 Paulette Goddard (div. 1942).
(4) 1943 Oona O'Neill 1*s*. 5*d*.

204

CHARLIE CHAPLIN

AUDACIR FORTIS

Few names, if any, can be cited by the connoisseur of cinema in the same breath as that of Charlie Chaplin, the man whose creative genius as actor, author, and director has graced the history of motion pictures for over 50 years. Sir Charles Cochran wrote that 'he and Disney are the greatest human products of the celluloid art'. Cochran added: 'Before Disney, Chaplin more than anybody had given it something which was specifically for this medium, and not merely an adaptation of the technique of the theatre.'

Chaplin himself has acknowledged his debt to one person whose talents surpassed his own. That was his mother, a music-hall performer before the advent of cinema. 'She was the most astounding mimic I ever saw', he has recalled. '. . . she was by far a greater artist than I will ever be.' His grandmother was a gipsy and he believes that his gifts came, in part, from her. His father was a drunken Vaudeville artist looking like Napoleon. Charlie saw little of him before he died at 37 of dropsy. Poverty was the cruel lot of the boy Chaplin. On one occasion the family was only rescued from complete destitution when his step-brother found a purse full of cash on a London bus. They welcomed it as a gift from heaven but despite this were obliged to throw themselves on the tender mercies of the Lambeth Borough workhouse for two months.

Charlie was only about eight when he made his first music-hall appearance with a group of clog dancers called the Eight Lancashire Lads. As make-up was scarce, the lads were encouraged to pinch their faces for colour. At 12 he was grateful for small stage parts at 50 shillings (about $10) a week. One of them was in *Sherlock Holmes*. Then he was a comedian with Fred Karno's company and made his first trip to America with Karno in 1910. Later he returned to America to win a screen test for Mack Sennett's Keystone Cops where he invented the character that made his name. Wearing baggy trousers, tight jacket, large shoes, and small hat, he had Sennett in stitches and got the job. In 1931 Sigmund Freud was to analyse the film Chaplin by reference to his childhood environment: 'He is undoubtedly a great artist – although he always plays one and the same part, the weak, poor, clumsy boy

205

Charlie Chaplin directed Sophia Loren in 'A Countess from Hong Kong' (Universal, 1966). He also composed the music for the film and made a brief appearance as a ship's steward.

for whom life turns out all right in the end . . . he invariably plays only himself as he was in his grim youth.'

Graduating from bit parts to what amounted to stardom in a short time, and confident of his capacity to take the initiative, Charlie persuaded Sennett to let him direct his own films. The demand for Chaplin comedies was accelerating across America and in 1914 no fewer than 35 silent shorts were released by Keystone. By 1916 his name was in lights in New York's Times Square and he had signed a contract for $670,000 (£167,500) a year with the Mutual Film Corporation. This contract completed he signed another to make eight two-reel comedies for First National which earned him $1,200,000 (£300,000).

Chaplin's output called for a consistent flow of ideas which did not come easily. Ideas develop, he has written, 'By sheer perseverance to the point of madness. One must have the capacity to suffer anguish and sustain enthusiasm over a long period of time.' According to Cecil B. de Mille, his humour 'was essentially humour of character rather than of situation'. But Charlie made use of slapstick within limits: 'If you kick a man in the rear, but not too hard, and he goes sprawling in a funny fashion but doesn't get hurt, it's funny. If you kick him hard, it's tragic.' He discerned, too, that comedy 'increases in refinement in inverse proportion to the refinement of the world in which it appears. This is why horseplay is not funny to the barbarians.'

Chaplin did not volunteer for service in World War I but participated in various Liberty Loan campaigns which raised large sums. At one luncheon, a wealthy lady paid $1,000 to the Red Cross for the privilege of sitting next to him. Following the war, Chaplin went into partnership with Mary Pickford and Douglas Fairbanks to form the United Artists Corpor-

ation. These studios produced the first full-length Chaplin comedies including *City Lights* which was shown by Royal Command at Balmoral Castle in 1931.

The Great Dictator was the first full-length film to which Chaplin brought his fullest talents as both actor and director. He himself played the title role, a magnificent send-up of Adolf Hitler. 'I did this picture', he explained, 'for the Jews of the world. I wanted to see the return of decency and kindness. I'm no Communist . . . just a human being who wants to see this country America a real democracy, and freedom from this infernal regimentation which is crawling over the rest of the world.' Long before the film was released, the Nazis recognized Chaplin's superficial likeness for Hitler and removed the moustache from the picture of Chaplin hanging in their museum of degenerate art.

Further films of inimitable quality followed World War II. In old age Chaplin showed little sign of slackening his productive capacity, writing his own film scripts and then directing the cast which he personally selected with great care. 'I dictate about 1,000 words a day', he has said, 'which averages me about 300 in finished dialogue for my films.' On the set he is meticulous in getting what he wants from his cast. Marlon Brando, directed by him in *A Countess from Hong Kong*, reported: 'In one scene I was waving smoke away from my face with two fingers. Charlie didn't like it and said I should use four.' Sophia Loren quoted Chaplin as telling her: 'You must have pride in everything you do. And you must always think you are the best. I myself shall go on making films until I die. And I shall always think the last one the greatest of them all.'

Of those who have gone on record for or against Chaplin, Winston Churchill told him he would make a good Labour Member of Parliament, Zsa Zsa Gabor was astonished to find him 'such a handsome man, with a quick, darting smile', and Errol Flynn, who never appeared in a Chaplin film, wrote: 'The outstanding thing to me about him was that, while he was gay and witty and charming, unless every bit of conversation centred around him he was deadly bored.'

Often labelled a 'Communist', Chaplin states in his autobiography that it is 'men like Dr Hewlett Johnson[1] and Canon Collins . . . that give vitality to the English church.' Although a confirmed Socialist he moved after 40 years in America, to take up residence in that well-known celebrity tax-haven, Switzerland.

His fourth wife, Oona, daughter of the playwright, Eugene O'Neill, was one-third his age when they married. At their first meeting he was captivated by her 'luminous beauty, with a sequestered charm and a gentleness that was most appealing'.

The Early Chaplin Films

1914
Making a Living
Kid Auto Races at Venice
Mabel's Strange Predicament
Between Showers
A Film Johnnie
Tango Tangles
His Favourite Pastime
Cruel, Cruel Love
The Star Boarder
Mabel at the Wheel
Twenty Minutes of Love
Caught in a Cabaret
Caught in the Rain
A Busy Day
The Fatal Mallet
Her Friend the Bandit
The Knockout
Mabel's Busy Day
Mabel's Married Life
Laughing Gas
The Property Man
The Face on the Bar-room Floor
Recreation
The Masquerader
His New Profession
The Rounders
The New Janitor
Those Love Pangs
Dough and Dynamite
Gentlemen of Nerve
His Musical Career
His Trysting Place
Tillie's Punctured Romance
Getting Acquainted
His Prehistoric Past

1915
His New Job
A Night Out
The Champion
In the Park
The Jitney Elopement

The Tramp
By the Sea
Work
A Woman
The Bank
Shanghaied
A Night in the Show

1916
Carmen
Police
The Floorwalker
The Fireman
The Vagabond
One a.m.
The Count
The Pawnshop
Behind the Screen
The Rink

1917
Easy Street
The Cure
The Immigrant
The Adventurer

1918
Triple Trouble
A Dog's Life
The Bond
Shoulder Arms

1919
Sunnyside
A Day's Pleasure

1920
The Kid
The Idle Class

1922
Hay Day

1923
The Pilgrim

Full-length Films

A Woman of Paris (1923)
The Gold Rush (1925)
The Circus (1928)
City Lights (1931)
Modern Times (1936)
The Great Dictator (1940)
Monsieur Verdoux (1947)
Limelight (1953)
The King in New York (1957)
The Chaplin Revue (1960)
A Countess from Hong Kong (1967)
The Freak (1970)

LP Recording

A Countess from Hong Kong
(soundtrack) (MCA DL71501)
including Chaplin's own composition *This is My Song*

---

[1] The Reverend Hewlett Johnson (1874-1966), 'Red' Dean of Canterbury and recipient of the 1951 Stalin Peace Prize. Johnson continued to support Soviet policy even after the Nazi-Soviet pact of 1939. In 1942 he asserted that the Soviet Union was 'the salvation of the world . . .'

In 1963 Irving Berlin was presented with the Milestone Award by the Screen Producers' Guild. On hand to see him honoured were Ginger Rogers and Fred Astaire who danced in the Berlin musical films 'Top Hat' (1935), 'Follow the Fleet' (1936), and 'Carefree' (1938).

Irving Berlin

Full name Israel Baline (changed to Irving Berlin in 1906).

Born Fri. 11 May 1888, Temun, USSR.

Characteristics Small and slight; brown eyes; black hair; chain-smoker when working; suffers from insomnia.

Married
(1) 1913 Dorothy Goetz (died 1913).
(2) 1926 Ellin Mackay 3*d*.

Unquestionably the greatest living composer of popular music is Irving Berlin. In the 'thirties George Gershwin was quoted in these terms: 'Berlin's songs are exquisite cameos of perfection. Each one of them is as beautiful as its neighbour. Irving Berlin is America's Schubert.' Jerome Kern was no less emphatic: 'Berlin has no place in American music. He *is* American music.' And Cole Porter admitted that his favourite numbers by another composer were: 'Any of Berlin's.' In 1943 the National Association for American Composers and Conductors, who normally concern themselves only with serious music, cited him as the 'outstanding composer of popular music'. He may also be described as the finest lyricist. Oscar Hammerstein II thought his line 'all alone by the telephone' was the most perfect in any lyric he knew.

The Baline family were driven out of their homes in Russia by Cossack marauders in 1892 and emigrated to America penniless. Young Israel worked as a singing waiter, drawing on the talent he inherited from three generations of Jewish cantors. His first published music was a song entitled *Marie from Sunny Italy* (1906) for which he composed the lyrics and scooped all of 37 cents in royalties. In 1909 he wrote lyrics for a song called *Dorando* after the famous marathon runner[1]; by this time was the proud owner of a contract bringing in $25 (£5) a week as a lyricist.

The man who wrote over 1,000 songs admitted that he had absolutely no musical education: 'I am unable to read notes. I play the piano in only one key, and I must say I play it terribly.' His product, usually given to an arranger to harmonize, never suffered from these basic handicaps. In 1911 he composed his first great number *Alexander's Ragtime Band* and made his mark in a booming sphere of popular music. Though not the originator of ragtime, he has been described as the 'interpreter-in-chief'. *Alexander's Ragtime Band* was heard for the first time at New York's Aeolian Hall in 1924 on the same day that Paul Whiteman first played George Gershwin's *Rhapsody in Blue*.

Before the days of motion pictures with sound and before World War I, Berlin

209

was already a great name in music. His first Broadway musical opened in 1911 and by 1919 when he wrote *A Pretty Girl is Like a Melody*, he had gone into partnership in a music publishing firm. He had already appeared at the London Hippodrome in 1917 and had a ready world audience for his numbers, many of them first heard in musicals. *The Music Box Revues* included such all-time favourites as *Say it With Music*, *All Alone*, and *What'll I Do*. Sometimes personal experiences gave rise to compositions. The death of his first wife inspired *When I Lost You*. Later when his prospective father-in-law was trying to prevent his marriage to Ellin Mackay he wrote *Remember* and *Always* (1925). In 1927, feeling that he had run out of creative energy, he wrote *The Song is Ended*.

Happily the lyric was not prophetic. The unforgettable numbers *Say it Isn't So* and *How Deep is the Ocean?* were published in 1932 and shortly Berlin broke into motion pictures on the grand scale. *Cheek to Cheek*, sung by Fred Astaire in *Top Hat*, won an 'Oscar' and there were other fine numbers in films starring Astaire: *Let's Face the Music and Dance* was composed for *Follow the Fleet*; *Change Partners* for *Carefree*. The film *On the Avenue* featured *I've Got My Love to Keep Me Warm*, and *The Barkleys of Broadway* had Astaire singing *It Only Happens When I Dance With You*.

Berlin's most popular number, in fact, the most successful commercial song of all time, was *White Christmas* which was first sung by Bing Crosby in the film *Holiday Inn* (1942). It won an 'Oscar' for the best screen song. *White Christmas* has been recorded by a least 400 other artists and, in the US and Canada alone, had sold 60,968,490 copies by the end of 1967. Berlin himself prefers to spend Christmas in sunny Florida.

After World War II the success of

Berlin's two greatest shows proved that he was still very much at the peak of his powers. Both went into motion pictures and included many more wonderful songs. *Annie Get Your Gun* had *You Can't Get a Man with a Gun*, *They Say It's Wonderful*, *My Defences are Down*, and *I Got the Sun in the Morning*. *Call me Madam*, a takeoff of Mrs Perle Mesta, President Harry S Truman's ambassador to Luxembourg, included other hits: *The Best Thing for You*, *You're Just in Love*, and *It's a Lovely Day Today*. Another number from *Call Me Madam* had the title *They Like Ike* and was used in the 1952 Presidential campaign. The title songs for three other motion pictures, *Blue Skies*, *Easter Parade*, and *There's No Business Like Show Business*, became standards that will always be linked with his name.

The patriotism of Irving Berlin was generously expressed in both world wars. The show *Yip, Yip, Yaphank* included the number *Oh How I Hate to Get Up in the Morning*, which World War I veterans sang with feeling. This show earned $83,000 (£20,750) for the US government.

This is the Army garnered nearly $10,000,000 (£2,250,000) for the US Army Emergency Relief Fund and a further $350,000 (£87,500) for British relief. For this Berlin was awarded the Medal of Merit by General George C. Marshall. More philanthropy resulted from the song *God Bless America* which was composed but not used in *Yip, Yip, Yaphank*. It was revived in the 1940 Presidential Convention and won the composer a special gold medal authorized by Congress in 1955 and presented by President Dwight D. Eisenhower. By 1968 it had earned royalties of $470,000 (£196,000) which were donated to the Boy Scouts, Girl Guides, and Campfire Girls.

In 1968 Berlin had completed a fresh selection of songs for a new Hollywood musical to be named after an early song hit, *Say it With Music*. Julie Andrews was reported to be the star under contract but plans were temporarily shelved in 1969.

---

[1] Dorando Pietri (Italy) who collapsed in the 1908 Olympic marathon in London. Dorando later met and was beaten by the Canadian Indian, Tom Longboat, giving rise to Berlin's song.

Shows and Revues

Jardin de Paris (1911)
Watch Your Step (1914)
Stop, Look and Listen (1915)
Yip, Yip, Yaphank (1918)
The Ziegfield Follies (1919)
The Ziegfield Follies (1920)
The Music Box Revue (1921)
The Music Box Revue (1922)
The Musix Box Revue (1923)
The Music Box Revue (1924)
The Music Box Revue (1925)
The Cocoanuts (1925)
The Ziegfield Follies (1927)
Face the Music (1931)
As Thousands Cheer (1933)
Louisiana Purchase (1935)
This is the Army (1942)
Annie Get Your Gun (1946)
Miss Liberty (1949)
Call Me Madam (1950)
Mr President (1962)
Say It With Music (1969)

Films

Puttin' on the Ritz (1919)
The Cocoanuts (1929)
Top Hat (1935)
Follow the Fleet (1936)
On the Avenue (1937)
Carefree (1938)
Alexander's Ragtime Band (1938)
Second Fiddle (1939)
Louisiana Purchase (1941)
Holiday Inn (1942)
Blue Skies (1946)
Easter Parade (1948)
The Barkleys of Broadway (1949)
Annie Get Your Gun (1950)
Call Me Madam (1953)
There's No Business Like Show Business (1954)
Sayonara (1957) theme music only

L.P. Records

Call Me Madam (soundtrack) (Ace of Hearts AH137)

Annie Get Your Gun (Mike Sammes Singers)
(Fontana SFL13021)

Irving Berlin Song Book (George Mitchell Minstrels)
(Columbia SX6267/SCX6267)

Irving Berlin (101 Strings) (Marble Arch MAL634)

Songs of Irving Berlin (3 LPs)
(World Record Club ST975/6/7)

N.B.: Hundreds of artists have recorded Berlin numbers. The above is a selection of recent LPs devoted to his music.

Artur Rubinstein

Full name Artur Rubinstein.

Born Thurs. 28 Jan. 1886, Lodz, Poland.

Characteristics About 5′ 8½″; brown hair; grey-blue eyes.

Married 1932 Aniela Mlynarski 2s. 2d.

A virtuoso with all the traits to equip half a dozen artists, Artur Rubinstein is beyond question the world's most durable concert pianist. He has said: 'It is simply my life, music. I love it, breathe it, talk with it. I am almost unconscious of it. No. I do not mean I take it for granted – one should never take for granted any of the gifts of God. But it is like an arm, a leg, part of me.'

Rubinstein commenced his musical studies at the age of three in 1889, and gave his first charity concert at four. By the time he was 10 he could pick up a sonata in the morning and grasp the essence of it in a day. His memory was really tested for the first time when he played Franck's Symphonic Variations in Madrid as a young man. 'I learned it in 36 hours on the train from Paris', he recalled. 'When I sat down at the rehearsal, it was still a little strange . . . in the evening it went better.' His musical memory operates rather like a magnetic tape: 'At breakfast I might pass a Brahms symphony in my head. Then I am called to the 'phone, and half an hour later I find it's been going on in my head all the time and I'm in the third movement.'

Rubinstein has recommended that the pianist should not be so dedicated to technical perfection as to be afraid of making mistakes: '. . . piano playing is a dangerous life; it must be lived dangerously.' He has emphasized that it is not good to over-practise: 'When you do the music seems to come out of your pockets.' If you play with a feeling of "Oh, I know this", you play without that little drop of fresh blood that is necessary – and the audience feels it. I am very nervous and tense before playing, but I think it is a good nervousness.' His natural exuberance has carried him through such schedules as the ten-day cycle which he offered at

Artur Rubinstein gave his first charity concert at the age of four. He was still playing the piano over 80 years later.

Carnegie Hall in 1962 when aged 76; this included 89 works (25 major ones) not counting 35 encores. His attitude to a concert is: 'I want to enjoy it more than the audience. That way the music can bloom anew. It's like making love. The act is always the same, but each time it's different.'

Helena Rubinstein, a close friend though unrelated to her namesake, wrote: 'Artur has a wonderful philosophy, and apart from his wonderful playing I love to hear him talk.' She quoted him as saying: 'The most important thing in life is to realize why one is alive. It is not only to build bridges and tall buildings, or to make money, but to do something truly important, to do something for humanity.' The maestro himself has philosophized: 'Life means living, not escaping. There is no *ersatz* for living. I prefer to die young than to sniff around life. People go to doctors and ask: What vitamins shall I eat? I ask you – what good are vitamins? Eat four lobsters; a pound of caviar – live! If you are in love with a beautiful blonde, don't be afraid. Marry her!'

Commissioned 30 years ago to write his autobiography, Rubinstein declined: 'I cannot write it. My life is too naughty. I am too shy about telling it.' Fans passing his home in New York can take encouragement from this revelation: '. . . sometimes when I sit down to practise and there is no one else in the room, I have to stifle an impulse to ring for the elevator man and offer him money to come in and hear me. I am happy to play to a crowded Carnegie Hall. But I am just as happy to play for 1,000 people, for 300, for 100, indeed anyone who cares to listen.'

Anyone who had the pleasure to listen would have a choice from a vast repertoire, including some pieces for pianoforte he has composed himself. He has made a large number of recordings and in America, where he has been a naturalized citizen since 1946, it has been estimated that his record albums have grossed as much as $500,000 (now £208,333) per annum. Igor Stravinsky is among the modern composers who have written music expressly for him, and his rendering of *The Ritual Fire Dance* was selected for the million-selling album 60 *Years of Music America Loves Best* (1959).

Artur Rubinstein: '. . . piano
playing is a dangerous life; it
must be lived dangerously.'

LP. Recordings

Albéniz: *Sevillana; Cantos (4)* (RCA Victor RB16067)

Brahms: *Piano Concerto No. 1 in D Minor*
(RCA Victor SB6726/RB6726)

Brahms: *Piano Quintet in F Minor*
(RCA Victor SB6737/RB6693)

Chopin: *Polonaises* (RCA Victor SB6640/RB6640)

Chopin: *Polonaise No. 7; Andante Spiamato* and *Grande
Polonaise; Impromptus Nos. 1–3; Fantaisie Impromptu*
(RCA Victor SB6649/RB6649)

Chopin: *Bacarolle; Preludes Nos. 25–27; Bolero; Fantasia;
Berceuse; Tarantelle*
(RCA Victor SB6683/RB6683)

Chopin: *Mazurkas Nos. 1–17*
(RCA Victor SB6702/RB6702)

Chopin: *Mazurkas Nos. 18–31*
(RCA Victor SB6703/RB6703)

Chopin: *Mazurkas Nos. 34–51*
(RCA Victor SB6704/RB6704)

Chopin: *Nocturnes Nos. 1–10*
(RCA Victor SB6731/RB6731)

Chopin: *Nocturnes Nos. 11–19*
(RCA Victor SB6732/RB6732)

Debussy: *Preludes Nos. 10 and 20, Images Nos. 2 and 6*
(RCA Victor SB5604/RB5604)

Falla: *Nights in the Gardens of Spain; El Sombrero*
(RCA Victor RB16067)

Fauré: *Nocturne No. 3* (RCA Victor SB6649/RB6649)

Granados: *Andaluza; Goyescas* (RCA Victor RB16067)

Liszt: *Sonata in B Minor* (RCA Victor SB6667/RB6667)

Mompou: *Canco I Dansa* (RCA Victor RB16067)

Poulenc: *Mouvements Perpetuel; Intermezzo No. 2*
RCA Victor RB6603

Prokofiev: *Visions Fugitives* (RCA Victor SB6504/RB6504)

Ravel: *Valses Nobles et Sentimentales; Miroirs 5*
(RCA Victor RB6603)

Schubert: *Fantasia in C (Wanderer)*
(RCA Victor SB6667/RB6667)

Schumann: *Piano Quintet* (RCA Victor SB6760/RB6760)

Schumann: *Noveletten* (RCA Victor SB6747/RB6747)

Szymanowski: *4 Mazurkas* (RCA Victor SB5604/RB5604)

Villa-Lobos: *Prole do Bebe* (RCA Victor SB5604/RB5604)

Picasso

Picasso at 84. 'We are all animals, more or less', he has observed. About three-quarters of the human race look like animals.

Full name

Pablo Diego José Francisco de Paula Juan Nepomuceno Crispin Crispiano de la Santisima Trinidad Ruiz y Picasso. (He chose to use his mother's maiden name, Picasso, because it was 'more musical' than his father's name, Ruiz.)

Born

23.30 hours, Tues. 25 Oct. 1881[1] at 36 (now 15) Plaza de la Merced, Malaga, Andalusia, Spain.

Characteristics

about 5′ 4″; sturdily built; originally black hair; hypnotic black eyes.

Married

1 1917 Olga Kochlova (separated 1935, died 1955) 1s. 1d.
2 1961 Jacqueline Roque.

Mistresses

1 1904–10 Fernande Olivier (died 1966).
2 1910–16 Marcelle (Éva) Humbert (died 1916).
3 1931–46 Marie Thérèse Walter 1d.
4 1935–45 Dora Maar.
5 1946–53 Françoise Gilot 1s. 1d.

According to *Picasso and His Women*, Jean-Paul Crespelle (Hodder, 1969), 'While he had only seven important liaisons, he had an enormous number of passing affairs, not to mention those paid encounters which he never disdained.'

The founder and leader of the Cubist school of art, seeing camouflage for the first time in World War I, exclaimed: 'Yes, it is we who made it – that is Cubism.' For the benefit of those requiring a fuller definition he has composed this more satisfying one: 'Cubism is neither a seed nor a foetus, but an art which is primarily concerned with form, and once form has been created, then it exists and goes on living its own life.'[2]

The artist who has made the greatest impact on the twentieth century has said: 'I want that internal surge – my creative dynamism – to propose itself to the viewer in the form of traditional painting violated.'

With Georges Braque (1882–1936) Picasso began the work of violation in the first decade of the century when his departure from the style of the Impressionists made itself felt.[3] His Blue and Rose periods happened because those colours were the cheapest then available.

Since then his style has undergone many radical changes. In more than seven decades of constant output it has been very roughly estimated that Picasso has created well over 20,000 works of art. Although thousands have been exhibited and catalogued, thousands more have never been named or publicly displayed. More than 500 such works exist in his villa *La Californie* near Cannes on the French Riviera. His other homes also have rooms full of artistic treasures yet to be appraised by experts. His most productive period was probably the month 2 April to 2 May 1936 when he completed no less than twenty-three major oil paintings.

Historically, Picasso's two most important paintings are probably *Les Demoiselles d'Avignon* (1907), named after a brothel in Barcelona, which can be seen at the Museum of Modern Art, New York, and *Guernica* (1937) which was inspired by the destruction of a Basque town in an air-raid on 28 April 1937. This painting is owned by Picasso and has been on loan to the Museum of Modern Art since 1939. It was reproduced on a Czech postage stamp issued in 1966.

[1] It was said that on this day the sun and moon both approached their nadir and a major confluence of stars and planets occurred.
[2] The dictionary definition of Cubism is 'A style of art in which objects are so represented as to give the effect of an assemblage of geometrical figures'.
[3] The Impressionists were a nineteenth-century school of painters who were more concerned with light and colour than with elaborate detail. Their name was derived from a painting called *Impression, Sunrise* (about 1872) by Claude Monet (1840–1926). Other notable Impressionists were Pierre-Auguste Renoir (1841–1919), Camille Pissaro (1831–1903), Paul Cézanne (1839–1906) and Edgar Degas (1834–1917).

Picasso

Picasso has explained that he paints as his passions tell him. 'What a miserable fate for a painter who adores blondes to have to stop himself putting them into a picture because they don't go with a basket of fruit.' He has also affirmed that it is quite wrong for a woman who does not smoke pipes to try and paint pipes. This basic standard of artistic integrity has not prevented him from consistently selecting subjects which prove to be lucrative, or from depicting at least a measure of beauty on his canvases. Like other artists, he has emphasized that it is not important to understand his work at first glance: 'You do not understand Chinese, perhaps, but it can be learnt.' The French writer, Jean Cocteau (1889–1963), opined that one of Picasso's greatest secrets was that: 'He runs faster than beauty. . . . There is nothing more fatal than running alongside with beauty or lagging behind it.'

Among those who have attempted to compare Picasso with the masters of the past, none has been more categorical than Salvador Dali. Describing him as 'the most vital man I have ever known', Dali has ranked Picasso the sixth greatest artist of all time. In his analysis, which takes into account technique, inspiration, colour, genius, composition, originality, mystery, and authenticity, Dali ranked himself fifth. The top four, in his view, are Jan Vermeer (1632–75), Sanzio Raphael (1483–1520), Diego Velasquez (1599–1660) and Leonardo da Vinci (1452–1519). That Picasso did not see himself as an immortal was apparent in a 1952 interview when he described himself as 'only an entertainer' and not 'an artist in the great and ancient sense of the word'.

The creator of the 'peace dove' of Communist propaganda, and a member of the French Communist Party, Picasso remains an ardent admirer of British royalty and has admitted to being especially fond of Princess Margaret. After seeing her wedding on TV, he told his son the next morning: 'If I had had that dream in the reign of Elizabeth I, I would certainly have been beheaded. I couldn't really be put in the Tower of London for that.'

The first Picasso painting to be sold at Sotheby's made £19 ($76) in 1922. Sales prices of Picasso's paintings only reached sizeable figures in 1958. The approximate sale of escalation in the commercial value of his works can be gauged from the following progressive table of top prices made at public auctions:

Year	Prices Made	
	£	$
1944	1,400	5,600
1954	4,410	12,348
1958	54,285	152,000
1959	55,000	154,000
1962	80,000	224,000
1967	190,000	532,000

In April 1967 the Chairman of Sotheby's estimated that Picasso's works had a total realizable value of over £100,000,000 ($280,000,000). In Dec. 1967 a wealthy American offered $2,560,000 (£1,066,666)

Approximate Dates of Some Important Periods in Picasso's Art

Blue Period (1901–04)
Rose Period (1904–06)
Period of Influence by African Sculpture
 (1906–09)
Early Cubist Period (1907–10)
Analytical Cubism (1910–12)

Synthetic Cubism (1913–18)
End of Cubism (1917–23)
Neo-Classic Period (1920–23)
Period of Big Compositions (1924–27)
Surrealist Period (1925–33)

---

for two Picassos, *Two Brothers* (1905) and *Seated Harlequin* (1922), exhibited in the Basel Museum of Arts, Switzerland, on loan from the Staechlin Foundation. As a special concession to the Museum, the Foundation allowed the Museum to keep the paintings for a payment of $1,950,000 (£812,500). It was estimated in 1968 that Picasso's output corresponded to potential earnings of £20,000 ($48,000) a day.

'I have pleased master and critic with all the changing oddities that have passed through my head, and the less they understood me the more they admired me.'

Recent highlights of Picasso's career have included the following:

1953 Picasso rebuked by the Central Committee of the French Communist Party for his 'unheroic' sketch of Joseph Stalin.

1956 Picasso rebuked the French Communist Party for its 'veil of silence' over the Hungarian revolution.

1958 The French Minister of Education banned the opening of his Museum of Peace in Paris.

1962 Picasso nominated as one of the recipients of the 1961 Lenin Peace Prize.

1966 In celebration of Picasso's 85th birthday an exhibition of 1,000 of his works was staged in Paris. It was arranged in three different palaces and insured for $60,000,000 (£21,430,000).

1967 Picasso donated to the Committee to rescue Italian works of art inundated in floods at Florence a sum of $105,000 (£37,500) made from the sale of *Reclinin Woman Reading* (1960) in a trans-Atlantic TV auction. Three froundations paid £100,000 ($280,000) for Picasso to execute the 50-foot high, 162-ton Cor-Ten steel sculpture for the new Civic Centre in Chicago, Illinois, USA.

Picasso's 'Maternite au Bord de la Mer' which made £190,000 ($532,000) at Sotheby's in 1967.

219

TOP SALE PRICES OF PICASSO'S WORKS

Date of Sale	Work	Price made £	$	Gallery
19 Nov. 1958	*Maternite*	54,285	152,000	Parke-Bernet
6 May 1959	*Hollandaise a la Coiffe* (1905)	55,000	154,000	Sotheby
12 Oct. 1960	*Femme Accroupie* (1902)	48,000	134,400	Sotheby
10 April 1962[1]	*Mort d'Harlequin* (1905)	80,000	224,000	Sotheby
	Femme Assise dans un Jardin (1905)			
21 Oct. 1964	*Verre, Bouquet, Guitare, Bouteille* (1919)	41,964	117,500	Parke-Bernet
14 April 1965	*Femme au Corsage Bleu* (1941)	41,071	115,000	Parke-Bernet
22 June 1965	*Femme Assise sur un Chaise* (1937–38)	50,000	140,000	Sotheby
23–24 April 1966	*Trois Baigneuses*	41,071	115,000	Parke-Bernet
26 April 1967	*Maternite au Bord de la Mer* (1902)	190,000[2]	532,000	Sotheby
28 June 1967	*Courses de Taureaux* (1900)	42,000	117,600	Sotheby
23 April 1968	*La Pointe de la Cite* (1912)	125,000	300,000	Sotheby
23 April 1968	*Ma Jolie : Guitare, Bouteille de Bass,*			
	Grappe de Raisin, et Verre (1914)	98,000	235,200	Sotheby
23 April 1968	*Nature Morte Dans Jn Paysage* (1915)	58,000	139,200	Sotheby
24 June 1968	*L'Embrassement* (1905)	84,400	202,560	Palais Galliera
3 July 1968	*Le Nu au Bas* (1901)	79,000	189,000	Sotheby
17 July 1968	Front curtain for the Diaghilev ballet			
	Le Train Bleu (1924)	69,000	165,000	Sotheby
10 Dec. 1969	*Bouteille de Rhum* (1911)	84,700	203,280	Palais Galliera

'If you want to kill a picture all you have to do is to hang it beautifully on a nail and soon you will see nothing of it but the frame. When it's out of place you see it better.'

'When I was a child my mother told me: "If you want to become a soldier, you will be a general. If you become a priest you will be Pope." I wanted to be a painter and I became Picasso.'

'We all know that art is not truth. Art is a lie that makes us realize truth, at least the truth that is given to us to understand. The artist must know the manner whereby to convince others or the truthfulness of his lies.'

In 1969, aged 87: 'I have been painting now for 77 years but I still have a lot to say. In 20 years' time when my task is completed I really will be famous.'

[1] Two-sided painting from the Somerset Maugham collection.

[2] This is the highest price paid at auction for a work by a living painter. The highest auction price for an Old Master is £821,429 ($2,300,000) for *Aristotle Contemplating the Bust of Homer* (1653) by Rembrandt Harmensz van Rijn (1606–69).

A selection of Picasso autographs from the period 1900–23. When once asked by a lady to sign one of his drawings he said: No, madame, absolutely not! If I signed it now, I would be committing a forgery. It would be my signature of 1943 applied to a canvas of 1922.

220

BERTRAND RUSSELL

Hailed at the time of his citation for the Nobel Prize for Literature as 'one of the time's most brilliant spokesmen of rationality and humanity and a fearless champion of free speech and free thought in the West', the 3rd Earl Russell also enjoys the distinction of being at once a convict[1] and a recipient of the Order of Merit. In his Nobel Prize acceptance speech on 11 Dec. 1950 he promulgated a novel proposal for the aversion of war. Suggesting that swimming pools should be constructed filled with man-eating sharks, or with artificial waterfalls over which people would ride in boats, he recommended that 'Everybody who preached primitive war should spend at least two hours a day among the sharks or in the boat.' Only two years before Russell had publicly called upon the West to attack Russia in a 'war to end wars'.

The century's most quoted philosopher and the protagonist of the attitude of methodological doubt, Russell has it to say that he dined in 1889 with the former Prime Minister of England, William Ewart Gladstone (1809-98). He embarked early on a literary career which was to produce over 50 learned works: 'I was 10 years old before I'd met anyone who hadn't written a book ... I had even written a book myself, when I was six. Not a very good one, but still a book.' His account of how he prepared to write a book is illuminating but not such as might serve to surmount the limitations of lesser minds: 'Having, by a time of intense concentration planted the problem in my subconscious, it would germinate underground until, suddenly the solution emerged with blinding clarity, so

---

[1] In Feb. 1918 he was sentenced to four months in prison for writing an article in *The Tribunal* allegedly critical of the American army. He spent the time writing his *Introduction to Mathematical Philosophy* (1919), a semi-popular version of *Principia Mathematica*.

221

that it only remained to write down what had appeared as if in a revelation.'

His most celebrated work was *Principia Mathematica* which his publisher estimated would involve a publishing loss of £600 ($2,400). Of this they agreed to bear half while the Royal Society guaranteed £200 ($800) 'We thus,' wrote Russell of himself and his co-author, Alfred North White-head, 'earned minus £50 by 10 years' work.' The bulky manuscript was delivered to the publisher in a horse-drawn cab.

Over age for military service at the beginning of World War I, Russell has nearly always been a pacifist. A member of the Fabian Society,[1] he has expressed his political philosophy in this way: 'I do not regard Socialism as a gospel of proletarian revenge, nor even, *primarily*, as a means of securing economic justice. I regard it as an adjustment to machine production de-manded by considerations of common sense and calculated to increase the happiness, not only of the proletarians, but of all except a tiny minority of the human race.' In *Portraits from Memory* he ex-plained why he was not a Communist: 'The theoretical doctrines of Communism are for the most part derived from Marx. My objections to Marx are of two sorts: one that he was muddle-headed; and the other, that his thinking was almost entirely inspired by hatred.' He added: 'I am completely at a loss to understand how it came about that some people who are both humane and intelligent could find some-thing to admire in the vast slave camp produced by Stalin.'

[1] A group of Socialists formed in 1883-84 whose objective was 'to reconstruct society according to the highest moral possibilities.'

In 1937 Lord Russell wrote his obituary for *The Times*, anticipating that it would be published in 1962. Among the self-revelations he drafted for posterity was this modest claim: 'His life, for all its waywardness, had a certain anachronistic consistency, reminiscent of that of the aristocratic rebels of the early 19th cen-tury.' His ability to survive not only 1962 but several of his own predictions that the world would end has inevitably invited many requests for advice from people anxious to benefit from his great experience. 'My first advice', he has stated unhelpfully, 'would be to choose your ancestors care-fully.' He has denied that longevity is promoted by austerity: 'I have never yet done anything on the ground that it is good for my health. I smoke what I like. I eat what I like. I have always found that to forget oneself is the best way to keep your health, if you are as naturally healthy as I am.' Russell's remarkable physical resilience was demonstrated in 1948 when he was ditched in a Norwegian flying boat which sank with the loss of 19 lives. The venerable peer, aged 76, swam fully clothed in icy seas until rescued.

Summing up in a few casual phrases the work of over half a century, Russell sketched this outline of his career in 1951: 'My intellect, such as it is, has been steadily decaying since the age of 20. When I was young I liked mathematics. When this became too difficult for me I took to philosophy, and when philosophy became too difficult I took to politics.' Russell stood three times for Parliament unsuccess-fully before deciding that politics were also too difficult.

'No great achievement is possible without persistent work, so absorbing and so difficult that little energy is left over for the more strenuous kinds of amusement.'

On his 80th birthday: 'I think the first war was a mistake . . . I think that if that hadn't happened, you would not have had the Communists, you would not have had the second world war, you would not have had the threat of the third.'

In the first volume of his memoirs Russell wrote: 'Intellectually, the month of September 1900 was the highest point of my life.' He further revealed that in 1902 he underwent a five-minute 'mystical illumination', in the course of which he was radically transformed: .'Having been an Imperialist, I became during those five minutes a pro-Boer and a Pacifist.' In the kaleidoscopic decades which succeeded his early intellectual pre-eminence, the following landmarks may be discerned:

Full name Bertrand Arthur William Russell, 3rd Earl Russell (created 1861), OM (1949).

Born Sat. 18 May 1872, Ravenscroft, near Trelleck, Monmouthshire, Wales.

Characteristics About 5′ 8″; about 117*lb.* (8*st.* 5*lb.*); brown hair; blue-grey eyes.

Married
(1) 1894 Alys Pearsall (div. 1921) 1*s.*
(2) 1921 Dora Winifred Black (div. 1935) 1*s.* 1*d.*
(3) 1936 Patricia Helen Spence (div. 1952) 1*s.*
(4) 1952 Edith Finch.

1946 Dismissed from his appointment at the Barnes Foundation, Merion, Pennsylvania, USA, for lecturing outside the foundation. Awarded $20,000 (£5,000) damages for breach of contract.

1948 Stated that the West should attack Russia in a 'war to end wars' before the Soviets get an atomic bomb.

1957 Sponsored a conference at Pugwash, Nova Scotia, on the misuse of nuclear power.

1958 Became President and founder member of Britain's Campaign for Nuclear Disarmament. Stated in a TV interview: 'If the Communists conquer the world, it would be very unpleasant for a while but if the human race is wiped out, that is the end.'

1960 Resigned as President of CND.

1961 Served seven days in jail for declining to call off a demonstration at the Polaris base at Holy Loch.

1962 Wrote to Nikita S. Khrushchev congratulating him on his 'courageous stand for sanity' after the Soviet Premier had denounced President John F. Kennedy's quarantine on Cuba.

1963 Condemned Khrushchev for his 30-megaton nuclear test. Resigned from the Committee of 100. Inaugurated the Bertrand Russell Peace Foundation.

1967 Told *The Times*: 'Since the Labour party turned Tory I have no political party.' Promulgated his so-called War Crimes Tribunal which was banned in Paris and later opened in Stockholm.

1968 Received £200,000 ($480,000) from McMaster University, Hamilton, Ontario, Canada, for a collection of 150,000 letters, diaries, manuscripts, journals, tapes, and other papers collected throughout his lifetime.

On his 89th birthday: 'If there were in the world today any large number of people who desired their own happiness more than they desired the unhappiness of others, we could have a paradise in a few years.'

At age 96: 'My views on religion remain those which I acquired at the age of 16. I consider all forms of religion not only false but harmful.'

Writing in the final volume of his memoirs, the Spanish-American philosopher, George Santayana (1863–1952), concluded that although as a great intellect Russell had 'petered out', he was the most gifted of all the men he had known: 'He had birth, genius, learning, indefatigable zeal and energy, brilliant intelligence, and absolute honesty and courage. His love of justice was as keen as his sense of honour. He was at home in mathematics, in natural science, and in history. He knew well all the more important languages and was well informed about everything going on in the world of politics and literature.' But, Santayana noted in an interview: 'Along with his genius he has a streak of foolishness.'

'The fact that a belief has a good moral effect on a man is no evidence whatsoever in favour of its truth.'

'Man is an animal, and his happiness depends upon his physiology more than he likes to think.'

Bertrand Russell at 90: 'I have never yet done anything on the ground that it is good for my health.'

Publications

German Social Democracy (1896)
Essays on the Foundation of Geometry (1897)
The Philosophy of Liebnitz (1900)
Principles of Mathematics (1903)
Philosophical Essays (1910)
Principia Mathematica (1910) with Dr A. N. Whitehead
Problems of Philosophy (1911)
Our Knowledge of the External World as a Field for Scientific Method in Philosophy (1914)
Principles of Social Reconstruction (1917)
Mysticism and Logic (1918)
Introduction to Mathematical Philosophy (1919)
The Practice and Theory of Bolshevism (1920)
The Analysis of Mind (1921)
The Problem of China (1922)
The ABC of Atoms (1923)
The Prospects of Industrial Civilization (1923) with Dora Russell
Icarus (1924)
What I Believe (1925)
The ABC of Relativity (1925)
On Education (1926)
The Analysis of Matter (1927)
An Outline of Philosophy (1927)
Sceptical Essays (1928)
Marriage and Morals (1929) (Nobel Prize)
The Conquest of Happiness (1930)
The Scientific Outlook (1931)
Education and the Social Order (1932)
Freedom and Organization, 1814–1914 (1934)
In Praise of Idleness (1935)

Which Way to Peace? (1936)
The Amberley Papers (1937) with Patricia Russell
Power: A New Social Analysis (1938)
An Inquiry into Meaning and Truth (1940)
History of Western Philosophy (1946)
Human Knowledge, Its Scope and Limits (1948)
Authority and the Individual (1949)
Unpopular Essays (1950)
New Hopes for a Changing World (1951)
The Impact of Science Upon Society (1952)
Satan in the Suburbs (1953)
Nightmares of Eminent Persons (1954)
Human Society in Ethics and Politics (1954)
Portraits from Memory (1956)
Why I am Not a Christian (1957)
Common Sense and Nuclear Warfare (1958)
My Philosophical Development (1959)
Wisdom of the West (1959)
Fact and Fiction (1961)
Has Man a Future? (1961)
Unarmed Victory (1963)
Political Ideals (1963)
The Autobiography of Bertrand Russell, 1872–1914 (1967)
The Autobiography of Bertrand Russell, 1914–1944 (1968)
The Autobiography of Bertrand Russell, 1944–1957 (1969)

'POLITICAL POWER GROWS OUT OF THE BARREL OF A GUN'

MAO TSE-TUNG

Full name Mao Tse-tung (meaning 'Hair Enrich-east'). Alternative personal name Jun-chih.

Born Tues. 26 Dec. 1893, Shao Shan, Hunan Province, China.

Characteristics About 5′ 8″; strongly built; walks like a duck; blue-black hair; dark brown eyes; a wart on his chin; suffers from Parkinson's disease.

Married
(1) A childhood betrothal, unconsummated.
(2) 1920 Yang Kai-hui (executed 1930) 2s.
(3) 193? Ho Tsu-chen (div. 1937) 5 children (one of his sons killed in Korea in 1950).
(4) 1938 Chiang Ching 2d.
Chairman Mao was reported to have suffered a stroke on 2 Sept. 1969 and to be in poor health.

'Every Communist must understand this truth: political power grows out of the barrel of a gun.' The saying with which Mao Tse-tung, Chairman of the Chinese People's Republic is often identified, was first made by him at the Sixth Plenum of the Central Committee of the Chinese Communist Party on 6 Nov. 1938. In the same speech he explained: 'As advocates of the abolition of war, we do not desire war; but war can only be abolished through war – in order to get rid of the gun, we must first grasp it in hand '

As a boy Mao's grasp was first exercised shovelling manure on the family farm, a

225

chore which he alternated with surreptitious study when he thought his father was not looking. One day the angry parent, who did not approve of his son's scholarly inclinations, found him reading and chided him. 'I have carried 15 baskets of munure', Mao protested. 'If you doubt my word, you may go to the field and count them for yourself . . . But please leave me in peace now. I want to read.' Mao finally escaped from the farm and from his father – 'I learned to hate him' – and by diligent application to his books caught up with his more literate contemporaries, acquiring an alleged capacity to read three or four times as fast as other students

A Marxist by 1920, Mao was already by 1923 making such anti-Capitalist statements as 'America is actually the most murderous of hangmen'. He helped to form the Chinese Communist Party and it was united under him in the struggle against both the Japanese and the Kuomintang[1] forces under Generalissimo Chiang Kai-shek. Said Mao in December 1935: 'We are convinced that it is only through a common struggle by ourselves and the people of Inner Mongolia that we can overthrow our common enemies – the Japanese imperialists and their running dog, Chiang Kai-shek; at the same time we are persuaded that is is only by fighting together with us that the people of Inner Mongolia can preserve the glory of the epoch of Genghis Khan . . .'[2] Mao's personal attitude has hardened by the loss of his first wife, garotted by the Koumintang in 1930, and his three brothers, also executed by the KMT. He also endured the bitter experiences of 'The Long March' (1934–35). In this remarkable exploit the First Red Army, under his command, carried out a 6,000-mile rearguard action, harassed by superior KMT forces, from South Central China to the far North, one of the longest marches in military history. Despite offers of up to $250,000 (£62,000)

on his head, Mao held the loyalty of his followers and survived with 22,000 of the original army of 90,000. The experience enabled him to write a primer on guerilla warfare; years later he told General Dwight D. Eisenhower his strategy for war was: 'Enemy advances, we retreat; enemy halts, we harass; enemy tires, we attack; enemy retreats, we pursue.'

In power Mao has exploited the gimmick of identifying sins against the Party by coined labels. Among them are 'subjectivism' (old-fashioned idea about love, flowers, beauty, and truth), 'closed-doorism' (shutting one's eyes to anything outside one's own work, especially to the West), and 'mountaintopism' (a persistent attitude of aloofness and superiority). His policies have been promoted by well-pointed political slogans. Among the more important of these were 'Let a Hundred[3] Flowers Bloom, Let Diverse Schools of Thought Contend', promulgated in a speech delivered by Mao on 2 May 1956, and 'The Correct Handling of Contradictions among the People', which was put out on 27 Feb. 1957. On the 'Hundred Flowers' theme Mao said: 'It is harmful to the growth of art and science if administrative measures are used to impose one particular style of art or school of thought and to ban another.' On the handling of contradictions he announced: 'Our policy is this: counter revolutionaries must be suppressed whenever they are found, mistakes must be corrected whenever they are discovered . . .'

The task of conditioning the masses, including those naïve enough to reveal themselves after his 'Hundred Flowers' snare as subscribing to other schools of thought than Mao's, proceeded methodically. In October 1952, Minister of Finance Po I-po had said: 'In the last three years we have liquidated more than two million bandits.'[4] Though the pace of extermination in the mid-fifties may have been less

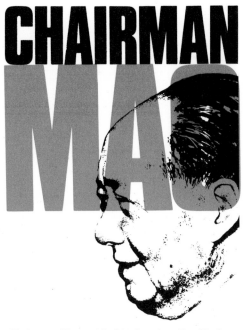

CHAIRMAN MAO

rapid, Lo Jui-ching,[5] Minister of State Security, testified that the overwhelming majority of the Chinese population had been 'educated' by witnessing public executions, and that millions of 'lesser criminals' were being sentenced to forced labour. An informed estimate of the total number of executions up to 1962 was 'more than 5,000,000 but less than 10,000,000. Meanwhile the masses took what cold comfort they could from such published propaganda as 'Today in the era of Mao Tse-tung, heaven is here on earth', and 'Mao Tse-tung ideology glows 100,000

Chairman Mao with his fourth wife. Madame Mao was born Li Ching Zun ('Azure Cloud'). She took the stage name Lan Ping ('Blue Apple') in 1937 but preferred to be known in political life by her chosen name, Chiang Ching. Her first husband was reported in 1967 to be the proprietor of a Chinese restaurant in Paris.

[1] The Kuomintang (literally 'National People's Party') ruled China from 1928-49. Chiang Kai-shek (*born* 31 Oct. 1887) still holds the title President of the Republic of China. He was re-elected for a third term in 1960 and resides as Taipei, Taiwan (formerly Formosa).
[2] Genghis Khan (real name Temujin) (1162-1227) the Mongolian King whose barbaric hordes, indulging in prolofic slaughters, conquered much of Central Asia and China, including Peking. Ironically, Mao in 1967 purged General Ulanfu, so-called strong man on Inner Mongolia, because he had set himself up as 'the 20th-century Genghis Khan'.
[3] The word hundred is not used in the numerical sense, but colloquially, to mean numerous.
[4] Counter-revolutionaries.
[5] In Jan. 1967 Po and Lo were reported to have attempted suicide; Lo succeeded.

feet high'. Mao's conviction that his message was getting across to his subjects sprung from ready grasp of their limitations, outlined in his 'Great Leap Forward' speech of 16 March 1958. 'Apart from their other characteristics', he pointed out, 'China's 600,000,000 people have two remarkable peculiarities; they are, first of all, poor, and secondly blank.' The total loss of lives in famine resulting from the Great Leap Forward has been estimated at 4,000,000.

Mao's views on international affairs were always distinctive. On 14 September 1939, shortly after the outbreak of World War II, he told a Party meeting at Yenan that 'it was not only Hitler but Chamberlain who wanted to fight', and that 'Today England has become the most reactionary country in the world, and the Number One anti-Soviet, anti-Communist, anti-democratic, and anti-popular leader, the enemy of all small peoples, is none other than Chamberlain...' Interviewed in August 1946, after President Harry S Truman's decision to end the war by using the atom bomb, Mao said: 'The atom bomb is a paper tiger ... All reactionaries are paper tigers.' Also classified as paper tigers were Hitler, Mussolini, Chiang Kai-shek, the Japanese, and the Americans.

Though he had once been expelled from the Communist Party by Stalin for 'deviationism', Mao issued a litany of praise on the death of the Soviet dictator

in 1953 (*see page* 286). On 14 Feb. 1955 Mao said: 'With the great co-operation between China and the Soviet Union . . . should the imperialists start a war of aggression we . . . will wipe them out clean from the surface of the globe.' In 1959, Nikita Khrushchev visited Mao in Peking and was asked by the Chinese leader for nuclear armaments. Mao told his guest: 'Comrade Khrushchev, you have only to provoke the Americans to military action and I will give you as many people as you wish – 100 divisions, 200 divisions, a thousand.' Khrushchev tactfully declined this offer and took credit for preserving world peace. But Sino-Soviet rapport had already taken a turn for the worse following Khrushchev's de-Stalinization speech in 1956, and divorce was virtually complete in 1962 when Mao again attacked Khrushchev over the Cuban missile crisis (*see page* 184).

Sealed off in almost total political isolation, Mao's attitudes have undergone no discernible change. In a Chinese Government Statement of 1 September 1963 Mao revealed that he had once discussed the question of nuclear war with the Indian Premier, Jawaharlal Nehru. Reported Mao: 'He believed that if an atomic war was fought, the whole of mankind would be annihilated. I said that if the worst came to the worst only half of mankind would be razed to the ground and the whole world would be socialist . . .'

On 14 April 1969 the Ninth Congress of the Chinese Communist Party in Peking named as Chairman Mao's successor the former Minister of Defence Lin Piao (real name Lin Yu-yung). Lin Piao (meaning 'Tiger-Cat' Lin) first came to prominence in the hierarchy during Mao's 1966 Cultural Revolution and was previously a distinguished army commander. The Ninth Congress also approved a resolution pledging China to 'fight to overthrow imperialism headed by the United States, the Soviet revisionist renegade clique, and reactionaries in all countries'.

'. . . the whole world can be remoulded only with the gun.'

'War is a special political technique for the realization of certain political objectives.'

'Some people have ridiculed us as the advocates of the "omnipotence of war"; yes, we are. We are the advocates of the omnipotence of the revolutionary war, which is not bad at all, but is good and Marxist.'

229

FIELD-MARSHAL EAR]

When, early in 1943, Churchill visited Tripoli to review the state of the North African campaign, then at its triumphant conclusion, his parting words to General Alexander were: 'Pray let me have a message which I can read in the House of Commons when I get back – and make it dramatic and colourful.' Never prolix in utterance, the Commander-in-Chief 18th Army Group addressed himself to the task and came up with a note of Wellingtonian brevity. 'Sir – The Orders which you gave me on August 15,[1] 1942, have been fulfilled. His Majesty's enemies together with their impedimenta have been completely eliminated from Egypt, Cyrenaica, Libya, and Tripolitania. I now await your further instructions.' The message was duly read by the Prime Minister in the House of Commons on 11 Feb., 1943. The victory it recorded will be remembered as one of the major turning points of World War II, and Alexander as the chief architect. The full magnitude of the British mastery over the German and Italian forces was sketched by Alexander when he reported: 'The final battle of Africa was an unusually complete example of annihilation. Never before had a great army been so completely destroyed. A quarter of a million laid down their arms in unconditional surrender. Only 663 escaped. The British losses in the final battle were less than 2,000 men.'

Soon Alexander was to lead the Allied invasion of Italy where he received the surrender of over a million of the enemy. The fall of Rome was an event of peculiar significance for him. All his life he had made a study of Hannibal (247–183 BC), the Carthaginian General who defeated the Romans but failed to capture Rome. Alexander did not fail nor did he spare himself the ordeal and risk of the front line. In one area, he was seen reviewing the

Full name Harold Rupert Leofric George Alexander, 1st Earl (1952), 1st Viscount (1946), 1st Baron Rideau (1952), KG (1946), GCB (1942), OM (1959), GCMG (1946), CSI (1936), DSO (1916), MC (1915), (PC 1952).

Born Thurs. 10 Dec. 1891, Caledon and Derg Lodge, Caledon, County Tyrone, Ireland.

Characteristics About 5′ 10″; about 164*lb.* (11*st.* 10*lb.*); dark brown hair; blue eyes.

Married 1931 Lady Margaret Diana Bingham 2*s.* 1*d.*, 1 adopted *d.*

Died Mon. 16 June 1969. Perforated aorta. **Estate** £120,176 ($288,422) net; duty paid £50,035 ($120,084).

action from an exposed position wearing his red-banded General's hat. A signal went out asking 'the gentleman in the red hat' to take note that he was drawing heavy enemy fire, a fact he was apparently unaware of.

Front line service was not new to Alexander. In World War I he went 'over the top' over thirty times, was wounded three times, and mentioned in dispatches five times. Home on leave when wounded in 1915, he became restive and set out to prove his fitness by taking a walk from his home in Ireland. His doctor was horrified to learn that the supposed gentle convalescent outing was a 64-mile marathon trudge through the snow of seventeen hours' duration. Alexander had, incidentally, already proved his athletic prowess by entering the Irish mile championship on Whit Monday, 1914, within months of leaving for the trenches. The report in the *Irish Times* evinced an economy of words of which Alexander might have approved. 'A big surprise was forthcoming in the mile', it

¹Actually August 10

ALEXANDER OF TUNIS

Field-Marshal Earl Alexander of Tunis was Commander-in-Chief Middle East (1942–43), Commander-in-Chief North Africa (1943), Commander-in-Chief Allied Armies in Italy (1943–44), Supreme Allied Commander, Mediterranean Theatre (1944–45), Governor-General of Canada (1946–52), and Minister of Defence (1952–54).

began. 'The holder, F. J. Ryder, retired 220 yards from the finish, and the Honourable H. R. Alexander of the Irish Guards, who went to the front after a lap and a half, experienced no difficulty in resisting the attention of J. Gamble of Ballymoney.'

It was conspicuous in the obituaries published at the time of Alexander's death that nobody could be found who had ever said a bad word about him. The Press were unanimous in their failure to detect a flaw in him. Aristocratic presence, elegant bearing, unfailing charm and courtesy, magnificent courage, epitomized, in the eyes of those who served under him, all the qualities of superlative leadership. But the high esteem of his senior colleagues and associates in time of war remains the finest

231

ALEXANDER
ALEXANDER
ALEXANDER

testimony of Alexander's greatness. General Dwight D. Eisenhower called him 'the ace card in the British Empire's hand'. Field-Marshal Montgomery wrote: 'I could not have served under a better chief; we were utterly different, but I liked him and respected him as a man.' General Omar Bradley[1] praised him as 'the outstanding General's General of the European war'. On the personal side, Lieutenant-General Sir Brian Horrocks[2] described him as 'a quiet man with a very pleasant personality. He gave me the impression of being remote from the battle, and on the few occasions I met him subsequently I always felt the same, that he lived in a world of his own which few others were encouraged to enter.' Clement Attlee saw him as a General 'who had a broad strategy of the war; he didn't just look at the battle, he looked ahead at what was going to happen. Rather more than Montgomery would and with a broad conception of things. He was the man for a campaign, Montgomery for a battle.' Harold Macmillan made an identical observation: 'If Montgomery was the Wellington,[3] Alexander was the Marlborough[4] of the war.'

Alexander emphasized his awareness of the wider implications of war when he pointed out that when 'whole nations are drawn into the struggle for survival, purely military strategy is not enough. Strategy must take account of the feelings and will of the people engaged in war; their morale is an important if not overriding factor.' His intense concern for the troops under his command was underlined in an address to war correspondents on 3 Nov. 1944: 'Always at the back of my mind when I make plans, is the thought that I am playing with human lives. Good chaps get killed and it's a terrible thing.'

It is known that Alexander was a favourite of Churchill's who noted his regard for him: 'He was the last British Commander at Dunkirk. Nothing ever disturbed or rattled him, and duty was a full satisfaction in itself, especially if it seemed hard. But all this was combined with so gay and easy a manner that the pleasure and honour of his friendship were prized by all those who enjoyed it, among whom I could count myself.'

Stories about Alexander at Dunkirk are legion. One was that he spent the last hours building castles in the sand; another that he appeared, spick and span, to enjoy his Dundee marmalade for breakfast in a shell-shattered house near the beach. When an aide remarked that they might have to surrender, the General replied: 'I don't know the form for surrendering. So it seems we can't.'

---

[1] Commander 1st US Army Normandy Campaign (1944).
[2] Horrocks commanded 10 corps in Egypt and Africa and 9 corps in Tunis.
[3] Field-Marshal the Duke of Wellington (1769–1852), victor of the Battle of Waterloo in 1815.
[4] John Churchill, 1st Duke of Marlborough (1650–1722), commanding officer of the English armies which defeated the French at the Battles of Ramillies (1706), Oudenarde (1708), and Malplaquet (1709). Marlborough was an ancestor of Sir Winston Churchill. He is buried at Windsor close to Alexander's residence.

Alexander of Tunis

Home on leave from the Italian campaign in 1944, Alexander dropped in at the United Service Club in London wearing civilian clothes to be greeted heartily by a friend who lived in Ireland. 'Hello Alex', he breezed, to the consternation of members, 'I haven't seen or heard of you since the war started. What have you been doing with yourself?' The Supreme Allied Commander, Mediterranean Theatre, was unabashed: 'I'm still soldiering', he smiled.

General Alexander's message to Churchill from North Africa. (Reproduced by the gracious permission of Her Majesty The Queen.)

ARMY FORM C-2130.
(Pads of 100.)

MESSAGE FORM.

Serial No.

CALL AND INSTRUCTIONS. IN

OUT

No. of Groups. GR.   Office Date Stamp

(ABOVE THIS LINE IS FOR SIGNALS USE ONLY.)

TO *Prime Minister*

FROM *Gen. Alexander*   Originator's Number.   Date. *4*   In Reply to Number.

Sir, the orders you gave me on Aug. 15th 1942 have been fulfilled O His Majesty's enemies together with their impedimenta have been completely eliminated from EGYPT, CYRENAICA, LIBYA and TRIPOLITANIA O I now await your further instructions

THIS MESSAGE MAY BE SENT AS WRITTEN BY ANY MEANS.   IF LIABLE TO BE INTERCEPTED OR FALL INTO ENEMY HANDS, THIS MESSAGE MUST BE SENT IN CIPHER.   ORIGINATOR'S INSTRUCTIONS DEGREE OF PRIORITY.   TIME OF ORIGIN. *1930 8/4*

SIGNED   SIGNED   (BELOW THIS LINE IS FOR SIGNALS USE ONLY.)   T.H.I. *1900/4*

SYSTEM IN	TIME IN	READER.	SENDER.	SYSTEM OUT	TIME OUT	READER.	SENDER.	SYSTEM OUT	TIME OUT	READER.	SENDER.

T.O.R.

MFP 3 C 1 (B)—(B-3)—5-6-40—38,000 Pads.

233

GENERAL DWIGHT D. EISENHOWER

Two boys in Kansas were once talking about what they would do when they grew up. 'I said I wanted more than anything else to be a baseball player', recalled Eisenhower. 'Then I asked him: "What do you want to be?" He answered "I want to be President of the United States." Neither of us got our wish.'

The boy who became President never lost his childhood passion for sports. As a cadet at West Point Military Academy, he played for the United States Army in the football match against Carlisle Indian School who fielded the legendary Jim Thorpe.[1] Years later, as Commander-in-Chief Allied Forces in North Africa (1942–44) and Supreme Commander of the Allied Expeditionary Forces in Western Europe (1944–45), General Eisenhower's military strategy was, according to Field-Marshal Montgomery, influenced by his enthusiasm for football. 'Eisenhower's

creed appeared to be that there must be aggressive action on the part of everyone at all times', wrote Montgomery. 'I remember Bedell Smith[2] once likened Eisenhower to a football coach; he was up and down the line all the time, encouraging everyone to get on with the game. This philosophy was expensive in life . . .' However, Monty still thought Ike 'a great Supreme Commander – a military statesman.' Field-Marshal Alexander averred that since Ike 'was not so conversant with modern methods as were his junior commanders, he very wisely trusted us to fight his battles – and as results proved he was right!' Testimony as to the quality of Eisenhower's leadership was furnished by Winston Churchill: 'Eisenhower was a broad-minded man – practical, serviceable, dealing with events as they came with cool selflessness'; Churchill's representative on the Chiefs of Staff Committee, General Ismay,

234

Full name
Dwight David Eisenhower. (Childhood nickname: 'Ike'.)

Born
Tues. 14 Oct. 1890, Denison, Texas, USA.

Characteristics
About 5' 10½"; about 175*lb*. (12*st*. 7*lb*.); sandy hair; blue eyes.

Married
1916 Mary (Mamie) Geneva Doud 2*s*

Died
Fri. 28 March 1969. Congestive heart failure (his seventh heart attack) and pneumonia.

'This world of individual nations is not going to be controlled by any one power or group of powers. This world is not going to be committed to any ideology. Please believe me when I say that the dream of world domination by one power or of world conformity is an impossible dream.'

noted in Ike 'no trace of conceit or pomposity. Frankness, sincerity, and friendliness were written all over him. But with it all, he was master in his own house, and he could be firm to the point of ruthlessness if the occasion demanded.' Lieutenant-General Sir Brian Horrocks described him as 'a large, friendly, shrewd person with a broad grin, who was a co-ordinator rather than a commander . . . His most endearing quality was his complete selflessness.' Harold Macmillan wrote: 'Whatever may be the final judgement about him, either as a soldier or a statesman, there can be no doubt about his quality as a leader of men. His services to the Allied cause were immeasurable. The experiment of a fully integrated staff, where British and American officers served side by side, was unique. Only Ike could have made it succeed.'

On VE Day, 8 May 1945, Eisenhower broadcast to the victorious forces under his command and paid tribute to: '. . . the truly heroic figure of this war. He is G.I. Joe, and his counterpart in the Air, the Navy, and the Merchant Marine of every one of the United Nations.' At a Press conference in Paris a month later he emphasized the part played by teamwork in victory: 'Franklin's old saying, "If we don't hang together, we'll hang separately",[3] applies in war more definitely than in peace.' When President Harry S Truman visited Europe for the Potsdam Conference in 1945 he told Eisenhower: 'General, there is nothing that you may want that I won't try to help you

[1] James Francis Thorpe (1888–1953) was voted the greatest football player and male athlete of the first half of the 20th century. He won the 1912 Olympic pentathlon and decathlon titles.

[2] Lt.-Gen. Walter Bedell Smith (1895–1961), Chief of staff to Eisenhower (1942–45).

[3] The actual remark of Benjamin Franklin (1706–1790) made at the signing of the Declaration of Independence on 4 July 1776 was: 'We must indeed all hang together or, most assuredly, we shall all hang separately.'

get. That definitely and specifically includes the Presidency in 1948.' It was the first hint the General had ever had of a future in public life. Returning home that year he said: 'I'm a soldier and I'm positive nobody thinks of me as a politician.' As it turned out, a large number of Americans did. They had, perhaps, noted his own view that: 'The people who know war, those who have experienced it ... I believe are the most earnest advocates of peace in the world.' He had also, through war, formed a broad concept of the role of the United States in world politics: 'We are not isolationists', he said at Abilene, Texas, on 23 June 1945, 'We are part of the great civilization of this world at this moment, and every part of the world where similar civilization prevails, is part of us.'

In the years preceding his inauguration as President, Eisenhower spoke frequently on the evils of war. At West Point in 1947 he reminded cadets: 'Though you follow the trade of the warrior, you do so in the spirit of Washington[1] – not of Genghis Khan.'[2] In an address at Pittsburgh he opined that: 'there is no such thing as preventive war ... no one has yet explained how war prevents war. Nor has anyone been able to explain away the fact that war begets conditions that beget further war.' On 20 Jan. 1953, the day of his inauguration as the 34th President, Eisenhower complained to the outgoing President that Truman had ordered Eisenhower's son, John, home from Korea for the ceremony. Truman later wrote: 'I thought this was a curious reaction by a father to the presence of his son on an occasion so historic for himself and his family. I could only account for it on the grounds that this was a manifestation of hostility towards me.'

In his State of the Union Message on 7 Feb. 1953 Eisenhower said: 'There is, in world affairs, a steady course to be followed between an assertion of strength that is truculent and a confession of helplessness which is cowardice.'

Ike had the satisfaction of seeing the Korean war draw to a close at the P'yongyang armistice of 27 July 1953 and of attending the Geneva Summit Conference. Speaking there on 21 July 1955, Ike said: 'The quest for peace is the statesman's most exacting duty. Security of the nation entrusted to his care is his greatest responsibility. Practical progress to peace is his fondest hope. Yet in pursuit of hope he must not betray the trust placed in him as guardian of the people's security.' On that occasion he failed to impress the Soviet Premier, Nikita S. Khrushchev. 'Such a President', commented Mr K., 'can take God knows what decisions, and his is a vast, great, and powerful nation. One shuddered that such great force was in such hands.'

Eisenhower made a further notable contribution to foreign affairs with his Eisenhower Doctrine (1957) which committed the United States to use force to resist the threat of Communist aggression.

On the home front, the Eisenhower administration introduced a Supreme Court ruling making racial segregation in schools unconstitutional. In Sept. 1957 Ike sent troops into Little Rock, Arkansas, during the segregation crisis. In 1958 the first US satellite, *Explorer I*, was launched, while in 1959 Alaska and Hawaii became the 49th and 50th States of the Union.

[1] George Washington (1732–99), President (1789–97).
[2] Genghis Khan (real name Temujin) (1162–1227), the Mongolian conqueror.

The President's health gave cause for international concern on several occasions. His addiction to golf, indulged in partly for reasons of health, was a frequent subject for news comment. Starting a round with Bob Hope he was once quoted as saying: 'I just lent Bolivia two million dollars for something or other, so we better hold this game down to a dollar.' Another golfing opponent, Sam Snead, took the liberty of offering America's first citizen a concise technical pointer which did not go down in the minutes of Federal business. Coached Snead: 'Stick your fanny[1] out, Mr President.' Ike profited from this guidance when he scored his first hole-in-one at the Swan Lakes Country Club in Palm Springs in Feb. 1968, sinking a 104-yard drive with his nine-iron at age seventy-seven.

The personal popularity which earned Eisenhowever the party slogan 'I like Ike' went with him everywhere, both in military and political life. It broke a record when he was re-elected President for a second term on 6 Nov. 1956 by the then largest popular vote: 35,581,003, or 57 per cent of the poll against 42 per cent of Adlai Stevenson. It was reflected in a message sent to Americans by Field-Marshal Montgomery when the President lay ill from a heart attack at Denver, Colorado, in 1955: 'He is not only your guy, he is our guy, he is our guy from a world point of view. It is frightfully important to get that right.' Elder statesman Bernard Baruch[2] explained Ike's secret in this way: 'Certainly no man in public life elicits affection and trust as he does. And this is because people respond to his essential decency and humility.' The view was endorsed by the American people who voted him the man they 'most admired' for each of the eight consecutive years 1953–60. He was again the man 'most admired' in 1967, some seven years after he had last held office as President.

---

[1] Fanny is American slang for backside.
[2] Bernard Mannes Baruch (1870–1965), Chairman of the War Industries Board in World War I, and US Representative on the UN Atomic Energy Commission in 1946. Baruch only gave up his round of shadow-boxing before breakfast when he reached the age of eighty.

LP Recordings

I Can Hear It Now (with Churchill and others).　　　　　　　　CBS BRG72256

Kennedy Memorial Album (with others).　　　　　　　　Diplomat 10000A-B

In 1951 a dinner was held in honour of General Eisenhower at the English-Speaking Union in London. Churchill, who attended, described Ike in his book as 'a broad-minded man – practical, serviceable, dealing with events as they came with cool selflessness.'

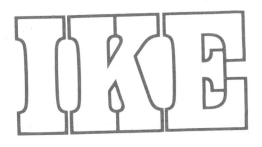

Full name
Robert Francis Kennedy.

Born
Fri. 20 Nov. 1925, Brookline, Massachusetts, USA.

Characteristics
About 5′ 10″; about 150*lb.* (10*st.* 10*lb.*) fair hair; blue eyes.

Married
1950 Ethel Skakel 7*s.* 4*d.*

Died
01.44 hours, Thurs 6 June 1968. Assassinated; shot by Sirhan Bishara Sirhan, a Jordanian expatriate, who fired eight shots from a calibre 0.22 pistol. Sirhan was sentenced on 21 May 1969 to die in the gas chamber.

The audience at the Royal Command Performance in 1962 were unanimous in their approbation. Bob Hope, with his unfailing capacity for slick yet kindly humour, had got to the essence of what the world knew and felt about the most celebrated family in United States political history. 'In America', said Hope succintly, 'we have two classes: the people and the Kennedys.'

His words were almost literally true. Joseph P. Kennedy was US Ambassador in London (1937–41). His eldest son, Joe, regarded by some as a potential future President, was killed in action with the USAF over Europe in 1944. His second son, John F. Kennedy, became the 35th President of the US and, as if in anticipation of the tragedy which was also to overtake him, he made this uncanny prediction: 'Just as I went into politics because Joe died, if anything happened to me tomorrow, my brother Bobby would run ... and if Bobby died, Teddy would take over for him.' He reinforced his message by giving his brother a cigarette box engraved with the legend: 'To Bob. When I've finished, why don't you start?'[1]

Robert Kennedy required no additional motivation. Born into the family tradition of leadership, he had been extended in various fields of action and responsibility long before his brother became President. At nineteen he served on the destroyer *Joseph P. Kennedy Jr.* before graduating from Harvard. He was not yet thirty when

ROBERT

the US Junior Chamber of Commerce named him as one of the 'ten outstanding young men' of 1954. Rising swiftly in the legal profession, he was retained as chief counsel to the Senate Rackets Committee[2] where his work won him a citation as 'Outstanding Investigator of the Year' in 1957, after he had exposed 'overwhelming evidence of corruption' in the powerful Teamsters Union. His findings were set out in his book *The Enemy Within* (1960).

His image was well established in its own right by the time Bobby made his vital contribution towards his brother's election to the Presidency in 1960. His masterly management of the campaign and his past record marked him out as an obvious candidate for high office but there were sour cries of 'nepotism' when the new President appointed him Attorney General. As loyal to his kin as to his convictions, JFK nonchalantly waved aside the howls of protest: 'I see nothing wrong with giving Robert some experience as Attorney General before he goes out to practice law.'

Bobby swiftly demonstrated his fitness for command, intensifying his pressure on organized crime and setting up machinery to cope with juvenile delinquency. Already recognized as a champion of the under-

privileged, he exerted his authority in support of the 1954 Supreme Court ruling on desegregation of schools. By sending Federal Marshals to Montgomery, Alabama, he successfully averted serious bloodshed in riots there. Again in 1962 he used troops to deter opposition to the enrolment of a Negro named James Meredith at the University of Mississippi.

Many of the big decisions of the John F. Kennedy administration had Bobby's support and counsel. Perhaps the most vital of these was the signing of the Nuclear Test Ban Treaty in 1963. Bobby referred specifically to this in a TV interview in 1968 when he acknowledged the part played by Harold Macmillan in this achievement and added: 'Whether England has the financial power or military power that she had thirty years ago is less important than the fact that she has a power no other country can share with her.' He generously conceded that by instilling the Rule of Law in many countries, Britain had made a contribution which even the United States could not match because America had obtained that Rule from the British in the first place.

On the assassination of President Kennedy, Bobby became the leader of the family and inheritor of the Kennedy mission but this did not preclude his wholehearted allegiance to President Lyndon B. Johnson whose policies he mainly endorsed until 1966. From that time his attitude on such issues as the war in Vietnam underwent a change and he became identified as a

---

[1] In 1969, following a motor accident in which his secretary was drowned, Senator Edward Kennedy announced that he would not stand for the Presidency in 1972.
[2] Correct title: the United States Senate Committee on Improper Practices in the Field of Labour and Management.

F. KENNEDY

possible rival to Johnson for the Presidential election. His formal announcement that he would run for the Democratic nomination did not come until 1968 and immediately it was seen that he had a large body of popular support, especially from the young and from minorities.

Kennedy's revised view of the role of the United States in the world scene arose from his feeling that America could no longer afford to fight aggression abroad as well as poverty at home. America's most important problem, he stated, was 'to end strife between our own people and solve their problems'. At the same time he did not accept the socialist attitude that the State should relieve men of the responsibility of solving their own problems. 'Welfare has proved ineffective and demeaning', he emphasized. 'The only answer is to create jobs. I'd do it through tax incentives to the private sector, using the government as employer of last resort.'

The personal qualities which made Bobby a formidable political quantity derived both from his Roman Catholic heritage and from the tough self-reliance characteristic of the Kennedys. His wife Ethel once said: 'Bobby sees only the goodies and the baddies, good things and bad things. Good things to him are virility, courage, action . . . He has no patience with the weak or the ditherers.' He was endowed with that superabundance of vitality which is often associated with leadership. Crowds loved to touch him and he travelled with a stock of inexpensive cuff-links to replace those he lost almost daily to the acquisitive fingers of admirers. His physical stamina was immense and he assiduously cultivated fitness in hard outdoor activity. A fine footballer at Harvard, he was, as recently as 1965, the first human to climb Mount Kennedy in Canada.

On the last morning of his life, within hours of ascending the victory rostrum at the California primary election, Bobby saved his twelve-year-old son David from drowning in the sea. David was already fully conscious of his place in the Kennedy orientation. Among his souvenirs is a photograph of himself at the White House. It was inscribed by his Uncle, the late President, with the words: 'A future President of the United States inspects his future property.'

A letter received by the author only five weeks before Robert F. Kennedy's tragic death. The Kennedy Coat of Arms appears on page 282.

ROBERT F. KENNEDY
NEW YORK

United States Senate
WASHINGTON, D.C. 20510

April 29, 1968

Dear Mr. Hildreth:

I regret very much the delay in replying to your letter. In any event, I am enclosing a copy of the Kennedy coat of arms as you requested.

With best regards,

Sincerely,

Robert F. Kennedy

Mr. P. Hildreth

240

Full name James Clark, OBE (1964).

Born Wed. 4 March 1936, Fife, Scotland.

Characteristics Just under 5′ 8″; about 150*lb*. (10*st*. 10*lb*.); brown hair; grey eyes; 6/6 vision in both eyes; according to Graham Hill he had very good muscular co-ordination, was light on his feet, had rhythm, excellent judgement, and very fast reactions; bit his nails constantly when not driving.

Died Sun. 7 April 1968, Hockenheim circuit, West Germany.

JIM CLARK

In a year when tragedy stalked the news in gruesome, almost daily headlines, the harsh bereavement inflicted on British and world sport by the death of Jim Clark in 1968 was among the cruellest. A shallow right-hand turn at 150 mph was a problem no stiffer than had faced him a thousand times. Yet this was the last drive for the man who once said: 'In motor racing there is a narrow margin between being right at the top and being a retirement or an also-ran'. Clark was denied retirement and was certainly no also-ran. Stirling Moss, who nearly lost his life in an accident like Clark's, as yet unexplained, rated him in 1963 'the greatest natural driving talent today'. Moss endorsed the point in 1965 when Jim broke his British record of sixteen Grand Prix victories. He said that John Surtees, Graham Hill, and Dan Gurney might be as technically good as Clark: 'But there is a difference between technique and brilliance. Clark has the brilliance.' The brilliance that was Jim came to fullest lustre in Jan. 1968 when his triumph in the South African Grand Prix brought his total of Formula I wins to twenty-five, surpassing the record twenty-four of Argentina's Juan Fangio. The five-time world champion himself was then reported as acknowledging Clark 'the greatest in the whole history of motor racing'.

With the rugged constitution born of Scottish air and country life, Jim's zest for things mechanical started early. He pedalled his own car at three, tinkered with the family farm tractor, and pranged the parental Alvis at age ten. The boy from Fife found time, too, for herding sheep but the thrill of driving was too much. He won a local sports car trial though ruled ineligible to compete, and then in 1956 showed his growing competence by crossing the line as sole finisher in a sprint for saloons over 2,000 cc. By 1958 he was a name to

approach found a place for the obvious as well as the esoteric in motoring. 'It's very, very important not to let your mind wander,' he emphasized once. In cornering he recognized that while there might be a theoretically correct line through every corner, it might be necessary to adjust this line to suit the handling of a car which might not be true. Another useful hint, valid in other sports as well, was that the best performance often follows a refreshing pause: 'I find that if I have been out in the car and then come into the pits and hang

JIM CLARK

FORMULA ONE GRAND PRIX VICTORIES

	Venue	GP Event	Car	Speed in mph
1962	Spa	Belgian	Lotus 25	131.90
	Aintree	British	Lotus 25	92.25
	Watkins Glen	United States	Lotus 25	108.61
1963	Spa	Belgian	Lotus 25	114.10
	Zandvoort	Dutch	Lotus 25	97.53
	Rheims	French	Lotus 25	125.31
	Silverstone	British	Lotus 25	107.75
	Monza	Italian	Lotus 25	127.74
	Mexico City	Mexican	Lotus 25	93.29
	East London	South African	Lotus 25	95.10
1964	Zandvoort	Dutch	Lotus 25	98.02
	Spa	Belgian	Lotus 25	132.51
	Brands Hatch	British	Lotus 25	94.14
1965	East London	South African	Lotus 33	100.33
	Spa	Belgian	Lotus 33	117.16
	Clermont-Ferrand	French	Lotus 25	89.22
	Silverstone	British	Lotus 33	112.02
	Zandvoort	Dutch	Lotus 33	101.30
	Nurburgring	German	Lotus 33	99.79
1966	Watkins Glen	United States	Lotus 43	114.94
1967	Zandvoort	Dutch	Lotus 49	104.45
	Silverstone	British	Lotus 49	117.64
	Watkins Glen	United States	Lotus 49	120.95
	Mexico City	Mexican	Lotus 49	101.42
1968	Kyalami	South African	Lotus 49	107.42

remember, winning 20 out of 42 events contested. Two more seasons saw him eighth in the world and on the brink of the big-time. In tenth place at Le Mans in 1959 – 'There are more difficulties at Le Mans than in any other race' – he also drove home seventh at Goodwood, lapping at similar speeds to the top men.

Clark was a thinking driver and absorbed the cumulative experience of 123 speed events before his first Formula I race, the 1960 Dutch Grand Prix. His cerebral

about for ten minutes or so I can usually set up a fast time on my third, fourth, or fifth laps on going out again.'

Clark's supremacy can be gauged as much as by the frequency with which he clocked fastest lap times in practice spins and the near misses he recorded as by his actual victories. In 1962 he lost the World Championship only by a mechanical failure in the final race; in 1964 it eluded him only on the last lap of the last Grand Prix. But the year 1963 saw him utterly in

242

command of Formula I racing. He won the first six Grand Epreuves in succession, then rounded off his staggering achievement with a seventh in the South African Grand Prix at East London. This not only consolidated the World Championship, making him at twenty-seven the youngest-ever winner, but also broke the six-in-a-season record of Alberto Ascari (Italy) who was killed in 1955. He was also second in the Indianapolis 500, a race which he dominated in 1965 to become the first man to win the world title and the

'Indy' in the same year. He averaged a record 150.686 mph at 'Indy' before the largest paying crowd in US sports history of 305,000. But Clark said: 'I still prefer road racing, where there are more problems and more interest.' Not that Indianapolis lacks problems. In the 53 races up to 1969 there were 54 fatalities among the drivers.

Dr Martin Luther
KING

When Dr Martin Luther King Jr. was nominated as a candidate for the 1964 Nobel Peace Prize, the field was reported to include such dignitaries as General Charles de Gaulle, General Dwight D. Eisenhower, and Konrad Adenauer. That King was finally selected over these powerful contenders is the finest tribute to his life and work. At thirty-five he was the youngest man ever to be so honoured. He was the third Negro[1] and the fourteenth American to win the coveted distinction, presented annually to the individual who is adjudged to have 'done most for the furtherance of brotherhood among men and to the abolishment or reduction of standing armies and for the extension of these purposes'. In his Nobel acceptance speech, King said with characteristic humility: 'I do not consider this merely an honour to me personally, but a tribute to the discipline, wise restraint, and majestic courage of the millions of gallant Negro and white persons of good will who have followed a non-violent course in seeking to establish a reign of justice and a rule of love across this nation of ours.'

Educated and ordained for the Baptist ministry, Luther King first became seriously involved in protests against racial discrimination in 1955. The arrest of a Negro seamstress for refusing to observe segregation on a public bus gave rise to a Negro boycott of the bus service which lasted 382 days. As President of the boycott committee King said at Montgomery, Alabama: 'If you will protest courageously, and yet with dignity and Christian love, when the history books are written in future generations, the historians will have to pause and say: "There lived a great people – a black people – who injected new meaning and dignity into the veins of civilization." '

King's development along the lines that were to make him a revered leader began early. In boyhood it was noted that he could always command the respect of his fellows and that they liked to listen to him. He was only six when he first told his mother of his love for words: 'You just wait and see. I'm going to get me some *big* words.' But words were not the only weapon of man who also had big ideals and strong faith. His conviction about the efficacy of non-violence was arrived at spiritually, not just as an accommodation of physical inadequacy, for King was physically tough. 'From my Christian background I gained my ideals', he stated, 'and from Gandhi my operational technique'. In fairness to the American it should be said that Gandhi could never have sustained King's output. In 1957 he delivered 208 speeches and travelled 780,000 miles in the cause of Negro Civil Rights: He was one of the speakers to address the crowds making the Prayer

Full name   Martin Luther King.
Born Tues. 15 Jan. 1929, Auburn Avenue, Atlanta, Georgia, USA.
Characteristics About 5′ 7″; black hair; brown eyes; described himself as an 'ambivert – half introvert and half extrovert.'
Married 1953 Coretta Scott 2s. 2d.
Died Thurs. 4 April 1968. Shot through the neck with a rifle bullet. The assassin, James Earl Ray, 41, was gaoled for 99 years at Memphis, Tennessee, on 10 March 1969.

Pilgrimage to the Lincoln Monument. This was before he went into Civil Rights work full-time. Already he was aware that each time out his performance would raise the level of expectation of his audiences: 'People will be expecting me to pull rabbits out of my hat for the rest of my life.'

In 1960 Luther King turned his entire attention to Civil Rights work, resigning his pastorship. He led several protest marches, the most important being the famous Washington March of 1963 on the Centenary of the Emancipation Proclamation of 1 Jan. 1863 which had abolished slavery. 'I have a dream',[2] intoned King on that occasion, making perhaps his most famous oration, 'that one day this nation will rise up and live out the true meaning of its creed: "We hold these truths to be self-evident, that all men are created equal." '[3] Some 250,000 people, 60,000 of them white, were at Washington for history's largest Civil Rights demonstration.

[1] The two previous Negro winners were Ralph J. Bunche (USA) in 1950 and Albert Luthuli (Union of South Africa) in 1960. Luthuli, a former Zulu chief, died in 1967.
[2] Shortly after King's death, Pat Boone recorded the song *I Have a Dream* and announced he would give all the royalties to Dr King's movement.
[3] From the original draft of the American *Declaration of Independence* by Thomas Jefferson (1743–1826): 'We hold these truths to be sacred and undeniable; that all men are created equal and independent. . . .'

Soon King's influence and his following had escalated to the point where *Time* magazine nominated him in Jan. 1964 as their 'Man of the Year' for 1963. The news magazine with the world's largest circulation described him at that time as 'the unchallenged voice of the Negro people and the disquieting conscience of the whites'. In 1964 King was received by the Pope, preached at St Paul's Cathedral in London, and predicted on BBC-TV that there would be a Negro President of the United States within twenty-five years. His cause made further important gains in 1965 with the enactment of the Voting Rights Law and the march on Selma, Alabama, where he was arrested for the seventeenth time in ten years.

But the rise of Negro violence in many American cities, despite his repeated condemnation of the use of force, proved a hindrance to the wider acceptance of King's pacifist ideals. A frequent victim of rough-handling, abuse, and threats, he had two miraculous escapes from violent death. In 1956 a twelve-stick dynamite bomb, hurled during the Montgomery boycott, failed to explode on his porch. Two years later he was stabbed in the chest by a deranged Negro woman. The surgeon who extracted the weapon reported that King had only to sneeze to be drowned in his own blood through a punctured aorta.

For over ten years, therefore, King had survived the menace of sudden death in a country where, since the turn of the century, over 750,000 Americans have been shot to death, more than lost their lives in the US armed services in both World Wars combined. King hinted at a premonition of his end in his last speech at Memphis the day before his assassination: 'Like anybody, I would like to live a long life; longevity has its grace. But I'm not concerned about that now. I just want to do God's will. And He's allowed me to go up to the mountain. And I've looked over, and I've seen the promised land.'

On 10 Dec. 1964 at Oslo, Dr Martin Luther King received the $54,600 (£19,500) Nobel Peace' Prize from Mr Gunnar Jahn, President of the Nobel Committee. Dr King donated the money to the Southern Christian Leadership Conference who subsequently placed his widow on their payroll at a salary of $12,000 (£5,000). The SCLC took out a $15,000 (now £6,250) insurance policy on Dr King's life which was also covered by a $50,000 (now £20,833) policy taken out by singer Harry Belafonte.

LP Recordings

In Search of Freedom
(Mercury 20119 SMCL)
The Great March to Freedom
(Tamla-Motown TML 11076)

YURI GAGARIN

'There is enough space in the cosmos for all.'

Full name Yuri Alexeyevich Gagarin (Gagarin means 'wild duck').

Born Fri. 9 March 1934, near Gzatsk, Smolensk, USSR.

Characteristics About 5′ 2″; about 153*lb.* (10*st.* 13*lb.*); brown hair; blue eyes; did not smoke or drink.

Married 1958 Valentina Ivanova 2*d.*

Died Wed. 27 March 1968. Killed in a jet crash. His ashes were interred at the foot of the Kremlin wall in Moscow.

The cosmonaut who figured in what Sir Bernard Lovell[1] described as 'the greatest scientific achievement in the history of man' left the launching pad in the $4\frac{1}{2}$-ton spaceship *Vostok* at 09.07 hours Moscow time on 12 April 1961. The rocket site at Baikonur in East Kazakhstan receded rapidly below him and within four minutes he had left the earth's atmosphere travelling at 17,560 mph. His first words to earth from a height of 203 miles were: 'I am in good spirits. The machine works perfectly.' He reported that when he emerged from the shadow of the earth the horizon looked different: 'There was a bright orange strip along it which again passed into a blue hue and once again into a dense black colour.' He said that during the 89.34-minute single orbit: 'One's legs, one's arms weigh nothing. Objects float in the cabin. Neither did I myself sit in the chair but hung in mid-air. I ate and drank and everything occurred just as it does here on earth.' When orbiting in *Vostok* he was in constant communication by radio with the ground, and was entertained with pop music and classics. 'I spoke to a lot of people from up there ... it made me feel pretty good. I remember them playing that song *Moscow Nights* and some Tschaikovsky and ballads and army songs I know. Somehow it didn't feel lonely up there.'

The most punishing part of Gagarin's space training had been the so-called 'corkscrew' descent on the parachute course. '... the body starts spinning at

flames raging all around the ship.' The last part of the return journey, travelling from South Africa to Russia, occupied less than 20 minutes.

On emerging from his vehicle in a field, Gagarin encountered a young woman who had been tending a calf. Frightened, she asked him: 'Who are you?' Responded Yuri, courteously doffing his space helmet: 'A friend, a friend.'

Soviet newspapers ran red headlines proclaiming the sensational event. In Moscow Gagarin was screened in a nation-wide TV hook-up speaking to Nikita S. Khrushchev on the telephone while the Soviet Premier was on holiday near the Black Sea. 'Let the capitalist countries try to catch up with our country, which has

great speed and it seems you are in the grip of a force that drives you through the air like a screw. Your head feels like lead; there is a sharp cutting pain in your eyes and your whole body is drained of strength. You lose all sense of direction.' According to experts, the most difficult section of the space flight was, in fact, the descending trajectory. 'The ship began to enter the dense layers of the atmosphere', said Gagarin. 'Its external skin rapidly became red-hot and through the porthole filters I saw the frightening crimson reflection of the

blazed the trail into space and launched the world's first cosmonaut',[2] exulted Mr K. Gagarin was named a Hero of the Soviet Union, the 11,375th citizen to attain that distinction, was promoted from Major to Colonel, and was cheered by a million people through the streets of Moscow. At a reception there on 14 April 1961 he was warmly embraced by Khrushchev. Later he toured the world and was entertained to luncheon at Buckingham Palace by Queen Elizabeth II.

Gagarin was born on a collective farm.

As a child he had read the science fiction novels of Jules Verne and gazed at the stars. He later joined a flying club at Saratov on the River Volga, qualified from an industrial college as a foundry worker and subsequently became an officer in the Soviet Air Force. After his conquest of the cosmos he became a member of the Supreme Soviet, the USSR Parliament.

Owing to damage to his inner-ear balance, reported to have been sustained in a domestic accident, Gagarin was not scheduled to make further space flights but he acted as control officer at the Baikonur Cosmodrome on several occasions. His opinion about lengthy space journeys of the future was necessarily guarded but he foresaw that the problems of feeding space-

After becoming the world's first spaceman in 1961, Gagarin rubbed shoulders on the tribune in Red Square, Moscow, with the then Soviet Premier, Nikita S. Khrushchev, and the future Secretary-General of the Communist Party, Leonid L Brezhnev.

men would be solved by having vehicles parked in orbit which would provide fresh fruit and vegetables from their floating hot-houses. He also observed that walking in space requires four or five times as much effort as during training on earth and that 'more thorough training in conditions of weightlessness' was imperative.

'We have faith in the boundless possibilities of the human intellect, and we want the achievements of modern science to be used for peaceful purposes.'

'The dream of outer space throws new light on the purpose of human existence. . . . There is enough space in the cosmos for all.'

[1] Director of Jodrell Bank Experimental Research Station, Cheshire, England.
[2] According to reliable sources there were up to ten previous Soviet attempts to launch a man into orbit, some of them with fatal results.

Sir Malcolm Sargent

Full name Harold Malcolm Watts Sargent, Kt (1947). (Nickname 'Flash Harry').

Born Mon. 29 April 1895, Bath Villas, Ashford, Kent, England.

Characteristics About 5′ 10½″; about 152*lb*. (10*st*. 12*lb*.); black hair; brown eyes; always wore a carnation when conducting, and sometimes carried his pet parakeet, Hughie, on his lapel.

Married 1923 Eileen Laura Harding (div. 1946) 1*s*. (1*d*. died 1944).

Died Tues. 3 Oct. 1967. Cancer of the pancreas. (In 1968 the Malcolm Sargent Cancer Fund for Children was set up.)

Estate £28,560 ($68,544) net.

As the air raid sirens wailed in a northern English town early in World War II, there was one group of people who did not hurry to the shelters. They had come to hear a concert and the conductor had assured them that even bombs would not deprive them of it. 'Anybody who wants to go can go now', he told them. 'But the orchestra will carry on. We may be killed but we shall play something that Hitler can never kill.' The orchestra began to play and the audience were made to forget the horrors of war in the sounds of music.

Malcolm Sargent sang alto in the choir at the age of six, played the organ at ten, and studied the piano under Benno Moseiwitch. An accidental occurrence made him turn to conducting. The man

250

'Music-making
is a
whole-time
job'

engaged for a rehearsal of *The Gondoliers* failed to appear and Sargent stood in. He was the youngest Doctor of Music when he qualified at Durham University in 1914. His debut proper took place at a Queen's Hall Promenade Concert in London in 1921 when he conducted his own composition *Impressions of a Windy Day*.

Sargent believed that music-making is a whole-time job: 'It calls for everything from us, from our body, from our mind, and from our spirit. . . .' He frequently took scores to bed with him and worked on them if he woke up in the night. He considered that music comes fundamentally from two sources: 'One is obviously the throat; it is because we have a voice with inflections that the art of melody arose . . . the other

part of our physical anatomy from which we get our rhythm is the legs. We have two legs of equal length, and because of that it is not possible for us to move without moving rhythmically, left-right, left-right. There we have the beginnings of a march rhythm.' The musical talisman of his life was Handel's *Messiah* of which he said: 'I have loved, rehearsed, and performed the *Messiah* for nearly forty years – a photographic facsimile of the original manuscript has been my musical Bible – but I am still conscious that the best of me is not worthy of this masterpiece.'[1]

[1] The *Messiah* is a three-part oratorio created in 24 days by the German-born, English-naturalized composer George Frederick Handel (1685–1759). It was first performed in Dublin in 1742 and was published in 1767 after revision. One of the most prolific composers of all time, Handel's complete works occupy 100 volumes.

As long ago as 1938 Sir Henry Wood (1869–1944) wrote: 'To my mind he is one of the finest living conductors.' In 1947 this truth was given official endorsement when Sir Malcolm succeeded Sir Henry as conductor of the famous Promenade Concerts at the Royal Albert Hall in London where he was to conduct some 500 proms in twenty years. Of this most exacting task Sir Malcolm said: 'For the first twenty-six concerts I give, I put in 225 hours of rehearsal – and that is only orchestral rehearsal, and does not include choral.' He took a holiday every year before the proms to get fit. The Albert Hall's much maligned accoustics were, he insisted, not so bad really: 'It is an English characteristic to run down everything in England, but in fact there is no place so big that is so good for sound ... it is true, as a general principle that the bigger the building the worse the sound. Granted this, the Albert Hall is almost certainly the best place in the world.' For the benefit of those going to the proms for the first time he explained that 'The conductor's right hand holds that baton and gives the beat to his players, while his left hand gives the shading.'

Sartorially impeccable at all times, Sir Malcolm wore a red carnation by day and a white one at night. His appearance at first earned him the nickname 'Flash Harry' from some of his musicians but this was contracted to 'Flash' by younger members of his audience when they called for him to take another bow. His showmanship, not just a veneer, carried with it a genuine affection for his audiences who reciprocated devotedly. He was highly sensitive and emotional, gave way not infrequently to tears, and was notoriously generous despite the modest fees which he earned. As an example, a 1958 contract earned him a total

A few months before his death, Sir Malcolm returned to the concert platform to conduct the Royal Choral Society with the Royal Philharmonic Orchestra.

of £1,000 ($2,800) for a dozen concerts, six in London and six in the provinces. Abroad he could command greater fees; in South America in 1950 he was paid £3,500 ($9,800) for twelve concerts.

Since 1936 Sargent had the additional burden of international commitments in many parts of the world, travelling as much as 40,000 miles a year. His valet complained that journeys were hard on his wardrobe. Among other things he wore out twenty-five tail suits in eighteen years and, in some climates, sweated his way through five changes of shirts in a day.

Until his last illness, which first manifested itself in 1966, he was working a nineteen-hour day and still managed to

LP Recordings   Tours

Piano Concerto No. 3; New Philharmonia Orchestra (HMV XLP50009/SXLP50009)

Elgar: Dream of Gerontius; Royal Liverpool Philharmonic Orchestra (World Record Club T658/9)

Ibert & Sullivan: Gondoliers; Pro Arte Orchestra (HMV ASD265/5 and ALP1504/5)

Gilbert & Sullivan: HMS Pinafore; Pro Arte Orchestra (HMV SXLP30088/9)

Gilbert & Sullivan: Iolanthe; Pro Arte Orchestra (HMV SXLP30112/3)

t & Sullivan: Princess Ida; Royal Philharmonic Orchestra (Decca SKL4845/LK4845)

Gilbert & Sullivan: Trial by Jury; Pro Arte Orchestra (HMV SXLP30088/9)

Gilbert & Sullivan: Yeomen of the Guard; Pro Arte Orchestra (HMV ASD364/5)

Handel: Messiah; Royal Liverpool Philharmonic Orchestra (HMV XLP30096)

Miscellaneous: Carols; Royal Choral Society (HMV SXLP50009/XLP50009)

Miscellaneous: Instruments of the Orchestra (Decca SXL2199/LXT5573)

Miscellaneous: Brains Trust (with others) (Argo DA38)

Miscellaneous: An Evening at the Proms; BBC Symphony Orchestra (World Record Club T602)

Prokofiev: Symphony No. 5; London Symphony Orchestra (Hallmark HM537)

Prokofiev: Cello Sinfonia; Royal Philharmonic Orchestra (World Record Club CM81)

maninov: Symphony No. 3; BBC Symphony Orchestra (Music for Pleasure MFP2078

Rachmaninov: Piano Concerto;

Rawsthorne: Piano Concerto No. 2; BBC Symphony Orchestra (HMV HQM1025)

spighi: Fountains of Rome – Pines; London Symphony Orchestra (Hallmark HM502)

Sibelius: Symphony No. 2; BBC Symphony Orchestra (Music for Pleasure MFP2052)

Tchaikowsky: Symphony No. 5; London Symphony Orchestra (Hallmark HM511)

Walton: Symphony No. 1; New Philharmonia Orchestra (HMV ASD2299/ALP2299)

Walton: Belshazzar's Feast; Royal Liverpool Philharmonic Orchestra (World Record Club T523)

Year	Tours
1936	Australia, New Zealand
1937	Palestine
1938	Australia, Palestine
1939	Australia, Palestine
1943	Stockholm
1945	Australia, New York, Stockholm
1946	Vienna
1947	Vienna, Brussels, Oslo
1948	Zurich, Rome, Johannesburg, Copenhagen
1949	Madrid, Portugal, Gibraltar, Milan, Gothenburg, Oslo
1950	Athens, Buenos Aires, Montevideo, Rio de Janeiro, Santiago
1952	Copenhagen, Buenos Aires, Santiago, Lima
1953	Malta
1954	Paris, Dusseldorf, Hamburg, The Hague, Amsterdam, Maastricht, Brussels, Japan
1955	Philadelphia, Washington, New York, Baltimore, Ascona
1956	Caracas, Copenhagen, Stockholm, Bergen, Helsinki, Johannesburg
1957	Houston, Canada, Moscow, Leningrad, Helsinki
1958	Vienna, Czechoslovakia, Belgium, Houston, Buenos Aires, Lisbon, Yugoslavia, Canada
1959	Vienna, Berlin
1960	Australia, Vienna, Houston
1961	Bonn, Houston
1962	Australia, Vienna, West Germany, Far East
1963	Canada, USA

maintain his zest for the concert platform. His sense of humour was seldom daunted. Asked once how he had contrived to conduct a choir in an overcrowded hall, he said that it was 'Like taking a jellyfish for a walk on an elastic lead.'

Among the tributes which flowed in on Sir Malcolm's death was one from Maria Callas: 'Sir Malcolm was a courageous and kind conductor. He was a complete gentleman and the kind of truly great person one no longer finds.' Colin Davis, who took over from him when illness prevented Sir Malcolm from conducting the 1967 Promenade Concerts, said that Proms would never be the same again: 'I don't think they will ever be centred around the personality of one man like Sir Henry Wood, who created them, or Sir Malcolm, who inherited them.' Many of his contemporaries referred to his great gift for choral performances. Sir Thomas Beecham (1879–1961), who celebrated the same birthday as Sir Malcolm (29 April), once described him as 'the greatest choirmaster of them all'.

'Escape is the whole art of living. Religion is the first and most important form of it. Music is the second.'

'I would say that jazz is the most successful way yet found of using the art of music to make money.'

253

WALT DISNEY

Among the host of unpublicized behind-the-scenes employees engaged for the film *Male and Female* (1919) was an eighteen-year-old commercial artist turning out advertising sketches for $12 a week. It was not until nearly forty years later that producer Cecil B. de Mille (1881–1959) discovered the identity of his former employee. 'The sketches', wrote de Mille in his autobiography with obvious pride, 'were among the first work done in Hollywood by one of Hollywood's very few authentically creative geniuses, Walt Disney.'

Disney's artistic bent had been put to profit since the age of ten when his barber used to give him a weekly haircut in exchange for a sketch on the shop wall. In the 'twenties he began to make his mark in what many regarded as a new art form, the animated cartoon. Disney himself preferred not to call it art. 'Art is never conscious', he said. 'We don't even let the word "art" be used around the studio. If anyone begins to get arty, we knock them down. What we strive for is entertainment.'

Disney created his first animated cartoons in 1920. His first films with animation – the first of over 700 Disney films – were *Alice in Cartoonland* (1923–26) and *Oswald the Rabbit* (1927). The idea of the cartoon creature really caught fire with the invention of Mickey Mouse who made his first appearance in the silent film *Plane*

'We are not in the business of duplicating human action. We can do better than that – much better.'

Full name   Walter Elias Disney.

Born   Thurs. 5 Dec. 1901 at Chicago, Illinois, USA.

Characteristics   About 5' 10½"; about 151*lb.* (11*st.* 11*lb.*); light brown hair; dark brown eyes.

Married   1925 Lillian Marie Bounds 2*d.*

Died   Thurs. 15 Dec. 1966. Circulatory collapse following surgery for lung cancer.

Estate   Stock in Walt Disney Productions worth about $18,000,000 (£6,428,570), plus deferred salary at about $1,666 (£595) a week for 7½ years from the date of his death, plus a percentage interest in many films. Disney's wife, daughter, brother, grandchildren, and other relations also owned stock in his corporations.

Crazy (1927) which was not released. His debut proper was in *Steamboat Willie* (1928), the first cartoon film ever to be produced with sound. Mickey came into existence partly by accident. 'Mice used to gather in my basket when I worked late at night', Disney recalled. 'I lifted them out and kept them in little cages in my desk. One of them was particularly friendly. I guess I do have a special feeling for mice.' Disney's own voice, lifted to falsetto, originally squeaked the words of Mickey on the sound track. The big-eared mouse has remained a children's favourite on television over thirty years later and has appeared in millions of comic strips and books in fifteen languages, a character well loved by about one-third of the world's population.

The first colour cartoons were the *Silly Symphonies* (1929) which were also the first motion pictures in colour. The first full-length cartoon, also in colour, was *Snow White and the Seven Dwarfs* (1937). This was reproduced in eight languages and cost $2,000,000 (£500,000) to produce, an unheard-of sum in those days. It grossed $10,000,000 (£2,500,000). Other cartoon characters were created, notably Donald Duck, Pluto, and Goofy, all of whom won a world-wide following.

During World War II Disney emerged as an educator. Among his propaganda films,

The New Spirit depicted Donald Duck paying his first income tax assessment. Incredibly, a Gallup poll revealed that 37 per cent of filmgoers had displayed a greater readiness to pay taxes as a result. The Allies' D-Day password in World War II, incidentally, was 'Mickey Mouse'.

In the post-war years the Disney film output increased both in number and variety. In addition to pure cartoon features, films which blended animation and live action, and real-life nature films were introduced by his studios. In films like *The Vanishing Prairie* limitless patience was exercised in accumulating authentic material. Camera crews sometimes waited weeks to capture shots which only occupied a few feet of edited film. In *The Legend of Lobo* a wolf was actually trained to walk a log at ascending heights until he could be filmed walking a 75-foot log over a chasm hundreds of feet deep.

The perfect blend of animation and live action was seen in what many believe to be Disney's greatest picture, *Mary Poppins*, which won five Academy Awards: best actress, Julie Andrews (*see page* 48), best song (*Chim chim cher-ee*), best music score, best visual effects, and best editing.

Walt's biggest venture was Disneyland, the 162-acre amusement park in Anaheim, California, which opened in 1955 and by 1967 represented an investment of

$100,000,000 now (£41,666,666). The idea had been cooking in Disney's mind since the mid-1930s. 'I put in all the things I wanted to do as a kid and couldn't, including getting into something without a ticket', he said. The park has almost every amusement and spectacle and is constantly being stocked with new ideas. Among the unique sights is a life-size model of President Abraham Lincoln capable of reproducing fifteen different facial expressions. Surprises in store for visitors included a 'haunted' house with shrinking rooms and wall-to-wall cobwebs. Disneyland draws about 6,000,000 visitors a year and has an annual revenue of about $27,000,000 (£11,250,000).

In 1965 plans were announced for the purchase of 27,443 acres in Florida for a new Disney World due to be opened in 1971. It will include a new amusement park, motel-hotel resort vacation centres, an industrial complex, an airport of the future, and his 'Experimental Prototype Community of Tomorrow'.

The motivation for all these enterprises clearly came from a man of exceptional drive. His brother, Roy, a partner in the business from the outset and now at its head, once recalled: 'As long as I can remember, Walt has been working. He worked in the daytime and he worked at night. Walt didn't play much as a boy.' Walt himself no longer sketched cartoons in recent years but filled a supervisory and catalystic role. 'I work on every script, writing dialogue, and planning scenes', he said. 'When the story is set, I turn it over to the boys, and they make it.' The product of Walt Disney Studios averages out at twenty-five new stories a year for TV and six films, plus ideas for Disneyland.

Hollywood's most honoured citizen, with more than 950 citations to his name, including thirty-three 'Oscars' and five 'Emmys' recognized the part played by teamwork in these distinctions. 'That first

"Oscar" was a special award for the creation of Mickey Mouse. The other Academy Awards belong to our group, a tribute to our combined efforts.' He also received the highest US civilian award, the Medal of Freedom, presented by President Lyndon B. Johnson on 14 Sept. 1964.

'... humans can't move as freely, gracefully, and comically as we can make animated figures move. We are not in the business of duplicating human action. We can do better than that – much better.'

'As I see it, a person's culture represents his appraisal of the things that make up life. And a fellow becomes cultured, I believe, by selecting that which is fine and beautiful in life, and throwing aside that which is mediocre and phoney.'

FULL-LENGTH FEATURE PRODUCTIONS

Snow White and the Seven Dwarfs (1937)
Pinocchio (1939)
Fantasia (1940)
The Reluctant Dragon (1941)
Dumbo (1941)
Bambi (1942)
Saludos Amigos (1942)
Victory Through Air Power (1943)
The Three Caballeros (1945)
Make Mine Music (1946)
Song of the South (1946)
Fun and Fancy Free (1947)
Melody Time (1948)
So Dear to My Heart (1949)
Ichabod and Mr Toad (1949)
Cinderella (1950)
Treasure Island (1950)
Alice in Wonderland (1951)
Robin Hood (1952)
Peter Pan (1953)
The Sword and the Rose (1953)
The Living Desert (1953)
Rob Roy (1954)
The Vanishing Prairie (1954)
Stormy (1954)
Twenty Thousand Leagues Under the Sea (1954)
Lady and the Tramp (1955, re-issued 1962)
Davy Crockett, King of the Wild Frontier (1955)
The Littlest Outlaw (1955)
The African Lion (1955)
The Great Locomotive Chase (1956)
Davy Crockett and the River Pirates (1956)
Secrets of Life (1956)
Westward Ho The Wagons! (1956)
Johnny Tremain (1957)
Perri (1957)
Old Yeller (1957)
The Light in the Forest (1958)
White Wilderness (1958)
Tonka (1958)
Sleeping Beauty (1959)
The Shaggy Dog (1959)
Darby O'Gill and the Little People (1959)
Third Man on the Mountain (1959)
Toby Tyler (1960)
Kidnapped (1960)

Walt Disney, with 33 'Oscars' and over 900 other citations, was Hollywood's most honoured citizen. (N.B.: The word 'Oscar' was first used in about 1931 when the then Secretary of the Academy of Motion Picture Arts and Sciences remarked that the golden figure reminded her of her Uncle Oscar.)

Disneyland LP Recordings on the Buena Vista Label

The Sign of Zorro (1960)
Pollyanna (1960)
Ten Who Dared (1960)
Jungle Cat (1960)
Swiss Family Robinson (1960)
The Absent Minded Professor (1961)
One Hundred and One Dalmatians (1961)
The Parent Trap (1961)
Nikki, Wild Dog of the North (1961)
Greyfriars Bobby (1961)
Babes in Toyland (1961)
Moon Pilot (1962)
Bon Voyage (1962)
Big Red (1962)
Almost Angels (*Born to Sing*) (1962)
The Legend of Lobo (1962)
In Search of the Castaways (1962)
Son of Flubber (1963)
Miracle of the White Stallions (*Flight of the White Stallions*) (1963)
Savage Sam (1963)
Summer Magic (1963)
The Incredible Journey (1963)
The Sword in the Stone (1963)
The Misadventures of Merlin Jones (1964)
A Tiger Walks (1964)
The Three Lives of Thomasina (1964)
The Moon-Spinners (1964)
Mary Poppins (1964)
Emil and the Detectives (1964)
Those Calloways (1965)
The Monkey's Uncle (1965)
That Darn Cat (1965)
The Ugly Dachshund (1966)
Lt Robinson Crusoe, USN (1966)
The Fighting Prince of Donegal (1966)
Follow Me Boys (1966)
Monkeys, Go Home (1967)
The Adventures of Bullwhip Griffin (1967)
The Gnome-Mobile (1967)
The Happiest Millionaire (1967)
The Jungle Book (1967)
Blackbeard's Ghost (1968)
Never A Dull Moment (1968)
The Horse in the Grey Flannel Suit (1969)
The Love Bug (1969)

DE-LUXE 12-INCH LPs WITH FULL-COLOUR ILLUSTRATED BOOK

Alice in Wonderland (ST3909)
Bambi (ST3903)
Best Loved Fairy Tales (ST3965)
Carnival of the Animals (Saint-Saens) (ST3900)
Cinderella (ST3908)
101 Dalmatians (ST3934)
Dumbo (ST3904)
Great Ballets (ST3932)
Great Piano Concertos (ST3933)
Hans Christian Andersen (ST3964)
Jungle Book (ST3948)
Lady and the Tramp (ST3917)
Mary Poppins (ST3922)
Maurice Chevalier's Musical Tour of France (ST3940)
Peter Pan (ST3910)
Peter and the Wolf (ST3926)
Pinocchio (ST3905)
Snow White (ST3906)
The Sound of Music (Mary Martin) (ST3936)
Three Little Pigs (ST3963)
When We Were Very Young (ST3976)
Winnie the Pooh and the Honey Tree (ST3928)
Winnie the Pooh and the Blustery Day (ST3953)
Winnie the Pooh, A Happy Birthday Party (ST3942)

12-INCH LPs IN THE 'DQ' SERIES

Best Loved Fairy Tales (DQ1284)
Goldilocks and the Three Bears (DQ1250)
Hans Christian Andersen (DQ1276)
Hansel and Gretel (DQ1253)
The Little Engine That Could! (DQ1259)
Mickey and the Beanstalk (DQ1248)
Mother Goose Nursery Rhymes (DQ1211)
The Nutcracker Suite (DQ1243)
The Severn Dwarfs (DQ1297)
The Three Little Pigs (DQ1310)

DISNEY'S 33 AWARDS FROM THE ACADEMY OF MOTION PICTURE ARTS AND SCIENCES

1932   *Flowers and Trees* (Best Cartoon Short Subject, 1931–32)

1932   Special Award to Walt Disney for the Creation of Mickey Mouse.

1933   *Three Little Pigs* (Best Cartoon Short Subject, 1932–33)

1935   *The Tortoise and the Hare* (Best Cartoon Production, 1934)

1936   *Three Orphan Kittens* (Best Cartoon Production, 1935)

1937   *The Country Cousin* (Best Cartoon Short Subject, 1936)

1938   *The Old Mill* (Best Cartoon Short Subject, 1937)

1938   Top Technical Award to Walt Disney Productions for the design and application to production of the Multi-Plane Camera, 1937

1939   *Ferdinand the Bull* (Best Cartoon Short Subject, 1938)

1939   Special Award to Walt Disney for *Snow White and the Seven Dwarfs*; recognized as a significant screen innovation; pioneered a great new entertainment field for the motion picture cartoon

1940   *The Ugly Duckling* (Best Cartoon Short Subject, 1939)

1942   Irving Thalberg Memorial Award to Walt Disney for 'the most consistent high quality of production achievement by an individual producer'

1942   Special Technical Award for 'outstanding contribution to the advancement of the use of sound in motion pictures through the production of *Fantasia*'

1942   *Lend A Paw* (Best Cartoon Short Subject, 1941)

1943   *Der Fuehrer's Face* (Best Cartoon Short Subject, 1942)

1949   *Seal Island* (Best Two-Reel Short Subject, 1948)

1951   *In Beaver Valley* (Best Two-Reel Short Subject, 1950)

1952   *Nature's Half Acre* (Best Two-Reel Short Subject, 1951)

1953   *Water Birds* (Best Two-Reel Short Subject, 1952)

1954   *The Living Desert* (Best Documentary Feature, 1953)

1954   *Bear Country* (Best Two-Reel Short Subject, 1953)

1954   *The Alaskan Eskimo* (Best Documentary Short Subject, 1953)

1954   *Toot, Whistle, Plunk & Boom* (Best Cartoon Short Subject, 1953)

1955   *The Vanishing Prairie* (Best Documentary Feature, 1954)

1955   *20,000 Leagues Under the Sea* (Best Achievement with Special Effects, 1954)

1956   *Men Against The Arctic* (Best Documentary Short Subject, 1955)

1958   *Wetback Hound* (Best Live-Action Short Subject, 1957)

1959   *White Wilderness* (Best Documentary Feature, 1958)

1959   *Grand Canyon* (Best Live-Action Short Subject, 1958)

1959   *Ama Girls* (Best Documentary Short Subject, 1958)

1961   *The Horse with the Flying Tail* (Best Documentary Feature, 1960)

1964   *Mary Poppins* (Best Actress, Best Editing, Best Special Effects, Best Song, *Chim Chim Cheree*, and Best Music Score)

1969   *Winnie the Pooh and the Blustery Day* (Best Cartoon, 1968)

ADULT SERIES OF 12-INCH LPs

Disney Songs the Satchmo Way
(Louis Armstrong) (BVS4044)
Happiest Millionaire (BV/BVS5001)
Jungle Book (BVS4041)
Man of La Mancha (BV/BVS3000)
Mary Poppins (BV/BVS4026)

SEVEN-INCH LPs WITH 24-PAGE BOOK IN COLOUR

Alice in Wonderland (LLP306)
Bambi (LLP309)
Black Beauty (LLP318)
Cinderella (LLP308)
101 Dalmatians (LLP305)
Dumbo (LLP324)
The Grasshopper and the Ant (LLP331)
Hansel and Gretel (LLP317)
Jungle Book (LLP319)
Lady and the Tramp (LLP307)
Little Red Riding Hood (LLP328)
Mary Poppins (LLP302)
Mother Goose Rhymes (LLP312)
Peter Pan (LLP304)
Pinocchio (LLP311)
The Seven Dwarfs (LLP314)
Sleeping Beauty (LLP301)
Snow White (LLP310)
Three Little Pigs (LLP303)
Winnie the Pooh and the Honey Tree (LLP313)

SOMERSET MAUGHAM

As an MP learns that the duty of the Opposition is to oppose, so an author becomes inured to the fact that critics must, for better or worse, criticize the literary endeavours of men they could not possibly hope to emulate. Thus Somerset Maugham, already established as the century's greatest story-teller, once made this rueful comment: 'In my twenties the critics said I was brutal, in my thirties they said I was flippant, in my forties they said I was cynical, in my fifties they said I was competent, and now in my sixties they say I am superficial.' To which panoramic review of his career one might add that only a remarkable craftsman could have attracted comment from the critics at all over such a period.

Maugham wrote and was hungry in Paris for ten years before making any ground as an author. His first novel was *Liza of Lambeth* (1897) and his first play *Shipwrecked* (1902). He was discovered by the London publisher, William Heinemann (1863–1920), whose firm still publishes the English editions of Maugham's books.

Conceding that there is in everyone something of the creative instinct, Maugham thought that 'the novelist must be something of an extrovert, since otherwise he will not have the urge to express himself; but he can make do with no more intelligence than is needed for a man to be a good lawyer or doctor.' He laid down that it was an abuse to use the novel as a pulpit or platform and that 'a novel should have an inner harmony' and 'a beautiful proportion.' His style was mainly influenced by the French novelist, Guy de Maupassant (1850–93). It is significant that in *Great Novelists and Their Novels* he

Full name William Somerset Maugham, CH (1954).

Born Sun. 25 Jan. 1874, Paris, France.

Characteristics About 5′ 8″; about 133*lb*. (9*st*. 7*lb*.); brown hair; brown eyes; cleft chin; spoke with a stammer.

Married 1915 Lady Syrie Wellcome (div. 1927) 1*d*.

Died Thurs. 16 Dec. 1965. Stroke.

included not one of his contemporaries. His verdict was: 'I think Balzac[1] is the greatest novelist the world has ever known, but I think Tolstoy's[2] *War and Peace* is the greatest novel.' Elsewhere he wrote that he considered the American writers, Raymond Chandler (1888–1959) and Dashiell Hammett (1895–1961), 'the two best novelists of the hard-boiled school'. Maugham's own stature as a writer was given full recognition on his eightieth birthday when the Garrick Club in London gave a dinner in his honour, a distinction only previously accorded to three other writers: William Makepeace Thackeray (1811–63), Charles Dickens (1812–70), and Anthony Trollope (1815–82).

Maugham's insights into people provided most of the material for his writings. 'I was not interested in men in general', he said, 'but in individuals – as possible material for my work. It was the obscure, not the famous, who attracted me. I've

[1] The French novelist, Honoré de Balzac (1799–1850).
[2] The Russian novelist Count Lev Nikolayevich Tolstoy (1828–1910)

MAUGHAM

usually found the famous rather unremarkable and superficial. But the ordinary are often themselves. They don't have to hide their emotions.' Another important observation was that human beings are never consistent: 'I have never seen people all of a piece. It has amazed me that the most incongruous traits should exist in the same person and for all that yield a plausible harmony.' A trait for which he advocated tolerance was homosexuality: '... in Siam they're sensible. They don't regard homosexuality as anything abnormal. They accept it as something perfectly natural. . . . And I believe that one day people will realize that there are people who are *born* homosexuals. And there is nothing whatsoever they can do about it.'

Photographer Yousuf Karsh has pinpointed what has been variously characterized as Maugham's cynicism or his fastidiousness when he described him as 'the kind of man who has seen everything and doesn't think much of any of it'. This outlook was well illustrated in *The Summing Up* where Maugham discussed the important values of truth, beauty, and goodness. Taking each in turn, he wrote: 'If truth is one of the ultimate values, it seems strange that no one seems quite to know what it is.' The concept of beauty, he thought, was subject to the vagaries of fashion and period: 'We can as little feel the beauty our ancestors felt as we can smell the roses they smelt.' His third axiom was that 'Goodness is shown in right action and who can tell in this meaningless world what right action is.'

The lifelong anguish of a stammer – 'I have a certain force of character which has enabled me to supplement my deficiencies' – has been cited as a motive force in Maugham's creativeness. The disability was symbolized by a club-foot in his best-selling work (about 11,000,000 copies), the autobiographical novel *Of Human Bondage* which was the subject of three different motion pictures. *Cakes and Ale* was another of his novels reputed to have sold 11,000,000 copies. *The Moon and Sixpence*, a novel based on the life of the French post-Impressionist painter, Paul Gauguin (1848–1903), was filmed both for cinema and television.

Maugham's reputation as a playwright reached its apogee in the 'twenties. Later his short stories also gained a wide currency. The most popular was *Rain* which was produced for the stage under various titles at least six different times in New York and London and was also screened three times. In all he wrote over eighty books and plays together with a large number of short stories and articles. Over forty films were made from his work. Up to 1956 total sales of his books had reached an estimated 66,000,000 copies. His books were translated not only into all the main European languages but also into Vietnamese, Oriya, Islandic, Yiddish, Hebrew, Serbo-Croat, Slovene, and Japanese.

Drafting his manuscripts in pencil, then editing in red ink, Maugham averaged £100 ($500) a year from his writings for the first ten years of his career. In the last thirty years of his life he was calculated to have averaged between £60,000 (now $144,000) and £100,000 (now $240,000) a year from all sources. His Villa Mauresque at Cap Ferrat in the South of France, which he bought for about £7,000 ($28,000) in 1926 was sold for a reported £312,500 ($750,000) in 1969. The contents of the home made £31,778 (now $76,267) in 1967. A sale at auction of thirty-five paintings collected by him during fifty years realized £523,800 ($1,466,640) in 1962. It was reported that he had earned 'millions of pounds' from his

Somerset Maugham in the grounds of his Villa Mauresque in the South of France which was sold in 1969 for a reported £312,500 ($750,000).

Novels & Books

Liza of Lambeth (1897)
The Making of a Saint (1898)
Orientations (1899)
The Hero (1901)
Mrs Craddock (1902)
The Venture (1903)
The Merry Go Round (1904)
The Land of the Blessed Virgin (1905)
The Bishop's Apron (1906)
The Explorer (1908)
The Magician (1908)
Of Human Bondage (1915)
The Moon and Sixpence (1919)
The Trembling of a Leaf (1922)
On a Chinese Screen (1922)
The Painted Veil (1925)
The Casuarina Tree (1926)
Ashenden (1928)
The Gentleman in the Parlour (1930)
Cakes and Ale (1930)
First Person Singular (1931)
The Book Bag (1932)
The Narrow Corner (1932)
Ah King (1932)
Traveller's Library (1933)
Altogether (1934)
The Judgement Seat (1934)
Don Fernando (1935)
Cosmopolitans (1936)
My South Sea Island (1936)
Theatre (1937)
The Summing Up (1938)
Christmas Holiday (1939)
Teller of Tales (1939)
Princess September and the
Nightingale (1939)
France at War (1940)
Books and You (1940)
The Mixture as Before (1940)
Up at the Villa (1941)
Strictly Personal (1942)
The Hour Before Dawn (1942)
Great Modern Reading (1943)
The Unconquered (1944)
The Razor's Edge (1944)
Then and Now (1946)
Creatures of Circumstance (1947)
Here and There (1948)
Catalina (1948)
Great Novelists and their Novels (1948)
A Writer's Notebook (1949)
The Vagrant Mood (1952)
Points of View (1958)
Seventeen Lost Stories (1969)

MAUGHAM

The ancient Moorish sign against the evil eye which Somerset Maugham adopted as his personal device. It is now the registered Coat of Arms of his nephew, Viscount (Robin) Maugham, who is also an author.

Plays

(dates of first performance)
Schiffbruchig (Shipwrecked) (1902)
A Man of Honour (1903)
Mademoiselle Zampa (1904)
Lady Frederick (1907)
Jack Straw (1908)
Mrs Dot (1908)
The Explorer (1908)
Penelope (1909)
The Noble Spaniard (1909)
Smith (1909)
The Tenth Man (1910)
Grace (1910)
Loaves and Fishes (1911)
The Perfect Gentleman (1913)
The Land of Promise (USA 1913, GB 1914)
Caroline (1916)
Our Betters (USA 1917, GB 1923)
Love in a Cottage (1918)
Caesar's Wife (1919)
Too Many Husbands (Home and Beauty)
                        (USA, GB 1919)
The Unknown (1920)
The Circle (1921)
East of Suez (1922)
The Camel's Back (USA 1923, GB 1924)
The Constant Wife (USA 1926, GB 1927)
The Letter (1927)
The Sacred Flame (USA 1928, GB 1929)
The Breadwinner (1930)
For Services Rendered (1932)
The Mask and the Face (USA 1933)
Sheppey (1933)

books. He was also reported to be a rouble millionaire but hesitated to visit Russia to spend the money because of his anti-Bolshevik activities in World War I, when he worked as a secret agent in the Soviet Union while ostensibly writing for *The Daily Telegraph*. During this period he had gleaned the material for his novel *Ashenden*.

Noël Coward once said: 'Willie was a very witty man with a bad stammer which he hated – and which he used. He was also capable of cruelty ... he hated people more easily than he loved them; I love people more easily than I hate them. That is the difference between me, Noël Coward, and Somerset Maugham.' Among the tributes paid to Maugham after his death was one from H. E. Bates: 'He was one of the greatest guardians of our despised orphan short story. Snob intellectuals who could never match him either in craftsmanship or versatility never forgave him for being successful.'

Maugham was offered a knighthood during the 'thirties but declined because he felt he would look silly if he went to a literary party and they announced 'Mr Arnold Bennett, Mr H. G. Wells, Mr Bernard Shaw – and Sir Somerset Maugham.' Shaw had already declined both a knighthood and a peerage.

'The love that lasts longest is the love that is never returned.'

'No man in his heart is quite as cynical as a well-bred woman.'

'The spirituality of man is most apparent when he is eating a hearty dinner.'

Film & TV Productions

Plays

Lady Frederick (1907), filmed as The Divorcee (1919)
Jack Straw (1908), filmed in 1920
The Explorer (1909), filmed in 1915
Smith (1909), filmed in 1915
The Tenth Man (1910), filmed in 1936
The Land of Promise (1913), filmed in 1917 and again as The Canadian (1926)
Our Betters (1917), filmed in 1933
Too Many Husbands (1919), filmed as a musical entitled Three for the Show (1955) starring Betty Grable
Caesar's Wife (1919), filmed as Infatuation (1925)
The Circle (1921), filmed with that title in 1925 and again as Strictly Unconventional (1930)
East of Suez (1922), filmed in 1924
The Constant Wife (1926), filmed as Charming Sinners (1929)
The Sacred Flame (1928), filmed in 1929 and again in 1935 entitled The Right to Live

Novels

The Magician (1908), filmed in 1926
Of Human Bondage (1915), filmed in 1934 starring Bette Davis, in 1946 starring Eleanor Powell, and in 1964 starring Kim Novak
The Moon and Sixpence (1919), filmed for cinema in 1942 starring George Sanders; adapted for TV in 1960 starring Sir Laurence Olivier, and again for TV in 1967 starring Charles Gray
The Painted Veil (1925), filmed in 1934 starring Greta Garbo
Ashenden (1928), filmed as Secret Agent (1937) starring John Gielgud
The Narrow Corner (1932), filmed as The Isle of Fury (1933), and again as Three in Eden (1936)
Theatre (1937), filmed as Adorable Julia (1963) starring Lilli Palmer
Christmas Holiday (1939), filmed in 1944
Up at the Villa (1941), adapted for TV in 1968
The Hour Before Dawn (1942), filmed in 1944
The Razor's Edge (1944), filmed in 1946 starring Tyrone Power

Short Stories

The Fall of Edward Barnard (1921), adapted for TV in 1969

Before the Party (1922), adapted for TV in 1969

P. & O. (1923), adapted for TV in 1969

Rain (1923), filmed as Sadie Thompson (1928) starring Gloria Swanson, as Rain (1932) starring Joan Crawford, and as Miss Sadie Thompson (1954) starring Rita Hayworth

The Letter (1924), filmed in 1929; filmed again in 1940 starring Bette Davis; adapted for TV in 1969

The Force of Circumstance (1924), due to be adapted for TV in 1970

Louise (1925), adapted for TV in 1969

The Creative Impulse (1926), adapted for TV in 1969

Footprints in the Jungle (1927), due to be adapted for TV in 1970

Virtue (1931), due to be adapted for TV in 1970

The Door of Opportunity (1931), due to be adapted for TV in 1970

The Human Element (1931), due to be adapted for TV in 1970

The Vessel of Wrath (1931), filmed in 1938 starring Charles Laughton and again as The Beachcomber (1955), starring Glynis Johns and Robert Newton. Due to be adapted for TV in 1970

The Back of Beyond (1933), adapted for TV in 1969

Three Fat Women of Antibes (1933), adapted for TV in 1969

The Book Bag (1933), due to be adapted for TV in 1970

A Casual Affair (1935), adapted for TV in 1969

A Man With A Conscience (1940), adapted for TV in 1969

Lord Mountdrago (1940) was one of the stories used in the composite film Three Cases of Murder (1955); adapted for TV in 1969

The Facts of Life (1940)
The Alien Corn (1931) } filmed as
The Kite (1947) } Quartet (1948)
The Colonel's Lady (1947)

The Verger (1924) } filmed as
Mr Know-All (1925) } Trio (1950)
Sanatorium (1947)

The Ant and the Grasshopper (1924) } filmed as
Winter Cruise (1947) } Encore
Gigolo and Gigolette (1935) } (1951)

A Woman of Fifty (1946), adapted for TV in 1969

Episode (1947), adapted for TV in 1969

Flotsam and Jetsam (1947), due to be adapted for TV in 1970

The Unconquered (1947), due to be adapted for TV in 1970

SIR
WINSTON
CHURCHILL

Whatever the tributes ultimately heaped upon him, the conviction that Winston Churchill had a future in politics did not widely prevail as the twentieth century faltered through its second decade and World War I devastated Europe. H. H. Asquith[1] had already expressed his reservations: 'It is a pity Winston has not a better sense of proportion ... I do not think he will ever get to the top in English politics with all his wonderful gifts.' Bonar Law[2] was emphatic in rejecting him as a potential member of the 1916 War Cabinet: 'I would rather have him against us every time.' David Lloyd George[3] had his doubts as well. However, though all but two of the Tory Ministers were opposed to having him on the War Cabinet, the Prime Minister gambled. 'I am convinced I was right to overrule the misgivings of my colleagues', he later reported, 'for Churchill rendered conspicuous service.' But, noted Lloyd George judiciously, 'Men of his ardent temperament and powerful mentality need exceptionally strong brakes.' Churchill's future, he considered, would depend on whether he could 'establish a reputation for prudence without audacity'.

According to Lord Beaverbrook,[4] who served in the Cabinet in both World Wars, Churchill was 'mentally, morally, and physically of stouter build than Lloyd George'. The verdict was reached, perhaps, with benefit of hindsight, a form of wisdom Churchill never needed. Equipped with a generous measure of the spirit that is

[1] Herbert Henry Asquith, 1st Earl of Oxford and Asquith (1852–1928), Liberal Prime Minister (1908–16).
[2] Andrew Bonar Law (1858–1923), Conservative Prime Minister (1922–23).
[3] David Lloyd George, 1st Earl Lloyd-George (1863–1945), Liberal Prime Minister (1916–22).
[4] William Maxwell Aitken, 1st Baron Beaverbrook (1879–1964).

According to Harold Macmillan 'the greatest Englishman of all time', Churchill had the longest span of service of any Member of Parliament: from Oct. 1900 to Aug. 1964 (63 years 10 months). He also enjoyed the longest life span of any Prime Minister of England, exceeding that of William Ewart Gladstone (1809–98) by one year 278 days. His Ministerial appointments were:

Under-Secretary of State for the Colonies (1906–08),
President of the Board of Trade (1908–10),
Home Secretary (1910–11),
First Lord of the Admiralty (1911–15),
Chancellor of the Duchy of Lancaster (1915),
Minister of Munitions (1917),
Secretary of State for War and Air (1919–21),
Secretary of State for Air and the Colonies (1921),
Secretary of State for the Colonies (1921–22),
Chancellor of the Exchequer (1924–29),
First Lord of the Admiralty (1939–40),
Minister of Defence (1940),
Prime Minister, First Lord of the Treasury, and Minister of Defence (1940–45),
Prime Minister and First Lord of the Treasury (1951–55), also Minister of Defence (1951–52).

Full name Winston Leonard Spencer-Churchill, KG (1953), OM (1946), CH (1922), TD, (PC 1922).
Born 01.30 hours Mon. 30 Nov. 1874 (two months prematurely after eight hours' labour), at Blenheim Palace, Woodstock, Oxfordshire, England.
Characteristics About 5' 8"; 210*lb.* (15*st.*) in later life; reddish hair; blue eyes.
Married 1908 Clementine Ogilvy Hozier 1*s.* 4*d.* (2*d.* survive).
Died Shortly after 08.00 hours, Sun. 24 Jan. 1965 at 27 Hyde Park Gate, London SW7, England. After one week's coma following a stroke.
Buried Bladen, Oxfordshire, England.
Estate £266,054 ($744,950) net; duty paid £109,093 ($305,460).

Churchill was one of over 100 Members of Parliament to have 'crossed the floor' of the House of Commons since 1900. He was Conservative (1900–04), Liberal (1904–22), and Conservative (1924–64). He represented Oldham (1900–06), North-West Manchester (1906–08), Dundee (1908–22), the Epping Division of Essex (1924–45), and the Woodford Division of Essex (1945–64).

genius, he had a realistic consciousness of destiny. 'We are all worms', he declared in 1906, 'but I do believe that I am a glow-worm.'

The statesman who served in more Ministerial offices than any other Englishman surmounted two handicaps on his path to immortality: a speech impediment and poor physical endowment. Churchill suffered all his life from an incapacity to enunciate the letter 's'. Weak and sickly as a child, his parents had reason more than once to fear for his life. 'I am cursed with a feeble body', he complained in 1893 as he qualified at the third attempt for entry into the Royal Military College, Sandhurst, measuring up with a less than martial height of 5 feet 6½ inches and an apparently fragile 31-inch chest.

In battle he led a charmed life, exposing himself under fire in Cuba, India, the Sudan, South Africa, the Netherlands, and France without being scathed. At the Battle of Omdurman in Sept. 1898 he rode into action with 200–300 men of the 21st Lancers against a section of the 60,000-strong Dervish army. 'It was I suppose the most dangerous two minutes I shall live to see', he reported factually. His only 'combat' wound was sustained in the House of Commons when a bound copy of the Orders of the House,[1] hurled by Ronald McNeill, a Member for Ulster, struck and gashed his forehead during the frenzied debate on the Home Rule Bill on 13 Nov. 1912.

Harold Macmillan recalled the Churchill of the 'twenties as 'unique, wayward, exciting, a man with a peculiar glamour of his own, that brought a sense of colour into our rather drab political life . . . no one could withhold admiration for the wit, humour, ingenuity, and oratorical skill which he deployed.' His legislative skill, overlooked by many who remember him only as a war leader, had already been vigorously deployed. He carried the Board of Trade Act (1909) with powers to impose minimum wages in the sweated industries and established labour exchanges throughout the country.[2] He framed the first unemployment insurance legislation, incorporated in the National Insurance Act (1911). James Herbert Wilson, father of the future Prime Minister, Harold Wilson, overheard Churchill say after a meeting at Manchester that if he had the powers of a dictator he would 'cause the word "Insure" to be inscribed on the lintel of every house in the land.' As Chancellor of the Exchequer,[3] Churchill announced in 1925 the introduction of contributory old-age pensions for the over-sixty-fives, a measure which also brought in widows and orphans for the first time.

The *leit motiv* of Churchill in the 'thirties was the rising menace of Nazi Germany. 'I dread the day', he said on 14 March 1934, 'when the means of threatening the heart of the British Empire should pass into the hands of the present rulers of Germany.' If his warnings went largely unheeded at home, and indeed helped to keep him out of office in this period, they generated a healthy respect in the mind of Adolf Hitler. 'I naturally cannot prevent the possibility of this gentleman entering the government in a couple of years', he stated in 1938, 'but I can assure you that I will prevent him from destroying Germany. . . . I can tell Churchill that it happened only once and that it will not happen again.'

With the Germans invading the Low Countries and the fall of France only a few days off, Churchill succeeded Neville Chamberlain to become the forty-first Prime Minister of England on 10 May

1940. Lloyd George expressed the confidence of the House of Commons when he said: 'I congratulate the country upon his elevation to the Premiership at this very, very critical and terrible moment.' The new Premier later recalled his feelings on the threshold of his massive task: 'I felt as if I were walking with Destiny, and that all my life had been but a preparation for this hour and for this trial. . . .'

Grappling with the dire consequences of other people's failure to arm Britain for her gravest emergency in nearly 900 years, Churchill injected the essence of resolve into the nation. 'We were inspired', wrote Macmillan, 'by the greatest Englishman of all time.' Clement Attlee, Churchill's deputy in the National Coalition Government (1940–45), furnished the most concise appraisal of his leadership: 'If somebody asked me what exactly Winston did to win the war, I would say: "Talk about it." '

Among the House of Commons speeches, more quoted than those of any other statesman in history, the most familiar are probably the pledge to the House of 13 May 1940: 'I have nothing to offer but blood, toil, tears, and sweat'; his rallying call of 18 June 1940: 'Let us therefore brace ourselves to our duties, and so bear ourselves that, if the British Empire and its Commonwealth last for a thousand years, men will still say: "This was their finest hour;" ' and his tribute to the Battle of Britain fighter pilots: 'Never in the field of human conflict was so much owed by so many to so few', spoken on 20 Aug. 1940. But beyond mere exhortation of others, Britain's leader, aged sixty-five, made it clear that he was ready personally to engage the enemy in mortal combat: 'If they come to London', he told Lord Halifax, 'I shall take a rifle (I'm not a bad shot with a rifle) and put myself in the pillbox at the bottom of Downing Street and shoot till I've no more ammunition, and then they can damned well shoot me.' At the time of the D-Day landings in 1944 it was only the written request of King George VI which prevented him from embarking with the Allied troops for Normandy.

In the darkest hours of war, Churchill consolidated the support of Britain's friends in the Commonwealth and secured American arms to help stem the setbacks of two years' almost unmitigated defeat. The US Secretary of State, Cordell Hull, confirmed: 'The President [*Franklin D. Roosevelt*] and I were convinced that, under Churchill's indomitable leadership, Britain intended to fight on. We believed that Mr Churchill meant what he said. Had we any doubt we would not have taken the steps we did.' The decision to declare war by the United States (8 Dec. 1941) gave Churchill the opportunity of addressing Congress on 16 Dec. 1941: 'I cannot help reflecting that if my father had been an American and my mother British, instead of the other way round, I might have got here on my own.'[4]

Churchill's contribution to the Allied war effort was universally applauded. General Lord Ismay wrote that in his grasp of the broad sweep of strategy he 'stood head and shoulders above his advisers'. Stalin said: 'There have been few cases in history where the courage of one man has been so important to the future of the world.' General de Gaulle pronounced: 'Sir Winston is, and will forever remain, the one who, in directing the final victory of the admirable effort of Great Britain, contributed powerfully to the salvation of the French people and to the liberty of the world. In the great drama, he was the greatest.'

Other statesmen noted Churchill's per-

---

[1] The book was later presented to Churchill by the Speaker of the House of Commons and exists at Churchill's former country home at Chartwell, Kent.
[2] At this time William Beveridge, who was later to earn distinction as author of the 'Beveridge Report', worked in Churchill's Ministry.
[3] The Financial Secretary at the Treasury at this time was the same McNeil who had in 1912 hurled a book at Churchill.

sonal power to move the men around him. Macmillan said: 'Perhaps the most endearing thing about him, in private talks, in the Cabinet, in the House of Commons, was his puckish humour, his tremendous sense of fun, and the quick alternation between grave and gay.' Sir Robert Menzies recorded that 'In the mood, he could make one feel as small as a pebble. But when the light came, it was a glorious awakening. The face became that of a cheerful schoolboy . . . a warm word would bring tears to his face.'

After the General Election of 1945 deprived him of office, Churchill's vision continued to set the trend in international affairs for the Western powers. On 5 March 1946 he made his famous speech at Fulton, Missouri, USA – 'An iron curtain has descended across the Continent' – warning of the growing menace of Communism in Europe. At Zurich on 19 Sept. 1946 he spoke of his ideal for Europe's future: 'Our constant aim must be to build and fortify the United Nations Organization. Under and within that world concept we must recreate the European family in a regional structure called, it may be, the United States of Europe. . . .'

In the concluding phase of the prodigious span of his life in public service, Churchill completed the link between the reigns of Queen Victoria (1819–1901) and Queen Elizabeth II whose accession saw him again at the head of British life as Prime Minister. He had declined a Dukedom[5] offered him by King George VI but was persuaded by the Queen to accept the Order of the Garter.

Among well over a hundred decorations, awards, and other honours showered upon him was the Nobel Prize for Literature awarded, according to the citation of 15 Oct. 1953, 'for his mastery in historical and biographic presentation and for his brilliant oratory, in which he stood forth as the defender of eternal human values.' The

The Churchill Commemorative Crown (1965), mintage 19,640,000.

most important of his literary works was the six-volume classic, *The Second World War*.

He also turned his creative talents to painting and produced more than 500 paintings (1915–58) over a hundred of which he gave away. The best known of his paintings was a view of Menaggio on Lake Como which he painted shortly after his defeat at the 1945 General Election. Sir Oswald Birley (1880–1952) said that if Churchill had given the time to painting that he gave to politics he would have been 'by all odds the world's greatest painter'.

On Churchill's retirement from Parliament, the House of Commons adopted on 28 July 1964 an all-Party vote of thanks expressing its 'unbounded admiration and gratitude for his services to Parliament, to the nation, and to the world'. The tribute was the first of its kind since the Duke of Wellington was similarly honoured on 1 July 1815. Macmillan told members that no man in the history of the House had combined in his person Churchill's many qualities and achievements. 'The life of the man we are today honouring', he said, 'is in this sense unique. The oldest among us can recall nothing to compare with it, and the

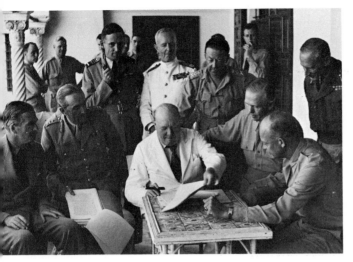

Churchill conferred with the fighting chiefs of Great Britain and the United States in North Africa in June 1943. They were, from left to right, Anthony Eden (now Lord Avon), General Sir Alan Brooke, Air Chief Marshal Sir Arthur Tedder, Admiral Sir Andrew Cunningham, General Sir Harold Alexander, General George C. Marshall, General Dwight D. Eisenhower, and General Sir Bernard Montgomery.

younger ones among you, no matter however long you live, will never see his like again'.

Attending an official function as Lord Warden of the Cinque Ports, Churchill lost an epaulette from his uniform. Describing the incident later he chuckled. 'It's a good job I personally fastened my braces.'

A photographer expressed the hope that he would take Churchill's picture on his 100th birthday. 'I don't see why not', said the Grand Old Man. 'You look reasonably fit and healthy.'

Churchill was watching *Oliver Twist* on TV with his poodle, Rufus, on his lap. When the point in the story was reached that Bill Sikes was about to drown the dog, Churchill covered Rufus' eyes with his hand and whispered: 'Don't look now. I'll tell you about it afterwards.'

A lady Member once accused Churchill of being 'drunk' in the House of Commons. He replied: 'And you, Madam, are ugly. But tomorrow I shall be sober.'

An MP named Wilfred Paling lost his temper and called Churchill 'a dirty dog'. In a flash the counter-attack was launched: 'Does the Honourable Member know what dirty dogs do to palings?'

---

[4] Churchill was a direct descendant of the Iroquois tribe through his American mother, Mrs Jennie Jerome Churchill. He was made the First Honorary Citizen of the United States and a member of the Congress of American Indians in 1963. President Lyndon B. Johnson called upon Americans to celebrate 'Sir Winston Churchill Day' on 30 Nov. 1964, Churchill's 90th birthday.

[5] Suggestions were Duke of London and Duke of Dover.

Films About Churchill

The Finest Hours (1964), based on *The Second World War*, with Orson Welles as narrator.

The Other Side of Winston Churchill (1964), based on *Painting as a Pastime* (1948), with Patrick Wymark as narrator.

My Early Life. Plans for a film based on this book with James Fox in the title role were announced in 1967.

Television

The Valiant Years (1961), a 26-part serial with Richard Burton as narrator.

Play

The Young Churchill (1969), a compilation of letters and biography.

TOP SALE PRICES OF CHURCHILL'S PAINTINGS

Date of Sale	Work	Price Made £	$	Gallery
11 May 1960	Cork Trees Near Mimizan (1924)	7,400	20,720	Sotheby
14 April 1965	Canal Scene (about 1938)	9,300	26,000	Parke-Bernet
24 May 1965	Menaggio, Lake Como (1945)	14,000	39,200	Parke-Bernet
12 Nov. 1965	Mimizan, Landes (about 1927)	9,975	27,930	Christie
12 Nov. 1965	Beaches Near Antibes (about 1925)	8,925	24,990	Christie
8–9 Dec. 1965	The Palladian Bridge at Wilton (1920s)	9,285	26,000	Parke-Bernet
20 April 1966	Igtham Moat (1930s)	8,000	22,400	Sotheby

CHURCHILL ON RECORD

The Voice of Winston Churchill (Decca LXT6200)
I Can Hear It Now (Argo BRG72256)
BBC Scrapbook for 1940 (with others) (Fontana 493014FDL)
BBC Scrapbook for 1945 (with others) (Fontana 493016FDL)
For Johnny (25th Anniversary of the Battle of Britain) (Fontana 49301FDL)
Sounds of Time 1934/1949 (CBS BPG62888)
The Prime Ministers (BBC Radio Enterprises REB39M)

PUBLICATIONS

Over 100 books concerning Churchill have been published. Apart from 17 volumes of selected speeches, and many contributions to periodical literature, his own publications comprised 35 volumes:

The Story of the Malakand Field Force (1898)
The River War (two volumes 1899)
Ian Hamilton's March (1900)
Savrola (1900)
Mr Brodrick's Army (1903)
Lord Randolph Churchill (two volumes 1906)
My African Journey (1908)
Liberalism and the Social Problem (1909)
The World Crisis (six volumes 1923–31). Earned reported royalties of £40,000 ($160,000)
My Early Life (1930)
Thoughts and Adventures (1932)
Marlborough: His Life and Times (four volumes 1933–38)
Great Contemporaries (1937)
Step by Step: 1936–39 (1939)
Painting as a Pastime (1948)

The Second World War (eight volumes 1948–54). Lord Camrose was reported to have paid £50,000 ($140,000) for the British serial rights alone.

A History of the English-Speaking Peoples (four volumes 1956–58).

iAN FLEMING

Full name Ian Lancaster Fleming.

Born Thurs. 28 May 1908, at 27 Green Street, Park Lane, Mayfair, London W1, England.

Characteristics About 6′ 1″; about 168*lb.* (12*st.*); wavy brown hair; blue eyes; broken nose sustained in a football game having collided with Henry Douglas-Home, brother of Sir Alec Douglas-Home; smoked 70 hand-made cigarettes a day.

Married 1952 Anne Lady Rothermere (née Anne Charteris) 1*s.*

Died Wed. 12 Aug. 1964. Heart attack.

Estate In Britain £289,170 ($809,676) net. A few months before his death Fleming sold to Booker Bros, McConnell for £100,000 ($280,000) a 51 per cent interest in Glidrose Productions, the company exploiting his earnings from the Bond books.

Ian Fleming's only children's story, 'Chitty Chitty Bang Bang', was filmed starring Dick Van Dyke (United Artists, 1968). Dick was the driver of 'Chitty Chitty Bang Bang'; his children in the film were played by Adrian Hall and Heather Ripley.

The paradox about the man who invented the century's most glorified fiction hero is that he did not really know what he was giving birth to. 'I didn't want Bond to be a glamorous figure at all. I merely sought to create an interesting man to whom extraordinary things happen. . . .' Certainly, Fleming never dreamed that James Bond would make him world famous and a millionaire in four years, or that he would one day be in a position to reject an offer of (£178,600) $500,000 plus 25 per cent of the profits for the film rights of one of the Bond films.

The man who wrote stories for 'warm-blooded heterosexuals in railways trains, aeroplanes, and beds' told an American reviewer: 'My books have no special significance, except a deleterious one; they're considered to have too much violence and too much sex.' Fleming was painfully self-conscious about his writing: 'I went to work like a blind man. After I had finished a page I used to hide it away under the others, never daring to look at it, in case I despaired that this utter rubbish, this piffle, was my handiwork. . . . I never went back and read what I had written nor corrected it. It was just a question of keep-ing my head down and typing like mad.' He worked to a daily stint of about 1,500 words and was most productive at his home in Jamaica. He once wrote to a friend 'I've got this bloody man Bond half way up a cliff and must leave him there if I'm to answer your letter.'

'Bond', explained Fleming, 'is the author's pillow fantasy, the feverish dream of the author of what he might have been. It is what you must expect with an adolescent mind like the one I happen to possess.' Bond, it could be added, also had some of Fleming's physical prowess: at Eton he twice (1925–26) won the Victor Ludorum as the best all-round athlete in the annual sports, and in 1927, wearing the pale-blue shorts of Sandhurst in the triangular match against Woolwich and Cranwell, finished second in the 120 yards high hurdles in $16\frac{1}{2}$ seconds. Fleming also enjoyed many of Bond's recreations, including golf and gambling: 'I like the excitement of gambling. I sometimes go over to Le Touquet for a couple of days and I take it fairly seriously', he was quoted as saying. 'I usually manage to meet my expenses out of winnings.' The name James Bond, inci-dentally, was borrowed from a famous

273

American ornithologist who wrote *Birds of the West Indies* (1936).

Raymond Chandler (1888–1954) was one popular author who admitted to being a Bond fan. 'I like Bond', he wrote, 'when he finally takes the beautiful girl in his arms and teaches her about one-tenth of the facts of life she already knew.' It was Fleming's passion for descriptive detail that made the fantasy of his stories more digestible. He wrote apologizing to one reader 'for making Bond order asparagus with Béarnaise instead of Mousseline sauce.' (See *Moonraker*, Chapter V.)

The Bond films made a millionaire of Sean Connery (*see page* 65), the star who carried the 007 label in *Dr No* (1963), *From Russia With Love* (1964), *Goldfinger* (1965), *Thunderball* (1966), and *You Only Live Twice* (1967). When Ian Fleming died, Connery (14 handicap in 1966), was playing a round of golf with Rex Harrison: 'We heard just as we were finishing lunch. Then we went out and played the other 18 holes.

Fleming would have liked us to do that.'

Noël Coward, a friend and neighbour of Fleming's in Jamaica, said of him: 'He was fabulously intelligent. Nobody quite appreciated how very, very good his descriptive passages were. . . . He asked me to play Dr No . . . I wish I could have.' Kingsley Amis who, under the pseudonym Robert Markham wrote another Bond novel called *Colonel Sun* (1968), assessed Fleming's place in literature alongside Jules Verne, Rider Haggard, and Conan Doyle.[1] 'Ian Fleming has set his stamp on the story of action and intrigue, bringing to it a sense of our time, a power and a flair that will win him readers when all the protests about his supposed deficiencies have been forgotten', wrote Amis. 'He leaves no heirs.' James Bond however has an heir. In Oct. 1967 the title *The Adventures of James Bond Jr – 003½* by R. D. Mascott was published.

---

[1] Jules Verne (1828–1905), the French author, and the English novelists Sir Henry Rider Haggard (1856–1925) and Sir Arthur Conan Doyle (1859–1930).

The James Bond Books by Ian Fleming

Casino Royale[1] (1953), adapted for TV in 1955 and for cinema in 1967
Live and Let Die (1954)
Moonraker (1955)
Diamonds are Forever (1956)
From Russia With Love (1957), filmed in 1964
Dr No (1958), filmed in 1963
Goldfinger (1959), filmed in 1965
For Your Eyes Only[2] (1960)
Thunderball[3] (1961), filmed in 1966
The Spy Who Loved Me (1962)
On Her Majesty's Secret Service (1963), filmed in 1969
You Only Live Twice (1964), filmed in 1967
The Man With The Golden Gun (1965)
Octopussy[2] (1965)

[1] The film *Casino Royale* (1967) was also discribed in advertising blurbs as having been suggested by Ian Fleming's novel; David Niven and Peter Sellers were among those who masqueraded in a weak send-up of James Bond.
[2] Short stories.
[3] *Thunderball* was Fleming's top-selling novel, ranking 21st in the United States' all-time fiction list published in 1968.

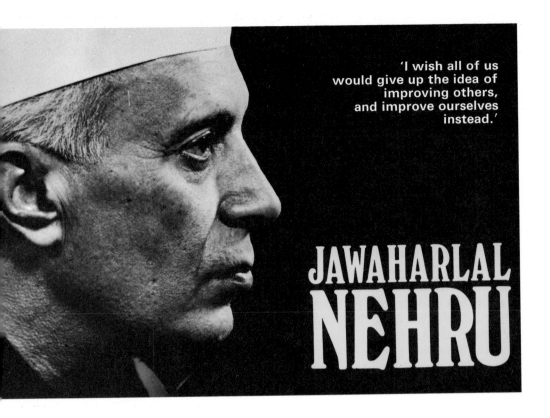

'I wish all of us would give up the idea of improving others, and improve ourselves instead.'

JAWAHARLAL NEHRU

The winner of the 880 yards race for Headmaster's House at Harrow School[1] in 1906 was a slender Indian boy who had also impressed his teachers by twice finishing top in class. The prize for his academic attainments was a volume of G. M. Trevelyan's biography of Garibaldi[2] which, Nehru later recalled, gave him the first stirrings of his ambition to bring independence to India. But ambitious and intellectually well endowed though he was, the gift of oratory did not come easily to the future Premier of India. 'I began what is called public speaking at a fairly late stage in my life,' he revealed in 1949. 'I was at college in Cambridge [*Trinity*]. I joined a well-known debating society. But I never had the courage to speak there, in spite of the fact that they actually had a system of fining members who did not speak every term. I gladly paid the fine.'

Nehru's father, whom he was to succeed as General Secretary of the All-India Congress Committee in 1929, was born on the same day (6 May 1861) as the poet Rabindranath Tagore (died 1941), and he saw this as an omen: 'I came into contact with Tagore rather in the later years when I had been conditioned more or less by my father and Gandhiji. Nevertheless, Rabindranath had a very considerable influence over me.' A leading disciple of Gandhi and his doctrine of non-violence (*see page* 287) since 1920, Nehru expressed his personal abhorrence of force in this way: 'I believe that the salvation of the whole world will come through non-violence. Violence has had a long career in the world. It has been weighed repeatedly and found wanting.' Previously a moderate, Nehru became increasingly disenchanted with the British Raj after the tragic Massacre of Amritsar.[3]

275

Full name Jawaharlal Nehru (Jawaharlal means 'darling jewel'). Nehru was commonly addressed as *Panditji*. The word *Pandit* is a term of respect originally used for people learned in Hindu history and law. The suffix *ji* is a mark of courtesy, roughly equivalent to 'sir'.

Born Thurs. 14 Nov. 1889, Allahabad, Central Provinces (now Uttar Pradesh), India.

Characteristics About 5′ 7″; about 140*lb.* (10*st.*); black hair; dark brown eyes.

Married 1916 Kamala Kaul (died 1936) 1*s.* (died in infancy in 1924) 1*d.* (Mrs Indira Priyadarshini Gandhi, no relation of Mahatma Gandhi).

Died Wed. 27 May 1964. Heart attack.

Jailed nine times by the British for a total of nearly nine years between 1921 and 1945 – 'One begins to appreciate the value of the little things of life in prison' – Nehru was a Marxist: 'I may not agree with everything the orthodox Communists have done,' he said in 1933. 'But I do think the basic ideology of Communism and its scientific interpretation of history is sound.' He was, too, an ardent admirer of Lenin[4] (*see page* 308). Further insight into his political philosophy was furnished in a letter written in 1939: 'I suppose I am temperamentally and by training an individualist, and intellectually a socialist. I hope that socialism does not kill or suppress individualism; indeed I am attracted to it because it will release innumerable individuals from economic and cultural bondage.' A Brahmin Hindu by upbringing, he was flexible in his attitude to religion: 'No orthodox religion attracts me, but if I had to choose, it would certainly be Buddhism.'

Winston Churchill once described Nehru as 'a man without malice or fear' and the Indian leader, even in 1936, eleven years before independence, showed relatively little bitterness towards the British Raj. 'To the British we must be grateful', he wrote in his autobiography, 'for one splendid gift of which they were the bearers, the gift of

276

science and its rich offspring. It is difficult, however, to forget or view with equanimity the efforts of the British Government in India to encourage the disruptive, obscurantist, reactionary, sectarian, and opportunist elements in this country.'

As a leading member of the Congress Party, Nehru worked for the reversal of these trends in close co-operation with Gandhi. But his most decisive step towards the leadership of independent India may, paradoxically, have been his divergence from Gandhi's pacifist ideals, a circumstance which contributed to the Mahatma's resignation from the Congress Party in 1941. Nehru's more practical and courageous outlook enabled him to discern that independence could only follow the successful repulse of the Japanese threat. That he had begun to see himself in an almost Churchillian role is suggested by his admission in 1946: 'Much as I hated war, the prospect of a Japanese invasion of Indian had in no way frightened me. At the back of my mind I was in a sense attracted to this coming of war, horrible as it was, to India. For I wanted a tremendous shake-up, a personal experience for millions of people, which would drag them from that peace of the grave that Britain had imposed on us.'

With British succour, India was spared the rigours of invasion and Nehru was duly elected India's first Prime Minister on 15 Aug. 1947. His qualifications for power were extolled by Clement (later Lord) Attlee, Prime Minister of the Labour Government at that time in office: 'It seems to me', said Attlee, 'that Nehru is a synthesis of the ideas of the East and the West. He understands both.' Attlee, who was responsible for the arrest of both Nehru and Gandhi during World War II, admitted in a 1965 TV interview which was not published until after his death in 1967 that 'they both accounted for a lot of trouble'.

The elation of Nehru's moment of destiny was unhappily vitiated by the tragic

HM The Queen visited New Delhi in 1967 and was welcomed by India's first Prime Minister, Jawaharlal Nehru. (Fashion note: The 'Nehru Jacket' was introduced to high fashion in London by Hardy Amies.)

dilemmas which accompanied the transition. Owing to the irreconcilable nature of the long-standing Hindu-Muslim communal problem, the Congress Party had been obliged to consent to partition of the sub-continent into the separate Dominions of India and Pakistan.[5] A year after the event, and the massacres[6] which accompanied it, Nehru reflected: 'We consented to it because we thought that thereby we were purchasing goodwill, though at a high price. . . . I do not know, now, if I had the same choice, how I would decide.' The most controversial of all his decisions was to use force in retaining the largely Muslim State of Kashmir in India, a choice influenced by the fact that both Nehru and his wife were Kashmiris, and made with the tacit acquiescence of Gandhi (*see page* 289). Concerning this decision, the Premier of the world's largest democracy told the Constituent Assembly of the Indian Parliament on 7 Sept. 1948: 'The Government of India and the Indian Army as a whole have done something which was inevitable, and each step which we have taken has been an inevitable step which, if we had not taken it, would have brought disgrace to us.'[7] Nehru's intransigence over Kashmir was the cause of over twenty years' tension, not to mention bloodshed, between India and Pakistan.

After the assassination of Gandhi, Nehru was more than ever the pre-eminent figure in the new nation. His foreign policy kept India conscious of her place in world affairs. Gandhi himself had said: 'Pandit Nehru is Indian to the core but, he being also an internationalist, has made us accustomed to looking at everything in the international light, instead of the parochial.' The essence of this doctrine was contained in Nehru's famous *panch sila* ('five points') – respect for sovereignty, non-aggression, non-interference with internal affairs, equality and mutual benefit, and peaceful co-existence – originally embodied in the 1953 Sino-Indian Treaty. Harold Wilson later paid tribute to Nehru's work telling the House of Commons on 1 Nov. 1962: 'Let there be no sneering about India's traditional neutrality. At crucial moments in the past ten years that neutrality has enabled India to exercise a decisive influence in securing peace: first in Korea and at a critical moment in Indo-China.' Nehru's Chinese flirtation proved disas-

PANDIT NEHRU

Jawaharlal Nehru

Right: *Mrs Indira Priyadarshini ('beautiful to behold') Gandhi, Pandit Nehru's daughter, was elected India's 3rd Prime Minister on 24 Jan. 1966 following the death of Lal Bahadur Shastri (11 Jan. 1966). She was re-elected Prime Minister for a five-year term on 12 March 1967.*

Born at Allahabad on 19 Nov. 1917, and married to Feroze Gandhi who died in 1960, Mrs Gandhi has two sons. She was Nehru's official hostess and companion for over 20 years until his death. He said of her: 'I have a great regard for her qualities and temperament, her energy and her integrity. I do not know what she has inherited from me; I am inclined to think she has derived these qualities from her mother.'

trous, however. The rape of Tibet by the Chinese, their provocations within the borders of Assam, and their political subversion in India were to have far-reaching deleterious effects.

Outside of politics, Nehru earned the affection of many for his charm and accessibility. Yehudi Menuhin found him a keen exponent of yoga (*see page* 110), and Charlie Chaplin commented on his 'exceedingly alert and sensitive mind'. Lord Avon wrote: 'I have always felt a sincere liking for

Mr Nehru personally which differences on policy could not affect.' The finest tribute paid to Nehru, other than in India, was when the honorary degree of Doctor of Laws was conferred on him at Columbia University. Dwight D. Eisenhower, reading the citation, said: 'His intellectual leadership has combined the profound knowledge of the West with the great heritage and enduring traditions of the East; a champion of under-privileged people, his devotion to the noble ideals of universal peace and understanding have won for him the respect and acclaim of all mankind.' Admiral of the Fleet Earl Mountbatten, great-grandson of Queen Victoria the former Empress of India, was the last British Viceroy. He described Nehru as 'a great statesman. He had a brilliant mind – he was quite amazingly quick to grasp a point, and very sensitive to situations.'

LP Recording

Sounds of Time 1934/1949 (with others) (CBS BPG62888)

---

[1] Harrow School, Middlesex, England was also the Alma Mater of Sir Winston Churchill.

[2] Giuseppe Garibaldi (1807–82) the Italian soldier patriot who overthrew the Bourbon government in Sicily and Naples with a small band of volunteers and brought most of the Italian peninsula under the rule of the house of Savoy.

[3] On 13 April 1919, an illegal public gathering in a public park at Amritsar called *Jallianwalla Bagh* was suppressed by British troops under General Dyer. Machine-gun fire killed 379 Indians. Dyer was relieved of his command.

[4] Lenin regarded the struggle between Capitalism and Communism as being dependent on the fact that the USSR, India, and China comprise the overwhelming majority of the world's population.

[5] Attlee announced partition on 3 June 1947. India and Pakistan were to become separate Dominions within the British Commonwealth with the right to secede if they wished. India became a Republic on 26 Jan. 1950; Pakistan on 23 March 1956. Both remained within the Commonwealth.

[6] Total deaths were estimated at between 180,000 and 2,000,000. Some 14,000,000 refugees crossed between the two countries.

[7] On 17 Dec. 1961 Indian troops also invaded the Portuguese enclaves of Goa, Daman, and Diu, forcibly imposing Indian rule.

JOHN F. KENNEDY

President John F. Kennedy described himself as an idealist without illusions.

Full name   John Fitzgerald Kennedy (usually called Jack).
Born   Tues. 29 May 1917, Brookline, Massachusetts, USA.
Characteristics   About 6′ 1″; about 166*lb.* (11*st.* 12*lb.*) reddish-brown hair; grey-green eyes; used a sun-lamp to maintain his tan throughout the year.
Married   1953 Jacqueline Bouvier 1*s.* 1*d.* (1*s.* died).
Died   Fri. 22 Nov. 1963.   Assassinated; struck in head and neck by rifle bullets fired by Lee Harvey Oswald; other unidentified assassins possibly implicated. Oswald was shot dead by Jack Ruby, a night-club owner, while in police custody awaiting trial, on 24 Nov. 1963.

   Three other Presidents were assassinated while in office: Abraham Lincoln was shot on 14 April 1865 and died on 15 April 1865; James Abram Garfield was shot on 2 July 1881 and died on 19 Sept. 1881; and William McKinley was shot on 6 Sept. 1901 and

The commander of a Japanese destroyer operating in the region of the Solomon Islands in Aug. 1943 was no respecter of Presidents of the United States, present or future. Knifing through the Pacific waters at a high rate of knots, the destroyer sliced clean through the USS PT-109 and sailed swiftly on leaving the crew of twelve to their fate. Thanks mainly to the heroism of their commander, Lieutenant John F. Kennedy, they lived to tell the tale. Swimming for 15 hours at a stretch, he guided his men to safety on a coral island, in one case actually towing a helpless member for three miles in a lifebelt with his teeth. For his gallantry, Kennedy was awarded the Navy and Marine Corps Medal and the Purple Heart. The citation read: 'His courage, endurance, and excellent leadership contributed to the saving of several lives and was in keeping with the highest traditions of the United States Naval Service.'

Kennedy's wife, Jacqueline, passed a most revealing comment on the then Senator in 1959. 'He has this curious, inquiring mind that is always at work', she said. 'If I were drawing him I would draw a tiny body with an enormous head.' She told one interviewer: 'He lived at such a pace because he wanted to know it all.' Kennedy's thirst for learning was already in operation at Harvard where he wrote a thesis entitled *Appeasement at Munich*. It was received *magne cum laude* and was to be a best-seller when published under the title *Why England Slept* (1941). He won literary distinction a second time with his book *Profiles in Courage* (1960) which was awarded the Pulitzer Prize. In it he wrote: 'The courage of life is often a less dramatic spectacle than the courage of a final moment; but it is no less a magnificent mixture of triumph and tragedy. A man does what he must – in spite of personal consequences, in spite of obstacles and dangers and pressures – and that is the

basis of all human morality.'

Kennedy's command of words was allied to a ready wit with which he often scored in speeches. At a fund raising dinner at Salt Lake City in 1960 he began: 'I am deeply touched – not as deeply touched as you have been by coming to this dinner, but nevertheless, it is a sentimental occasion.' At a White House dinner for Nobel Prize winners on 29 April 1962 he said: 'I think this is the most extraordinary collection of talent, of human knowledge, that has ever been gathered together at the White House – with the possible exception of when Thomas Jefferson dined alone.' Soon after becoming President, he attended a National Football Foundation dinner in New York and made light of the Democratic Party's narrow success at the election: 'There are not so many differences between politics and football. Some Republicans have been unkind enough to suggest that this close election was somewhat similar to the Notre Dame-Syracuse game.' The game was won by Notre Dame with a disputed penalty.

Kennedy the Democrat succeeded in establishing warm rapport with the outgoing Republican President, Dwight D. Eisenhower. 'In our conversations I was struck by his pleasing personality, his concentrated interest, and his receptiveness', wrote Ike. On 20 Jan. 1961, the day of his inauguration as the 35th and youngest elected President of the United States, Kennedy said: 'In the long history of the world, only a few generations have been granted the role of defending freedom in its hour of maximum danger. I do not shrink from this responsibility – I welcome it.'

During Kennedy's administration the threat of World War III was at its worst. In a campaign address at Michigan State Fair in 1960, he had said: 'Mr Khrushchev says with confidence that our children and grandchildren will be Communists. I think

we should say with the same confidence that his children will be free.' After their meeting at Vienna in 1961, Khrushchev told Russian televiewers: 'Our conversations with President Kennedy revealed that we have different conceptions of peaceful co-existence.' One of the differences, clearly, was that Kennedy recognized the danger to the United States of a Communist regime in Cuba, which he planned to overthrow by sponsoring an attempt by anti-Castro exiles to invade Cuba. After the failure of the abortive Bay of Pigs landing in April 1961 Kennedy spoke philosophically: 'We can't win them all. And I have been close enough to disaster to realize that these things which seem world-shaking at one moment, you can barely remember the next. We got a big kick in the leg – and we deserved it.' On 22 Oct. 1962 Kennedy announced the imposition of a 'quarantine' on Cuba due to the existence of Russian missile bases on the island. The crisis blew over when Khrushchev, acting on Kennedy's ultimatum, announced his agreement to halt the building of missile bases on 28 Oct. 1962. Said Kennedy: 'I welcome Chairman Khrushchev's statesmanlike decision to stop building bases in Cuba, dismantling offensive weapons, and returning them to the Soviet Union under the United Nations' verification. This is an important and constructive contribution to world peace.' Khrushchev recorded his respect for Kennedy in a taped TV interview, released in 1967, in which he said JFK was 'A real statesman. He completely filled his post. I liked the way he – unlike Eisenhower – had his personal opinions on all questions we discussed. Kennedy was entirely different from Eisenhower and had a precisely formulated answer for every question.' Khrushchev went so far, in this interview, as to claim credit for Kennedy's election as President (*see page* 185).

Following the crisis of 1962 Kennedy moderated the pressures of people within

The 50 Cent Kennedy (1964) ; a second mintage was issued in 1965.

his own administration who were opposed to negotiation with Soviet Russia. Said the President: 'Winston Churchill said it is better to jaw, jaw than war, war,[1] and we shall continue to jaw, jaw and see if we can produce a useful result.' The useful result ultimately achieved by Kennedy, with the help of the British Prime Minister, Harold Macmillan (*see page* 191), was the ratification of the Nuclear Test Ban Treaty on 8 Oct. 1963. He also promoted measures affecting international trade through his proposals in the US Trade Expansion Act of 1962 which was the inspiration for the 'Kennedy Round' talks.[2]

Kennedy's ability to establish contact with people outside the sphere of politics was a great strength in a modern President. He showed recognition to distinguished writers and artists by inviting them to his inauguration and was a friend of show business personalities: Frank Sinatra had

281

a 'Kennedy slept here' plaque at his home in California, while Bob Hope was the recipient of a Presidential nod for his war work (*see page* 157).

An acute sufferer from slipped disc – his brother testified that 'At least half of the days he spent on this earth were days of intense physical pain' – Kennedy also had an organic complaint diagnosed as Addison's disease.[3] He told reporters: 'The doctors say I've got a sort of slow-motion leukaemia, but they tell me I'll probably last until I'm 45.' As it happened, the prognosis was only a year out. The President was forty-six when the assassin's bullet cruelly ended his career. Macmillan, who had noted on meeting him: 'It was the gay things that linked us together and made it possible for us to talk about the terrible things,'[4] expressed the shock of millions after Kennedy's death: 'Why was this feeling – this sorrow – at once so universal and so individual? Was it not because he seemed, in his person, to embody all the hopes and aspirations of this new world that was struggling to emerge – to rise, phoenix-like, from the ashes of the old?'

The incoming President, Lyndon B. Johnson, announced a day of national mourning, hailing his predecessor as: 'A man of wisdom, strength, and peace, he moulded and moved the power of our nation in the service of a world of growing liberty and order.'

On 14 May 1965 a monument was dedicated to the late President by Queen Elizabeth II at Runnymede, Surrey, England where King John (1167–1216) signed the Magna Carta (15 June 1215). The dedication was made in these terms: 'This acre of English ground was given to the United States of America by the people of Great Britain in memory of John Fitzgerald Kennedy.'

[1] The precise wording of Churchill's remark made at the White House, Washington, DC, on 26 June 1954 was: 'Talking jaw to jaw is better than going to war.'

[2] The 'Kennedy Round' talks took place under the auspices of the General (Geneva) Agreement on Tariffs and Trade (GATT) beginning in 1964. On 15 May 1967 it was announced that 53 nations had reached agreement on tariff reductions affecting about 60,000 items, representing an overall reduction of about one-third in world industrial tariffs over five years. In Jan. 1968 President Johnson said: 'The Kennedy Round achieved the greatest reduction in tariff barriers in all the history of trade negotations.'

[3] Deficiency of the suprarenal cortex of which the symptoms are brown pigmentation of the skin, wasting, and debility.

[4] In 1969, Macmillan revealed that during the 1962 Cuba crisis Kennedy had telephoned him two or three times a night.

A copy of the Kennedy Coat of Arms was sent to the author by Senator Robert F. Kennedy in April 1969 (see page 240).

LP Recordings
Memorial Album (speeches by Kennedy and others) (Diplomat 10000A-B)
Memorial Album (speeches narrated by Ed. Brown) (Decca ACL-R1168)
John Fitzgerald Kennedy – As We Remember Him (with Lyndon B. Johnson, Richard M. Nixon and others) (CBS L2L1017)
The President in Ireland (HMV CLP1732)
Four Days That Shook the World (Colpix PXL2500)
The Kennedy Wit (narrated by David Brinkley) (RCA Victor RB6614)

STALIN

Generalissimo Joseph Stalin waved a nonchalant salute to the Scots Guards at Potsdam in 1945. At the Conference, Churchill made some remark about the Pope. Stalin sneered: 'How many divisions has the Pope?'

Full name Joseph Vissarionovich Djugashvili. Stalin ('Steel man') was one of at least 17 aliases or pseudonyms employed by him, including: Koba, Ko, K. St., K. Kato, K., J. G—shishvili, David Bars (meaning leopard), Gayoz Nizheradze, Beshoshvili, Zakhar Gregoryan Melikyants, Ogoness Vartanovich Totomyants, Ivanovich, K. Salin, K. Solin, and K. Stephin.

Born Sun. 21 Dec. 1879, Gori, Georgia, USSR.

Characteristics Just under 5′ 4″; dark hair and eyes; swarthy, pock-marked face; withered left arm; second and third toes of the left foot attached.

Married
(1) 1904 Yekaterina Svanidze (died 1907) 1s.
(2) 1919 Nadejda Sergeyevna Alliluieva (committed suicide 1932) 1s. 1d.
(3) ? (According to unconfirmed reports) Rosa Kaganovich.

Died 21.30 hours, Thurs. 5 March 1953. Cerebral haemorrhage. According to Svetlana Stalin, he was slowly asphyxiated for 12 hours, his face became dark and unrecognizable, his lips turned black, and he choked to death in terrible agony.

'Everybody is familiar with the cogent and invincible force of Stalin's logic, the crystal clarity of his mind, his iron will, his devotion to the Party, his ardent faith in the people. . . .' The words could only have come from someone who knew his subject intimately. That someone was the anonymous writer of a book entitled *Joseph Stalin: A Short Biography*. The work had been published some years before the writer's identity was revealed. The revelation came from Nikita S. Khrushchev; the writer's name: Joseph Stalin.

The son of a Georgian peasant shoe-maker, Stalin rounded off his education at a religious seminary from which he was expelled as a trouble maker. Between 1902 and 1917 he was arrested and exiled six times for seditious activities. Though he did not play an important part in the 1917 revolution, he was an energetic and able Party man and was once editor of *Pravda*. His militant posture made an impression on Lenin whose political testament, dated Dec. 1922, included this observation: 'Stalin is excessively rude, and this defect, which can be freely tolerated in our midst and in contacts among us Communists, becomes a defect which cannot be tolerated in the position of Secretary-General.' At the time Stalin had already been Secretary-General for a few months and succeeded in surviving Lenin's bid to oust him.

According to Leon Trotsky[1], Stalin's most powerful rival in the succession to Lenin, Stalin confided to Trotsky that in Feb. 1923, when Lenin was paralysed and losing the power of speech, he wanted to commit suicide and asked Stalin for poison. Wrote Trotsky: 'Whether Stalin sent the poison to Lenin with the hint that the physicians left no hope for his recovery or whether he resorted to more direct means I do not know. But I am firmly convinced that Stalin could not have waited passively when his fate hung by a thread.'

Stalin's struggle against Trotsky was virtually decided in 1928 when the latter went into exile. On 21 Aug. 1940, Trotsky, then exiled in Mexico, died after being struck down by one of Stalin's assassins wielding an ice-axe.[2] Trotsky's son, Serge Serdov, had 'disappeared' in Russia in 1935.

The central theme of Stalin's domestic policy was his drive to transform Russia from a mainly agricultural nation into an industrial one by collectivizing farms in order to release labour for industry. This policy was carried out with such ruthless efficiency that enormous numbers of the population starved. According to Winston Churchill, who asked Stalin about the loss of life arising from his policy in the period 1933–34, the Soviet dictator estimated the number of his victims at 10,000,000, emphasizing the gruesome statistics by raising his ten fingers while the interpreter translated. It was, added Stalin, 'difficult but necessary'.[3]

H. G. Wells visited Moscow in 1934 and elicited these remarks from Stalin: 'I do not stand for any kind of order. I stand for order that corresponds to the interests of the working class.' He also assured Wells: '. . . you are wrong if you think that the Communists are enamoured of violence. They would be very pleased to drop violent methods, if the ruling class agreed to give way to the working class. But the experience of history speaks against such an assumption.'

During World War II, Russia's contribution to the Allied victory was vital though it began only in 1941 after Adolf Hitler had betrayed the Molotov-Ribbentrop Pact of 1939 and hurled his armies right up to the suburbs of Moscow.[4] The heroic Russian stand and subsequent counter-offensive was galvanized by Stalin's message of 3 July 1941: 'In occupied regions conditions must be made unbearable for the enemy and all his accomplices. They must be hounded and annihilated at every step, and all their measures frustrated.' The turning point came in Feb. 1943 when the Red Army completed a crushing victory over the German Sixth Army at the Battle of Stalingrad.

The impressions of statesmen who met Stalin were not unmixed. Anthony Eden (now Lord Avon) recorded after meeting him in 1943: '. . . he still has that disconcerting habit of not looking at one when he speaks or shakes hands. A meeting with him would be in all respects a creepy, even sinister experience if it weren't for his

readiness to laugh, when his whole face creases and his little eyes open. He looks more and more like bruin.' Marshal Tito noted that Stalin 'could not bear to be contradicted. In conversation with the men around him he was coarse and touchy.' Franklin D. Roosevelt, duped by Stalin into surrendering much of Eastern Europe to Soviet rule, complained bitterly of the dictator's bad faith after the Yalta Conference in Feb. 1945: 'Stalin can't be trusted! He has broken his word on every promise he made to me at Yalta.' Harry S Truman endorsed his predecessor's conclusion: 'The only thing was that we found Stalin such a blooming liar. I liked him a lot. It was much easier to make an agreement with Stalin. But Churchill kept his agreements and Stalin did not.' General de Gaulle has provided one of the most definitive word pictures of the Soviet tyrant: 'Stalin was possessed by the will to power. After a lifetime of machinations he was used to disguising his features as well as his inmost soul, to dispensing with illusions, pity, or sincerity, and to see in each man an obstacle or a threat. He was all strategy, suspicion, and stubbornness.' Briefer, but no less pointed, was the

posthumous demerit awarded by Alexei N. Kosygin, Soviet premier since 1964. He rated Stalin a 'pock-marked bastard'.

In 1937 Stalin's disciple, Khrushchev, had been fulsome in his hymn of praise: 'Stalin is our hope, he is the beacon which guides all progressive humanity. Stalin is our banner! Stalin is our victory!' The eulogy was in striking contrast to Khrushchev's 1956 denunciation, delivered a safe three years after his former chief had died: 'Stalin was a very deceitful man, diseased with suspicion.... After the war he became even more capricious, irritable, and brutal; in particular his suspicion grew. His persecution mania grew to unbelievable dimensions.' Mr K. completed his demolition of the character and reputation of the Generalissimo by depicting him as 'a sadist, a mass-murderer, a coward, a military bungler, a falsifier of history'.

In private, Khrushchev's admission to the US diplomat, Averell Harriman, gave an alternative account of his personal feelings on the death of Stalin: 'I wept. After all, we were his pupils and owed him everything. Like Peter the Great,[5] Stalin fought barbarism with barbarism but he was a great man.' The account is not inconsistent with the awe in which Stalin's associates held him. A story, possibly apocryphal, is told of how Lavrentia Beria[6] danced a jig of delight around Stalin's inert body when he first appeared to have died. When Stalin unexpectedly opened one eye, Beria was transformed instantly into a posture of abject servility.

The refusal of China to follow the 1956 Khrushchev line of 'de-Stalinization' widened the split already evident in the unity of the Communist camp. On the death of Stalin, Mao Tse-tung had said: 'Stalin was the greatest genius of the present age ... dearest friend and great teacher of the Communist people.' In 1956 Mao was reported to have told Anastas Mikoyan that far from being the monster Khrushchev made him out to be, 'Stalin's merits outweighed his faults'. Other Communist leaders were disenchanted, none more so than Milovan Djilas, former Vice-President of Yugoslavia, who was released from prison by Tito on 31 Dec. 1966 after serving half of an eight-year sentence passed for revealing 'State secrets' in his book *Conversations with Stalin* (1962). It was not made clear whether the summing up of Stalin published by Djilas was regarded as classified information, but it remains the most sweeping condemnation of a Communist by a fellow-Communist ever printed: 'Whatever standards we use to take his measure, he has the glory of being the greatest criminal in history – and, let us hope, for all time to come. For in him was joined the criminal senselessness of a Caligula[7] with the refinement of a Borgia[8] and the brutality of a Tsar Ivan the Terrible.[9]'

Stalin's body had first been put on public display in Moscow with that of Lenin but on 30 Oct. 1961 a resolution was passed by the Central Committee that 'abuses of power, the mass reprisals against honest Soviet people and other actions during the period of the personality cult makes it impossible to leave his body in the Lenin mausoleum.' The next day his name was effaced from the tomb on Red Square and on 1 Nov. his body was re-interred at the foot of the Kremlin wall. The city of Stalingrad[10] was renamed Volgograd, innumerable Stalin statues were pulled down, and his name was removed from towns, streets, factories, and farms all over Eastern Europe. At the Jubilee Celebrations in 1967, the name of the man who had ruled the USSR for nearly 30 out of 50 years of Communist history was conspicuously ignored, while his daughter, Svetlana, defected to the United States to publish memoirs damningly critical of both her father's and the current Soviet regime.

'We Communists are people of a special mould. We are made of special material.'

'What is the sharpening of the class struggle due to? It is due to the fact that the Capitalist elements will not depart from the scene voluntarily.'

'English Capitalism was, is, and always will be the most ruthless strangler of revolutions of the peoples.'

'For the good of the Party, every method is permissible.'

[1] Real name Lev Davidovitch Bronstein (1879–1940).

[2] Trotsky's assassin, Jacques Mornard, alias Ramon Mercador del Rio, was released from prison at Mexico City on 4 May 1960 after serving twenty years. He was flown to Cuba with two Czech embassy officals. Trotsky's widow, Natalia I. Trotsky, applied for rehabilitation of her husband's name in 1956 after Stalin's disgrace, and again in 1961, but without success. She died in 1962.

[3] According to *The Great Terror: Stalin's Purge of the Thirties*, Robert Conquest (Macmillan, 1968) a figure of 20,000,000 dead 'is almost certainly too low'.

[4] Stalin had participated with Hitler in the subjugation of Poland in 1939 and up to June 1941 was still sending munitions and supplies to Hitler, some of which were used against Russia. Stalin was alerted to Hitler's treachery by Churchill's message of 3 April 1941. Hitler launched his attack on Russia on 22 June 1941.

[5] Peter I, called 'the Great' (1672–1725), founder of the Russian navy and of the city of St Petersburg, who was acclaimed Emperor of All Russia in 1721.

[6] Beria, once regarded as a possible successor to Stalin, was executed for treason on 23 Dec. 1953. Khrushchev is said to have personally participated in the execution. Beria's house in Moscow, which was said to have been haunted, had to be exorcized following his death before it could be put into service as an embassy.

[7] Gaius Caesar Caligula (AD 12–41), Roman Emperor (AD 37–41), who degenerated through insanity to abysmal depths of cruelty and vice.

[8] The Borgias were an Italian Renaissance family of whom the most notorious was Cesare Borgia (1476–1507), son of Pope Alexander VI. Cesare was an adventurer of treacherous and ferocious reputation, some of which was wrongly ascribed to his sister Lucrezia Borgia (1480–1519).

[9] Ivan IV, called 'the Terrible' (1530–84), Tsar of Moscow, whose reign was characterized by vicious brutality and the massacre of rebellious sections of the population. He also murdered his own son.

[10] Originally Tsaritsyn but re-named Stalingrad in 1925 after Stalin had successfully led the defence of the city against the counter-revolutionary White Army.

GANDHI

'I think that most people meeting him would be conscious, as I was conscious, of a very powerful personality, and this, independent of physical endowment, which indeed is unfavourable. Small, wizened, rather emaciated, no front teeth, it is a personality poorly adorned with the world's trimmings. And yet you cannot help feeling the force of character behind the sharp little eyes and immensely active and acutely working mind.' So wrote Lord Irwin who, as Lord Halifax,[1] visited Adolf Hitler in 1937 and was offered that tyrant's unsolicited views on how he should have handled Indian nationalism. 'Shoot Gandhi', rapped the Führer, 'and if that does not suffice to reduce them to submission, shoot a dozen leading members of Congress; and if that does not suffice, shoot 200, and so on until order is established.'

Gandhi was, in fact, to die by the hand of an Indian assassin eleven years later but not before he had performed a leading role in advancing independence[2] for his country, fulfilling his belief that 'freedom won through non-violence will mean the inauguration of a new order in the world'. The precept of non-violence was enshrined in the expression *Satyàgraha* (soul-force or truth-force) which, he explained, 'is an insistence upon truth which, dynamically expressed, means love; and by the law of love we are required not to return hatred for hatred, violence for violence, but to return good for evil'. Gandhi started the *Satyàgraha* movement in 1915. He learned the rule of non-violence from his wife, to whom he was

287

betrothed at seven and married at fourteen: 'Her determined resistance to my will on the one hand, and her quiet submission to the suffering my stupidity involved on the other, ultimately made me ashamed of myself and cured me of my stupidity in thinking I was born to rule over her.' The key words in his policy for India were *ahimsà* (non-violence) and *swaràj* (self-rule). The term used for his group of disciples was *ashram*.

As a child Gandhi had promised his mother to fight the recurring temptations of meat, wine, and women. Thus he also preached *brahmacharya* (celibacy) and recommended a vegetarian diet: 'My experience teaches me', he said, 'that for those whose minds are working towards self-restraint, dietetic restriction and fasting are very helpful. In fact without their help concupiscence cannot be completely rooted out of the mind.' He stressed that 'the strength of the soul grows in proportion as you subdue the flesh'. Gandhi's personal example in this respect was irreproachable – he remained abstinent for the last forty-two years of his life, during thirty-eight of which years he was married.

In 1920 Gandhi proclaimed a campaign of 'non-violent non-co-operation' with British rule in India, urging his followers to boycott government service, the courts of law, and public services.[3] Sentenced to six years' imprisonment in 1922 for conspiring to overthrow the government, he served only two years before being released. In 1930 he served a year for urging civil disobedience by violating the salt excise laws. A third sentence was cut short owing to the supposed danger to his health occasioned by his so-called 'fast unto death' from 8–29 May 1933.[4] His fasts, designed to incite Indian national feeling against the British, probably constituted no health hazard. Gandhi himself once predicted that his life span would be 125, even 133 years.

Among those who were sceptical of Gandhi's methods was Lord Reading[5]: 'I have always thought that he became more the politician than the holy man and in the former capacity had to say and do things which were not strictly compatible with the latter.' Winston Churchill was a vociferous opponent of the Mahatma (Great Soul). In a speech at the West Essex Unionist Association on 23 Feb. 1931 he said it was 'alarming and also nauseating to see Mr Gandhi, a seditious Middle Temple lawyer, now posing as a fakir of a type well known in the East, striding half-naked up the steps of the Viceregal Palace, while he is still organizing and conducting a defiant campaign of civil disobedience, to parley on equal terms with the representative of the King-Emperor.' Lord

---

Full name Mohandas Karamchand Gandhi (Gandhi means 'perfume merchant'). Gandhi was known affectionately to his followers as *Bapu* - father.

Born Sat. 2 Oct. 1869, Porbandar, Kathiawar (now Saurashtra), India.

Characteristics About 5′ 7″; weighed as little as 107*lb.* (7*st.* 9*lb.*) during his last fast; black hair; brown eyes; vegetarian; drank goat's milk and offered it to his visitors.

Married 1882 Kasturbai Makanji (died 1944) 4*s.*

Died Fri. 30 Jan. 1948. Shot at point-blank range by Nathuran Godse, 35, a Hindu nationalist; three pistol bullets entered Gandhi's chest and stomach. His last words were *'He Ram'* ('Oh God'). Of the eight conspirators arrested, Godse and Narayan Apte were hanged. Godse, unrepentant, twitched for 15 minutes on the noose before expiring.

288

Birkenhead[6] thought Gandhi 'as pathetic a figure with his spinning wheel as the last minstrel with his harp, but not able to secure so charming an audience!'

Though there were some who would not have shared these views they were to recognize the extent of Gandhi's intransigence during World War II when demands for independence continued unabated. Sir Stafford Cripps (1889–1952), leader of the Cripps Mission to India in March 1942, commented that Gandhi's non-co-operation was 'calculated to endanger the Allied war effort and to bring the greatest aid and comfort to our common enemies. Mr Gandhi was not prepared to wait. He would rather jeopardize freedom and the whole cause of the United Nations.'

Churchill's report to the House of Commons following the Cripps Mission crystallized the factors on which Indian security depended: 'It is fortunate indeed,' he said, 'that the Congress Party has no influence whatever with the martial races, on whom the defence of India, apart from British forces, largely depends.'[7] Gandhi had earlier been so convinced that Britain would be crushed by Germany that he even went so far as to call on 'every Briton to adopt ... a nobler and braver way' of surrender to Hitler. Fortunately the Congress Party was not with Gandhi in his pacifist ideals and he resigned on 30 Dec.

1941 shortly after Japan entered the war. Despite his opposition the defence of India was thus assured and the way to independence made secure.

Gandhi envisaged a united independent India but he was unable to maintain harmony between the irreconcilable religious groups involved.[8] Mohammed Ali Jinnah (1876–1948) leader of the Muslim League, said in 1944: 'We are a nation with our own distinctive culture and civilization, language and literature, art and architecture, names and nomenclature, sense of value and proportion, legal laws and moral codes, customs and calendar, history and traditions, aptitudes and ambitions.... By all canons of international law, we are a nation.' His words embodied the view that independent India would have to be divided into two nations. But Gandhi strenuously opposed the idea of partition: 'Even if the whole of India burns, we shall not concede Pakistan, no, not if they demand it at the point of a sword.' He was disillusioned and unhappy about the massacres which accompanied partition:[9] 'I do not agree with what my closest friends have done or are doing: thirty-two years of work have come to an inglorious end.' However, he made no attempt to influence Jawaharlal Nehru in his decision to use force to keep Kashmir in India (see page 277). Recalled Nehru:

Gandhi with Sir Stafford Cripps, leader of the Cripps Mission to India in 1942.

Films About Gandhi
Mahatma Gandhi – 29th Century Prophet (1953)
Nine Hours to Rama (1963)

LP Recording
Mahatma Gandhi Centenary Record
(HMV ALP2113)

'Gandhi said nothing to indicate his disapproval. It was a great relief, I must say. If Gandhi, the vigorous non-violent, didn't demur, it made my job a lot easier. This strengthened my view that Gandhi could be adaptable.'

Clement (later Lord) Attlee, Prime Minister of the Labour Government that passed the Indian Independence Act of 1947, also noted Gandhi's duality, characterizing him as 'A combination of saint and astute politician – Gladstone[10] must have been a bit like him – but with ideas difficult to reconcile with modern views of progress, difficult for the West to appreciate anyway.' Lord Irwin had also found a degree of

ambivalence in Gandhi: 'There was a directness about him which was singularly winning, but this could be accompanied by a subtlety of intellectual process which could sometimes be disconcerting.'

On the assassination of the Mahatma, Prime Minister Nehru spoke to the Indian nation: 'In ages to come, centuries and maybe millennia after us, people will think of this generation when this man of God trod on earth and will think of us who, however small, could also follow his path and tread the holy ground where his feet had been.' Cripps wrote: 'I know of no other man in our time or, indeed, in recent history, who so fully demonstrated the power of the spirit over material things.'

At least two films about Gandhi have been screened and a whole department of the Central Government of India was engaged in collating his complete works, in readiness for the celebrations in 1969 of the centenary of his birth.

'My love of the British is equal to that of my own people. I claim no merit for it for I have equal love for all mankind without exception. It demands no reciprocity. I own no enemy on earth. That is my creed.'

'Faith is not a thing to grasp; it is a state to grow to. And growth comes from within.'

'I would far rather that India perished than that she won freedom at the sacrifice of truth.'

---

[1] Lord Irwin was Viceroy of India (1926–31). The Canadian journalist, Negley Farson, wrote: 'If Gandhi was a holy man, Lord Irwin certainly was a saint.'
[2] The British period in India comprised about 300 years of trading, 200 years of political power, and 130 years of general supremacy. Eventual independence had been envisaged ever since Queen Victoria's proclamation of 1858.
[3] The preamble of the Government of India Act (1919), implementing the declaration of 20 Aug. 1917, provided for 'the increasing association of Indians in every branch of the administration and the gradual development of self-governing institutions with a view to the progressive realization of responsible government in British India as an integral part of the British Empire.'
[4] Gandhi spent 249 days in jail in South Africa and 2,089 days in jail in India, some of them in conditions of great comfort in the Aga Khan's palace at Poona.
[5] Rufus Daniel Isaacs, 1st Marquess of Reading (1860–1935), Viceroy of India (1921–26).
[6] Frederick Edwin Smith, 1st Earl of Birkenhead (1872–1930), Secretary of State for India (1924–28).
[7] According to captured Japanese documents, the Gurkhas were the most formidable troops they encountered in the war.
[8] The census of 1941 showed a total population for undivided India of 386,551,733, broken down by religions as follows: Hindus 254,930,506; Muslims, 92,058,096; Christians, 6,316,549; Sikhs, 5,691,447; Jains, 1,449,286; Buddhists, 232,003; Others, 25,873,846.
[9] Between 180,000 and 2,000,000 were estimated to have lost their lives; about 14,000,000 refugees were reported to have crossed between the two countries.
[10] William Ewart Gladstone (1809–1898), Prime Minister (1868–74, 1880–85, 1886, and 1892–94).

ADOLF
HITLER

Adolf Hitler in person with the Italian dictator, Benito Mussolini. Hitler sometimes used doubles for parades. On One occasion he 'appeared' at two different functions at the same time, causing considerable confusion in newspaper reports.

Full name Adolf Hitler (his father changed his name from Schicklgruber to Hitler 12 years before Adolf was born).

Born 18.30 hours, Sat. 20 April 1889 in the Gasthof zum Ponner (an inn), Braunau am Inn, Austria.

Characteristics About 5′ 9″; rather slight build; black hair; staring blue eyes; non-smoker; partial vegetarian; fanatical believer in the occult; devoid of humour; enjoyed pornographic books and films.

Doubles Hitler had three doubles whose names were a closely-kept secret; their nicknames were Little Willi, Old Bismarck, and Putzi.

Married 1945 Eva Braun (died 1945).

Mistresses (*inter alia*)
(1) His half-sister's daughter, Geli Raubal (committed suicide).
(2) Renate Muller (committed suicide).
(3) Tillie Fleischer, 1936 Olympic javelin champion (reported to be still alive in 1966).
(4) Jenny Jugo.
(5) Sigrid von Lappus.

Died Mon. 30 April 1945. Suicide by discharging a revolver at his temple. Eva Braun took poison. Both bodies were saturated in petrol and burned according to Hitler's orders. Owing to the conflicting rumours which circulated in the post-war period, Hitler's death was formally confirmed by a German court on 25 Oct. 1956.

'A thousand years will pass and the guilt of Germany will not be erased.' Such was the lament of Hans Frank, Nazi Governor-General of Poland, before submitting to the hangman's noose at Nuremberg in 1946. It was a sentiment that would never have sprung to the lips of the man pre-

eminently responsible for German guilt, Adolf Hitler, who, it is said, wept only twice – over the grave of his mother, and on hearing that Germany had lost World War I. At the time he lay in hospital, temporarily blinded by British chlorine gas in the Battle of Ypres on 13 Oct. 1918. 'I stumbled back with burning eyes', he recalled, 'taking with me my last report of the war. A few hours later my eyes had turned to burning coals; it had grown dark around me'. Corporal Hitler, who had narrowly missed coming to grips with Major Anthony Eden a few months earlier (*see* page 176), regretted only one thing: that Germany had lost. 'In these nights hatred grew in me', he wrote, 'hatred for those responsible for his deed. . . . Miserable and degenerate criminals! The more I tried to achieve clarity on the monstrous event of this hour, the more the shame of indignation and disgrace burned my brow. What was all the pain in my eyes compared to this misery?'

Hitler's foul designs were disseminated in the notorious and ponderously prolix work *Mein Kampf* (Volume I, 1925; Volume II, 1927). In it he propounded his racial prejudices: '. . . it is never by war that nations are ruined, but by the loss of their powers of resistance, which are exclusively a characteristic of pure racial blood. In this world everything that is not of sound racial stock is like chaff'; his anti-semitism: '. . . one really cannot be surprised if in the imagination of our people the Jew is pictured as the incarnation of Satan and the symbol of evil'; and his nefarious views on propaganda: '. . . the broad masses of a nation are always more easily corrupted in the deeper strata of their emotional nature than consciously or voluntarily, and thus in the primitive simplicity of their minds they more readily fall victims to the big lie than the small lie.'

Hitler dictated the turgid paragraphs while serving a sentence for treason passed in 1924 for his abortive attempt to seize power in the infamous 'Beer Hall Putsch' at Munich on 8 Nov. 1923. His scribe and fellow-criminal was Rudolf Hess[1] who was to become number three in the Nazi hierarchy and deputy leader of Hitler's Nazi[2] wartime regime. *Mein Kampf* (My Struggle) sold only 9,473 copies in 1925 but in 1933, the year Hitler became Chancellor, sales leaped to over a million, bringing him royalties of over $300,000 (£75,000) and making him Germany's most prosperous author. By 1940 over 6,000,000 copies of *Mein Kampf* had been sold in Germany.

Examining the manner in which the German people were corrupted, C. G. Jung (1875–1961), the psychologist, wrote in 1936: 'Perhaps we can sum up this general phenomenon as *Ergriffenheit* – a state of being seized or possessed. . . . The impressive thing about the German phenomenon is that one man who is obviously "possessed" has infected a whole nation. . . .'

Hitler's *entente* with Benito Mussolini lacked cordiality from the outset. In 1932 he wrote to Rome asking for a signed photograph of the Fascist dictator. The Italian Foreign Office sent a terse note to their Berlin embassy saying: 'Please thank the above-named gentleman for his sentiment and tell him in whatever terms you consider best that the Duce does not think fit to accede to his request.' By 1934 relations were still far from convivial; at their meeting in that year Hitler expounded his theory that all peoples of the Mediterranean area had a Negro strain, upon which Mussolini called him 'a buffoon' to his face. Benito was to reveal on another occasion that he had no illusions as to the Führer's real depravity: 'He is a cruel and ferocious character and calls to mind legendary characters of the past . . . Attila.'[3]

The Nazi dictator's personality impressed itself vividly on the former US President Herbert Hoover[4] who said he was 'forceful, highly intelligent, had a remarkable and accurate memory, a wide range of information, and a capacity for lucid exposition. . . . From his clothing and hair-do he was obviously a great deal of an exhibitionist. He seemed to have trigger spots in his mind which, when touched, set him off like a man in a furious anger.' Anthony Eden (later Lord Avon) drew an interesting comparison between Hitler and the other great dictators of the day: 'Unlike Stalin as I was to know him, or Mussolini, he appeared negative to me, certainly not compelling; he was also rather shifty. Stalin and Mussolini were, in their separate ways, men whose personality would be felt in any company. Hitler was essentially the man who would pass in the crowd.' This impression was shared by Lord Halifax[5] when visiting Berchtesgarden in 1937; at first he actually mistook Hitler for the footman. The Duke of Windsor, on the other hand, proved susceptible to Hitler's hubris: 'His eyes were piercing and magnetic. I confess frankly that he took me in. I believed him when he implied that he sought no war with Britain.' There were others, too, who failed utterly to divine his evil intentions. David Lloyd George, who met the Führer at Obersalsburg in 1936, hailed him as 'a great man' who had the vision and the will to solve a nation's problems. Neville Chamberlain[6] found him to be 'the commonest little dog' yet wrote

[1] Hess fled from Nazi Germany and parachuted into Scotland on 10 May 1941 with the declared intention of making overtures to the British. Tried as a major war criminal at Nuremberg in 1945–46, he was still serving a life sentence at Spandau jail in 1969.

[2] The acronym Nazi stood for *Nationalsozialistische Deutsche Arbeiter Partei* (National Socialist German Labour Party).

[3] Attila, King of the Huns from 434 until his death in 453. Known as the 'Scourge of God', he ruled over territories extending roughly from the Baltic and the Alps in the west to the Caspian Sea in the east.

[4] Herbert Clark Hoover (1874–1964), President (1929–33).

[5] Edward Frederick Lindley Wood, 1st Earl of Halifax (1881–1959), Secretary of State for War (1935), Lord Privy Seal (1935–37), Lord President of the Council (1937–38), and British Ambassador in Washington (1941–46). As Lord Irwin he was Viceroy of India (1926–31).

[6] Arthur Neville Chamberlain (1869–1940), Prime Minister (1937–40).

to his sister: 'I got the impression that here was a man who could be relied upon when he had given his word.' Harold Macmillan wrote that 'the British people found it difficult, when they first heard of him, to take Hitler too seriously, with his Charlie Chaplin moustache[1] and his everlasting raincoat. Naturally, nobody to read *Mein Kampf*. Nor could anybody see below the apparent insignificance of his appearance the deep, cunning, malignant brain.'

The Chancellor of the Third Reich (1933–45) was not hampered by doubts as to his omnipotence. At a military conference on 22 Aug. 1939 he boasted: 'There will probably never again in the future be a man with more authority than I have.' Cynically, he paraded his utter disregard for the consequences of his decisions: 'In starting and waging war it is not right that matters, but victory. Close your hearts to pity! Act brutally! Eighty million people must obtain what is their right. . . .'

After the fall of France Hitler made his so-called Peace Offer in a Reichstag speech on 19 July 1940. Predicting that Churchill would soon flee to Canada he added: 'I can see no reason why this war need go on. I am grieved to think of the sacrifices it must claim. . . . Possibly Mr Churchill will brush aside this statement of mine by saying it is merely born of fear and doubt of final victory. In that case I shall have relieved my conscience in regard to the things to come.' Churchill was to comment: 'If Hitler invaded Hell, I would make at least a favourable reference to the Devil in the House of Commons.'

During the war Hitler's public utterances conjured wildly with the truth. On 21 June 1941 he wrote to Mussolini: 'England has lost this war. Like a drowning person, she grasps at every straw.' At the time, the Battle of Britain had been fought and won – by Britain, and Hitler's armies were

[1] The Nazis recognized the likeness and removed the moustache from the picture of Chaplin hanging in their museum of degenerate art.

occupied in the disastrous invasion of the USSR. On 3 Nov. 1942, when the Axis armies were already in trouble at the battle of El Alamein, he wrote to Field-Marshal Rommel: 'I and the German people are watching the heroic defensive battle waged in Egypt with faithful trust in your powers of leadership and in the bravery of the German-Italian troops under your command.' The tide had also turned in Europe in Feb. 1943 when the Soviets inflicted a crushing defeat on the Nazis at Stalingrad (now Volgograd).

Among Hitler's other problems were at least nine attempts on his life by disaffected Germans in 1943 and 1944. His narrowest escape was when a bomb, placed in a black briefcase in the conference room, killed a shorthand writer but succeeded only in blowing off Hitler's trousers.

The invasion of Western Europe by Allied forces took place at midnight on 5–6 June 1944, heralding the final, remorseless stages of the annihilation of the Nazi scourge. As the Allied forces closed in on Berlin, Hitler took refuge in his bunker saying: 'After a six-years' war which, in spite of all setbacks will one day go down in history as the most glorious and heroic manifestation of a people's will to live, I cannot forsake the city which is the capital of this state.' To avoid the execution and public exhibition which had been the fate of Mussolini a few days earlier (*see page 296*), he ordered that his body and that of his wife of a few days, Eva Braun, should be burned. In his Political Testament he reverted to a familiar theme: 'It is not true that I, or anybody else in Germany, wanted war in 1939. It was wanted and provoked by those international politicians who either came of Jewish stock or worked for Jewish interests.'

The magnitude of Hitler's crimes is difficult to appraise. At the Nuremburg Trials of Major War Criminals in 1945–46 it was estimated that about 5,750,000 Jews had been exterminated by the Nazis. The total loss of life in Hitler's war was about 54,800,000. The aptest testimonial on history's vilest human came from the man who, though they never met, played the foremost role in bringing about his downfall. 'This wicked man' said Churchill. 'The repository and embodiment of many forms of soul-destroying hatred, this monstrous product of former wrongs and shames. . . .'

Celluloid fame was thrust upon Hitler when Donald Duck starred in 'Der Fuehrer's Face' (1942). The film won Walt Disney an 'Oscar' in 1943 for the best cartoon short subject.

Extracts from the military papers of Corporal Adolf Hitler:
(1) Date and place of birth: 20 April 1889, Braunau am Inn, Austria. (2) Profession: painter. (3) Religion: Catholic. (4) Height: 1.76 metres. (5) Awarded the Iron Cross, Second Class, on 2 Dec. 1914. (6) Served in France 1914/15/16. (7) Wounded on 5 Oct. 1916 at Le Barque in the upper thigh.

MUSSOLINI

Full name Benito Amilcare Mussolini.

Born 14.00 hours, Sun. 29 July 1883, Predappio, Romagnana, Italy.

Characteristics About 5′ 6″; stocky build tending to corpulence; shaven head; dark eyes.

Married About 1910 Rachele Guidi[1] 3*s*. 2*d*.

Died 16.10 hours, Sat. 28 April 1945. Executed by order of the Italian Communist Party. Five rifle bullets entered Mussolini's body.

[1] An Italian court ruled in May 1969 that Signora Mussolini was entitled to a pension of about £90 ($216) a month plus arrears of about £9,600 ($23,040) in respect of Mussolini's service for the State between 1902 and 1931.

On 26 June 1940 the Fascist dictator of Italy penned a message to his partner in crime, Adolf Hitler: 'Now the time has come to thrash England. I remind you of what I said to you at Munich about the direct participation of Italy in the assault of the Isle. I am ready to take part with land and air forces, and you know how much I desire it.' To those acquainted with the Duce's bullying propensities, this was a natural sequal to his statement on visiting Germany in 1937: 'My visit . . . is wholly a matter of the heart . . . . The two peoples will clasp hands . . . and will march side by side in the future, for this future belongs to us. . . . My visit is a demonstration for a common policy of strong peace.'

When it came to the crunch, Mussolini had shown no marked readiness for the fray. His proclaimed policy, on the outbreak of World War II, had been that of non-belligerent. Only when Hitler appeared to have England at his mercy did the 'strong man' of Italy grow bold. His only pretence to military fame had been the rape of Abyssinia (1935–36), an atrocity committed with vastly superior forces against virtually unarmed opposition. His martial prowess in World War I had been restricted to wounding his hand with a grenade during a military exercise.

On 23 March 1919 Mussolini had founded the *Fasci di Combattimento*, a new political movement which gained support as a vigorous front against the much-feared threat of a Bolshevik revolution. The Fascist Party grew in strength, crushing its opponents by force, its armed squads giving brutal effect to Mussolini's 1913 contention that Italy needed 'a bath of blood'. The first Fascist government came to power in 1922 and in the succeeding years Mussolini introduced measures giving himself special prerogatives as Prime Minister. On 26 May 1927 the Premier was able to assure the Italian Senate: 'An opposition is not necessary to the function of a healthy political system. An opposition is silly and superfluous in a totalitarian regime such as the Fascist regime.'

The personable side of Mussolini did not fail to impress British politicians. Winston Churchill, who met him in 1926, remarked: 'That he is a great man I do not deny.' Lord Vansittart[1] wrote that 'he took such obvious pleasure in his own company' that he was reminiscent of 'a boxer in a flashy dressing-gown shaking hands with himself'. Vansittart added: 'He was a bounder, but bounding is no sin in the sun.'

Listeners to many a raucous public utterance might have been excused for reaching a less tolerant conclusion about

297

Mussolini listened politely to Neville Chamberlain at Munich in 1938. He told his friends: 'Chamberlain is not aware that to present himself to Hitler in the uniform of a bourgeois pacifist and parliamentarian is the equivalent of giving a wild beast a taste of blood.'

his political posture. 'Liberty is not an end. It is a means. As a means it must be controlled and dominated,' was one characteristic epigram. Another was: 'The crowd loves a strong man. The crowd is like a woman . . . Everything turns upon one's ability to control it like an artist.' Apologizing once for the liberality of his early political attitudes he remarked: 'If when I was a socialist, I had had a knowledge of the Italian middle class, not purely theoretical reading from Karl Marx, but practical, based on experience such as I have now, I would have launched a revolution so pitiless that, by comparison, the revolution of Comrade Lenin would have been child's play.'

Anthony Eden (later Lord Avon), who first met Mussolini in 1934 found him 'lively, vigorous, and entertaining'. Eden felt then and later that 'Mussolini envied Hitler, not the man or his characteristics, but his power over the German people. . . .'

The Duce's public attitude to the Führer was one of patronage both when he met him (*see page* 293) and when he airily advised the Germans to 'allow themselves to be guided by me if they wish to avoid unpardonable blunders. In politics it is undeniable that I am more intelligent than Hitler.' Adolf had appeared to endorse this when in 1936 he hailed Mussolini as 'the leading statesman in the world, to whom none may even remotely compare himself'. He had, perhaps, forgotten this eulogy when, on another occasion, Hitler went so far as to make a deferential comparison with himself: 'The Duce himself is my equal. He may perhaps even be my superior from the point of view of his ambitions for his people.'

There was melodrama in Mussolini's announcement to the nation of Italy's entrance into the war on 10 June 1940: 'An hour marked by destiny is striking in the sky of your country. . . .' But destiny

'Better to live one day like a lion than 100 years like a sheep.'

'For my part I prefer fifty-thousand rifles to five million votes.'

The DUCE

proved less glorious in the reality than in the boast. At the Battle of El Alamein, nine Italian generals were captured and eight divisions reduced to a shambles. Groping for excuses for failure Mussolini, whom Churchill had variously described as 'this whipped jackal' and as Hitler's 'tattered lackey', harangued the Fascist Party Directorate in Jan. 1943: 'How did it come about that the battle of El Alamein was decisive? Because the other arm of the pincers was lacking. The German troops should have poured down from the Caucasus.'

In his last speech to mass Fascism in Milan on 16 Dec. 1944, with Italy already overrun by Allied forces, Mussolini made a hollow appeal to the credibility of his listeners: 'It is time to tell our Italian, German, and Japanese comrades that the contribution made by Republican Italy to the common cause since September 1943 – in spite of the temporary reduction of the territory of the republic – is far superior to what is commonly believed.'[2] In 1945, when the end was near: 'I am the captain of a ship in a storm. My ship has broken up and I am floating on a piece of wreckage in a tumultuous sea. It is impossible to act or save the situation! No one hears my voice and I now withdraw into silence. But one day the world will listen to me.' A last pathetic truism was spoken a few weeks before his death at the hands of Communist partizans: 'Everything that has entered into history cannot be erased.'

After his execution, the body of Mussolini together with that of his mistress, Clara Petacci, and four others, was strung up by the heels from the beams of a petrol station. They were buried in the pauper's section of the *Cimitero Maggiore* in Milan. Mussolini's body was transferred to his birthplace in 1957.

'Women are trusting, confiding little animals. Women cannot create. They are what men desire them to be.'

[1] Permanent Under-Secretary of State for Foreign Affairs (1930–38).

[2] According to a German account, one contribution was a supply of tins of tough Italian beef issued to Axis troops in North Africa. They carried the initials 'A.M.' which German troops took to mean *'Asinus Mussolini'*.

299

Franklin D. Roosevelt

President Franklin D. Roosevelt with Churchill and Stalin at the Yalta Conference in 1945. Later Roosevelt was to lament: 'Stalin can't be trusted. He has broken his word on every promise he made to me at Yalta.'

The signatures of the 'Big Three' as they appeared on the Yalta agreement.

Full name   Franklin Delano Roosevelt.

Born   08.45 hours, Mon. 30 Jan. 1882, Hyde Park, New York, USA.

Characteristics   About 6′ 2″; about 188*lb.* (13*st.* 6*lb.*); dark hair; high forehead; wore pince-nez spectacles and used a long cigarette holder.

Married   1905 Anna Eleanor Roosevelt (died 1963) 5*s.* 1*d.*

Died   Thurs. 12 April 1945. Massive cerebral haemorrhage.

300

The only President of the United States to serve three terms, and then take the oath for a fourth term as well, Franklin D. Roosevelt ranks among the foremost statesmen of his era. Winston Churchill referred to him in 1941 as 'this formidable politician who has imposed his will for nearly ten years upon the American scene, and whose heart seemed to respond to many of the impulses that stirred my own.' Bernard Baruch (1870–1965), United States elder statesman, wrote of him: 'He thought of liberty, justice, equality of opportunity not in abstract terms but in terms of human beings. And because he dedicated himself to helping men realize these ideals – and because he succeeded in such great measure – his place in history and in the memory of the people will endure.'

Roosevelt came to power at a time of economic depression in America. At the Democratic Party National Convention on 2 July 1932 he declared: 'I pledge you, I pledge myself, to a new deal for the American people. Let us all here assembled constitute ourselves prophets of a new order of competence and courage.' Surviving an attempt on his life on 15 Feb. 1933,[1] Roosevelt was duly elected the 32nd President. In his Inaugural Address at

[1] Five shots killed the Mayor of Chicago and injured five others at Miami, Florida. The assailant, a mental defective named Guiseppe Zangara, was executed on 20 March 1933.

Washington on 4 March 1933 he said: This great nation will endure as it has endured, will revive and will prosper ... let me assert my firm belief that the only thing we have to fear is fear itself.' This was the prelude to the 'Hundred Days' in which measures were taken to restore confidence in the economy and stimulate business enterprise. Roosevelt proclaimed: 'I believe, I have always believed, and I will always believe, in private enterprise as the backbone of well-being in the United States.' His New Deal proved effective over the ensuing years and one of those who gave their support to it was a young Senator from Texas, Lyndon B. Johnson. Said Johnson of Roosevelt: 'He caused you to feel you wanted to do what he wanted you to do. And he had about the quickest mind of any man I've ever known. It was hard to keep up with him in conversation. He was always a jump or two ahead.'

Roosevelt's outstanding reputation outside of the United States, as well as at home, was founded on his broad view of international affairs. In 1933 he launched his 'Good Neighbour' policy for Latin American countries; this was cemented by trade treaties in 1934–37. In his Armistice Day address on 11 Nov. 1935 he said: '... we cannot and must not build walls around ourselves and hide our heads in the sand, we must go forward with all our

The Roosevelt 10 Cent was issued from 1946 to 1964 in silver, and in 1965 in cupro-nickel.

ROOSEVELT

British statesman hailed him as 'the greatest American friend we have ever known, and the greatest champion of freedom who has ever brought help and comfort from the new world to the old'.

Lord Halifax, British Ambassador in Washington (1941–46), while admitting in private correspondence that FDR was 'never within streets of Winston's quality', supplied this insight into his character: 'He was genuinely interested in human beings as human beings; problems stood before his mind's eye always as human situations; the treatment of them spelt greater happiness or greater unhappiness for men and women; and all the time it was on the relations of men and women that the whole of the world turned.' Allied to this enlightened purpose, Roosevelt exercised great personal charm and erudition. Harry S Truman wrote: 'I don't think I have ever come into contact with anyone who had read more or was more familiar with the history and background of the country.' Clement (later Lord) Attlee found him a 'charming companion, a brilliant raconteur, and was full of ideas'. General Dwight D. Eisenhower was 'struck with his phenomenal memory for detail', and rated him 'a very inspirational leader'.

General de Gaulle commented on a different level: 'Roosevelt was a star and disliked sharing the spotlight. He had difficulties in getting along with anyone like Churchill, for example, who is also a star, but whom Roosevelt did not like, although both made great pretence of friendship.' Anthony Eden (later Lord Avon) wrote: 'Roosevelt was, above all else, a consummate politician. Few men could see more clearly their immediate objective, or show greater artistry in obtaining it.' But Eden found that 'as a price of these gifts, his long-range vision was not so sure'. Eden also cited FDR's dislike of colonialism and credited him with the hope that former

strength and stress and strive for international peace.' Although his offer of help to the British Prime Minister, Neville Chamberlain, in the critical days before the outbreak of World War II was rejected, he did not hesitate, on the outbreak of hostilities in Europe, to let the world know in his Fireside Chat[1] on 3 Sept. 1939 where the heart of America lay: 'When peace has been broken anywhere, the peace of all countries everywhere is in danger.'

The President initiated a policy of aid to the nations combating the Axis powers and, following his re-election, Congress sanctioned on 11 March 1941 the Lend-Lease Act authorizing continued aid in this vital direction. In that year Japan signed a mutual aid pact with Germany and Italy, strengthening the probability of the United States entering the war. The hour of precipitation was reached on 7 Dec. 1941 when Japan attacked the US Pacific fleet without warning in Pearl Harbour, Hawaii. Declaring war the next day, FDR said this was 'a date that will live in infamy'.

In assuming full powers as Commander-in-Chief of the United States Armed Forces, Roosevelt drew on his immense reserves of courage in America's emergency. A victim of polio since 1921, he was never again able to walk unaided or without metal leg braces. The handicap did not deter him from performing prodigies of leadership, acknowledged by Churchill on many occasions, not least on his death when the

colonial territories would ultimately become dependent upon the United States. Eden also opined that in his anxiety not to make it appear that the United States was ganging up with Britain against Russia, Roosevelt 'created some confusion in Anglo-American relations which profited the Soviets'. Harold Macmillan made similar observations in his memoirs, discerning that 'With all his apparent sincerity and charm, there lay behind the outward show of friendship a feeling of hostility – perhaps even of jealousy – of the great Imperial story of the Old Country . . . and the liquidation of the British Empire was, whether consciously or unconsciously, one of his aims.' Macmillan also quoted in his memoirs a letter from Roosevelt to Churchill in which FDR stated: 'I think I can personally handle Stalin better than either your Foreign Office or my State Department. Stalin hates the guts of all your top people. He thinks he likes me better, and I hope he will continue to do so.'

In failing health, Roosevelt attended the Yalta Conference (3–11 Feb. 1945) to discuss the future of occupied Europe with Churchill and Stalin. With the United States by then in the position of senior partner in the balance of Western power, Roosevelt's role was paramount. The outcome of the Conference was that the whole of Eastern Europe, which had been occupied by the Red Armies in beating back the scourge of Nazism, came into the Communist orbit and were deprived of democratic rule. Churchill, powerless to act alone, was obliged to watch his worst fears concerning the future of Europe being realised. 'We can now see', he wrote later in his memoirs, 'the deadly hiatus which existed between the fading of President Roosevelt's strength and the growth of President Truman's grip on the vast world problem. In this melancholy void one President could not act and the other could not know.'

Roosevelt died the day before he was scheduled to deliver a speech on the 202nd anniversary of the birth of Thomas Jefferson (1743–1826), President (1801–09). In his script were drafted these words: 'The only limit to our realization of tomorrow will be our doubts of today. Let us move forward with strong and active faith.' The United States House of Representatives approved legislation for the posthumous award of the Congressional Medal of Honour in recognition of 'his peerless leadership as Commander-in-Chief, his heroic courage as a pioneer of new frontiers of freedom, his gallant and unselfish devotion to the service of his country, and his everlasting contribution to the cause of world peace'.

A poll of 75 historians was conducted in 1962 by the *New York Times* who drew up a ranking list of Presidents of the United States. Of the 31 Presidents reviewed, it found that only five qualified for the epithet 'great' and rated Roosevelt third after Abraham Lincoln (1809–65), President (1861–65), and George Washington (1732–99), President (1789–97).

'In the future days which we seek to make secure, we look forward to a world founded on four essential freedoms. The first is freedom of speech and expression – everywhere in the world. The second is freedom of every person to worship God in his own way – everywhere in the world. The third is freedom from want. . . . The fourth is freedom from fear.'

---

[1] Roosevelt was the first President to make regular use of sound radio to address the nation. He was also the first President to appear on television.

LENIN

Full name Vladimir Ilyich Ulyanov (the name Lenin meaning 'Man of Stone' was assumed in 1896. Other pseudonyms were Jacob Richter, Tulin, Ilin, William Frey, and Nicolai Petrovich. As a young man his nickname has been *Starik* meaning 'Old Man').

Born Fri. 22 April 1870, Simbirsk (now Ulyanovsk), on the River Volga, USSR.

Characteristics About 5' 5½"; stocky physique; reddish-grey hair and beard, becoming nearly bald in later life; dark, dark brown eyes, squinting; a forehead 'like Socrates'.

Married 1898 Madezhda Konstantinova Krupskaya.

Died 18.50 hours, Tues. 21 Jan. 1924. Stroke arising from arteriosclerosis; death possibly hastened by poison.

Said Lenin: 'Three-quarters of mankind may perish so that the rest may experience Communism.' After 50 years of Communist history, it was estimated in 1967 that the total number of deaths attributable to the spread and enforcement of Communism throughout the world was in excess of 90,000,000, a toll greater than the loss of human lives in both World Wars combined.

According to David Lloyd George: 'One of the greatest leaders of men ever thrown up in any epoch', Lenin was the founder and 'spiritual father' of the Communist International, and remains the pre-eminent figure in the annals of world Communism. He came to power as a result of the historic Oct.–Nov. 1917 *coup d'état*, known as the October Revolution. In the parliamentary elections which had just been concluded, the Bolshevik[1] Party, which Lenin headed, polled 9,000,000 votes out of a total of 34,000,000. Since 21,000,000 had voted for the Social Revolutionaries, the newly formed Constituent Assembly did not find favour with the Bolsheviks who forcibly ousted it.

Lenin was of mixed German, Swedish, and Chuvash, but not Russian blood. He was a qualified barrister and developed his political attitudes through an intensive study of the works of Karl Marx. When his brother Alexander was hanged in 1887 for planning to assassinate the Tsar Alexander III, Lenin was heard to say: 'I'll make them pay for this. I swear it!' On 16 July 1918 he was to arrange for the murder of the ex-Tsar Nicholas II (a cousin of King George V of England) and his wife and four daughters.[2]

In 1902 Lenin has visited London. He lived at 30 Holford Square, Pentonville, and, under the name Jacob Richter, held a ticket to the British Museum Reading Room where Karl Marx had written *Das Kapital*.[3] Lenin made a point of attending working class meetings and reported to his

wife: 'They are just bursting with Socialism! If a speaker starts talking rot a worker gets up right away and takes the bull by the horns, shows up the very essence of Capitalism.' His wife wrote: 'Ilyich always had a remarkable flair for deeply sensing the moods of the working class at a given moment.' She also revealed that he was a keen chess player and even talked about it in his sleep. But for the good of the Party, chess had to go: 'Chess is too absorbing', he concluded. 'It interferes with your work.' Lenin's output as a writer was a major preoccupation in these years. It was announced in 1960 that his works had sold 304,750,000 copies since 1917.[4] As recently as 1966 Lenin was the most translated author with 201 translations in that year. The *Bible* was second with 197.

Noted as a student for an excessive tendency to isolation and reserve, Lenin was terrifyingly articulate in power. Outlining the tactics of social democracy, he thundered: 'The proletariat must carry to completion the democratic revolution, by allying to itself the mass of the peasantry in order to crush by force the resistance of the autocracy and to paralyse the instability of the bourgeoisie.'[5] Further, he threatened: 'The existence of the Soviet Republic side by side with the Imperialist States for a long time is unthinkable. One or other must triumph in the end. And before that end supervenes a series of frightful collisions between the Soviet Republic and the bourgeois States will be inevitable.' In his exposition of 'revolutionary morality' he

305

recommended these methods: 'The Communists must be prepared to make every sacrifice, and, if necessary, even resort to all sorts of cunning, schemes, and stratagems, to employ illegal methods, to evade and conceal the truth, in order to penetrate into the trade unions, to remain in them, and conduct the Communist work in them at all costs.' His most extravagant boast was: 'When we conquer on a world scale we will build lavatories of gold on the streets of several of the biggest cities of the world.'

Lavish in his plans for public conveniences, Lenin was parsimonious in his personal budget. In a letter to the business manager of the Council of People's Commissars, of which Lenin himself was Chairman, he once wrote: 'In view of non-fulfillment by you of my insistent demand to notify me on what grounds my salary was raised from 500 to 800 roubles[6] per month as from 1 March 1918, and in view of the obvious illegality of such a rise, which you have made . . . in direct violation of the decrees of the Council of People's Commissars dated 23 Nov. 1917, I herewith severely reprimand you.' Though he used a Rolls-Royce, Lenin was austere in his way of life. He started work at 11 o'clock each morning and pursued his relentless schedule until 5 or 6 o'clock the next morning.

The mightiest of the Bolsheviks was not an imposing figure. 'What was my disappointment when I saw the most ordinary-looking individual', wrote Joseph Stalin of his first meeting with Lenin in 1905, 'below middle height, distinguished from ordinary mortals by nothing, literally nothing.' Bertrand Russell, who had an interview with Lenin in 1920, was similarly unimpressed: 'Nothing in his manner of bearing suggests the man who has power. He looks at his visitor very close and screws up one eye.' Maxim Gorky (1868–1936), one of the most eminent Soviet writers, said that

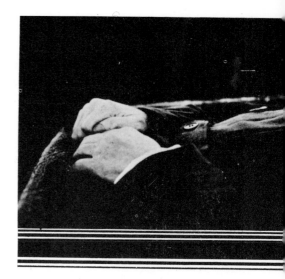

Lenin 'enjoyed fun, and when he laughed, his whole body shook, really bursting with laughter, sometimes until tears came into his eyes.' Gorky added an intriguing description. Lenin, he said, was 'squat and solid, with a skull like Socrates and the all-seeing eyes of a great deceiver, he often liked to assume a strange and somewhat ludicrous posture: throw his head backwards, then incline it to the shoulder, put his hands under the armpits, behind the vest.' Gorky's opinion of Lenin as a politician is also worth noting. 'We must recognise', he declaimed, 'that Lenin is not an omnipotent magician, but a cold-blooded trickster, who spares neither the honour nor the lives of the proletariat.' Stalin later accorded full recognition to Gorky by bestowing on him the Order of Lenin and persuading him to form the first Union of Soviet Writers.

On Fri. 30 Aug. 1918 as he was emerging from a labour rally in Moscow, Lenin was shot at point-blank range by a nearly blind woman named Fanya Kaplan. Three bullets struck him, one passing through his neck, missing the aorta by a fraction of an inch, another lodging in his neck, and a third in his left shoulder. Kaplan was executed on 3 Sept. 1918 and her corpse

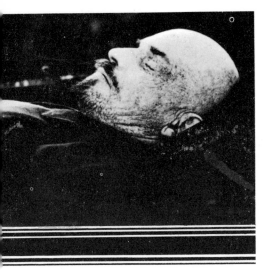

The embalmed body of Lenin lying in state in Moscow in 1924. After 1928 visitors were reported to have marvelled at his 'fresh and lifelike appearance'. The total number of visitors to the Lenin Mausoleum up to 1967 was estimated at 62,312,000. The total for 1966 alone was 3,220,000. The average daily attendance is between 6,000 and 8,000.

destroyed so that not a trace remained. Lenin recovered but in 1922 an operation was performed for the removal of one of the bullets. On extraction it was found to be a dum-dum bullet which had failed to spread on entry. Another strange discovery was that the bullet had been smeared with curare, a deadly poison, which had also failed to carry out its fatal mission.

In the intervening years a growing accumulation of evidence pointed to the conclusion that revolution had only served to introduce vastly greater evils than it had set out to remedy. Following heavy Russian losses in World War I, the 1917 Revolution accounted for about 1,500,000 deaths. Then during the three-year civil war and subsequent period of famine there were a further estimated 13,000,000 deaths. Lenin strove to make light in public of these horrors, describing the massacre at his order of 35,000 men in the 1921 Kronstadt rebellion as 'an absolutely insignificant incident'. In the same year he established the first slave labour camp on Solovetsky Island in the Arctic Circle. An estimate of the number of deaths in slave labour camps in the Soviet Union between 1921 and 1960 put the tally of victims at no fewer than 19,000,000.

The 'patron saint' of world Communism preferred to ride in Capitalist comfort. Lenin's Rolls-Royce was restored in 1959 and can be seen in the Lenin Museum in Moscow.

307

Lenin's health degenerated speedily in the years of dictatorship. Already suffering from the effects of venereal disease, he was afflicted by blinding headaches, insomnia, and depression. The last of three strokes finally brought him to a state of paralytic helplessness from which death at last delivered him after a nine-month agonizing purgatory. Evidence that death may have been speeded by poison, probably administered by Stalin, is regarded by some scholars as substantial (*see page* 284).

In his last months Lenin appeared to have felt remorse for the pitiless tyrannies which he had set in motion. One letter, dictated from his sickbed, opened with the confession: 'I am, I believe, strongly guilty before the workers of Russia. . . .' But the workers did not get to hear of this remarkable revelation. When he died in 1924 the name of the city of Petrograd, which had been changed from St Petersburg in 1914, was changed again to Leningrad. At the same time his birthplace, Simbirsk, was re-named Ulyanovsk after his real name. The legend of Lenin was launched.

In 1927 the young Jawaharlal Nehru visited Moscow and wrote these reflections of what he saw in the Lenin mausoleum on Red Square: 'In life they say he was not beautiful to look at. . . . But in death there is a strange beauty and his brow is peaceful and unclouded. On his lips there hovers a smile and there is a suggestion of pugnacity, of work done and success achieved. He has a uniform on and one of his hands is tightly clenched. Even in death he is a dictator.'

It is likely that Nehru was among the last to see the actual corpse. In 1928 the mausoleum was closed for 'repairs'. Although with the assistance of an imported German specialist, the cadaver had been immersed in a solution of alcohol, glycerine, formalin, and potassium acetate, its state of preservation was apparently no longer adequate for public display. A

visitor in 1930 commented that there was no protrusion where's Lenin's feet should have been; this omission was duly rectified. Other visitors, marvelling at his 'fresh and lifelike' appearance, questioned whether death could actually have cured his baldness.

For many years pathologists examined the brain of Lenin (weight 1,340 grams or 2.948 pounds) for evidence of special characteristics suggestive of genius. They sliced the grey matter into 31,000 sections. Among their conclusions was that the brain of the guiding light of world Communism contained some 200 fields of localization, many of the same type as had been identified in the brains of apes.

'Put Europe to the flames. . . .'
'We shall destroy everything and on the ruins we shall build our temple.'

'Our task is total, terrible, universal, and merciless destruction. . . .'

'Liberty is indeed a precious commodity—so precious that it must be rationed.'

[1] The Russian Marxists were divided into two main groups, the Bolsheviks and the Mensheviks (Reds and Whites). Bolshevik means 'majority', Menshevik means 'minority'
[2] There is evidence that one daughter, Anastasia, may have survived. The film *Anastasia* (1957) was based on her story, starring Yul Brynner and Ingrid Bergman.
[3] Karl Marx (1771–1858), the German author of *Das Kapital* (Volume I–1867, Volume II–1885, Volume III–1894) which is the cornersLne of Communist ideology.
[4] The first complete edition in English comprised 38 volumes, the last of which appeared in 1968.
[5] The Marxist term for the ruling class of Capitalists.
[6] About £50–£80 or 1200–1320.

LATE ADDITIONS AND AMENDMENTS

CREDITS FOR ILLUSTRATIONS

Numbers refer to pages on which illustrations appear

CONCISE BIBLIOGRAPHY

Actors on Acting (Crown Publishers, 1949).

Actors Talk About Acting, Lewis Funke and John E. Boothby (Thames & Hudson, 1961).

Afternoon Light, Sir Robert Menzies (Cassell, 1967).

Alexander, James A. Robinson (Banbridge Chronicle Press, 1946).

Alexander of Tunis, Norman Hillson (W. H. Allen, 1952).

Arnold Palmer, Mark H. McCormack (Cassell, 1967).

The Art of Animation, Bob Thomas (Simon & Schuster, 1958).

The Art of Cricket, Sir Donald Bradman (Hodder & Stoughton, 1958).

The Art of Margot Fonteyn (Joseph, 1965).

The Art of Walt Disney, Robert D. Field (Macmillan, 1942).

The Autobiography of Bertrand Russell (Allen & Unwin, 1967, 1968, 1969).

The Autobiography of Cecil B. de Mille, ed. Donald Hayne (W. H. Allen, 1959).

The Battle of Matapan, S. W. C. Pack (Batsford, 1961).

The Beatles, Hunter Davies (Heinemann, 1968).

Benito Mussolini, Christopher Hibbert (Longmans, 1962).

Bernard Shaw, Hesketh Pearson (Collins, 1942).

Bertrand Russell: A Life, Herbert Gottschalk (Baker, 1965).

Bertrand Russell: The Passionate Sceptic, Alan Wood (Allen & Unwin, 1957).

The Blast of War, 1939–1945, Harold Macmillan (Macmillan, 1967).

Blonde Venus, Leslie Frewin (MacGibbon & Kee, 1955).

Bogart: The Man and the Legend, Jonathan Hill and Jonah Ruddy (Mayflower-Dell, 1966).

The Brutal Friendship, F. W. Deakin (Weidenfeld, 1962).

Bull Fever, Kenneth Tynan (Longmans, 1966).

A Bunch of Old Letters (Asia Publishing House, 1958).

Callas, George Jellinek (Gibbs & Phillips, 1960).

Callas La Divina, Stelios Galatopolous (Dent, 1966).

Call Me Lucky, Bing Crosby (Muller, 1953).

The Captain General, General Leslie Hollis (Jenkins, 1961).

The Case of Salvador Dali, Fleur Cowles (Heinemann, 1959).

A Cellarful of Noise, Brian Epstein (Souvenir Press, 1964).

The Celluloid Sacrifice, Alexander Walker (Joseph, 1966).

Chaplin – The Immortal Tramp, R. J. Minney (Newnes, 1954).

Churchill and Beaverbrook, Kenneth Young (Eyre & Spottiswoode, 1966).

Churchill: Portrait of Greatness, Relman Morin (Sidgwick & Jackson, 1965).

Clem Attlee (Panther, 1967).

Cole Porter, The Life That Late He Led, George Eels (W. H. Allen, 1967).

Collected Letters of George Bernard Shaw, ed. D. H. Lawrence (Rheinhardt, 1965).

Conversations, Kenneth Harris (Hodder, 1967).

Conversations with Stalin, Milovan Djilas (Hart-Davis, 1962).

Cosmonaut Yuri Gagarin, Wilfred Burchett and Anthony Purdy (Gibbs & Phillips, 1961).

Crusade in Europe, Dwight D. Eisenhower (Heinemann, 1948).

Daily Mail Book of Golden Discs, Joseph Murrells (McWhirter Twins, 1966).

De Gaulle: The Crucial Years, A. L. Funk (University of Oklahoma Press, 1959).

The Decline and Fall of Lloyd George, Lord Beaverbrook (Collins, 1963).

Diary of a Genius, Salvador Dali (Hutchinson, 1966).

Dietrich, Leslie Frewin (Frewin, 1967).

Double Exposure, Roddy McDowall (Delacorte Press, 1966).

Duke Ellington, ed. Peter Gammond (Phoenix House, 1958).

Duke Ellington, G. E. Lambert (Cassell, 1959).

Duke Ellington, Barry Ulanov (Musicians Press, 1947).

Dunlop Book of Facts, Norris and Ross McWhirter (Dreghorn Publications, 1966).

The Eden Memoirs, Facing the Dictators, The Rt. Hon. the Earl of Avon (Cassell, 1962).

The Eden Memoirs, Full Circle, Sir Anthony Eden (Cassell, 1960).

The Eden Memoirs, The Reckoning, The Rt. Hon. the Earl of Avon (Cassell, 1965).

Eisenhower Speaks, ed. R. L. Trenenfels (Thos. Crowell, 1948).

Eisenhower the President, Merlo J. Pusey (Macmillan, New York, 1956).

Elizabeth Taylor, Ruth Waterbury (Mayflower-Dell, 1965).

The Essential Gandhi, ed. Louis Fischer (Allen & Unwin, 1962).

Fab: The Anatomy of a Phenomenon, Peter Leslie (MacGibbon & Kee, 1965).

Face to Face, ed. Hugh Burnett (Nonesuch Press, 1961).

Facts About the Presidents, Joseph Nathan Kane (H. W. Wilson, 1964, 1965).

Franklin D. Roosevelt, Frank Friedel (McClelland, 1952).

From the Third Programme, ed. John Morris (BBC, 1956).

Frost, Anatomy of a Success, Wallace Reyburn (Macdonald, 1968).

A Full Life, Lieutenant-General Sir Brian Horrocks (Collins, 1960).

Fullness of Days, Lord Halifax (Collins, 1957).

Future Indefinite, Noël Coward (Heinemann, 1954).

M. K. Gandhi, An Autobiography (Cape, 1949).

The Glass of Fashion, Cecil Beaton (Weidenfeld, 1954).

The Grand Tactician, Lazar Pistrak (Thames & Hudson, 1960).

Great Acting, ed. Hal Burton (BBC, 1967).

Great Companions, Max Eastman (Museum Press, 1959).

Great Contemporaries, Winston S. Churchill (Butterworth, 1937).

The Guinness Book of Records, Norris and Ross McWhirter (Guinness Superlatives, 1965–69).

H.R.H. The Duke of Edinburgh, Marguerite D. Peacocke (Phoenix House, 1961).

H.R.H. Prince Philip, Sportsman, Mrs Helen Cathcart (Stanley Paul, 1961).

Halifax, The Earl of Birkenhead (Hamilton, 1965).

Harold Wilson, Dudley Smith, MP (Hale, 1964).

Harold Wilson, Leslie Smith (Hodder, 1964).

Harold Wilson and the 'New Britain', Gerard Eyre Noel (Gollancz, 1964).

Hear Me Talkin' To Ya, Nat Shapiro and Nat Hentoff (Peter Davies, 1965).

High Adventure, Sir Edmund Hillary (Hodder, 1962).

High Tide and After, Hugh Dalton (Muller, 1962).

Hitler: A Study in Tyranny, Alan Bullock (Odhams, 1958).

How to be Rich, J. Paul Getty (W. H. Allen, 1966).

I Owe Russia $1,200 Bob Hope (Hale, 1963).

Ian Fleming: The Man with the Golden Pen, Richard Gant (Mayflower-Dell, 1966).

In Praise of Idleness, Bertrand Russell (Allen & Unwin, 1963).

In Search of Greatness, Yousuf Karsh (Cassell, 1962).

The Incredible Crosby, Barry Ulanov (McGraw-Hill, 1948).

The Inner Circle, Sir Ivone Kirkpatrick (Macmillan, 1959).

It Gives Me Great Pleasure, Cecil Beaton (Weidenfeld, 1955).

J. Paul Getty, The Richest American, Ralph Hewins (Sidgwick & Jackson, 1961).

The James Bond Dossier, Kingsley Amis (Cape, 1966).

Jawaharlal Nehru, An Autobiography (John Lane, 1942).

Jawaharlal Nehru, Frank Moraes (Macmillan, New York 1956).

Jim Clark, Portrait of a Great Driver, Graham Gauld (Hamlyn, 1968).

The Jim Clark Story, Bill Gavin (Frewin, 1967).

Julie Andrews, John Cottrell (Barker, 1968).

Kennedy, Theodore C. Sorenson (Hodder, 1965).

Kennedy Without Tears, Tom Wicker (Morrow, New York, 1964).

Khrushchev, Edward Crankshaw (Collins, 1966).

Khrushchev, Mark Frankland (Penguin, 1966).

Khrushchev, Konrad Kellen (Thames & Hudson, 1961).

Khrushchev: The Road to Power, George Paloczi-Horvath (Secker & Warburg, 1960).

The Kremlin and the Embassy, Sir William Hayter (Hodder, 1966).

The Last Days of Hitler, H. R. Trevor-Roper (Macmillan, 1956).

Lenin, David Shubb (Penguin, 1966).

Lenin and the Bolsheviks, Adam B. Ulam (Secker & Warburg, 1966).

Lenin: The Compulsive Revolutionary, Stefan T. Possony (Allen & Unwin, 1966).

Leninism, Alfred G. Meyer (Harvard University Press, 1957).

The Letters of Sigmund Freud, ed. Ernst L. Freud (Hogarth Press, 1961).

The Life and Death of Lenin, Robert Payne (W. H. Allen, 1964).

The Life and Times of Khrushchev, Roy MacGregor Hastie (Hamilton, 1959).

The Life and Times of Lord Mountbatten, John Terraine (Hutchinson, 1968).

The Life of Ian Fleming, John Pearson (Cape, 1966).

The Life of Lenin, Louis Fischer (Weidenfeld, 1965).

The Life of Mahatma Gandhi, Louis Fischer (Cape, 1951).

The Life of Sir Richard Stafford Cripps, Colin Cooke (Hodder, 1957).

Life with Picasso, Françoise Gilot and Carlton Lake (Nelson, 1965).

Limelighters, Oriana Fallaci (Joseph, 1968).

Looking at My Heart, Dr Philip Blaiberg (Heinemann, 1969).

Lord Reading, H. Montgomery Hyde (Heinemann, 1967).

Macmillan: A Study in Ambiguity, Anthony Sampson (Allen Lane, 1967).

Malcolm Sargent, Charles Reid (Hamilton, 1968).

Man of Everest, James Ramsey Ullman (Harrap, 1955).

Mandate for Change, Dwight D. Eisenhower (Heinemann, 1962).

Mao Tse-tung, Stuart Schram (Penguin, 1966).

Mao Tse-tung and I Were Beggars, Siao-Yu (Hutchinson, 1961).

Mao Tse-tung, Emperor of the Blue Ants, George Paloczi-Horvath (Secker & Warburg, 1962).

Margot Fonteyn, Elizabeth Frank (Chatto & Windus, 1958).

Maughmiana, Raymond Toole Stott (Heinemann, 1950).

Maxim Gorky, Richard Hare (Oxford University Press, 1962).

Mein Kampf, Adolf Hitler (Hutchinson, 1940).

The Memoirs of Field-Marshal Earl Alexander of Tunis (Cassell, 1962).

The Memoirs of Field-Marshal Montgomery (Collins, 1958).

The Memoirs of General the Lord Ismay (Heinemann, 1960),

Memoirs of a Professional Cad, George Sanders (Hamilton. 1960).

Memories, Dreams, Reflections, C. G. Jung (Collins, 1963).

Memories and Reflections, Volumes I and II, The Earl of Oxford and Asquith (Cassell, 1928).

The Millionaire Mentality, Michael Pearson (Secker & Warburg, 1961).

Montgomery, Alan Moorehead (Four Square, 1958).

The Montgomery Legend, R. W. Thompson (Allen & Unwin, 1967).

Movies, Richard Schickel (MacGibbon & Kee, 1965).

The Multi-Millionaires, Goronwy Rees (Chatto & Windus, 1961).

The Murder of the Mahatma, G. D. Khosla (Chatto & Windus, 1963).

Music on My Mind, Willie 'The Lion' Smith (MacGibbon & Kee, 1965).

Mussolini, Laura Fermi (Chicago University Press, 1961).

Mussolini: Study of a Demagogue, Sir Ivone Kirkpatrick (Odhams, 1964).

My Autobiography, Charlie Chaplin (Bodley Head, 1964).

My Contemporaries, Jean Cocteau (Owen, 1967).

My Daughter, Maria Callas, Evangelia Callas (Frewin, 1967).

My 55 Ways to Lower Your Golf Score, Jack Nicklaus (Hodder, 1955).

My Father, Charlie Chaplin, Charles Chaplin Jr (Longmans, 1960).

My Life and Fortunes, J. Paul Getty (Allen & Unwin, 1964).

My Record of Music, Compton Mackenzie (Hutchinson, 1955).

Nehru: A Political Biography, Michael Brecher (Oxford University Press, 1959).

The Nemesis of Power, John Wheeler-Bennett (Macmillan, 1953).

The Nine Lives of Mike Todd, Art Cohn (Prentice-Hall, 1959).

Nobel, The Man and His Prizes (Elsevier, 1962).

Nureyev, Alexander Bland (Hodder, 1962).

Onassis, Willi Frischauer (Meredith Press, 1968).

Or I'll Dress You in Mourning, Larry Collins and Dominique Lapierre (Simon & Schuster, 1968).

Pakistan, Ian Stephens (Benn, 1963).

Panditji, A Portrait of Jawaharlal Nehru, Marie Seton (Dobson, 1967).

Parliamentary Debates (Hansard).

The Path to Leadership, Field-Marshal Montgomery (Collins, 1952).

A Pattern of Rulers, Francis Williams (Longmans, 1965).

Persona Grata, Cecil Beaton and Kenneth Tynan (Wingate, 1957).

Petain and de Gaulle, Jean-Raymond Tournoux (Heinemann, 1961).

Peter Ustinov, Geoffrey Willans (Peter Owen, 1957).

Picasso, Wilhelm Boeck and Jaime Sabartés (Thames & Hudson, 1955).

Picasso, Lothar-Günther Bucheim (Thames & Hudson, 1959).

Picasso, Antonina Vallentin (Cassell, 1963).

Picasso and Co., Brassaï (Thames & Hudson, 1967).

Picasso: His Life and Work, Roland Penrose (Gollancz, 1958).

Points of View, Somerset Maugham (Heinemann, 1958).

The Political Thought of Mao Tse-tung, Stuart Schram (Pall Mall Press, 1963).

Portrait of a Revolutionary: Mao Tse-tung, Robert Payne (Abelard-Schuman, 1961).

Portrait of a Statesman, Dennis Bardens (Muller, 1955).

Portraits from Memory, Bertrand Russell (Allen & Unwin, 1956).

Pragmatic Premier, Ernest Kay (Frewin, 1967).

Present Indicative, Noël Coward (Heinemann, 1937).

President Kennedy, Bruce Lee (Blandford, 1961).

Prince Philip Speaks, ed. Richard Ollard (Collins, 1960).

Prince Rainier of Monaco, Peter Hawkins (Kimber, 1966).

The Private Life of Josif Stalin, Jack Fishman and Bernard Hutton (W. H. Allen, 1966).

Profiles in Courage, John F. Kennedy (Hamilton, 1960).

The Prophet Outcast, Isaac Deutscher (Oxford University Press, 1959).

Public Papers of the Presidents (US National Archives).

The Public Years, Bernard Baruch (Odhams, 1960).

Quant by Quant (Putnam's, 1966).

The Quintessence of Nehru, K. T. Narasimha Char (Allen & Unwin, 1961).

"R.A.B.": Study of a Statesman, Gerald Sparrow (Odhams, 1965).

The Red Barbarians, Roy MacGregor Hastie (Boardman, 1961).

Reminiscences of Lenin, N. K. Krupskaya (Foreign Languages Publishing House, 1959).

Richard Burton, Ruth Waterbury (Mayflower-Dell, 1965).

The Rise and Fall of Sir Anthony Eden, Randolph Churchill (MacGibbon & Kee, 1959).

The Rise and Fall of Stalin, Robert Payne (W. H. Allen, 1966).

The Rise and Fall of the Third Reich, William L. Shirer (Secker & Warburg, 1962).

Road to the Stars, Yuri Gagarin (Foreign Languages Publishing House, 1962).

311

Roosevelt in Retrospect, John Gunther (Hamilton, 1950).
Royal Riviera, Charles Graves (Heinemann, 1957).

Satchmo, Louis Armstrong (Peter Davies, 1955).
Sean Connery: Gilt-Edged Bond, Richard Gant (Mayflower-Dell, 1966).
The Second World War, Volume I, The Gathering Storm, Winston S. Churchill (Cassell, 1948).
The Second World War, Volume II, Their Finest Hour, Winston S. Churchill (Cassell, 1949).
The Second World War, Volume III, The Grand Alliance, Winston S. Churchill (Cassell, 1950).
The Second World War, Volume IV, The Hinge of Fate, Winston S. Churchill (Cassell, 1951).
The Secret Life of Salvador Dali (Vision Press, 1942).
Shocking Life, Elsa Schiaparelli (Dent, 1954).
Showman Looks On, C. B. Cochran (Dent, 1945).
Simply Churchill, Roy Howells (Hale, 1965).
Sinatra, Robin Douglas-Home (Joseph, 1962).
Sinatra, Arnold Shaw (W. H. Allen, 1968).
Sir Anthony Eden, Lewis Broad (Hutchinson, 1955).
Sir Anthony Eden, William Rees-Mogg (Rockliff, 1956).
Sir Malcolm Sargent, Phyllis Matthewman (Cassell, 1959).
Six and Out, Donald Bradman (Robertson 1965).
Somerset and All the Maughams, Robin Maugham (Heinemann, 1966).
Sophia Loren, Renaud de Laborderie (World Distributors, 1964).
Stage Directions, Sir John Gielgud (Heinemann, 1963).
Steps in Time, Fred Astaire (Heinemann, 1959).
The Story of American Golf, ed. Herbert Warren Wind (Farrar, Strauss, 1948).
The Story of Irving Berlin, David Ewen (Holt, 1950).
The Strategy of Peace, John F. Kennedy (Hamilton, 1960).
A Study of Nehru, ed. Rafiq Zakaria (Times of India, 1959).
Suez, The Seven Day War, A. J. Barker (Faber, 1964).

Theatrical Companion to Coward, Raymond Mander and Joe Mitchenson (Rockliff, 1957).
Theatrical Companion to Maugham, Raymond Mander and Joe Mitchenson (Rockliff, 1955).
Theatrical Companion to Shaw, Raymond Mander and Joe Mitchenson (Rockliff, 1955).
This Guy Marciano, Wilfrid Diamond (World's Work, 1955).
A Thousand Days, John F. Kennedy in the White House, Arthur M. Schlesinger (Deutsch, 1965).
The Three Lives of Charles de Gaulle, David Schoenbrun (Hamilton, 1966).
Till We Reach the Stars, Kwaja Ahmad Abbas (Asia Publishing House, 1961).
Tito Speaks, Vladimir Dedijer (Weidenfeld, 1953).
Towards Peace in Indo-China, The Rt. Hon. The Earl of Avon (Oxford University Press, 1966).
The Triumph of Integrity, Duncan Grinnel-Milne (Bodley Head, 1961).
The True Story of the Beatles, Billy Shepherd (Beat Publications, 1964).

Variety of Men, Lord Snow (Macmillan, 1967).
A Victorian in Orbit, Sir Cedric Hardwicke (Methuen, 1961).
Waging Peace, Dwight D. Eisenhower (Heinemann, 1966).
Walt Disney, Richard Schickel (Weidenfeld, 1968).
War Memoirs, Volume III, Salvation, General Charles de Gaulle (Weidenfeld, 1960).
The War Memoirs of David Lloyd George (Odhams, 1938).
The Way of a Transgressor, Negley Farson (Gollancz, 1935).
Why England Slept, John F. Kennedy (Funk & Wagnall, 1941).
Winds of Change, 1914–1939, Harold Macmillan (Macmillan, 1966).
Winston Churchill as I Knew Him, Violet Bonham Carter (Eyre & Spottiswoode, 1965).
Winston S. Churchill, Volume I, Youth, 1874–1900, Randolph S. Churchill (Heinemann, 1966).
Winston S. Churchill, Volume II, Young Statesman, 1901–1914, Randolph S. Churchill (Heinemann, 1967).

Winston Churchill, The Years of Achievement, Lewis Broad (Sidgwick & Jackson, 1964).
The Wit of Politicians, Leon Harris (Cassell, 1964).
With Rommel in the Desert, H. W. Schmidt (Harrap, 1951).
Wiv a Little Bit O' Luck, Stanley Holloway (Frewin, 1967).
Writers at Work (Secker & Warburg, 1963).

Yehudi Menuhin, Bernard Gavoty (Kister, Geneva, 1955).
Yehudi Menuhin, Robert Magidoff (Hale, 1956).
Yehudi Menuhin, Norman Wymer (Phoenix House, 1961).
Yes, I Can, Sammy Davis Jr (Cassell, 1965).

The author also had reference to a large number of newspapers and periodicals, including the following:

Annabel
Collier's
Coronet
Cosmopolitan
Daily Express
Daily Mail
The Daily Telegraph
Dance Magazine
Ebony
Elle
Esquire
Evening News
Evening Standard
Fashion
The Financial Times
Fortune
Golf Digest
Golf Illustrated
Harper's
Harper's Bazaar
Holiday
House and Garden
Ladies' Home Journal
Life
The Listener
Look
McCall's
The National Geographic Magazine
New York Times
Newsweek
Nova
The Observer
Penthouse
Photoplay
Reader's Digest
Saturday Evening Post
The Saturday Review
She
Sports Illustrated
The Star
Sun
Sunday Express
Sunday Telegraph
The Sunday Times
Theatre Arts
Time
The Times
Town
True
Vogue
Weekend Telegraph
Woman
Woman's Home Companion
Woman's Journal
Woman's Magazine
Woman's Mirror
Woman's Own
World Sports

INDEX

Bold type refers to main profile subjects